AYN RAND ON:

Objectivism: "A book salesman asked me whether I could present the essence of my philosophy while standing on one foot. I did, as follows: 1. *Metaphysics*: Objective Reality. 2. *Epistemology*: Reason. 3. *Ethics*: Self-interest. 4. *Politics*: Capitalism." (Introducing Objectivism)

The Vietnam War: "It was a shameful war ... because it served no national interest, because we had nothing to gain from it, because the lives and heroism of thousands of American soldiers were sacrificed in pure compliance with the ethics of altruism, selflessly and senselessly." (The Lessons of Vietnam)

The Death of Marilyn Monroe: "Anyone who ever felt resentment against the good for being good and has given voice to it, is the murderer of Marilyn Monroe." (Through Your Most Grievous Fault)

Apollo 11: "For once, if only for seven minutes, the worst among those who saw the lift-off had to feel—not 'How small is man by the side of the Grand Canyon!'—but 'How great is man and how safe is nature when he conquers it!'" (Apollo 11)

DR. LEONARD PEIKOFF worked closely with Ayn Rand for many years and was designated by her as heir to her estate. He has taught philosophy at Hunter College, Long Island University, and New York University, and he lectures on Ayn Rand's philosophy throughout the country. Dr. Peikoff is the author of *The Ominous Parallels: The End of Freedom in America* (Mentor), and the editor of *The Early Ayn Rand* (Signet).

D0032591

THE WRITINGS OF AYN RAND

The Voice of Reason
Essays in Objectivist Thought

Ayn Rand

**Edited and with an Introduction
by Leonard Peikoff
and with Additional Essays
by Leonard Peikoff and Peter Schwartz**

A MERIDIAN BOOK

MERIDIAN
Published by the Penguin Group
Penguin Group (USA) Inc., 375 Hudson Street, New York, New York 10014, U.S.A.
Penguin Group (Canada), 90 Eglinton Avenue East, Suite 700, Toronto, Ontario,
Canada M4P 2Y3 (a division of Pearson Penguin Canada Inc.)
Penguin Books Ltd., 80 Strand, London WC2R 0RL, England
Penguin Ireland, 25 St. Stephen's Green, Dublin 2, Ireland
(a division of Penguin Books Ltd.)
Penguin Group (Australia), 250 Camberwell Road, Camberwell, Victoria 3124,
Australia (a division of Pearson Australia Group Pty. Ltd.)
Penguin Books India Pvt. Ltd., 11 Community Centre, Panchsheel Park,
New Delhi – 110 017, India
Penguin Group (NZ), 67 Apollo Drive, Rosedale, North Shore 0632, New Zealand
(a division of Pearson New Zealand Ltd.)
Penguin Books (South Africa) (Pty.) Ltd., 24 Sturdee Avenue,
Rosebank, Johannesburg 2196, South Africa

Penguin Books Ltd., Registered Offices: 80 Strand, London WC2R 0RL, England

Published by Meridian, a member of Penguin Group (USA) Inc.
The Voice of Reason previously appeared in an NAL BOOKS edition.

First Meridian Printing, June 1990
40 39 38 37 36 35 34 33 32

 REGISTERED TRADEMARK—MARCA REGISTRADA

Library of Congress Cataloging-in-Publication Data

Rand, Ayn.
    The voice of reason ; essays in objectivist thought / Ayn Rand ;
with an introduction by Leonard Peikoff ; and additional essays by
Leonard Peikoff and Peter Schwartz.
        p.   cm.
    ISBN 978-0-452-01046-8
    1. Philosophy.   2. Political science—Philosophy.
3. Civilization, Modern—1950–   4. Rand, Ayn.   I. Peikoff, Leonard.
II. Schwartz, Peter.   III. Title.
B945.R231   1988
191—dc19   88-18192
                                                            CIP

Printed in the United States of America
Set in Fairfield
Original hardcover designed by Julian Hamer

Permission requests for college or textbook use should be addressed to the Estate of
Ayn Rand, Box 177, Murray Hill Station, New York, N.Y. 10157.

Information about other books by Ayn Rand and her philosophy, Objectivism, may
be obtained by writing to OBJECTIVISM, Box 177, Murray Hill Station, New York,
New York, 10157 USA.

Contents

Part Three: Politics

Introduction

This is the final collection of Ayn Rand's articles and speeches that I plan to publish. It may be regarded as the best of the non-anthologized Ayn Rand. None of the pieces (with one exception) has appeared before in book form.

Some of these twenty-six pieces are brief comments addressed to readers of her newspaper column in the *Los Angeles Times* or of her own magazines. Others are longer articles from her magazines, or lectures delivered to various kinds of audiences. The material spans a period of twenty years, from 1961, when she gave the first of her annual talks at the Ford Hall Forum in Boston, to 1981, when she gave what was to be her last talk, to a businessmen's group in New Orleans.

I have also included six essays written after Miss Rand's death in 1982: five are the Ford Hall Forum talks I have been giving in her stead in recent years. The sixth is an article by Peter Schwartz, editor of *The Intellectual Activist*, a publication that covers current events from an Objectivist viewpoint.

The contents of this book vary widely in scope and subject matter. As the subtitle indicates, however, all are "essays in Objectivist thought." That is, all take as their frame of reference Ayn Rand's unique philosophy of Objectivism. Objectivism upholds *capitalism* in politics, on the basis of *egoism* in ethics, on the basis of *reason* in epistemology. Everything in this book, accordingly, is an application of this last tenet, which is the root and essence of Objectivism. If one accepts reason—in its full, philosophical definition and implications—all the rest follows. Thus the title of the present collection.

The culture of our time, a legacy of two centuries of Kantianism, is shaped by the opposite ideas; it is a product of mysticism, altruism, collectivism. All around us we see rebels against the Enlightenment, who openly avow their disdain for the mind—in favor of brain-drowning drugs or obedience to the State or cults urging "back to nature" or "back to the Bible." In this kind of era, there is only one true rebel: the man or woman who challenges the root of the evil sweeping the world, i.e., the radical who champions reason.

Reason is man's faculty of integrating sensory data into concepts, and thereby of expanding incalculably the power of his consciousness. Such integration is man's distinctive method of cognition and the source of all his achievements: it is his only means of understanding and dealing with the facts of reality. The mind, in other words, is a practical attribute, the most practical one we possess. Reason is man's basic means of survival.

A faculty so vital cannot be compromised or sabotaged with impunity. It cannot perform its life-sustaining function if it is treated as an occasional indulgence alternating with bouts of divine revelation or the equivalent. It must be identified as the essential principle of human existence, then upheld as an absolute.

Human virtue, in the Objectivist approach, consists not in faith or social conformity or arbitrary emotion, but in thought, objectivity, *rationality*, the relentless exercise of one's intelligence in the task of achieving the values, spiritual and material, which human life requires. Thus Ayn Rand's ethics of rational self-interest. If such rationality is to be possible, however, the individual must be treated as a sovereign agent and left unmolested by physical force; he must be left free to think and then to act on his own best judgment. Thus Ayn Rand's defense of the original American system of government, the system founded on the recognition of man's inalienable individual rights.

Ayn Rand came to the United States from Soviet Russia in 1926, at the age of twenty-one. The founding principles of the United States, she thought, made it the greatest country in history and the exact opposite of Russia, which she hated. In many ways the United States lived up to her expectations. She found here the freedom to write and speak; she became famous as a champion of individualism; she met her husband, Frank O'Connor, whom she loved for fifty years. Intellectually, however, the United States was a disappointment. When she arrived, the intellectuals were on the threshold of what is now called the Red Decade. They were increasingly skeptical about the efficacy of reason, and they were, to her, astonishingly anti-American. At first, she could hardly believe that in the bastion of capitalism (as she had imagined it to be), she was hearing everywhere the same fundamental ideas that she had heard in Russia, the very ideas from which she had run for her life.

She had no choice but to fight the trend. She had seen what it led to, including the expropriation of her father's business under Lenin and, later, the death of her family under Stalin. She proceeded with every fiber of her being to fight for man's mind and his liberty, and all the major intellectual groups reacted by denouncing her: the liberals attacked her as a reactionary; the conservatives, as a radical; the Communists, as a pro-capitalist; the Church, as an atheist (which she was). By her own choice and conviction, she was miles outside the intellectual mainstream—she was fighting to reverse that mainstream—and there was no influential group anywhere to act as her ally.

No group perhaps, but the American people, from whom she received an outpouring of admiration. I have read her fan mail through the years, from soldiers and physicians and dancers and CEO's and truck drivers and countless solemn teenagers and even some professors and priests—all struggling to thank her for the vision of man and life presented in her novels, a vision that gave them the courage to carry on their own lives at a moment when they desperately needed it. I have seen her being mobbed by students feeling the same response at dozens of college campuses, from Harvard, Yale and Princeton on down. I have seen the lines of people waiting in the sometimes bitter Boston cold for ten hours or more until the doors to the lecture hall would open and her Ford Hall speech begin. Ayn Rand offered people something they could not get elsewhere, and in return they gave her love, awe, wealth. From the intellectuals, however, she evoked for the most part the opposite: hatred.

There were a few distinguished exceptions, among the most prominent of which was the Ford Hall Forum, a Boston organization that annually invites a series of nationally known speakers to discuss current issues and then submit to questioning from an audience. Like the rest of our intellectual establishment, the Forum professes to be fair; it claims to be open to all viewpoints. Unlike most of our colleges and media, however, the Forum is not an exercise in hypocrisy; it *is* fair. It actually says to real dissenters on fundamental issues: "Come and tell us what you think. We will not necessarily agree, but we will listen." I have observed few other examples of such fairness in the thirty-five years I have lived in this country. The Boston *Globe* a few years ago described the Forum as "fiercely independent, so far uncorrupted and radical," and added that it "has never allowed itself to be co-opted, diluted, or rendered 'cautious' and uncontroversial." The Forum's treatment of Ayn Rand proves that this tribute is not rhetoric, but simple truth.

When Miss Rand was first invited to speak in 1961, she was reluctant to accept. She did not know the Forum's distinguished history, and expected a group of unruly antagonists; but she went anyway, with misgivings—and she loved it. The audience that evening did not agree with her, but they listened, then peppered her with intelligent questions, the kind she always enjoyed answering. "The Forum," she told me later, "sponsors many speakers with whom I disagree totally. But it is honest. Since it is open to new ideas, it truly is an intellectual organization and it deserves to be supported." Accordingly, she agreed to return year after year, and her admirers came to expect it; they started to gather every April in Boston from all over the country (and then the world). *The New York Times* once described these gatherings as the "Objectivist Easter." I accept the term, since the word "Easter" comes from Eos, the Greek goddess of the dawn, and means, symbolically, the festival celebrating the rebirth of light after the darkness of winter.

I want to thank the Ford Hall Forum for making these Easter gatherings—and along with them, ten of the longest chapters in this book—possible. (Many of Miss Rand's other Ford Hall talks have been reprinted in other anthologies of hers.) In particular, I want to salute the guiding spirit of the Forum, Frances Smith. Her sense of intellectual honor and rigor, her scrupulous objectivity, her authentic enthusiasm for ideas and for philosophy— all this, in our age, is a rare value, for which the citizens of Boston should be (and I think are) deeply grateful.

Now let me explain the structure and contents of the present anthology.

Part I, Philosophy, consists of pieces that elaborate on the Objectivist philosophy. It includes a brief overview of the Objectivist viewpoint (Chapter 1), an indication of its kinship with the ideas of Aristotle (Chapter 2), and several important new discussions of ethics. These focus on the need of objectivity in ethics (Chapters 3 and 4), on the crucial distinction between psychological diagnosis and moral judgment (Chapter 5), and on the non-objective nature of the ethics of altruism (Chapters 6 and 7). Part I concludes with a denunciation of religion, which Objectivism regards as the rejection of reason (Chapters 8 and 9).

Part II, Culture, begins with a discussion of the bankruptcy of today's intellectuals (Chapter 10), then turns to some of this bankruptcy's most ominous manifestations: today's cultural vacuum (Chapter 11), and the worldwide "ethnic" upsurge (Chapter 12). There follows a more specific consideration of the flaws of three groups: liberal pragmatists (Chapter 13), conservatives (Chapter 14), and businessmen, whom Miss Rand regards as being the unwitting financiers of their own destroyers, the universities (Chapter 15). Two eloquent cultural events are then analyzed. One is tragic: the death of Marilyn Monroe (Chapter 16); the other is exultant: the flight of Apollo 11 (Chapter 17). This last piece, one of Ayn Rand's personal favorites, is her eyewitness account of the moon rocket's lift-off; it conveys the sensory reality, the emotional resonance, and the deepest philosophical cause of an historic event; it is the kind of reportage possible only to a great thinker who is at the same time a literary artist. The end of the Apollo program is the subject of Chapter 18. Part II ends with a pair of my lectures on the American educational system. One documents the anti-Americanism rampant in our universities (Chapter 19); the other, the anti-conceptual methodology that is wrecking our grade schools (Chapter 20).

Part III, Politics, considers a number of political issues from the standpoint of an advocate of laissez-faire capitalism. It includes attacks on the quota system (Chapter 21), public TV (Chapter 22), antitrust legislation (Chapter 24), foreign aid (Chapter 25), and socialized medicine (Chapters 29 and 30). It also offers a practical proposal to break up the government's monopoly in the field of education (Chapter 23); a discussion of the role of wealth in an industrial economy (Chapter 27); an identification of the cause of world hunger (Chapter 28); and an explanation of Ayn Rand's view that a rational woman would not desire to serve as president of the United States (Chapter 26). Part III concludes with a penetrating analysis by Peter Schwartz of the political movement known as Libertarianism. Ayn Rand was always opposed to Libertarianism, regarding it as the opposite of her philosophy. The Schwartz piece explains why.

The epilogue to this book—"My Thirty Years With Ayn Rand: An Intellectual Memoir"—is my report on the mental processes of a genius. Until a full-scale, authorized biography of Miss Rand is completed (which will be years from now), this lecture is my answer to the question: "What was Ayn Rand really like?"

Now a few words about editorial matters. I have begun each chapter with a sentence or two indicating the original source of the article or lecture. Aside from minor copy editing, mainly involving the removal of some commas, Miss Rand's pieces are reproduced unchanged. Occasionally I have inserted into her text, using brackets, an historical explanation or an unavoidable change in wording. (Please note that brackets *within* a quotation or parentheses are Miss Rand's, and represent her own interpolations.) As a rule, I have followed Miss Rand's practice of leaving footnote references in brackets within the text itself, except in a few cases where this would be cumbersome; in such cases, references are numbered and collected at the end of the chapter.

I want to thank a dedicated assistant, Diane LeMont, for her cheerfulness under pressure, and for her patient, meticulous work in helping to prepare the manuscript.

The selection I have made for the present volume is, to a real extent, arbitrary. There are many excellent articles by Ayn Rand and her associates that I have been forced by space limitations to omit. If you would like to receive information about the complete back issues of the relevant periodicals—*The Objectivist Newsletter, The Objectivist, The Ayn Rand Letter, The Objectivist Forum,* and *The Intellectual Activist*—as well as information about the Objectivist movement today, please write to Objectivism VR, Box 177, Murray Hill Station, New York, NY 10157. I regret that owing to the thousands of inquiries we receive, personal replies to such letters are not possible. But in due course inquirers will receive literature from several sources indicating the direction to pursue if they wish to investigate Ayn Rand's ideas further.

—LEONARD PEIKOFF
South Laguna, California
February 1988

Part One:
Philosophy

1

Introducing Objectivism
by Ayn Rand

This is the first of Ayn Rand's newspaper columns. It appeared in the Los Angeles Times *on June 17, 1962.*

At a sales conference at Random House, preceding the publication of *Atlas Shrugged*, one of the book salesmen asked me whether I could present the essence of my philosophy while standing on one foot. I did, as follows:

1. *Metaphysics:* Objective Reality
2. *Epistemology:* Reason
3. *Ethics:* Self-interest
4. *Politics:* Capitalism

If you want this translated into simple language, it would read: 1. "Nature, to be commanded, must be obeyed" or "Wishing won't make it so." 2. "You can't eat your cake and have it, too." 3. "Man is an end in himself." 4. "Give me liberty or give me death."

If you held these concepts with total consistency, as the base of your convictions, you would have a full philosophical system to guide the course of your life. But to hold them with total consistency—to understand, to define, to prove, and to apply them—requires volumes of thought. Which is why philosophy cannot be discussed while standing on one foot—nor while standing on two feet on both sides of every fence. This last is the predominant philosophical position today, particularly in the field of politics.

In the space of a column, I can give only the briefest summary of my position, as a frame of reference for all my future columns. My philosophy, Objectivism, holds that:

3

1. Reality exists as an objective absolute—facts are facts, independent of man's feelings, wishes, hopes, or fears.
2. Reason (the faculty which identifies and integrates the
   material provided by man's senses) is man's only means of
   perceiving reality, his only source of knowledge, his only
   guide to action, and his basic means of survival.
3. Man—every man—is an end in himself, not the means to
   the ends of others. He must exist for his own sake, neither
   sacrificing himself to others nor sacrificing others to himself. The pursuit of his own *rational* self-interest and of his
   own happiness is the highest moral purpose of his life.
4. The ideal political–economic system is laissez-faire capitalism. It is a system where men deal with one another, not as
   victims and executioners, nor as masters and slaves, but as
   traders, by free, voluntary exchange to mutual benefit. It is
   a system where no man may obtain any values from others
   by resorting to physical force, and *no man may initiate the
   use of physical force against others.* The government acts only
   as a policeman that protects man's rights; it uses physical
   force *only* in retaliation and *only* against those who initiate
   its use, such as criminals or foreign invaders. In a system of
   full capitalism, there should be (but, historically, has not
   yet been) a complete separation of state and economics, in
   the same way and for the same reasons as the separation of
   state and church.

Capitalism was the system originated in the United States. Its
success, its progress, its achievements are unprecedented in
human history. America's political philosophy was based on
man's right to his own life, to his own liberty, to the pursuit of
his own happiness, which means: on man's right to exist for his
own sake. That was America's *implicit* moral code, but it had not
been formulated explicitly. This was the flaw in her intellectual
armor, which is now destroying her. America and capitalism are
perishing for lack of a moral base.

The destroyer is the morality of altruism.

Altruism holds that man has no right to exist for his own sake,
that service to others is the only moral justification of his existence, and that self-sacrifice is his highest moral duty. The
political expression of altruism is collectivism or *statism*, which
holds that man's life and work belong to the state—to society, to
the group, the gang, the race, the nation—and that the state may

dispose of him in any way it pleases for the sake of whatever it deems to be its own tribal, collective good.

"From her start, America was torn by the clash of her political system with the altruist morality. Capitalism and altruism are incompatible; they cannot coexist in the same man or in the same society. Today, the conflict has reached its ultimate climax; the choice is clear-cut: either a new morality of rational self-interest, with its consequences of freedom, justice, progress and man's happiness on earth—or the primordial morality of altruism, with its consequences of slavery, brute force, stagnant terror, and sacrificial furnaces." *[For the New Intellectual]*

You may observe the practical results of altruism and statism all around us in today's world—such as the slave-labor camps of Soviet Russia, where twenty-one million political prisoners work on the construction of government projects and die of *planned* malnutrition, human life being cheaper than food—or the gas chambers and mass slaughter of Nazi Germany—or the terror and starvation of Red China—or the hysteria of Cuba where the government offers men for sale—or the wall of East Berlin, where human beings leap from roofs or crawl through sewers in order to escape, while guards shoot at fleeing *children*.

Observe these atrocities, then ask yourself whether any of it would be possible if men had not accepted the idea that man is a sacrificial animal to be immolated for the sake of the "public good." Read the speeches of those countries' political leaders and ask yourself what arguments would be left to them if the word "sacrifice" were regarded not as a moral ideal, but as the anti-human evil which it is.

And *then*, listen to the speeches of our present [Kennedy] Administration—and ask yourself the same question.

2

Review of Randall's *Aristotle*
by Ayn Rand

*John Herman Randall's book on Aristotle was pub-
lished by Columbia University Press in 1960. This
review appeared in* The Objectivist Newsletter,
May 1963.

If there is a philosophical Atlas who carries the whole of
Western civilization on his shoulders, it is Aristotle. He has
been opposed, misinterpreted, misrepresented, and—like an
axiom—used by his enemies in the very act of denying him.
Whatever intellectual progress men have achieved rests on his
achievements.

Aristotle may be regarded as the cultural barometer of Western history. Whenever his influence dominated the scene, it
paved the way for one of history's brilliant eras; whenever it
fell, so did mankind. The Aristotelian revival of the thirteenth
century brought men to the Renaissance. The intellectual counterrevolution turned them back toward the cave of his antipode:
Plato.

There is only one fundamental issue in philosophy: the cognitive efficacy of man's mind. The conflict of Aristotle versus
Plato is the conflict of reason versus mysticism. It was Plato
who formulated most of philosophy's basic questions—and doubts.
It was Aristotle who laid the foundation for most of the answers.
Thereafter, the record of their duel is the record of man's long
struggle to deny and surrender or to uphold and assert the
validity of his particular mode of consciousness.

Today, philosophy has sunk below the level of Aristotle versus Plato, down to the primitive gropings of Parmenides versus Heraclitus; whose disciples were unable to reconcile the

concept of intellectual certainty with the phenomenon of change: the Eleatics, who claimed that change is illogical, that in any clash between mind and reality, reality is dispensable and, therefore, change is an illusion—versus the Heraclitean Sophists, who claimed that mind is dispensable, that knowledge is an illusion and nothing exists but change. Or: consciousness without existence versus existence without consciousness. Or: blind dogmatism versus cynical subjectivism. Or: Rationalism versus Empiricism.

Aristotle was the first man who integrated the facts of identity and change, thus solving that ancient dichotomy. Or rather, he laid the foundation and indicated the method by which a full solution could be reached. In order to resurrect that dichotomy thereafter, it was necessary to ignore and evade his works. Ever since the Renaissance, the dichotomy kept being resurrected, in one form or another, always aimed at one crucial target: the concept of *identity*—always leading to some alleged demonstration of the deceptiveness, the limitations, the ultimate impotence of reason.

It took several centuries of misrepresenting Aristotle to turn him into a straw man, to declare the straw man invalidated, and to release such a torrent of irrationality that it is now sweeping philosophy away and carrying us back past the pre-Socratics, past Western civilization, into the prehistorical swamps of the Orient, via Existentialism and Zen Buddhism.

Today, Aristotle is the forgotten man of philosophy. Slick young men go about droning the wearisome sophistries of the fifth century B.C., to the effect that man can know nothing, while unshaven young men go about chanting that they *do* know by means of their whole body from the neck down.

It is in this context that one must evaluate the significance of an unusual book appearing on such a scene—*Aristotle* by John Herman Randall, Jr.

Let me hasten to state that the above remarks are mine, not Professor Randall's. He does not condemn modern philosophy as it deserves—he seems to share some of its errors. But the theme of his book is the crucial relevance and importance of Aristotle to the philosophical problems of our age. And his book is an attempt to bring Aristotle's theories back into the light of day—of *our* day—from under the shambles of misrepresentation by medieval mystics and by modern Platonists.

"Indeed," he writes, "[Aristotle's] may well be the most passionate mind in history: it shines through every page, almost every line. His crabbed documents exhibit, not 'cold thought,' but the passionate search for passionless truth. For him, there is no 'mean,' no moderation, in intellectual excellence. The 'theoretical life' is not for him the life of quiet 'contemplation,' serene and unemotional, but the life of *nous*, of *theoria*, of intelligence, burning, immoderate, without bounds or limits."

Indicating that the early scientists had discarded Aristotle in rebellion against his religious interpreters, Professor Randall points out that their scientific achievements had, in fact, an unacknowledged Aristotelian base and were carrying out the implications of Aristotle's theories.

Blaming the epistemological chaos of modern science on the influence of Newton's mechanistic philosophy of nature, he writes:

> It is fascinating to speculate how, had it been possible in the seventeenth century to reconstruct rather than abandon Aristotle, we might have been saved several centuries of gross confusion and error.... Where we are often still groping, Aristotle is frequently clear, suggestive, and fruitful. This holds true of many of his analyses: his doctrine of natural teleology; his view of natural necessity as not simple and mechanical but hypothetical; his conception of the infinite as potential, not actual; his notion of a finite universe; his doctrine of natural place; his conception of time as not absolute, but rather a dimension, a system of measurement; his conception that place is a coordinate system, and hence relative. On countless problems, from the standpoint of our present theory, Aristotle was right, where the nineteenth-century Newtonian physicists were wrong.

Objecting to "the structureless world of Hume in which 'anything may be followed by anything,' " Professor Randall writes:

> To such a view, which he found maintained by the Megarians, Aristotle answers, No! Every process involves the operation of determinate powers. There is nothing that can become anything else whatsoever. A thing can become only what it has the specific power to become, only what it already *is*, in a sense, potentially. And a thing can be understood only as that kind of thing that has that kind of a specific power; while the process can be understood only as the operation, the actualization, the functioning of the powers of its subject or bearer.

To read a concise, lucid presentation of Aristotle's system, written by a distinguished modern philosopher—written in terms of basic principles and broad fundamentals, as against the senseless "teasing" of trivia by today's alleged thinkers—is so rare a value that it is sufficient to establish the importance of Professor Randall's book, in spite of its flaws.

Its flaws, unfortunately, are numerous. Professor Randall describes his book as "a philosopher's delineation of Aristotle." Since there are many contradictory elements and many obscure passages in Aristotle's own works (including, in some cases, the question of their authenticity), it is a philosopher's privilege (within demonstrable limits) to decide which strands of a badly torn fabric he chooses to present as significantly "Aristotelian." But nothing—particularly not Aristotle—is infinite and indeterminate. And while Professor Randall tries to separate his presentation from his interpretation, he does not always succeed. Some of his interpretations are questionable; some are stretched beyond the limit of the permissible.

For instance, he describes Aristotle's approach to knowledge as follows: "Knowing is for him an obvious fact. . . . The real question, as he sees it, is, 'In what kind of a world is knowing possible?' What does the fact of knowing imply about our world?" *This* is a form of "the prior certainty of consciousness"—the notion that one can first possess knowledge and then proceed to discover what that knowledge is of, thus making the world a derivative of consciousness—a Cartesian approach which would have been inconceivable to Aristotle and which Professor Randall himself is combating throughout his book.

Most of the book's flaws come from the same root: from Professor Randall's inability or unwillingness to break with modern premises, methods, and terminology. The perceptiveness he brings to his consideration of Aristotle's ideas seems to vanish whenever he attempts to equate Aristotle with modern trends. To claim, as he does, that: "In modern terms, Aristotle can be viewed as a behaviorist, an operationalist, and a contextualist" (and, later, as a "functionalist" and a "relativist"), is either inexcusable or so loosely generalized as to rob those terms of any meaning.

Granted that those terms have no specific definitions and are used, like most of today's philosophical language, in the manner of "mobiles" which *connote* rather than denote—even so, their accepted "connotations" are so anti-Aristotelian that one is forced, at times, to wonder whether Professor Randall is trying to put something over on the moderns or on Aristotle. There are passages in the book to support either hypothesis.

On the one hand, Professor Randall writes: "That we can know things as they are, that such knowledge is possible, is the fact that Aristotle is trying to explain, and not, like Kant and his followers, trying to deny and explain away." And: "Indeed, any construing of the fact of 'knowledge,' whether Kantian, Hegelian, Deweyan, Positivistic, or any other, seems to be consistent and fruitful, and to avoid the impasses of barren self-contradiction, and insoluble and meaningless problems, only when it proceeds from the Aristotelian approach, and pushes Aristotle's own analyses further . . . only, that is, in the measure that it is conducted upon an Aristotelian basis." (Though one wonders what exactly would be left of Kant, Hegel, Dewey, or the Positivists if they were stripped of their non-Aristotelian elements.)

On the other hand, Professor Randall seems to turn Aristotle into some foggy combination of a linguistic analyst and a Heraclitean, as if language and reality could be understood as two separate, unconnected dimensions—in such passages as: "When [Aristotle] goes on to examine what is involved in 'being' anything . . . he is led to formulate two sets of distinctions: the one set appropriate to understanding any 'thing' or *ousia* as a subject of discourse, the other set appropriate to understanding any 'thing' or *ousia* as the outcome of a process, as the operation or functioning of powers, and ultimately as sheer functioning, activity."

It is true that Aristotle holds the answer to Professor Randall's "structuralism–functionalism" dichotomy and that his answer is vitally important today. But his answer eliminates that dichotomy altogether—and one cannot solve it by classifying him as a "functionalist" who believed that things are "sheer process."

The best parts of Professor Randall's book are Chapters VIII, IX, and XI, particularly this last. In discussing the importance of Aristotle's biological theory and "the biological motivation of Aristotle's thought," he brings out an aspect of Aristotle which has been featured too seldom in recent discussions and which is much more profound than the question of Aristotle's "functionalism": the central place given to living entities, to the phenomenon of *life*, in Aristotle's philosophy.

For Aristotle, *life* is not an inexplicable, supernatural mystery, but a fact of nature. And consciousness is a natural attribute of certain living entities, their natural power, their specific mode of action—*not* an unaccountable element in a mechanistic universe, to be explained away somehow in terms of inanimate matter, nor a mystic miracle incompatible with physical reality, to be attributed to some occult source in another dimension. For Aristotle, "living" and "knowing" are facts of reality; man's mind is neither unnatural nor supernatural, but *natural*—and *this* is the root of Aristotle's greatness, of the immeasurable distance that separates him from other thinkers.

Life—and its highest form, man's life—is the central fact in Aristotle's view of reality. The best way to describe it is to say that Aristotle's philosophy is *"biocentric."*

This is the source of Aristotle's intense concern with the study of living entities, the source of the enormously "pro-life" attitude that dominates his thinking. In some oddly undefined manner, Professor Randall seems to share it. This, in spite of all his contradictions, seems to be his real bond with Aristotle.

"Life is the end of living bodies," writes Professor Randall, "since they exist for the sake of living." And: "No kind of thing, no species is subordinated to the purposes and interests of any other kind. In biological theory, the end served by the structure of any specific kind of living thing is the good—ultimately, the 'survival'—of that kind of thing." And, discussing the ends and conclusions of natural processes: "Only in human life are these ends and conclusions consciously intended, only in men are purposes found. For Aristotle, even God has no purpose, only man!"

The blackest patch in this often illuminating book is Chapter XII, which deals with ethics and politics. Its contradictions are apparent even without reference to Aristotle's text. It is astonishing to read the assertion: "Aristotle's ethics and politics are actually his supreme achievement." They are not, even in their original form—let alone in Professor Randall's version, which transforms them into the ethics of pragmatism.

It is shocking to read the assertion that Aristotle is an advocate of the "welfare state." Whatever flaws there are in Aristotle's political theory—and there are many—he does not deserve that kind of indignity.

Professor Randall, who stresses that knowledge must rest on empirical evidence, should take cognizance of the empirical fact that throughout history the influence of Aristotle's philosophy (particularly of his epistemology) has led in the direction of individual freedom, of man's liberation from the power of the state—that Aristotle (via John Locke) was the philosophical father of the Constitution of the United States and thus of *capitalism*—that it is Plato and Hegel, not Aristotle, who have been the philosophical ancestors of all totalitarian and welfare states, whether Bismarck's, Lenin's, or Hitler's.

An "Aristotelian statist" is a contradiction in terms—and this, perhaps, is a clue to the conflict that mars the value of Professor Randall's book.

But if read critically, this book is of great value in the study of Aristotle's philosophy. It is a concise and comprehensive presentation which many people need and look for, but cannot find today. It is of particular value to college students: by providing a frame of reference, a clear summary of the whole, it will help them to grasp the meaning of the issues through the fog of the fragmentary, unintelligible manner in which most courses on Aristotle are taught today.

Above all, this book is important culturally, as a step in the right direction, as a recognition of the fact that the great physician needed by our dying science of philosophy is Aristotle— that if we are to emerge from the intellectual shambles of the present, we can do it only by means of an *Aristotelian* approach.

"Clearly," writes Professor Randall, "Aristotle did not say everything; though without what he first said, all words would be meaningless, and when it is forgotten they usually are."

3

To Young Scientists
by Ayn Rand

*These remarks were delivered at the Massachusetts
Institute of Technology in March 1962. They were
addressed to "the students who are to be America's
future scientists." Reprinted from an edited version
in* The Objectivist Newsletter, *October 1962.*

We are living in an age when every social group is struggling frantically to destroy itself—and doing it faster than
any of its rivals or enemies could hope for—when every man is
his own most dangerous enemy, and the whole of mankind is
rolling, at supersonic speed, back to the Dark Ages, with a
nuclear bomb in one hand and a rabbit's foot in the other.

The most terrible paradox of our age is the fact that the
destruction of man's mind, of reason, of logic, of knowledge, of
civilization, is being accomplished in the name and with the
sanction of *science*.

It took centuries and volumes of writing to bring our culture
to its present state of bankruptcy—and volumes would have to
be written to expose, counteract, and avert the disaster of a total
intellectual collapse. But of all the deadly theories by means of
which you are now being destroyed, I would like to warn you
about one of the deadliest and most crucial: the alleged dichotomy of science and ethics.

You have heard that theory so often and from so many authorities that most of you now take it for granted, as an axiom, as the
one absolute taught to you by those who proclaim that there are
no absolutes. It is the doctrine that man's science and ethics—or
his knowledge and values, or his body and soul—are two separate, antagonistic aspects of his existence, and that man is caught

13

between them, as a precarious, permanent traitor to their conflicting demands.

Science, they tell you, is the province of reason—but ethics, they say, is the province of a higher power, which man's impotent, fallible intellect must not be so presumptuous as to challenge. What power? Why, *feelings*.

Before you accept that doctrine, identify concretely and specifically what it means. (Remember that ethics is a code of values to guide man's choices and actions, the choices and actions that determine the purpose and course of his life.) It means that *you*, as scientists, are competent to discover new knowledge—but not competent to judge for what purpose that knowledge is to be used. *Your* judgment is to be disqualified, if, when, and *because* it is rational—while human purposes are to be determined by the representatives of nonreason. *You* are to create the means—but *they* are to choose the ends. *You* are to work and think and strain all the power, energy and ingenuity of your mind to its utmost logical best, and produce great achievements—but those "superior" others will dispose of your achievements, by the grace and guidance of their *feelings*. Your *mind* is to be the tool and servant of their *whims*. You are to create the H-bomb—but a blustering Russian anthropoid will decide when he *feels* like dropping it and on whom. Yours is not to reason why—yours is just to do and provide the ammunition for others to die.

From Plato's *Republic* onward, all statist-collectivists have looked longingly up at an anthill as at a social ideal to be reached. An anthill is a society of interdependent insects, where each particular kind or class is physiologically able to perform only one specific function: some are milch cows, some are toilers, a few are rulers. Collectivist planners have dreamed for a long time of creating an ideal society by means of eugenics—by breeding men into various castes physiologically able to perform only one specific function. *Your* place, in such a society, would be that of toiling milch-brains, of human computers who would produce anything on demand and would be biologically incapable of questioning the orders of the anthropoid who'd throw them their food rations.

Does your self-esteem accept such a prospect?

No, I am not saying that that dream will ever be achieved physiologically. But I am saying that it has already been achieved politically and intellectually: politically, among your so-called colleagues in Soviet Russia—intellectually, in the mind of any man who accepts the science-ethics dichotomy.

I believe that many of you were attracted to the field of science precisely by reason of that dichotomy: in order to escape from the hysterical mystic-subjectivist-emotionalist shambles to which philosophers have reduced the field of ethics—and in order to find a clean, intelligible, rational, *objective* realm of activity.

You have not found it—not because it doesn't exist, but because it cannot be found without the help of a clean, intelligible, rational, *objective* philosophy, part of which is ethics. It cannot be found until you realize that man cannot exist as half-scientist, half-brute—that *all* the aspects of his existence are, can be, and *should* be subject to the study and the judgment of his intellect—and that of all human disciplines, it is *ethics*, the discipline which sets his goals, that should be elevated into a science.

No man and no class of men can live without a code of ethics. But if there are degrees of urgency, I would say that it is *you*, the scientists, who need it most urgently. The nature of your power and of your *responsibility* is too obvious to need restatement. You can read it in every newspaper headline. It is obvious why you should know—before you start out—to what purpose and service you choose to devote the power of your mind.

If you do not care to know—well, I would like to say that there is a character in *Atlas Shrugged* who was dedicated to *you* as a warning, with the sincere hope that it would not be necessary. His name is Dr. Robert Stadler.

Many things have happened [in recent months] to demonstrate the ultimate consequences of the science–ethics dichotomy.

If a professional soldier were to accept a job with Murder, Inc. and claim that he is merely practicing his trade, that it is not his responsibility to know who is using his services or for what purpose—he would be greeted by a storm of indignation and regarded as a moral psychopath. Yet at his bloodiest worst, he could not perpetrate a fraction of the horrors achieved by any haughty ascetic of science who merely places a slip of paper with some mathematical computations into the hands of Khrushchev or Mao Tse-tung or any of their imitators in America, and, having read no newspapers since 1914, declares himself to be "above the battle."

It is thus that the world reached the nightmare spectacle which surpasses any horror story of science fiction: two Soviet capsules circling in "outer space," as the alleged triumph of an advanced science—while here on earth, a young boy lies bleeding to death and screaming for help, at the foot of the wall in East Berlin, shot for attempting to escape and left there by the prehistorical monsters from twenty thousand centuries deep: the Soviet rulers.

No, this is not the worst evil on today's earth; there is one still worse: the conscience of those Western scientists who are still willing to associate on civilized terms with those colleagues of theirs who champion unilateral disarmament.

If you are now starting on a career in science, you do not have to share the guilt of those men, but you do have to reclaim the field and the honor of science.

There is only one way to do it: by accepting the moral principle that one does not surrender one's mind into blind servitude to thugs, and one does not accept the job of munitions maker for Attila's conquest of the world; not for any Attila, actual or potential, foreign or domestic.

There is only one way to implement that principle. Throughout history, with only a few exceptions, governments have claimed the "right" to rule men by means of physical force, that is: by terror and destruction. When the potential of terror and destruction reaches today's scale, it should convince every *human* being that if mankind is to survive, Attila's concept of government must be discarded, along with the alleged "right" of any men to impose their ideas or wishes on others by *initiating* the use of physical force. This means that men must establish a free, noncoercive society, where the government is only a policeman protecting *individual* rights, where force is used only in retaliation and self-defense, where no gang can seize the legalized power to unleash a reign of terror. Such a society does not have to be invented: it had existed, though not fully. Its name is capitalism.

Needless to say, capitalism does not force individuals or nations into the collectivist slave pen of a world government. The so-called One World is merely "one neck ready for one leash." Capitalism leaves men free for self-defense, but gives no one the political means to initiate force or war.

This—not physical but *political* disarmament, the renunciation of legalized brute force as a way of life—is the only means of saving the world from nuclear destruction.

4

Who Is the Final Authority in Ethics?
by Ayn Rand

Written in answer to a reader's question, this article appeared in the "Intellectual Ammunition Department" of The Objectivist Newsletter, *February 1965.*

There are certain questions that must be questioned—that is, challenged at their root—because they consist of smuggling a false premise into the mind of a careless listener. "Who created the universe?" is one such question. "Do you still beat your wife?" is another. And so is the question above.

It comes up in many different ways, directly and indirectly. It is usually asked in some formulation such as: "Who *decides* what is right or wrong?"

Students of Objectivism are not likely to ask this question, but they may hear it from others and fail to understand its nature. I was astonished, however, to find it addressed to this department, in the following form: "Is it intellectual plagiarism to accept and even to use philosophical principles and values discovered by someone else?"

It may not appear to be the same question, but it is—in the sense that it comes from the same fundamental error.

The nature of the error will become apparent if one applies that question to the physical sciences: "Who *decides* what is right or wrong in electronics?" Or: "Is it scientific plagiarism to accept and even to use medical principles and therapeutic techniques discovered by someone else?"

It is obvious that the root of such questions is a certain kind of conceptual vacuum: the absence of the concept of *objectivity* in the questioner's mind.

Objectivity is both a metaphysical and an epistemological concept. It pertains to the relationship of consciousness to existence. Metaphysically, it is the recognition of the fact that reality exists independent of any perceiver's consciousness. Epistemologically, it is the recognition of the fact that a perceiver's (man's) consciousness must acquire knowledge of reality by certain means (reason) in accordance with certain rules (logic). This means that although reality is immutable and, in any given context, only one answer is true, the truth is not automatically available to a human consciousness and can be obtained only by a certain mental process which is required of every man who seeks knowledge—that there is no substitute for this process, no escape from the responsibility for it, no shortcuts, no special revelations to privileged observers—and that there can be no such thing as a final "authority" in matters pertaining to human knowledge. Metaphysically, the only authority is reality; epistemologically—one's own mind. The first is the ultimate arbiter of the second.

The concept of objectivity contains the reason why the question, "Who decides what is right or wrong?" is wrong. Nobody "*decides*." Nature does not *decide*—it merely *is*; man does not *decide*, in issues of knowledge, he merely *observes* that which is. When it comes to applying his knowledge, man decides what he chooses to do, according to what he has learned, remembering that the basic principle of rational action in *all* aspects of human existence, is: "Nature, to be commanded, must be obeyed." This means that man does not *create* reality and can achieve his values only by making his decisions consonant with the facts of reality.

Who "decides" what is the right way to make an automobile, to cure an illness or to live one's life? Any man who cares to acquire the appropriate knowledge and to judge, at and for his own risk and sake. What is his criterion of judgment? Reason. What is his ultimate frame of reference? Reality. If he errs or evades, who penalizes him? Reality.

It took centuries (and the influence of Aristotle) for men to acquire a precarious hold on the concept of objectivity in regard to the physical sciences. How precarious that hold actually is, can be observed in the fact that most men are incapable of extending that concept to *all* human knowledge including the so-called humanities, the sciences dealing with man. In regard to the humanities, consciously or subconsciously, explicitly or implicitly, most people revert to the epistemology of prehistorical savages, i.e., to *subjectivism.*

Subjectivism is the belief that reality is not a firm absolute, but a fluid, plastic, indeterminate realm which can be altered, in whole or in part, by the consciousness of the perceiver—i.e., by his feelings, wishes or whims. It is the doctrine which holds that man—an entity of a specific nature, dealing with a universe of a specific nature—can, somehow, live, act, and achieve his goals apart from and/or in contradiction to the facts of reality, i.e., apart from and/or in contradiction to his own nature and the nature of the universe. (This is the "mixed," moderate or middle-of-the-road version of subjectivism. Pure or "extreme" subjectivism does not recognize the concept of identity, i.e., the fact that man or the universe or anything possesses a specific nature.)

Morality has been the monopoly of mystics, i.e., of subjectivists, for centuries—a monopoly reinforced and reaffirmed by the neo-mystics of modern philosophy. The clash between the two dominant schools of ethics, the mystical and the social, is only a clash between personal subjectivism and social subjectivism: one substitutes the supernatural for the objective, the other substitutes the collective for the objective. Both are savagely united against the introduction of objectivity into the realm of ethics.

Most men, therefore, find it particularly difficult to regard ethics as a science and to grasp the concept of a rational, *objective* ethics that leaves no room for anyone's arbitrary "decision."

Subjectivism is the smuggled premise at the root of both variants of the question under discussion. Superficially, the two variants may appear to come from opposite motives. Actually, they are two sides of the same subjectivist coin.

The man who asks: "Who decides what is right or wrong?" is obviously a subjectivist who believes that reality is ruled by human whims and who seeks to escape from the responsibility of independent judgment by one of two means: either by cynicism or by blind faith, either by negating the validity of all moral standards or by looking for an "authority" to obey.

But the man who asks: "Is it intellectual plagiarism to accept and even to use philosophical principles and values discovered by someone else?" is not a sovereign consciousness seeking independence from others, as he wants to make himself appear. He has no better grasp of objectivity than the first man; he is a subjectivist who sees reality as a contest of whims and wants it to be ruled by *his* whims—which he proposes to accomplish by discarding as false everything discovered by others. His primary concern, in regard to philosophical principles, is not: "Is it true or false?" but: "Who discovered it?"

On such a premise, he would have to make fire by rubbing sticks together (if he discovers that much), since he is not Edison and cannot accept electric light. He would have to maintain that the earth is flat, since Columbus beat him to the demonstration of its shape. He would have to advocate statism, since he is not Adam Smith. And he would have to discard the laws of logic, since he is obviously not Aristotle.

The division of labor in the pursuit of knowledge—the fact that men can transmit knowledge and learn from one another's discoveries—is one of man's great advantages over all other living species. Only a subjectivist, who equates *facts* with *arbitrary assertions*, could imagine that to "*learn*" means to "*accept on faith*"—as this questioner seems to imply.

It is also possible that the motive of such a mentality is the wish not to discard the ideas of others, but to *appropriate* them. "Plagiarism" is a concept that pertains, not to the acceptance, but to the *authorship* of an idea. Needless to say, to accept someone's idea and then to pose as its originator *is* plagiarism of the lowest order. But this has nothing to do with a legitimate, rational process of learning. The truth of an idea and its authorship are two separate issues, which are not difficult to keep apart.

This particular variant of the question was worth noting only as an extreme example of subjectivism—of the degree to which ideas have no reality and no connection to reality in a subjectivist's mind. It is an illustration of the extent to which the concept of objectivity is still alien to a great many men, and of the extent to which mankind needs it.

Observe that most modern collectivists—the alleged advocates of human brotherhood, benevolence, and cooperation—are committed to subjectivism in the humanities. Yet reason—and, therefore, *objectivity*—is the only common bond among men, the only means of communication, the only universal frame of reference and criterion of justice. No understanding, communication, or cooperation is possible to men on the basis of unintelligible feelings and subjective "urges"; nothing is possible but a contest of whims resolved by the rule of brute force.

In politics, the subjectivist question of "Who 'decides'?" comes up in many forms. It leads many alleged champions of freedom to the notion that "the will of the people" or of the majority is the ultimate sanction of a free society, which is a contradiction in terms, since such a sanction represents the doctrine of unlimited majority rule.

The answer, here as in all other moral-intellectual problems, is that nobody "*decides*." Reason and reality are the only valid criteria of political theories. Who determines which theory is true? *Any man who can prove it.*

Theories, ideas, discoveries are not created collectively; they are the products of individual men. In politics, as in every other field of human endeavor, a group can only accept or reject a product (or a theory); it cannot, *qua* group, participate in its creation. The participants are those who choose that particular field of activity, each to the extent of his ability and ambition. And when men are free, irrational theories can win only temporarily and only through the errors or the default of the thinkers, i.e., of those who do seek the truth.

In politics, as in every other field, the men who do not care to think are merely ballast: they accept, by default, whatever the intellectual leaders of the moment have to offer. To the extent to which men do think, they follow the man who offers the best (i.e., the most rational) idea. This does not happen instantaneously or automatically or in every specific case and detail, but this is the way knowledge spreads among men, and this has been the pattern of mankind's progress. The best proof of the power of ideas—the power of reason for men of all levels of intelligence— is the fact that no dictatorship was ever able to last without establishing censorship.

The number of its adherents is irrelevant to the truth or falsehood of an idea. A majority is as fallible as a minority or as an individual man. A majority vote is not an epistemological validation of an idea. Voting is merely a proper political device— within a strictly, constitutionally delimited sphere of action— for choosing the practical *means* of implementing a society's basic principles. But those principles are not determined by vote. By whom, then, are they determined? By the facts of reality—as identified by those thinkers who chose the field of political philosophy. This was the pattern of the greatest political achievement in history: the American Revolution.

In this connection, it is important to note the *epistemological* significance of a free society. In a free society, the pursuit of truth is protected by the free access of any individual to any field of endeavor he may choose to enter. (A free access does not mean a guarantee of success, or of financial support, or of anyone's acceptance and agreement—it means the absence of any forced restrictions or legal barriers.) This prevents the formation of any coercive "elite" in any profession—it prevents the legalized enforcement of a "monopoly on truth" by any gang of power seekers—it protects the free market place of ideas—it keeps all doors open to man's inquiring mind.

Who "decides"? In politics, in ethics, in art, in science, in philosophy—in the entire realm of human knowledge—it is *reality* that sets the terms, through the work of those men who are able to identify its terms and to translate them into *objective* principles.

5

The Psychology of Psychologizing
by Ayn Rand

This article was published in The Objectivist,
March 1971.

In certain passages of *Atlas Shrugged*, I touched briefly on issues which I wanted to discuss theoretically at a later date and at greater length.

One such passage is the scene in which Hank Rearden, struggling to understand his wife's behavior, wonders whether the motive of her constant, spiteful sarcasm is "not a desire to make him suffer, but a confession of her own pain, a defense for the pride of an unloved wife, a secret plea—so that the subtle, the hinted, the evasive in her manner, the thing begging to be understood, was not the open malice, but the hidden love."

Struggling to be just, he gives her the benefit of the doubt and suppresses the warning of his own mind. "He felt a dim anger, like a voice he tried to choke, a voice crying in revulsion: Why should I deal with her rotten, twisted lying?—why should I accept torture for the sake of pity?—why is it I who should have to take the hopeless burden of trying to spare a feeling she won't admit, a feeling I can't know or understand or try to guess?—if she loves me, why doesn't the damn coward say so and let us both face it in the open?"

Rearden was the innocent victim of a widespread game that has many variants and ramifications, none of them innocent, a game that could be called a racket. It consists, in essence, of substituting psychology for philosophy.

Today, many people use psychology as a new form of mysticism: as a substitute for reason, cognition and objectivity, as an escape from the responsibility of moral judgment, both in the role of the judge and the judged.

23

Mysticism requires the notion of the unknowable, which is revealed to some and withheld from others; this divides men into those who feel guilt and those who cash in on it. The two groups are interchangeable, according to circumstances. When being judged, a mystic cries: "I couldn't help it!" When judging others, he declares: "You can't know, but *I* can." Modern psychology offers him both opportunities.

Once, the power superseding and defeating man's mind was taken to be predetermined fate, supernatural will, original sin, etc.; now it is one's own subconscious. But it is still the same old game: the notion that the wishes, the feelings, the beliefs— and, today, the *malfunction*—of a human consciousness can absolve a man from the responsibility of cognition.

Just as reasoning, to an irrational person, becomes rationalizing, and moral judgment becomes moralizing, so psychological theories become *psychologizing*. The common denominator is the corruption of a cognitive process to serve an ulterior motive.

Psychologizing consists in condemning or excusing specific individuals on the grounds of their psychological problems, real or invented, in the absence of or contrary to factual evidence.

As a science, psychology is barely making its first steps. It is still in the anteroom of science, in the stage of observing and gathering material from which a future science will come. This stage may be compared to the pre-Socratic period in philosophy; psychology has not yet found a Plato, let alone an Aristotle, to organize its material, systematize its problems, and define its fundamental principles.

A conscientious psychotherapist, of almost any school, knows that the task of diagnosing a particular individual's problems is extremely complex and difficult. The same symptom may indicate different things in different men, according to the total context and interaction of their various premises. A long period of special inquiry is required to arrive even at a valid hypothesis.

This does not stop the amateur psychologizers. Armed with a smattering not of knowledge, but of undigested slogans, they rush, unsolicited, to diagnose the problems of their friends and acquaintances. Pretentiousness and presumptuousness are the psychologizer's invariable characteristics: he not merely invades the privacy of his victims' minds, he claims to understand their minds better than they do, to know more than they do about their own motives. With reckless irresponsibility, which an old-fashioned mystic oracle would hesitate to match, he ascribes to his victims any motivation that suits his purpose, ignoring their denials. Since he is dealing with the great "unknowable"—which used to be life after death or extrasensory perception, but is now man's subconscious—all rules of evidence, logic, and proof are suspended, and anything goes (which is what attracts him to his racket).

The harm he does to his victims is incalculable. People who have psychological problems are confused and suggestible; unable to understand their own inner state, they often feel that any explanation is better than none (which is a very grave error). Thus the psychologizer succeeds in implanting new doubts in their minds, augmenting their sense of guilt and fear, and aggravating their problems.

The unearned status of an "authority," the chance to air arbitrary pronouncements and frighten people or manipulate them, are some of the psychologizer's lesser motives. His basic motive is worse. Observe that he seldom discovers any virtuous or positive elements hidden in his victims' subconscious; what he claims to discover are vices, weaknesses, flaws. What he seeks is a chance to condemn—to pronounce a negative moral judgment, not on the grounds of objective evidence, but on the grounds of some intangible, unprovable processes in a man's subconscious untranslated into action. This means: a chance to subvert morality.

The basic motive of most psychologizers is *hostility*. Caused by a profound self-doubt, self-condemnation, and fear, hostility is a type of projection that directs toward other people the hatred which the hostile person feels toward himself. Blaming the evil of others for his own shortcomings, he feels a chronic need to justify himself by demonstrating their evil, by seeking it, by hunting for it—and by inventing it. The discovery of actual evil in a specific individual is a painful experience for a moral person. But observe the almost triumphant glee with which a psychologizer discovers some ineffable evil in some bewildered victim.

The psychologizer's subversion of morality has another, corollary aspect: by assuming the role of a kind of moral Grand Inquisitor responsible for the psychological purity of others, he deludes himself into the belief that he is demonstrating his devotion to morality and can thus escape the necessity of applying moral principles to his own actions.

This is his link to another, more obvious, and, today, more fashionable type of psychologizer who represents the other side of the same coin: the humanitarian cynic. The cynic turns psychology into a new, "scientific" version of determinism and—by means of unintelligible jargon derived from fantastically arbitrary theories—declares that man is ruled by the blind forces of his subconscious, which he can neither know nor control, that he can't help it, that nobody can help what he does, that nobody should be judged or condemned, that morality is a superstition and anything goes.

This type has many subvariants, ranging from the crude cynic, who claims that innately all men are swine, to the compassionate cynic, who claims that anything must be forgiven and that the substitute for morality is love.

Observe that both types of psychologizers, the Inquisitor and the cynic, switch roles according to circumstances. When the Inquisitor is called to account for some action of his own, he cries: "I couldn't help it!" When the humanitarian cynic confronts an unforgiving, moral man, he vents as virulent a stream of denunciations, hostility, and hatred as any Inquisitor—forgetting that the moral man, presumably, can't help it.

The common denominator remains constant: escape from cognition and, therefore, from morality.

Psychologizing is not confined to amateurs acting in private. Some professional psychologists have set the example in public. As an instance of the Inquisitor type of psychologizing, there was the group of psychiatrists who libeled Senator Barry Goldwater [in 1964], permitting themselves the outrageous impertinence of diagnosing a man they had never met. (Parenthetically, Senator Goldwater exhibited a magnificent moral courage in challenging them and subjecting himself to their filthy malice in the ordeal of a trial, which he won. The Supreme Court, properly, upheld the verdict.) [*Goldwater* v. *Ginzburg et al.* 396 U.S. 1049]

As an example of the cynic type of psychologizing, there are the psychologists who rush to the defense of any murderer (such as Sirhan Sirhan), claiming that he could not help it, that the blame rests on society or environment or his parents or poverty or war, etc.

These notions are picked up by amateurs, by psychologizing commentators who offer them as excuses for the atrocities committed by "political" activists, bombers, college-campus thugs, etc. The notion that poverty is the psychological root of all evil is a typical piece of psychologizing, whose proponents ignore the fact that the worst atrocities are committed by the children of the well-to-do.

As examples of eclectic mixtures, there are the psychologizing biographies of historical figures that interpret the motives of men who died centuries ago—by means of a crude, vulgarized version of the latest psychological theories, which are false to begin with. And there are the countless psychologizing movies that explain a murderer's actions by showing that his domineering mother did not kiss him good night at the age of six—or account for a girl's frigidity by revealing that she once broke a doll representing her father.

Then there is the renowned playwright who was asked in a television interview why his plays always had unhappy endings, and who answered: "I don't know. Ask my psychiatrist."

While the racket of the philosophizing mystics rested on the claim that man is unable to know the external world, the racket of the psychologizing mystics rests on the claim that man is unable to know his own motivation. The ultimate goal is the same: the undercutting of man's mind.

Psychologizers do not confine themselves to any one school of psychology. They snatch parts of any and all psychological theories as they see fit. They sneak along on the fringes of any movement. They exist even among alleged students of Objectivism.

The psychologizers' victims are not always innocent or unwilling. The "liberation" from the responsibility of knowing one's own motives is tempting to many people. Many are eager to switch the burden of judging their own moral stature to the shoulders of anyone willing to carry it. Men who do not accept the judgment of others as a substitute for their own in regard to the external world, turn into abject secondhanders in regard to their inner state. They would not go to a quack for a medical diagnosis of their physical health, but they entrust their mental health to any psychologizer who comes along. The innocent part of their reasons is their failure of introspection and the painful chaos of their psychological conflicts; the non-innocent part is fear of moral responsibility.

Both the psychologizers and their victims ignore the nature of consciousness and of morality.

An individual's consciousness, as such, is inaccessible to others; it can be perceived only by means of its outward manifestations. It is only when mental processes reach some form of expression in action that they become perceivable (by inference) and can be judged. At this point, there is a line of demarcation, a division of labor, between two different sciences.

The task of evaluating the processes of man's subconscious is the province of psychology. Psychology does not regard its subject morally, but medically—i.e., from the aspect of health or malfunction (with cognitive competence as the proper standard of health).

The task of judging man's ideas and actions is the province of philosophy.

Philosophy is concerned with man as a conscious being; it is for conscious beings that it prescribes certain principles of action, i.e., a *moral code*.

A man who has psychological problems is a conscious being; his cognitive faculty is hampered, burdened, slowed down, but not destroyed. *A neurotic is not a psychotic*. Only a psychotic is presumed to suffer from a total break with reality and to have no control over his actions or the operations of his consciousness (and even this is not always true). A neurotic retains the ability to perceive reality, and to control his consciousness and his actions (this control is merely more difficult for him than for a healthy person). So long as he is not psychotic, this is the control that a man *cannot* lose and *must not* abdicate.

Morality is the province of philosophical judgment, not of psychological diagnosis. Moral judgment must be objective, i.e., based on perceivable, demonstrable facts. *A man's moral character must be judged on the basis of his actions, his statements, and his conscious convictions*—not on the basis of inferences (usually spurious) about his subconscious.

A man is not to be condemned or excused on the grounds of the state of his subconscious. His psychological problems are his private concern which is not to be paraded in public and not to be made a burden on innocent victims or a hunting ground for poaching psychologizers. Morality demands that one treat and judge men as responsible adults.

This means that one grants a man the respect of assuming that he is conscious of what he says and does, and one judges his statements and actions *philosophically*, i.e., as what they *are*—not *psychologically*, i.e., as leads or clues to some secret, hidden, unconscious meaning. One neither speaks nor listens to people in code.

If a man's consciousness is hampered by malfunction, it is the task of a psychologist to help him correct it—just as it is the task of a doctor to help correct the malfunction of a man's body. It is not the task of an astronaut-trainer or a choreographer to adjust the techniques of space flying or of ballet dancing to the requirements of the physically handicapped. It is not the task of philosophy to adjust the principles of proper action (i.e., of morality) to the requirements of the psychologically handicapped—nor to allow psychologizers to transform such handicaps into a moral issue, one way or the other.

It is not man's subconscious, but his *conscious* mind that is subject to his direct control—and to moral judgment. It is a specific individual's *conscious* mind that one judges (on the basis of objective evidence) in order to judge his moral character.

Every kind of psychologizing involves the false dichotomy whose extremes are represented by the Inquisitor and the cynic. The alternative is not: rash, indiscriminate moralizing or cowardly, evasive moral neutrality—i.e., condemnation without knowledge or the refusal to know in order not to condemn. These are two interchangeable variants of the same motive: escape from the responsibility of cognition and of moral judgment.

In dealing with people, one necessarily draws conclusions about their characters, which involves their psychology, since every character judgment refers to a man's consciousness. But it is a man's *subconscious* and his *psychopathology* that have to be left alone, particularly in moral evaluations.

A layman needs some knowledge of medicine in order to know how to take care of his own body—and when to call a doctor. The same principle applies to psychology: a layman needs some knowledge of psychology in order to understand the nature of a human consciousness; but theoretical knowledge does not qualify him for the extremely specialized job of diagnosing the psychopathological problems of specific individuals. Even self-diagnosis is often dangerous: there is such a phenomenon as psychological hypochondriacs, who ascribe to themselves every problem they hear or read about.

Allowing for exceptions in special cases, it is not advisable to discuss one's psychological problems with one's friends. Such discussions can lead to disastrously erroneous conclusions (since two amateurs are no better than one, and sometimes worse) —and they introduce a kind of medical element that undercuts the basis of friendship. Friendship presupposes two firm, independent, reliable, and responsible personalities. (This does not mean that one has to lie, put on an act and hide from one's friends the fact that one has problems; it means simply that one does not turn a friend into a therapist.)

The above applies to psychological discussions between two honest persons. The opportunities such discussions offer to the dishonest are obvious: they are an invitation for every type of psychologizer to pounce upon. The Inquisitor will use them to frighten and manipulate a victim. The cynic will use them to attract attention to himself, to evoke pity, to wheedle special privileges. The old lady who talks about her operation is a well-known bore; she is nothing compared to the youngish lady who talks on and on and on about her psychological problems, with a lameness of imagination that prevents them from being good fiction.

Psychological problems as such are not a disgrace; it is what a person does about them that frequently is.

Since a man's psychological problems hamper his cognitive judgment (particularly the problems created by a faulty psycho-epistemology), it is his responsibility to delimit his problems as much as possible, to think with scrupulous precision and clarity before taking an action, and never to act blindly on the spur of an emotion (it is emotions that distort cognition in all types of psychological problems). In regard to other men, it is his responsibility to preserve the principle of *objectivity*, i.e., to be consistent and *intelligible* in his behavior, and not to throw his neurosis at others, expecting them to untangle it, which none of them can or should do.

This brings us to the lowest type of psychologizing, exemplified by Lillian Rearden.

Though her behavior was a calculated racket, the same policy is practiced by many people, in many different forms, to varying extents, moved by various mixtures of cunning, inertia, and irresponsibility. The common denominator is the conscious flouting of objectivity—in the form of the self-admitted inability and/or unwillingness to explain one's own actions. The pattern goes as follows: "Why did you do this?" "I don't know." "What were you after?" "I don't know." "Since I can't understand you, what do you expect me to do?" "I don't know."

This policy rests on the notion that the content of one's consciousness need not be processed.

It is only a newborn infant that could regard itself as the helplessly passive spectator of the chaotic sensations which are the content of its consciousness (but a newborn infant would not, because its consciousness is intensely busy processing its sensations). From the day of his birth, man's development and growth to maturity consists in his mastery of the skill of processing his sensory-perceptual material, of organizing it into concepts, of integrating concepts, of identifying his feelings, of discovering their relation to the facts of reality. This processing has to be performed by a man's own mind. No one can perform it for him. If he fails to perform it, he is mentally defective. It is only on the assumption that he *has* performed it that one treats him as a conscious being.

The evil of today's psychologizing culture—fostered particularly by Progressive education—is the notion that no such processing is necessary.

The result is the stupor and lethargy of those who are neither infants nor adults, but miserable sleepwalkers unwilling to wake up. Anything can enter the spongy mess inside their skulls, nothing can come out of it. The signals it emits are chance regurgitations of any chance splatter.

They have abdicated the responsibility for their own mental processes, yet they continue to act, to speak, to deal with people—and to expect some sort of response. This means that they throw upon others the burden of the task on which they defaulted, and expect others to understand the unintelligible.

The number of people they victimize, the extent of the torture they impose on merciful, conscientious men who struggle to understand them, the despair of those whom they drive to the notion that life is incomprehensible and irrational, cannot be computed.

It should not be necessary to say it, but today it is: anyone who wants to be understood, has to make damn sure that he has made himself intelligible.

This is the moral principle that Hank Rearden glimpsed and should have acted upon at once.

It is only with a person's conscious mind that one can deal, and it is only with his conscious mind that one can be concerned. The unprocessed chaos inside his brain, his unidentified feelings, his unnamed urges, his unformulated wishes, his unadmitted fears, his unknown motives, and the entire cesspool he has made of his stagnant subconscious are of no interest, significance, or concern to anyone outside a therapist's office.

The visible image of an "unprocessed" mentality is offered by non-objective art. Its practitioners announce that they have failed to digest their perceptual data, that they have failed to reach the conceptual or fully conscious level of development, and that they offer you the raw material of their subconscious, whose mystery is for you to interpret.

There is no great mystery about it.

The mind is a processing organ; so is the stomach. If a stomach fails in its function, it throws up; its unprocessed material is vomit.

So is the unprocessed material emitted by a mind.

6

Altruism as Appeasement
by Ayn Rand

This article was published in The Objectivist, *January 1966.*

In March 1962, on the occasion of giving a lecture at M.I.T., I met a young student who was earnestly, intelligently concerned with opposing the trend to collectivism. I asked him his views on why so many of today's young intellectuals were becoming "liberals." He could not give me a full answer. But a few weeks later, he wrote me a remarkable letter.

He explained that he had given a great deal of thought to my question and had reached certain conclusions. The majority of college students, he wrote, do not choose to think; they accept the status quo, conform to the prescribed code of values, and evade the responsibility of independent thought. "In adopting this attitude, they are encouraged by teachers who inspire imitation, rather than creation."

But there are a few who are not willing to renounce their rational faculty. "They are the intellectuals—and they are the outsiders. Their willingness to think makes them shine forth as a threat to the stagnant security of the levelers in which they are immersed. They are teased and rejected by their schoolmates. An immense amount of faith in oneself and a rational philosophical basis are required to set oneself against all that society has ever taught.... The man who preaches individual integrity, pride, and self-esteem is today virtually nonexistent. Far more common is the man who, driven by the young adult's driving need for acceptance, has compromised. And here is the key—[the result of] *the compromise is the liberal.*

"The man who sets himself against society by seeking to be

32

rational is almost certain to succumb to the extent of accepting a strong guilt complex. He is declared 'guilty' by his rejection of the omnipresent 'equality in mediocrity' doctrine of today. . . . So the intellectual, to atone for a false guilt, becomes today's liberal. He proclaims loudly the brotherhood of all men. He seeks to serve his escapist brothers by guaranteeing them their desire for social security. He sanctions their mediocrity, he works for their welfare, above all he essentially seeks their approval—to atone for the guilt that they have thrust upon him in the guise of an absolute moral system which is not open to question."

This young man deserves credit for an extraordinary psychological perceptiveness. But the situation he describes is not new; it is as old as altruism; nor is it confined to "liberals."

Shortly after receiving that letter, I met a distinguished historian, a man of great intellect and scholarship, an advocate of capitalism, who was then in his late seventies. I had been puzzled by the fact that in his many works, the rigorous logic of his arguments was inexplicably contradicted and undercut by his acceptance of "the common good" as the criterion of morality—and I asked him his reasons. "Oh, one must say that to the masses," he answered, "otherwise, they won't accept capitalism."

Between these two extremes of age—from college years to the culmination of a lifetime's struggle—lies a silent psychological horror story. It is the story of men who spend their lives apologizing for their own intelligence.

The following pattern does not enmesh all men of superior mental endowment; some manage to escape it; but in our antirational culture, it strangles too many of them.

By the time he reaches college, a bright, sensitive, precociously observant youth has acquired the sense of being trapped in a nightmare universe where he is resented not for his flaws, but for his greatest attribute: his intelligence. It is merely a *sense*, not a firm conviction; no teenager can draw such a conclusion with certainty or fully believe so enormous an evil. He senses only that he is "different," in some way which he cannot define—that he does not get along with people, for some reason which he cannot name—that he wants to understand things and issues, *big* issues, about which no one else seems to care.

His first year in college is, usually, his psychological killer. He had expected college to be a citadel of the intellect where he would find answers, knowledge, meaning, and, above all, some companions to share his interest in ideas. He finds none of it. One or two teachers may live up to his hope (though they are growing rarer year by year). But as to intellectual companionship, he finds the same gang he had met in kindergarten, in playgrounds, and in vacant lots: a leering, screeching, aggressively mindless gang playing the same games, with a latinized jargon replacing the mud pies and baseball bats.

There are many wrong decisions he can make at this crossroads, but the deadliest—psychologically, intellectually, and morally—is the attempt to join the gang at the price of selling his soul to uninterested buyers. It is an attempt to apologize for his intellectual concerns and to escape from the loneliness of a thinker by professing that his thinking is dedicated to some social-altruistic goal. It is an attempt that amounts to the wordless equivalent of the plea: "I'm not an outsider! I'm your friend! Please forgive me for using my mind—I'm using it only in order to serve *you!*"

Whatever remnants of personal value he may preserve after a deal of that kind, self-esteem is not one of them.

Such decisions are seldom, if ever, made consciously. They are made gradually, by subconscious emotional motivation and semiconscious rationalization. Altruism offers an arsenal of such rationalizations: if an unformed adolescent can tell himself that his cowardice is humanitarian love, that his subservience is unselfishness, that his moral treason is spiritual nobility, he is hooked. By the time he is old enough to know better, the erosion of his self-esteem is such that he dares not face or reexamine the issue.

Some degree of social metaphysics [secondhandedness] is almost always involved in the psychology of such a man, but it is hard to tell whether it led to or resulted from his surrender. In either case, his basic motivation is different and, in a certain sense, worse. Basically, a social metaphysician is motivated by the desire to escape the responsibility of independent thought, and he surrenders the mind he is afraid to use, preferring to follow the judgments of others. But an intellectual appeaser surrenders morality, the realm of values, *in order to be permitted to use his mind.* The degree of self-abasement is greater; the implicit view of values—as irrelevant to the mind—is disastrous; the implicit view of the mind—as functioning by permission of the mindless—is unspeakable. (Nor does the appeaser often care to speak about it.)

There are as many variants of the consequences as there are men who commit this particular type of moral treason. But certain scars of psychological deformity can be observed in most of them as their common symptoms.

Humanitarian love is what the altruist-appeaser never achieves. Instead, his salient characteristic is a mixture of bitter contempt and intense, profound hatred for mankind, a hatred impervious to reason. He regards men as evil by nature, he complains about their congenital stupidity, mediocrity, depravity—yet slams his mind ferociously shut to any argument that challenges his estimate. His view of the people at large is a nightmare image—the image of a mindless brute endowed with some inexplicably omnipotent power—and he lives in terror of that image, yet resists any attempt to revise it.

If questioned, he can give no grounds for his view. Intellectually, he admits that the average man is not a murderous brute ready to attack him at any moment; emotionally, he keeps feeling the brute's presence behind every corner.

An accomplished young scientist once told me that he was not afraid of gangsters, but waiters and gas-station attendants filled him with terror, even though he could not say what it was he expected them to do to him. An elderly, extremely successful businessman told me that he divided people into three classes according to their intelligence: the above average, the average, and the below average; he did not mind the first two classes, but those of below average intelligence threw him into uncontrollable panic. He had spent his life expecting a bloody uprising of brutes who would seize, loot, wreck, and slaughter everything in sight; no, he was not a "conservative"; he was a "liberal."

There is an element of truth in that image of the brute: not *factual* truth, but *psychological* truth, not about people at large, but about the man who fears them. The brute is the frozen embodiment of mankind as projected by the emotions of an adolescent appeaser. The brute's omnipotent power to perpetrate some unimaginable horror is merely an adult's rationalization; physical violence is not what he fears. But his terror is real: a monster that had the power to make him surrender his mind is, indeed, a terrifying evil. And the deepest, the unconfessed source of his terror lies in the fact that the surrender was not demanded or extorted—that the monster was the victim's own creation.

This is the reason why the appeaser has a vested interest in maintaining his belief in the brute's existence: even a life of terror, with the excuse that he could not help it, is preferable to facing the full enormity of the fact that he was not robbed of self-esteem, but threw it away—and that his chronic sense of guilt does not come from the spurious sin of possessing intelligence, but from the actual crime of having betrayed it.

A corollary symptom, in most intellectual appeasers, is the "elite" premise—the dogmatic, unshakable belief that "the masses don't think," that men are impervious to reason, that thinking is the exclusive prerogative of a small, "chosen" minority.

In the field of politics, this leads the more aggressive type of appeasers, the "liberals," to the belief in rule by physical force, to the doctrine that people are unfit for freedom and should be ruled—"for their own good"—by a dictatorship of the "elite." Hence the craving of such "liberals" for governmental recognition, and their extreme susceptibility to bribes by any strong-arm government, foreign or domestic, in the form of minor jobs, loud titles, official honors or simply dinner invitations. Hence the tolerant sympathy of such "liberals" for the regimes of Soviet Russia or Red China, and their appalling indifference to the wholesale atrocities of those countries.

The more timorous type of appeasers, the "conservatives," take a different line: they share the notion of an intellectual "elite" and, therefore, they discard intellectuality as numerically unimportant, and they concentrate on cajoling the brute ("the masses") with baby talk—with vapid slogans, flattering bromides, folksy speeches in two-syllable words, on the explicit premise that reason does not work, that the brute must be won through appeals to his emotions and must, somehow, be fooled or cheated into taking the right road.

Both groups believe that dictatorships are "practical"—the "liberals" boldly and openly, the "conservatives" fearfully. Behind the ineffectual, half-hearted, apologetic attempts of the "conservatives" to defend freedom, lies the often confessed belief that the struggle is futile, that free enterprise is doomed. Why? The unconfessed answer is: Because men are brutes.

Moral cowardice is the necessary consequence of discarding morality as inconsequential. It is the common symptom of all intellectual appeasers. The image of the brute is the symbol of an appeaser's belief in the supremacy of evil, which means—not in conscious terms, but in terms of his quaking, cringing blinding panic—that when his mind judges a thing to be evil, his emotions proclaim its power, and the more evil, the more powerful.

To an appeaser, the self-assertive confidence of the good is a reproach, a threat to his precarious pseudo-self-esteem, a disturbing phenomenon from a universe whose existence he cannot permit himself to acknowledge—and his emotional response is a nameless resentment. The self-assertive confidence of the evil is a metaphysical confirmation, the sign of a universe in which he feels at home—and his emotional response is bitterness, but obedience. Some dictators—who boastfully stress their reign of terror, such as Hitler and Stalin—count on this kind of psychology. There are people on whom it works.

Moral cowardice is fear of upholding the good *because* it is good, and fear of opposing the evil *because* it is evil. The next step leads to opposing the good in order to appease the evil, and rushing out to seek the evil's favor. But since no mind can fully hide this policy from itself, and no form of pseudo-self-esteem can disguise it for long, the next step is to pounce upon every possible or impossible chance to blacken the nature of the good and to whitewash the nature of the evil.

Such is the relationship of mind to values—and such is the fate of those who sought to preserve their intellect by dispensing with morality.

The appeaser's inner state is revealed in the field of esthetics. His sense of life dominates modern art and literature: the cult of depravity—the monotonous projection of cosmic terror, guilt, impotence, misery, doom—the compulsive preoccupation with the study of homicidal maniacs, a preoccupation resembling the mentality of a superstitious savage who fashions a voodoo doll in the belief that to reproduce is to master.

This does not mean that all the practitioners of modern art or modern politics are men who betrayed their own intelligence: most of them had nothing to betray. But it *does* mean that such practices would not have spread without the sanction of the intellectual traitors—and that they brought their own nightmare universe into reality by creating a cultural bandwagon for pretentious mediocrities and worse.

Not all of the intellectual appeasers reach the public arena. A great many of them perish on the way, torn by their inner conflicts, paralyzed by an insufficient capacity to evade, petering out in hopeless lethargy after a brilliantly promising start. A great many others drag themselves on, by an excruciating psy-

chological effort, functioning at a small fraction of their potential. The cost of this type of appeasement—in frustrated,
hampered, crippled, or stillborn talent—can never be computed.

An appeaser's professional success or failure, as well as the
degree of his precarious psychological adjustment, depends on
the slowness or speed of a process common to all appeasers: the
erosion of his sense of values. The renunciation of values—the
acceptance of an irrational morality—was the specific form of
his surrender. The pretense at any belief in altruism vanishes
from his mind in a very few years, and there is nothing left to
replace it: his independent capacity to value has been repressed—
and his fear of the brute makes the pursuit of values seem
hopelessly impractical. What sets in, thereafter, is the dry rot of
cynicism—like a kind of premature senility of the spirit—a thin
coating of belligerent amorality over a swamp of lifeless resignation. The result is a muted, impoverished, extinguished personality, the *impersonal* personality of a man with an ever shrinking
range of concern, with nothing to seek, to achieve, to admire or
oppose, and—since self-assertion is the assertion of one's values—
with no self to assert. One of the bitter penalties of the appeasers is that even the most brilliant of them turn out, as persons,
to be conventional, empty, *dull.*

If their initial crime was the desire to be "one of the boys,"
this is the way in which they do succeed.

Their ultimate penalty is still worse. A wrong premise does
not merely fail, it achieves its own opposite. After years of
intellectual faking, diluting, corner-cutting—in order to smuggle
his ideas past an imaginary censor, in order to placate irrationality, stupidity, dishonesty, prejudice, malice, or vulgarity—the
appeaser's own mind assumes the standards of those he professes to despise. A mind cannot maintain a double standard of
judgment indefinitely (if at all). Any man who is willing to
speak or write "down," i.e., to *think* down—who distorts his own
ideas in order to accommodate the mindless, who subordinates
truth to fear—becomes eventually indistinguishable from the
hacks who cater to an alleged "public taste." He joins the hordes
who believe that the mind is impotent, that reason is futile, that
ideas are only means of fooling the masses (i.e., that ideas are
important to the unthinking, but the thinkers know better)—the
vast, stagnant underworld of anti-intellectuality. Such is the
dead end of the road he has chosen to take, he who had started
out as a self-sacrificial priest of the intellect.

Hatred for reason is hatred for intelligence; today's culture is saturated with both. It is the ultimate product of generations of appeasers, past and present—of men who, fearing an imaginary brute, upheld and perpetuated the irrational, inhuman, brutalizing morality of altruism.

No, men are not brutes; neither are they all independent thinkers. The majority of men are not intellectual initiators or originators; they accept what the culture offers them. It is not that they don't think; it is that they don't sustain their thinking consistently, as a way of life, and that their abstract range is limited. To what extent they are stunted by the anti-rational influences of our cultural traditions, is hard to say; what *is* known, however, is that the majority of men use only a small part of their potential intellectual capacity.

The truly and deliberately evil men are a very small minority; it is the appeaser who unleashes them on mankind; it is the appeaser's intellectual abdication that invites them to take over. When a culture's dominant trend is geared to irrationality, the thugs win over the appeasers. When intellectual leaders fail to foster the best in the mixed, unformed, vacillating character of people at large, the thugs are sure to bring out the worst. When the ablest men turn into cowards, the average men turn into brutes.

No, the average man is not morally innocent. But the best proof of his non-brutality, of his helpless, confused, inarticulate longing for truth, for an intelligible, rational world—and of his response to it, when given a chance he cannot create on his own—is the fact that no dictatorship has ever lasted without establishing censorship.

No, it is not the intelligent man's moral obligation to serve as the leader or teacher of his less endowed brothers. His foremost moral obligation is to preserve the integrity of his mind and of his self-esteem—which means: to be proud of his intelligence—regardless of their approval or disapproval. No matter how hard this might be in a corrupt age like ours, he has, in fact, no alternative. It is his only chance at a world where intelligence can function, which means: a world where he—and, incidentally, they—can survive.

7

The Question of Scholarships
by Ayn Rand

This article was published in The Objectivist, *June 1966.*

Many students of Objectivism are troubled by a certain kind of moral dilemma confronting them in today's society. [I am] frequently asked the questions: "Is it morally proper to accept scholarships, private or public?" and: "Is it morally proper for an advocate of capitalism to accept a government research grant or a government job?"

I shall hasten to answer: *"Yes"*—then proceed to explain and qualify it. There are many confusions on these issues, created by the influence and implications of the altruist morality.

1. There is nothing wrong in accepting *private* scholarships. The fact that a man has no claim on others (i.e., that it is not their moral duty to help him and that he cannot demand their help as his right) does not preclude or prohibit good will among men and does not make it immoral to offer or to accept voluntary, non-sacrificial assistance.

    It is altruism that has corrupted and perverted human benevolence by regarding the giver as an object of immolation and the receiver as a helplessly miserable object of pity who holds a mortgage on the lives of others—a doctrine which is extremely offensive to both parties, leaving men no choice but the roles of sacrificial victim or moral cannibal. A man of self-esteem can neither offer help nor accept it on such terms.

    As a consequence, when people need help, the best of them (those who need it through no fault of their own) often prefer to starve rather than accept assistance—while the worst of them (the professional parasites) run riot and cash in on it to the full. (For instance, the student "activists" who, not satisfied with free education, demand ownership of the university as well.)

To view the question in its proper perspective, one must begin by rejecting altruism's terms and all of its ugly emotional aftertaste—then take a fresh look at human relationships. It is morally proper to accept help, when it is offered not as a moral duty, but as an act of good will and generosity, when the giver can afford it (i.e., when it does not involve self-sacrifice on his part), and when it is offered in response to the receiver's virtues, *not* in response to his flaws, weaknesses, or moral failures, and *not* on the ground of his need as such.

Scholarships are one of the clearest categories of this proper kind of help. They are offered to assist *ability*, to reward intelligence, to encourage the pursuit of knowledge, to further achievement—*not* to support incompetence.

If a brilliant child's parents cannot send him through college (or if he has no parents), it is not a moral default on their part or his. It is not the fault of "society," of course, and he cannot demand the *right* to be educated at someone else's expense; he must be prepared to work his way through school, if necessary. But *this* is the proper area for voluntary assistance. If some private person or organization offers to help him, in recognition of his ability, and thus to save him years of struggle—he has the moral right to accept.

The value of scholarships is that they offer an ambitious youth a *gift of time* when he needs it most: at the beginning.

(The fact that in today's moral atmosphere, those who give or distribute scholarships are often guilty of injustices and of altruistic motives, does not alter the principle involved. It represents *their* failure to live up to the principle; their integrity is not the recipient's responsibility and does not affect his right to accept the scholarship in good faith.)

2. A different principle and different considerations are involved in the case of public (i.e., governmental) scholarships. The right to accept them rests on the right of the victims to the property (or some part of it) which was taken from them by force.

The recipient of a public scholarship is morally justified *only so long as he regards it as restitution and opposes all forms of welfare statism.* Those who advocate public scholarships have no right to them; those who oppose them have. If this sounds like a paradox, the fault lies in the moral contradictions of welfare statism, not in its victims.

Since there is no such thing as the right of some men to vote away the rights of others, and no such thing as the right of the government to seize the property of some men for the unearned benefit of others—the advocates and supporters of the welfare state are morally guilty of robbing their opponents, and the fact that the robbery is legalized makes it morally worse, not better. The victims do not have to add self-inflicted martyrdom to the injury done to them by others; they do not have to let the looters profit doubly, by letting them distribute the money exclusively to the parasites who clamored for it. Whenever the welfare-state laws offer them some small restitution, *the victims should take it.*

It does not matter, in this context, whether a given individual has or has not paid an amount of taxes equal to the amount of the scholarship he accepts. First, the sum of his individual losses cannot be computed; this is part of the welfare-state philosophy, which treats everyone's income as public property. Second, if he has reached college age, he has undoubtedly paid—in hidden taxes—much more than the amount of the scholarship. Or, if his parents cannot afford to pay for his education, consider what taxes *they* have paid, directly or indirectly, during the twenty years of his life—and you will see that a scholarship is too pitifully small even to be called a restitution.

Third—and most important—the young people of today are not responsible for the immoral state of the world into which they were born. Those who accept the welfare-statist ideology assume their share of the guilt when they do so. But the anti-collectivists are innocent victims who face an impossible situation: it is welfare statism that has almost destroyed the possibility of working one's way through college. It was difficult but possible some decades ago; today, it has become a process of close-to-inhuman torture. There are virtually no part-time jobs that pay enough to support oneself while going to school; the alternative is to hold a full-time job and to attend classes at night—which takes *eight* years of unrelenting twelve-to-sixteen-hour days, for a four-year college course. If those responsible for such conditions offer the victim a scholarship, his right to take it is incontestable—and it is too pitifully small an amount even to register on the scales of justice, when one considers all the other, the nonmaterial, nonamendable injuries he has suffered.

The same moral principles and considerations apply to the issue of accepting social security, unemployment insurance, or other payments of that kind. It is obvious, in such cases, that a man receives his own money which was taken from him by force, directly and specifically, without his consent, against his own choice. Those who advocated such laws are morally guilty, since they assumed the "right" to force employers and unwilling coworkers. But the victims, who opposed such laws, have a clear right to any refund of their own money—and they would not advance the cause of freedom if they left their money, unclaimed, for the benefit of the welfare-state administration.

3. The same moral principles and considerations apply to the issue of government research grants.

The growth of the welfare state is approaching the stage where virtually the only money available for scientific research will be government money. (The disastrous effects of this situation and the disgraceful state of government-sponsored science are apparent already, but that is a different subject. We are concerned here only with the moral dilemma of scientists.) Taxation is destroying private resources, while government money is flooding and taking over the field of research.

In these conditions, a scientist is morally justified in accepting government grants—*so long as he opposes all forms of welfare statism.* As in the case of scholarship recipients, a scientist does not have to add self-martyrdom to the injustices he suffers. And he does not have to surrender science to the Dr. Floyd Ferrises [this refers to a villain in *Atlas Shrugged* who is a government scientist].

Government research grants, for the most part, have no strings attached, i.e., no controls over the scientist's intellectual and professional freedom (at least, not yet). When and if the government attempts to control the scientific and/or political views of the recipients of grants, *that* will be the time for men of integrity to quit. At present, they are still free to work—but, more than any other professional group, they should be on guard against the gradual, insidious growth of pressures to conform and of tacit control-by-intimidation, which are implicit in such conditions.

4. The same moral principles and considerations apply to the issue of taking government jobs.

The growth of government institutions has destroyed an incalculable number of private jobs and opportunities for private employment. This is more apparent in some professions (as, for instance, teaching) than in others, but the octopus of the "public sector" is choking and draining the "private sector" in virtually every line of work. Since men have to work for a living, the opponents of the welfare state do not have to condemn themselves to the self-martyrdom of a self-restricted labor market—particularly when so many private employers are in the vanguard of the advocates and profiteers of welfare statism.

There is, of course, a limitation on the moral right to take a government job: one must not accept any job that demands *ideological* services, i.e., any job that requires the use of one's mind to compose propaganda material in support of welfare statism—or any job in a regulatory administrative agency enforcing improper, non-objective laws. The principle here is as follows: it is proper to take the kind of work which is not wrong per se, except that the government should not be doing it, such as medical services; it is improper to take the kind of work that *nobody* should be doing, such as is done by the F.T.C., the F.C.C., etc.

But the same limitation applies to a man's choice of private employment: a man is not responsible for the moral or political views of his employers, but he cannot accept a job in an undertaking which he considers immoral, or in which his work consists specifically of violating his own convictions, i.e., of propagating ideas he regards as false or evil.

5. The moral principle involved in all the above issues consists, in essence, of defining as clearly as possible the nature and limits of one's own responsibility, i.e., the nature of what is or is not in one's power.

The issue is primarily *ideological*, not financial. Minimizing the financial injury inflicted on you by the welfare-state laws, does not constitute support of welfare statism (since the purpose of such laws *is* to injure you) and is not morally reprehensible. Initiating, advocating, or expanding such laws is.

In a free society, it is immoral to denounce or oppose that from which one derives benefits—since one's associations are voluntary. In a controlled or mixed economy, opposition becomes obligatory—since one is acting under force, and the offer of benefits is intended as a bribe.

So long as financial considerations do not alter or affect your convictions, so long as you fight against welfare statism (and *only* so long as you fight it) and are prepared to give up any of its momentary benefits in exchange for repeal and freedom—so long as you do not sell your soul (or your vote)—you are morally in the clear. The essence of the issue lies in your own mind and attitude.

It is a hard problem, and there are many situations so ambiguous and so complex that no one can determine what is the right course of action. *That* is one of the evils of welfare statism: its fundamental irrationality and immorality force men into contradictions where *no* course of action is right.

The ultimate danger in all these issues is psychological: the danger of letting yourself be bribed, the danger of a gradual, imperceptible, subconscious deterioration leading to compromise, evasion, resignation, submission. In today's circumstances, a man is morally in the clear only so long as he remains *intellectually* incorruptible. Ultimately, these problems are a test—a hard test—of your own integrity. You are its only guardian. Act accordingly.

8

Of Living Death
by Ayn Rand

This lecture on the July 29, 1968 papal encyclical
Humanae Vitae *was delivered at the Ford Hall
Forum on December 8, 1968. Because* The Objectivist *was behind schedule at the time, the lecture was
published in the issues dated September–November
1968.*

Those who wish to observe the role of philosophy in human
existence may see it dramatized on a grand (and gruesome)
scale in the conflict splitting the Catholic church today.

Observe, in that conflict, men's fear of identifying or challenging philosophical fundamentals: both sides are willing to
fight in silent confusion, to stake their beliefs, their careers,
their reputations on the outcome of a battle over the effects of
an unnamed cause. One side is composed predominantly of men
who dare not name the cause; the other, of men who dare not
discover it.

Both sides claim to be puzzled and disappointed by what they
regard as a contradiction in the two recent encyclicals of Pope
Paul VI. The so-called conservatives (speaking in religious, not
political, terms) were dismayed by the encyclical *Populorum
Progressio (On the Development of Peoples)*—which advocated global
statism—while the so-called liberals hailed it as a progressive
document. Now the conservatives are hailing the encyclical
Humanae Vitae (Of Human Life)—which forbids the use of
contraceptives—while the liberals are dismayed by it. Both sides
seem to find the two documents inconsistent. But the inconsis-
tency is theirs, not the pontiff's. The two encyclicals are strictly,
flawlessly consistent in respect to their basic philosophy and

ultimate goal: both come from the same view of man's nature and are aimed at establishing the same conditions for his life on earth. The first of these two encyclicals forbade ambition, the second forbids enjoyment; the first enslaved man to the physical needs of others, the second enslaves him to the physical capacities of his own body; the first damned achievement, the second damns love.

The doctrine that man's sexual capacity belongs to a lower or animal part of his nature has had a long history in the Catholic church. It is the necessary consequence of the doctrine that man is not an integrated entity, but a being torn apart by two opposite, antagonistic, irreconcilable elements: his body, which is of this earth, and his soul, which is of another, supernatural realm. According to that doctrine, man's sexual capacity—regardless of how it is exercised or motivated, not merely its abuses, not unfastidious indulgence or promiscuity, but *the capacity as such*—is sinful or depraved.

For centuries, the dominant teaching of the church held that sexuality is evil, that only the need to avoid the extinction of the human species grants sex the status of a *necessary* evil and, therefore, only procreation can redeem or excuse it. In modern times, many Catholic writers have denied that such is the church's view. But what *is* its view? They did not answer.

Let us see if we can find the answer in the encyclical *Humanae Vitae*.

Dealing with the subject of birth control, the encyclical prohibits all forms of contraception (except the so-called "rhythm method"). The prohibition is total, rigid, unequivocal. It is enunciated as a moral absolute.

Bear in mind what this subject entails. Try to hold an image of horror spread across space and time—across the entire globe and through all the centuries—the image of parents chained, like beasts of burden, to the physical needs of a growing brood of children—young parents aging prematurely while fighting a losing battle against starvation—the skeletal hordes of unwanted children born without a chance to live—the unwed mothers slaughtered in the unsanitary dens of incompetent abortionists—the silent terror hanging, for every couple, over every moment of love. If one holds this image while hearing that this nightmare is not to be stopped, the first question one will ask is: *Why?* In the name of humanity, one will assume that some inconceivable, but crucially important reason must motivate any human being who would seek to let that carnage go on uncontested.

So the first thing one will look for in the encyclical, is that reason, an answer to that *Why?*

"The problem of birth," the encyclical declares, "like every other problem regarding human life, is to be considered ... in the light of an integral vision of man and of his vocation, not only his natural and earthly, but also his supernatural and eternal, vocation." [Paragraph 7]

And:

> A reciprocal act of love, which jeopardizes the responsibility to transmit life which God the Creator, according to particular laws, inserted therein, is in contradiction with the design constitutive of marriage, and with the will of the author of life. To use this divine gift, destroying, even if only partially, its meaning and its purpose, is to contradict the nature both of man and of woman and of their most intimate relationship, and therefore it is to contradict also the plan of God and His will. [13]

And *this* is all. In the entire encyclical, this is the only reason given (but repeated over and over again) why men should transform their highest experience of happiness—their love—into a source of lifelong agony. Do so—the encyclical commands—because it is God's will.

I, who do not believe in God, wonder why those who do would ascribe to him such a sadistic design, when God is supposed to be the archetype of mercy, kindness, and benevolence. What *earthly* goal is served by that doctrine? The answer runs like a hidden thread through the encyclical's labyrinthian convolutions, repetitions, and exhortations.

In the darker corners of that labyrinth, one finds some snatches of argument, in alleged support of the mystic axiom, but these arguments are embarrassingly transparent equivocations. For instance:

> ... to make use of the gift of conjugal love while respecting the laws of the generative process means to acknowledge oneself not to be the arbiter of the sources of human life, but rather the minister of the design established by the Creator. In fact, just as man does not have unlimited dominion over his body in general, so also, with particular reason, he has no such dominion over his creative faculties as such, because of their intrinsic ordination toward raising up life, of which God is the principle. [13]

What is meant here by the words "man does not have unlimited dominion over his body in general"? The obvious meaning is that man cannot change the *metaphysical* nature of his body; which is true. But man has the power of choice in regard to the *actions* of his body—specifically, in regard to "his creative faculties," and the responsibility for the use of these particular faculties is most crucially his. "To acknowledge oneself not to be the arbiter of the sources of human life" is to evade and to default on that responsibility. Here again, the same equivocation or package deal is involved. Does man have the power to determine the nature of his procreative faculty? No. But granted that nature, is he the arbiter of bringing a new human life into existence? He most certainly is, and he (with his mate) is the *sole* arbiter of that decision—and the consequences of that decision affect and determine the entire course of his life.

This is a clue to that paragraph's intention: if man believed that so crucial a choice as procreation is not in his control, what would it do to his control over his life, his goals, his future?

The passive obedience and helpless surrender to the physical functions of one's body, the necessity to let procreation be the inevitable result of the sexual act, is the natural fate of *animals*, not of men. In spite of its concern with man's higher aspirations, with his soul, with the sanctity of married love—it is to the level of animals that the encyclical seeks to reduce man's sex life, in fact, in reality, on earth. What does this indicate about the encyclical's view of sex?

Anticipating certain obvious objections, the encyclical declares:

> Now, some may ask: In the present case, is it not reasonable in many circumstances to have recourse to artificial birth control if, thereby, we secure the harmony and peace of the family, and better conditions for the education of children already born? To this question it is necessary to reply with clarity: The church is the first to praise and recommend the intervention of intelligence in a function which so closely associates the rational creature with his Creator; but she affirms that this must be one with respect for the order established by God. [16]

To what does this subordinate man's intelligence? If intelligence is forbidden to consider the fundamental problems of man's existence, forbidden to alleviate his suffering, what does this indicate about the encyclical's view of man—and of reason?

History can answer this particular question. History has seen a period of approximately ten centuries, known as the Dark and Middle Ages, when philosophy was regarded as "the handmaiden of theology," and reason as the humble subordinate of faith. The results speak for themselves.

It must not be forgotten that the Catholic church has fought the advance of science since the Renaissance: from Galileo's astronomy, to the dissection of corpses, which was the start of modern medicine, to the discovery of anesthesia in the nineteenth century, the greatest single discovery in respect to the incalculable amount of terrible suffering it has spared mankind. The Catholic church has fought medical progress by means of the same argument: that the application of knowledge to the relief of human suffering is an attempt to contradict God's design. Specifically in regard to anesthesia during childbirth, the argument claimed that since God intended woman to suffer while giving birth, man has no right to intervene. (!)

The encyclical does not recommend unlimited procreation. It does not object to all means of birth control—only to those it calls "artificial" (i.e., scientific). It does not object to man "contradicting God's will" nor to man being "the arbiter of the sources of human life," provided he uses the means it endorses: *abstinence*.

Discussing the issue of "responsible parenthood," the encyclical states: "In relation to physical, economic, psychological and social conditions, responsible parenthood is exercised, either by the deliberate and generous decision to raise a numerous family, or by the decision, made for grave motives and with due respect for the moral law, to avoid for the time being, or even for an indeterminate period, a new birth." [10] To avoid—by what means? By abstaining from sexual intercourse.

The lines preceding that passage are: "In relation to the tendencies of instinct or passion, responsible parenthood means the necessary dominion which reason and will must exercise over them." [10] How a man is to force his reason to obey an irrational injunction and what it would do to him psychologically, is not mentioned.

Further on, under the heading "Mastery of Self," the encyclical declares:

> To dominate instinct by means of one's reason and free will undoubtedly requires ascetic practices ... Yet this discipline which is proper to the purity of married couples, far from harming conjugal love, rather confers on it a higher human value. It demands continual effort yet, thanks to its beneficent influence, husband and wife fully develop their personalities, being enriched with spiritual values.... Such discipline ... helps both

parties to drive out selfishness, the enemy of true love; and deepens their sense of responsibility. [21]

If you can bear that style of expression being used to discuss such matters—which I find close to unbearable—and if you focus on the meaning, you will observe that the "discipline," the "continual effort," the "beneficent influence," the "higher human value" refer to the torture of sexual frustration.

No, the encyclical does not say that sex as such is evil; it merely says that sexual abstinence *in marriage* is "a higher human value." What does this indicate about the encyclical's view of sex—and of marriage?

Its view of marriage is fairly explicit. "[Conjugal] love is first of all fully human, that is to say, of the senses and of the spirit at the same time. It is not, then, a simple transport of instinct and sentiment, but also, and principally, an act of the free will, intended to endure and to grow by means of the joys and sorrows of daily life, in such a way that husband and wife become one only heart and one only soul, and together attain their human perfection.

"Then this love is total; that is to say, it is a very special form of personal friendship, in which husband and wife generously share everything, without undue reservations or selfish calculations." [9]

To classify the unique emotion of *romantic love* as a form of *friendship* is to obliterate it: the two emotional categories are mutually exclusive. The feeling of friendship is asexual; it can be experienced toward a member of one's own sex.

There are many other indications of this kind scattered through the encyclical. For instance: "These acts, by which husband and wife are united in chaste intimacy and by means of which human life is transmitted, are, as the council recalled, 'noble and worthy.' " [11] It is not *chastity* that one seeks in sex, and to describe it this way is to emasculate the meaning of marriage.

There are constant references to a married couple's *duties*, which have to be considered in the context of the sexual act— "duties toward God, toward themselves, toward the family and toward society." [10] If there is any one concept which, when associated with sex, would render a man impotent, it is the concept of "duty."

To understand the full meaning of the encyclical's view of

sex, I shall ask you to identify the common denominator—the common *intention*—of the following quotations: .

> [The church's] teaching, often set forth by the Magisterium, is founded upon the inseparable connection, willed by God and unable to be broken by man on his own initiative, between the two meanings of the conjugal act: the unitive meaning and the procreative meaning. Indeed, by its intimate structure, the conjugal act, while most closely uniting husband and wife, capacitates them for the generation of new lives. [12]

"[The conjugal acts] do not cease to be lawful if, for *causes independent of the will of husband and wife*, they are foreseen to be infecund." [11, emphasis added.]

The church forbids: "every action which, either in anticipation of the conjugal act or its accomplishment, or in the development of its natural consequences, proposes, whether as an end or as a means, to render procreation impossible." [14]

The church does not object to "an impediment to procreation" which might result from the medical treatment of a disease, *"provided such impediment is not, for whatever motive, directly willed."* [15, emphasis added.]

And finally, the church "teaches that each and every marriage act (*'quilibet matrimonii usus,'*) must remain open to the transmission of life." [11]

What is the common denominator of these statements? It is not merely the tenet that sex as such is evil, but deeper: it is the commandment by means of which sex will *become* evil, the commandment which, if accepted, will divorce sex from love, will castrate man spiritually and will turn sex into a meaningless physical indulgence. That commandment is: *man must not regard sex as an end in itself, but only as a means to an end.*

Procreation and "God's design" are not the major concern of that doctrine; they are merely primitive rationalizations to which man's self-esteem is to be sacrificed. If it were otherwise, why the stressed insistence on forbidding man to impede procreation by his conscious will and choice? Why the tolerance of the conjugal acts of couples who are infecund by nature rather than by choice? What is so evil about that choice? There is only one answer: that choice rests on a couple's conviction that the justification of sex is their own enjoyment. And *this* is the view which the church's doctrine is intent on forbidding at any price.

That such is the doctrine's intention, is supported by the

church's stand on the so-called "rhythm method" of birth control, which the encyclical approves and recommends.

> The church is coherent with herself when she considers recourse to the infecund periods to be licit, while at the same time condemning, as being always illicit, the use of means directly contrary to fecundation, even if such use is inspired by reasons which may appear honest and serious. . . . It is true that, in the one and the other case, the married couple are concordant in the positive will of avoiding children for plausible reasons, seeking the certainty that offspring will not arrive; but it is also true that only in the former case are they able to renounce the use of marriage in the fecund periods when, for just motives, procreation is not desirable, while making use of it during infecund periods to manifest their affection and to safeguard their mutual fidelity. By so doing, they give proof of a truly and integrally honest love. [16]

On the face of it, this does not make any kind of sense at all—and the church has often been accused of hypocrisy or compromise because it permits this very unreliable method of birth control while forbidding all others. But examine that statement from the aspect of its intention, and you will see that the church is indeed "coherent with herself," i.e., consistent.

What is the *psychological* difference between the "rhythm method" and other means of contraception? The difference lies in the fact that, using the "rhythm method," a couple cannot regard sexual enjoyment as a right and as an end in itself. With the help of some hypocrisy, they merely sneak and snatch some personal pleasure, while keeping the marriage act "open to the transmission of life," thus acknowledging that childbirth is the only moral justification of sex and that only by the grace of the calendar are they unable to comply.

This acknowledgment is the meaning of the encyclical's peculiar implication that "to renounce the use of marriage in the fecund periods" is, somehow, a virtue (a renunciation which proper methods of birth control would not require). What else but this acknowledgment can be the meaning of the otherwise unintelligible statement that by the use of the "rhythm method" a couple "give proof of a truly and integrally honest love"?

There is a widespread popular notion to the effect that the Catholic church's motive in opposing birth control is the desire to enlarge the Catholic population of the world. This may be superficially true of some people's motives, but it is not the full truth. If it were, the Catholic church would forbid the "rhythm method" along with all other forms of contraception. And, more important, the Catholic church would not fight for anti-birth-control legislation all over the world: if numerical superiority were its motive, it would forbid birth control to its own followers and let it be available to other religious groups.

The motive of the church's doctrine on this issue is, philosophically, much deeper than that and much worse; the goal is not metaphysical or political or biological, but psychological: if man is forbidden to regard sexual enjoyment as an end in itself, he will not regard love or his own happiness as an end in itself; if so, then he will not regard his own life as an end in itself; if so, then he will not attain self-esteem.

It is not against the gross, animal, physicalistic theories or uses of sex that the encyclical is directed, but against the *spiritual* meaning of sex in man's life. (By "spiritual" I mean pertaining to man's consciousness.) It is not directed against casual, mindless promiscuity, but against romantic love.

To make this clear, let me indicate, in brief essentials, a rational view of the role of sex in man's existence.

Sex is a physical capacity, but its exercise is determined by man's mind—by his choice of values, held consciously or subconsciously. To a rational man, sex is an expression of self-esteem—*a celebration of himself and of existence.* To the man who lacks self-esteem, sex is an attempt to fake it, to acquire its momentary illusion.

Romantic love, in the full sense of the term, is an emotion possible only to the man (or woman) of unbreached self-esteem: it is his response to his own highest values in the person of another—an integrated response of mind and body, of love and sexual desire. Such a man (or woman) is incapable of experiencing a sexual desire divorced from spiritual values.

I quote from *Atlas Shrugged*: "The men who think that wealth comes from material resources and has no intellectual root or meaning, are the men who think—for the same reason—that sex is a physical capacity which functions independently of one's mind, choice or code of values. . . . But, in fact, a man's sexual choice is the result and the sum of his fundamental convictions. . . . Sex is the most profoundly selfish of all acts, an act which [man] cannot perform for any motive but his own enjoyment—just try to think of performing it in a spirit of selfless charity!—an act which is not possible in self-abasement, only in self-exaltation, only in the confidence of being desired and being worthy of desire. . . . Love is our response to our highest values—and can be nothing else. . . . Only the man who extols the purity of a love devoid of desire, is capable of the depravity of a desire devoid of love."

In other words, sexual promiscuity is to be condemned not because sex as such is evil, but because it is *good*—too good and too important to be treated casually.

In comparison to the moral and psychological importance of sexual happiness, the issue of procreation is insignificant and irrelevant, except as a deadly threat—and God bless the inventors of the Pill!

The capacity to procreate is merely a potential which man is not obligated to actualize. The choice to have children or not is morally optional. Nature endows man with a variety of potentials—and it is his *mind* that must decide which capacities he chooses to exercise, according to his own hierarchy of rational goals and values. The mere fact that man has the capacity to kill does not mean that it is his duty to become a murderer; in the same way, the mere fact that man has the capacity to procreate does not mean that it is his duty to commit spiritual suicide by making procreation his primary goal and turning himself into a stud-farm animal.

It is only animals that have to adapt themselves to their physical background and to the biological functions of their bodies. Man adapts his physical background and the use of his biological faculties to himself—to his own needs and values. *That* is his distinction from all other living species.

To an animal, the rearing of its young is a matter of temporary cycles. To man, it is a lifelong responsibility—a grave responsibility that must not be undertaken causelessly, thoughtlessly, or accidentally.

In regard to the moral aspects of birth control, the primary right involved is not the "right" of an unborn child, or of the family, or of society, or of God. The primary right is one which—in today's public clamor on the subject—few, if any, voices have had the courage to uphold: *the right of man and woman to their own life and happiness*—the right not to be regarded as the means to any end.

Man is an end in himself. Romantic love—the profound, exalted, lifelong *passion* that unites his mind and body in the sexual act—is the living testimony to that principle.

This is what the encyclical seeks to destroy; or, more precisely, to obliterate, as if it does not and cannot exist.

Observe the encyclical's contemptuous references to sexual desire as "instinct" or "passion," as if "passion" were a pejorative term. Observe the false dichotomy offered; man's choice is either mindless, "instinctual" copulation—or marriage, an institution presented not as a union of *passionate* love, but as a relationship of "chaste intimacy," of "special personal friendship," of "discipline proper to purity," of unselfish duty, of alternating bouts with frustration and pregnancy, and of such unspeakable, Grade-B-movie-folks-next-door kind of boredom that any semi-living man would have to run, in self-preservation, to the nearest whorehouse.

No, I am not exaggerating. I have reserved—as my last piece of evidence on the question of the encyclical's view of sex—the paragraph in which the coils and veils of euphemistic equivocation got torn, somehow, and the naked truth shows through.

It reads as follows:

> Upright men can even better convince themselves of the solid grounds on which the teaching of the church in this field is based, if they care to reflect upon the consequences of methods of artificial birth control. Let them consider, first of all, how wide and easy a road would thus be opened up toward conjugal infidelity and the general lowering of morality. Not much experience is needed in order to know human weakness, and to understand that men—especially the young, who are so vulnerable on this point—have need of encouragement to be faithful to the moral law, so that they must not be offered some easy means of eluding its observance. It is also to be feared that the man, growing used to the employment of anticonceptive practices, may finally lose respect for the woman and, no longer caring for her physical and psychological equilibrium, may come to the point of considering her as a mere instrument of selfish enjoyment, and no longer as his respected and beloved companion. [17]

I cannot conceive of a rational woman who does not want to be precisely *an instrument of her husband's selfish enjoyment*. I cannot conceive of what would have to be the mental state of a woman who could desire or accept the position of having a husband who does *not* derive any selfish enjoyment from sleeping with her. I cannot conceive of anyone, male or female, capable of believing that sexual enjoyment would destroy a husband's love and respect for his wife—but regarding her as a brood mare and himself as a stud, would cause him to love and respect her.

Actually, this is too evil to discuss much further.

But we must also take note of the first part of that paragraph. It states that "artificial" contraception would open "a wide and easy road toward conjugal infidelity." Such is the encyclical's actual view of marriage: that marital *fidelity* rests on nothing better than fear of pregnancy. Well, "not much experience is needed in order to know" that that fear has never been much of a deterrent to anyone.

Now observe the inhuman cruelty of that paragraph's reference to the young. Admitting that the young are "vulnerable on this point," and declaring that they need "encouragement to be faithful to the moral law," the encyclical forbids them the use of contraceptives, thus making it cold-bloodedly clear that its idea of moral encouragement consists of terror—the sheer, stark terror of young people caught between their first experience of love and the primitive brutality of the moral code of their elders. Surely the authors of the encyclical cannot be ignorant of the fact that it is not the young chasers or the teenage sluts who would be the victims of a ban on contraceptives, but the *innocent* young who risk their lives in the quest for love—the girl who finds herself pregnant and abandoned by her boyfriend, or the boy who is trapped into a premature, unwanted marriage. To ignore the agony of such victims—the countless suicides, the deaths at the hands of quack abortionists, the drained lives wasted under the double burden of a spurious "dishonor" and of an unwanted child—to ignore all that in the name of "the moral law" is to make a mockery of morality.

Another, and truly incredible mockery, leers at us from that same paragraph 17. As a warning against the use of contraceptives, the encyclical states:

> Let it be considered also that a dangerous weapon would thus be placed in the hands of those public authorities who take no heed of moral exigencies. . . . Who will stop rulers from favoring, from even imposing upon their peoples, if they were to consider it necessary, the method of contraception which they judge to be most efficacious? In such a way men, wishing to avoid individual, family or social difficulties encountered in the observance of the divine law, would reach the point of placing at the mercy of the

intervention of public authorities the most personal and most reserved sector of conjugal intimacy.

No public authorities have attempted—and no private groups have urged them to attempt—to force contraception on Catholics. But when one remembers that it is the Catholic church that has initiated anti-birth-control legislation the world over and thus has placed "at the mercy of the intervention of public authorities the most personal and most reserved sector of conjugal intimacy"—that statement becomes outrageous. Were it not for the politeness one should preserve toward the papal office, one would call that statement a brazen effrontery.

This leads us to the encyclical's stand on the issue of abortion, and to another example of inhuman cruelty. Compare the coiling sentimentality of the encyclical's style when it speaks of "conjugal love" to the clear, brusque, military tone of the following: "We must once again declare that the direct interruption of the generative process already begun, and, above all, directly willed and procured abortion, *even if for therapeutic reasons*, are to be absolutely excluded as licit means of regulating birth." [14, emphasis added.]

After extolling the virtue and sanctity of motherhood, as a woman's highest duty, as her "eternal vocation," the encyclical attaches a special risk of death to the performance of that duty—an unnecessary death, in the presence of doctors forbidden to save her, as if a woman were only a screaming huddle of infected flesh who must not be permitted to imagine that she has the right to live.

And *this* policy is advocated by the encyclical's supporters in the name of their concern for "the sanctity of life" and for "rights"—the rights of the embryo. (!)

I suppose that only the psychological mechanism of projection can make it possible for such advocates to accuse their opponents of being "*anti-life*."

Observe that the men who uphold such a concept as "the rights of an embryo," are the men who deny, negate, and violate the rights of a living human being.

An embryo *has no rights*. Rights do not pertain to a *potential*, only to an *actual* being. A child cannot acquire any rights until it is born. The living take precedence over the not yet living (or the unborn).

Abortion is a moral right—which should be left to the sole

discretion of the woman involved; morally, nothing other than her wish in the matter is to be considered. Who can conceivably have the right to dictate to her what disposition she is to make of the functions of her own body? The Catholic church is responsible for this country's disgracefully barbarian anti-abortion laws, which should be repealed and abolished.

The intensity of the importance that the Catholic church attaches to its doctrine on sex may be gauged by the enormity of the indifference to human suffering expressed in the encyclical. Its authors cannot be ignorant of the fact that man has to earn his living by his own effort, and that there is no couple on earth—on any level of income, in any country, civilized or not—who would be able to support the number of children they would produce if they obeyed the encyclical to the letter.

If we assume the richest couple and include time off for the periods of "purity," it will still be true that the physical and psychological strain of their "vocation" would be so great that nothing much would be left of them, particularly of the mother, by the time they reached the age of forty.

Consider the position of an *average* American couple. What would be their life, if they succceded in raising, say, twelve children, by working from morning till night, by running a desperate race with the periodic trips to maternity wards, with rent bills, grocery bills, clothing bills, pediatricians' bills, strained-vegetables bills, school book bills, measles, mumps, whooping cough, Christmas trees, movies, ice cream cones, summer camps, party dresses, dates, draft cards, hospitals, colleges—with every salary raise of the industrious, hardworking father mortgaged and swallowed before it is received—what would they have gained at the end of their life except the hope that they might be able to pay their cemetery bills, in advance?

Now consider the position of the majority of mankind, who are barely able to subsist on a level of prehistorical poverty. No strain, no backbreaking effort of the ablest, most conscientious father can enable him properly to feed one child—let alone an open-end progression. The unspeakable misery of stunted, disease-eaten, chronically undernourished children, who die in droves before the age of ten, is a matter of public record. Pope Paul VI—who closes his encyclical by mentioning his title as earthly representative of "the God of holiness and mercy"—cannot be ignorant of these facts; yet he is able to ignore them.

The encyclical brushes this issue aside in a singularly irresponsible manner:

> We are well aware of the serious difficulties experienced by public authorities in this regard, especially in the developing countries. To their legitimate preoccupations we devoted our encyclical letter *Populorum Progressio*. . . . The only possible solution to this question is one which envisages the social and economic progress both of individuals and of the whole of human society, and which respects and promotes true human values.
>
> Neither can one, without grave injustice, consider Divine Providence to be responsible for what depends, instead, on a lack of wisdom in government, on an insufficient sense of social justice, on selfish monopolization or again on blameworthy indolence in confronting the efforts and the sacrifices necessary to insure the raising of living standards of a people and of all its sons. [23]

The encyclical *Populorum Progressio* advocated the abolition of capitalism and the establishment of a totalitarian, socialist-fascist, global state—in which the right to "the minimum essential for life" is to be the ruling principle and "all other rights whatsoever, including those of property and of free commerce, are to be subordinated to this principle." (For a discussion of that encyclical, see my article "Requiem for Man" in [*Capitalism: The Unknown Ideal*].)

If, today, a struggling, desperate man, somewhere in Peru or China or Egypt or Nigeria, accepted the commandments of the present encyclical and strove to be moral, but saw his horde of children dying of hunger around him, the only practical advice the encyclical would give him is: Wait for the establishment of a collectivist world state. What, in God's name, is he to do in the meantime?

Philosophically, however, the reference to the earlier encyclical, *Populorum Progressio*, is extremely significant: it is as if Pope Paul VI were pointing to the bridge between the two documents and to their common base.

The global state advocated in *Populorum Progressio* is a nightmare utopia where all are enslaved to the physical needs of all; its inhabitants are selfless robots, programmed by the tenets of altruism, without personal ambition, without mind, pride, or self-esteem. But self-esteem is a stubborn enemy of all utopias of that kind, and it is doubtful whether mere economic enslavement would destroy it wholly in men's souls. What *Populorum*

Progressio was intended to achieve from without, in regard to the physical conditions of man's existence, *Humanae Vitae* is intended to achieve from within, in regard to the devastation of man's consciousness.

"Don't allow men to be happy," said Ellsworth Toohey in *The Fountainhead*. "Happiness is self-contained and self-sufficient. . . . Happy men are free men. So kill their joy in living. . . . Make them feel that the mere fact of a personal desire is evil. . . . Unhappy men will come to you. They'll need you. They'll come for consolation, for support, for escape. Nature allows no vacuum. Empty man's soul—and the space is yours to fill."

Deprived of ambition, yet sentenced to endless toil; deprived of rewards, yet ordered to produce; deprived of sexual enjoyment, yet commanded to procreate; deprived of the right to live, yet forbidden to die—condemned to this state of living death, the graduates of the encyclical *Humanae Vitae* will be ready to move into the world of *Populorum Progressio*; they will have no other place to go.

"If some man like Hugh Akston," said Hank Rearden in *Atlas Shrugged*, "had told me, when I started, that by accepting the mystics' theory of sex I was accepting the looters' theory of economics, I would have laughed in his face. I would not laugh at him now."

It would be a mistake, however, to suppose that in the subconscious hierarchy of motives of the men who wrote these two encyclicals, the second, *Humanae Vitae*, was merely the spiritual means to the first, *Populorum Progressio*, which was the material end. The motives, I believe, were the reverse: *Populorum Progressio* was merely the material means to *Humanae Vitae*, which was the spiritual end.

". . . with our predecessor Pope John XXIII," says Pope Paul VI in *Humanae Vitae*, "we repeat: no solution to these difficulties is acceptable 'which does violence to man's essential dignity' and is based only '*on an utterly materialistic conception of man himself and of his life.*' " [23, emphasis added.] They mean it—though not exactly in the way they would have us believe.

In terms of reality, nothing could be more *materialistic* than an existence devoted to feeding the whole world and procreating to the limit of one's capacity. But when they say "materialistic," they mean pertaining to man's mind and to this earth; by "spiritual," they mean whatever is anti-man, anti-mind, anti-life, and, above all, anti-possibility of human happiness on earth.

The ultimate goal of these encyclicals' doctrine is not the material advantages to be gained by the rulers of a global slave state; the ultimate goal is the spiritual emasculation and degradation of man, the extinction of his love of life, which *Humanae Vitae* is intended to accomplish, and *Populorum Progressio* merely to embody and perpetuate.

The means of destroying man's spirit is *unearned guilt*.

What I said in "Requiem for Man" about the motives of *Populorum Progressio* applies as fully to *Humanae Vitae*, with only a minor paraphrase pertaining to its subject. "But, you say, the encyclical's ideal will not work? It is not intended to work. It is not intended to [achieve human chastity or sexual virtue]; it is intended to induce guilt. It is not intended to be accepted and practiced; it is intended to be accepted and broken—broken by man's 'selfish' desire to [love], which will thus be turned into a shameful weakness. Men who accept as an ideal an irrational goal which they cannot achieve, never lift their heads thereafter—and never discover that their bowed heads were the only goal to be achieved."

I said, in that article, that *Populorum Progressio* was produced by the sense of life not of an individual, but of an institution—whose driving power and dominant obsession is the desire to break man's spirit. Today, I say it, with clearer evidence, about the encyclical *Humanae Vitae*.

This is the fundamental issue which neither side of the present conflict is willing fully to identify.

The conservatives or traditionalists of the Catholic church seem to know, no matter what rationalizations they propound, that such is the meaning and intention of their doctrine. The liberals seem to be more innocent, at least in this issue, and struggle not to have to face it. But they are the supporters of global statism and, in opposing *Humanae Vitae*, they are merely fighting the right battle for the wrong reasons. If they win, their social views will still lead them to the same ultimate results.

The rebellion of the victims, the Catholic laymen, has a touch of healthy self-assertiveness; however, if they defy the encyclical and continue to practice birth control, but regard it as a matter of their own weakness and guilt, the encyclical will have won: this is precisely what it was intended to accomplish.

The American bishops of the Catholic church, allegedly struggling to find a compromise, issued a pastoral letter declaring that contraception is an *objective evil*, but individuals are not necessarily guilty or sinful if they practice it—which amounts to a total abdication from the realm of morality and can lead men only to a deeper sense of guilt.

Such is the tragic futility of attempting to fight the existential consequences of a philosophical issue, without facing and challenging the philosophy that produced them.

This issue is not confined to the Catholic church, and it is deeper than the problem of contraception; it is a moral crisis approaching a climax. The core of the issue is Western civilization's view of man and of his life. The essence of that view depends on the answer to two interrelated questions: Is man (man the individual) an end in himself?—and: Does man have the right to be happy on this earth?

Throughout its history, the West has been torn by a profound ambivalence on these questions: all of its achievements came from those periods when men acted as if the answer were "Yes"—but, with exceedingly rare exceptions, their spokesmen, the philosophers, kept proclaiming a thunderous "No," in countless forms.

Neither an individual nor an entire civilization can exist indefinitely with an unresolved conflict of that kind. Our age is paying the penalty for it. And it is our age that will have to resolve it.

9

Religion Versus America
by Leonard Peikoff

This lecture was delivered at the Ford Hall Forum on April 20, 1986, and published in The Objectivist Forum, *June 1986.*

A specter is haunting America—the specter of religion. This, borrowing Karl Marx's literary style, is my theme tonight.

Where do I see religion? The outstanding political fact of the 1980s is the rise of the New Right, and its penetration of the Republican party under President Reagan. The bulk of the New Right consists of Protestant Fundamentalists, typified by the Moral Majority. These men are frequently allied on basic issues with other religiously oriented groups, including conservative Catholics of the William F. Buckley ilk and neoconservative Jewish intellectuals of the *Commentary* magazine variety.

All these groups observed the behavior of the New Left awhile back and concluded, understandably enough, that the country was perishing. They saw the liberals' idealization of drugged hippies and nihilistic yippies; they saw the proliferation of pornography, of sexual perversion, of noisy Lib and Power gangs running to the Democrats to demand ever more outrageous handouts and quotas; they heard the routine leftist deprecation of the United States and the routine counsel to appease Soviet Russia—and they concluded, with good reason, that what the country was perishing from was a lack of values, of ethical absolutes, of morality.

Values, the Left retorted, are subjective; no lifestyle (and no country) is better or worse than any other; there is no absolute right or wrong anymore—unless, the liberals added, you believe in some outmoded ideology like religion. Precisely, the New

64

Rightists reply; that is our whole point. There *are* absolute truths and absolute values, they say, which are the key to the salvation of our great country; but there is only one source of such values: not man or this earth or the human brain, but the Deity as revealed in scripture. The choice we face, they conclude, is the skepticism, decadence, and statism of the Democrats, *or* morality, absolutes, Americanism, and their only possible base: religion—old-time, Judeo-Christian religion.

"Religious America is awakening, perhaps just in time for our country's sake," said Mr. Reagan in 1980. "In a struggle against totalitarian tyranny, traditional values based on religious morality are among our greatest strengths."[1]

"Religious views," says Congressman Jack Kemp, "lie at the heart of our political system. The 'inalienable rights' to life, liberty, and the pursuit of happiness are based on the belief that each individual is created by God and has a special value in His eyes. . . . Without a common belief in the one God who created us, there could be no freedom and no recourse if a majority were to seek to abrogate the rights of the minority."[2]

Or, as Education Secretary William Bennett sums up this viewpoint: "Our values as a free people and the central values of the Judeo-Christian tradition are flesh of the flesh and blood of the blood."[3]

Politicians in America have characteristically given lip service to the platitudes of piety. But the New Right is different. These men seem to mean their religiosity, and they are dedicated to implementing their religious creeds politically; they seek to make these creeds the governing factor in the realm of our personal relations, our art and literature, our clinics and hospitals, and the education of our youth. Whatever else you say about him, Mr. Reagan has delivered handsomely on one of his campaign promises: he has given the adherents of religion a prominence in setting the national agenda that they have not had in this country for generations.

This defines our subject for tonight. It is the new Republican inspiration and the deeper questions it raises. Is the New Right the answer to the New Left? What *is* the relation between the Judeo-Christian tradition and the principles of Americanism? Are Ronald Reagan and Jack Kemp, as their admirers declare, leading us to a new era of freedom and capitalism—or to something else?

In discussing these issues, I am not going to say much about the New Right as such; its specific beliefs are widely known. Instead, I want to examine the movement within a broader, philosophical context. I want to ask: what is religion? and then: how does it function in the life of a nation, any nation, past or present? These, to be sure, are very abstract questions, but they are inescapable. Only when we have considered them can we go on to judge the relation between a particular religion, such as Christianity, and a particular nation, such as America.

Let us begin with a definition. What is religion as such? What is the essence common to all its varieties, Western and Oriental, which distinguishes it from other cultural phenomena?

Religion involves a certain kind of outlook on the world and a consequent way of life. In other words, the term "religion" denotes a type (actually, a precursor) of *philosophy*. As such, a religion must include a view of knowledge (which is the subject matter of the branch of philosophy called epistemology) and a view of reality (metaphysics). Then, on this foundation, a religion builds a code of values (ethics). So the question becomes: what type of philosophy constitutes a religion?

The *Oxford English Dictionary* defines "religion" as "a particular system of faith and worship," and goes on, in part: "Recognition on the part of man of some higher unseen power as having control of his destiny, and as being entitled to obedience, reverence, and worship."

The fundamental concept here is *"faith."* "Faith" in this context means belief in the absence of evidence. This is the essential that distinguishes religion from science. A scientist may believe in entities which he cannot observe, such as atoms or electrons, but he can do so only if he proves their existence logically, by inference from the things he does observe. A religious man, however, believes in "some higher unseen power" which he cannot observe and cannot logically prove. As the whole history of philosophy demonstrates, no study of the natural universe can warrant jumping outside it to a supernatural entity. The five arguments for God offered by the greatest of all religious thinkers, Thomas Aquinas, are widely recognized by philosophers to be logically defective; they have each been refuted many times, and they are the best arguments that have ever been offered on this subject.

Many philosophers indeed now go further: they point out that God not only is an article of faith, but that this is essential to religion. A God susceptible of proof, they argue, would actually wreck religion. A God open to human logic, to scientific study, to rational understanding, would have to be definable, delimited, finite, amenable to human concepts, obedient to scientific law, and thus incapable of miracles. Such a thing would be merely one object among others within the natural world; it would be merely another datum for the scientist, like some new kind of galaxy or cosmic ray, not a transcendent power running the universe and demanding man's worship. What religion rests on is a true God, i.e., a God not of reason, but of faith.

If you want to concretize the idea of faith, I suggest that you visit, of all places, the campuses of the Ivy League, where, according to *The New York Times*, a religious revival is now occurring. Will you find students eagerly discussing proofs or struggling to reinterpret the ancient myths of the Bible into some kind of consistency with the teachings of science? On the contrary. The students, like their parents, are insisting that the Bible be accepted as literal truth, whether it makes logical sense or not. "Students today are more reconciled to authority," one campus religious official notes. "There is less need for students to sit on their own mountaintop"—i.e., to exercise their own independent minds and judgment. Why not? They are content simply to believe. At Columbia University, for instance, a new student group gathers regularly not to analyze, but "to sing, worship, and speak in tongues." "People are coming back to religion in a way that some of us once went to the counterculture," says a chaplain at Columbia.[4] This is absolutely true. And note what they are coming back to: not reason or logic, but *faith*.

"Faith" names the method of religion, the essence of its epistemology; and, as the *Oxford English Dictionary* states, the belief in "some higher unseen power" is the basic content of religion, its distinctive view of reality, its metaphysics. This higher power is not always conceived as a personal God; some religions construe it as an impersonal dimension of some kind. The common denominator is the belief in the supernatural—in some entity, attribute, or force transcending and controlling this world in which we live.

According to religion, this supernatural power is the essence of the universe and the source of all value. It constitutes the realm of true reality and of absolute perfection. By contrast, the world around us is viewed as only semi-real and as inherently imperfect, even corrupt, in any event metaphysically unimportant. According to most religions, this life is a mere episode in the soul's journey to its ultimate fulfillment, which involves leaving behind earthly things in order to unite with Deity. As a pamphlet issued by a Catholic study group expresses this point: Man "cannot achieve perfection or true happiness in this life here on earth. He can only achieve this in the eternity of the next life after death. . . . Therefore . . . what a person has or lacks in terms of worldly possessions, privileges or advantages is not important."[5] In New Delhi a few months ago, expressing this viewpoint, Pope John Paul II urged on the Indians a life of "asceticism and renunciation." In Quebec some time earlier, he decried "the fascination the modern world feels for productivity, profit, efficiency, speed, and records of physical strength." Too many men, he explained in Luxembourg, "consciously organize their way of life merely on the basis of the realities of this world without any heed for God and His wishes."[6]

This brings us to religious ethics, the essence of which also involves faith, faith in God's commandments. Virtue, in this view, consists of obedience. Virtue is not a matter of achieving *your* desires, whatever they may be, but of seeking to carry out God's; it is not the pursuit of egoistic goals, whether rational or not, but the willingness to renounce your own goals in the service of the Lord. What religion counsels is the ethics of self-transcendence, self-abnegation, *self-sacrifice*.

What single attitude most stands in the way of this ethics, according to religious writers? The sin of pride. Why is pride a sin? Because man, in this view, is a metaphysically defective creature. His intellect is helpless in the crucial questions of life. His will has no real power over his existence, which is ultimately controlled by God. His body lusts after all the temptations of the flesh. In short, man is weak, ugly, and low, a typical product of the low, unreal world in which he lives. Your proper attitude toward yourself, therefore, as to this world, should be a negative one. For earthly creatures such as you and I, "Know thyself" means "Know thy worthlessness"; simple honesty entails humility, self-castigation, even self-disgust.

Religion means orienting one's existence around faith, God, and a life of service—and correspondingly of downgrading or condemning four key elements: reason, nature, the self, and man. Religion cannot be equated with values or morality or even philosophy as such; it represents a specific approach to philosophic issues, including a specific code of morality.

What effect does this approach have on human life? We do

not have to answer by theoretical deduction, because Western history has been a succession of religious and unreligious periods. The modern world, including America, is a product of two of these periods: of Greco-Roman civilization and of medieval Christianity. So, to enable us to understand America, let us first look at the historical evidence from these two periods; let us look at their stand on religion and at the practical consequences of this stand. Then we will have no trouble grasping the base and essence of the United States.

Ancient Greece was not a religious civilization, not on any of the counts I mentioned. The gods of Mount Olympus were like a race of elder brothers to man, mischievous brothers with rather limited powers; they were closer to Steven Spielberg's Extra-Terrestrial visitor than to anything we would call "God." They did not create the universe or shape its laws or leave any message of revelations or demand a life of sacrifice. Nor were they taken very seriously by the leading voices of the culture, such as Plato and Aristotle. From start to finish, the Greek thinkers recognized no sacred texts, no infallible priesthood, no intellectual authority beyond the human mind; they allowed no room for faith. Epistemologically, most were staunch individualists who expected each man to grasp the truth by his own powers of sensory observation and logical thought. For details, I refer you to Aristotle, the preeminent representative of the Greek spirit.

Metaphysically, as a result, Greece was a secular culture. Men generally dismissed or downplayed the supernatural; their energies were devoted to the joys and challenges of life. There was a shadowy belief in immortality, but the dominant attitude to it was summed up by Homer, who has Achilles declare that he would rather be a slave on earth than "bear sway among all the dead that be departed."

The Greek ethics followed from this base. All the Greek thinkers agreed that virtue is egoistic. The purpose of morality, in their view, is to enable a man to achieve his own fulfillment, his own happiness, by means of a proper development of his natural faculties—above all, of his cognitive faculty, his intellect. And as to the Greek estimate of man—look at the statues of the Greek gods, made in the image of human strength, human grace, human beauty; and read Aristotle's account of the virtue—yes, the virtue—of pride.

I must note here that in many ways Plato was an exception to the general irreligion of the Greeks. But his ideas were not dominant until much later. When Plato's spirit did take over, the Greek approach had already died out. What replaced it was the era of Christianity.

Intellectually speaking, the period of the Middle Ages was the exact opposite of classical Greece. Its leading philosophic spokesman, Augustine, held that faith was the basis of man's entire mental life. "I do not know in order to believe," he said, "I believe in order to know." In other words, reason is nothing but a handmaiden of revelation; it is a mere adjunct of faith, whose task is to clarify, as far as possible, the dogmas of religion. What if a dogma cannot be clarified? So much the better, answered an earlier Church father, Tertullian. The truly religious man, he said, delights in thwarting his reason; that shows his commitment to faith. Thus Tertullian's famous answer, when asked about the dogma of God's self-sacrifice on the cross: "Credo quia absurdum" ("I believe it because it is absurd").

As to the realm of physical nature, the medievals characteristically regarded it as a semi-real haze, a transitory stage in the divine plan, and a troublesome one at that, a delusion and a snare—a delusion because men mistake it for reality, a snare because they are tempted by its lures to jeopardize their immortal souls. What tempts them is the prospect of earthly pleasure.

What kind of life, then, does the immortal soul require on earth? Self-denial, asceticism, the resolute shunning of this temptation. But isn't it unfair to ask men to throw away their whole enjoyment of life? Augustine's answer is: what else befits creatures befouled by original sin, creatures who are, as he put it, "crooked and sordid, bespotted and ulcerous"?

What were the practical results—in the ancient world, then in the medieval—of these two opposite approaches to life?

Greece created philosophy, logic, science, mathematics, and a magnificent, man-glorifying art; it gave us the base of modern civilization in every field; it taught the West how to think. In addition, through its admirers in ancient Rome, which built on the Greek intellectual base, Greece indirectly gave us the rule of law and the first idea of man's rights (this idea was originated by the pagan Stoics). Politically, the ancients never conceived a society of full-fledged individual liberty; no nation achieved that before the United States. But the ancients did lay certain theoretical bases for the concept of liberty; and in practice, both in some of the Greek city-states and in republican Rome, large numbers of men at various times were at least relatively free.

They were incomparably more free than their counterparts ever had been in the religious cultures of ancient Egypt and its equivalents.

What were the practical results of the medieval approach? The Dark Ages were dark on principle. Augustine fought against secular philosophy, science, art; he regarded all of it as an abomination to be swept aside; he cursed science in particular as "the lust of the eyes." Unlike many Americans today, who drive to church in their Cadillac or tape their favorite reverend on the VCR so as not to interrupt their tennis practice, the medievals took religion seriously. They proceeded to create a society that was antimaterialistic *and* anti-intellectual. I do not have to remind you of the lives of the saints, who were the heroes of the period, including the men who ate only sheep's gall and ashes, quenched their thirst with laundry water, and slept with a rock for their pillow. These were men resolutely defying nature, the body, sex, pleasure, all the snares of this life—and they were canonized for it, as, by the essence of religion, they should have been. The economic and social results of this kind of value code were inevitable: mass stagnation and abject poverty, ignorance and mass illiteracy, waves of insanity that swept whole towns, a life expectancy in the teens. "Woe unto ye who laugh now," the Sermon on the Mount had said. Well, they were pretty safe on this count. They had precious little to laugh about.

What about freedom in this era? Study the existence of the feudal serf tied for life to his plot of ground, his noble overlord, and the all-encompassing decrees of the Church. Or, if you want an example closer to home, jump several centuries forward to the American Puritans, who were a medieval remnant transplanted to a virgin continent, and who proceeded to establish a theocratic dictatorship in colonial Massachusetts. Such a dictatorship, they declared, was necessitated by the very nature of their religion. You are owned by God, they explained to any potential dissenter; therefore, you are a servant who must act as your Creator, through his spokesmen, decrees. Besides, they said, you are innately depraved, so a dictatorship of the elect is necessary to ride herd on your vicious impulses. And, they said, you don't really own your property either; wealth, like all values, is a gift from Heaven temporarily held in trust, to be controlled, like all else, by the elect. And if all this makes you unhappy, they ended up, so what? You're not supposed to pursue happiness in this life anyway.

There can be no philosophic breach between thought and action. The consequence of the epistemology of religion is the politics of tyranny. If you cannot reach the truth by your own mental powers, but must offer obedient faith to a cognitive authority, then you are not your own intellectual master; in such a case, you cannot guide your behavior by your own judgment, either, but must be submissive in action as well. This is the reason why, historically—as Ayn Rand has pointed out—faith and force are always corollaries; each requires the other.

The early Christians did contribute some good ideas to the world, ideas that proved important to the cause of future freedom. I must, so to speak, give the angels their due. In particular, the idea that man has value *as an individual*—that the individual soul is precious—is essentially a Christian legacy to the West; its first appearance was in the form of the idea that every man, despite original sin, is made in the image of God (as against the pre-Christian notion that a certain group or nation has a monopoly on human value, while the rest of mankind are properly slaves or mere barbarians). But notice a crucial point: this Christian idea, by itself, was historically impotent. It did nothing to unshackle the serfs or stay the Inquisition or turn the Puritan elders into Thomas Jeffersons. Only when the religious approach lost its power—only when the idea of individual value was able to break free from its Christian context and become integrated into a rational, secular philosophy—only then did this kind of idea bear practical fruit.

What—or who—ended the Middle Ages? My answer is: Thomas Aquinas, who introduced Aristotle, and thereby *reason*, into medieval culture. In the thirteenth century, for the first time in a millennium, Aquinas reasserted in the West the basic pagan approach. Reason, he said in opposition to Augustine, does not rest on faith; it is a self-contained, natural faculty, which works on sense experience. Its essential task is not to clarify revelation, but rather, as Aristotle had said, to gain knowledge of this world. Men, Aquinas declared forthrightly, must use and obey reason; whatever one can prove by reason and logic, he said, is true. Aquinas himself thought that he could prove the existence of God, and he thought that faith is valuable as a supplement to reason. But this did not alter the nature of his revolution. His was the charter of liberty, the moral and philosophical sanction, which the West had desperately needed. His message to mankind, after the long ordeal of faith, was in effect: "It is all right. You don't have to stifle your mind anymore. You can think."

The result, in historical short order, was the revolt against the authority of the Church, the feudal breakup, the Renaissance. Renaissance means "rebirth," the rebirth of reason and of man's concern with this world. Once again, as in the pagan era, we see secular philosophy, natural science, man-glorifying art, and the pursuit of earthly happiness. It was a gradual, tortuous change, with each century becoming more worldly than the preceding, from Aquinas to the Renaissance to the Age of Reason to the climax and end of this development: the eighteenth century, the Age of Enlightenment. This was the age in which America's founding fathers were educated and in which they created the United States.

The Enlightenment represented the triumph (for a short while anyway) of the pagan Greek, and specifically of the Aristotelian, spirit. Its basic principle was respect for man's intellect and, correspondingly, the wholesale dismissal of faith and revelation. *Reason the Only Oracle of Man*, said Ethan Allen of Vermont, who spoke for his age in demanding unfettered free thought and in ridiculing the primitive contradictions of the Bible. "While we are under the tyranny of Priests," he declared in 1784, ". . . it ever will be their interest, to invalidate the law of nature and reason, in order to establish systems incompatible therewith."[7]

Elihu Palmer, another American of the Enlightenment, was even more outspoken. According to Christianity, he writes, God "is supposed to be a fierce, revengeful tyrant, delighting in cruelty, punishing his creatures for the very sins which he causes them to commit; and creating numberless millions of immortal souls, that could never have offended him, for the express purpose of tormenting them to all eternity." The purpose of this kind of notion, he says elsewhere, "the grand object of all civil and religious tyrants . . . has been to suppress all the elevated operations of the mind, to kill the energy of thought, and through this channel to subjugate the whole earth for their own special emolument." "It has hitherto been deemed a crime to think," he observes, but at last men have a chance—because they have finally escaped from the "long and doleful night" of Christian rule, and have grasped instead "the unlimited power of human reason"—"reason, which is the glory of our nature."[8]

Allen and Palmer are extreme representatives of the Enlightenment spirit, granted; but they *are* representatives. Theirs is the attitude which was new in the modern world, and which, in a less inflammatory form, was shared by all the founding fathers as their basic, revolutionary premise. Thomas Jefferson states the attitude more sedately, with less willful provocation to religion, but it is the same essential attitude. "Fix reason firmly in her seat," he advises a nephew, "and call to her tribunal every fact, every opinion. Question with boldness even the existence of a God; because, if there be one, he must more approve of the homage of reason, than that of blindfolded fear."[9] Observe the philosophic priorities in this advice: man's mind comes first; God is a derivative, if you can prove him. The absolute, which must guide the human mind, is the principle of reason; every other idea must meet this test. It is in *this* approach—in this fundamental rejection of faith—that the irreligion of the Enlightenment lies.

The consequence of this approach was the age's rejection of all the other religious priorities. In metaphysics: this world once again was regarded as real, as important, and as a realm not of miracles, but of impersonal, natural law. In ethics: success in this life became the dominant motive; the veneration of asceticism was swept aside in favor of each man's pursuit of happiness— his own happiness on earth, to be achieved by his own effort, by self-reliance and self-respect leading to self-made prosperity. But can man really achieve fulfillment on earth? Yes, the Enlightenment answered; man has the means, the potent faculty of intellect, necessary to achieve his goals and values. Man may not yet be perfect, people said, but he *is* perfectible; he must be so, because he is the rational animal.

Such were the watchwords of the period: not faith, God, service, but reason, nature, happiness, man.

Many of the founding fathers, of course, continued to believe in God and to do so sincerely, but it was a vestigial belief, a leftover from the past which no longer shaped the essence of their thinking. God, so to speak, had been kicked upstairs. He was regarded now as an aloof spectator who neither responds to prayer nor offers revelations nor demands immolation. This sort of viewpoint, known as deism, cannot, properly speaking, be classified as a religion. It is a stage in the atrophy of religion; it is the step between Christianity and outright atheism.

This is why the religious men of the Enlightenment were scandalized and even panicked by the deist atmosphere. Here is the Rev. Peter Clark of Salem, Mass. in 1739: "The former Strictness in Religion, that ... Zeal for the Order and Ordinances of the Gospel, which was so much the Glory of our Fathers, is very much abated, yea disrelished by too many: and a Spirit of Licentiousness, and Neutrality in Religion ... so opposite to the Ways of God's People, do exceedingly prevail in the midst of us."[10] And here, fifty years later, is the Rev. Charles Backus of Springfield, Mass. The threat to divine religion, he says, is the "indifference which prevails" and the "ridicule." Mankind, he warns, is in "great danger of being laughed out of religion."[11] This was true; these preachers were not alarmists; their description of the Enlightenment atmosphere is correct.

This was the intellectual context of the American Revolution. Point for point, the founding fathers' argument for liberty was the exact counterpart of the Puritans' argument for dictatorship— but in reverse, moving from the opposite starting point to the opposite conclusion. Man, the founding fathers said in essence (with a large assist from Locke and others), is the rational being; no authority, human or otherwise, can demand blind obedience from such a being—not in the realm of thought or, therefore, in the realm of action, either. By his very nature, they said, man must be left free to exercise his reason and then to act accordingly, i.e., by the guidance of his best rational judgment. Because this world *is* of vital importance, they added, the motive of man's action should be the pursuit of happiness. Because the individual, not a supernatural power, is the creator of wealth, a man should have the right to private property, the right to keep and use or trade his own product. And because man is basically good, they held, there is no need to leash him; there is nothing to fear in setting free a rational animal.

This, in substance, was the American argument for man's inalienable rights. It was the argument that reason demands freedom. And this is why the nation of individual liberty, which is what the United States was, could not have been founded in any philosophically different century. It required what the Enlightenment offered: a rational, secular context.

When you look for the source of an historic idea, you must consider philosophic essentials, not the superficial statements or errors that people may offer you. Even the most well-meaning men can misidentify the intellectual roots of their own attitudes. Regrettably, this is what the founding fathers did in one crucial respect. All men, said Jefferson, are endowed "by their Creator" with certain unalienable rights, a statement that formally ties individual rights to the belief in God. Despite Jefferson's eminence, however, his statement (along with its counterparts in Locke and others) is intellectually unwarranted. The principle of individual rights does *not* derive from or depend on the idea of God as man's creator. It derives from the very nature of man, whatever his source or origin; it derives from the requirements of man's mind and his survival. In fact, as I have argued, the concept of rights is ultimately incompatible with the idea of the supernatural. This is true not only logically, but also historically. Through all the centuries of the Dark and Middle Ages, there was plenty of belief in a Creator; but it was only when religion began to fade that the idea of God as the author of individual rights emerged as an historical, nation-shaping force. What then deserves the credit for the new development—the age-old belief or the new philosophy? What is the real intellectual root and protector of human liberty—God or reason?

My answer is now evident. America does rest on a code of values and morality—in this, the New Right is correct. But, by all the evidence of philosophy and history, it does not rest on the values or ideas of religion. It rests on their opposite.

You are probably wondering here: "What about Communism? Isn't it a logical, scientific, atheistic philosophy, and yet doesn't it lead straight to totalitarianism?" The short answer to this is: Communism is *not* an expression of logic or science, but the exact opposite. Despite all its anti-religious posturings, Communism is nothing but a modern derivative of religion: it agrees with the essence of religion on every key issue, then merely gives that essence a new outward veneer or cover-up.

The Communists reject Aristotelian logic and Western science in favor of a "dialectic" process; reality, they claim, is a stream of contradictions which is beyond the power of "bourgeois" reason to understand. They deny the very existence of man's mind, claiming that human words and actions reflect nothing but the alogical, predetermined churnings of blind matter. They do reject God, but they replace him with a secular stand-in, Society or the State, which they treat not as an aggregate of individuals, but as an unperceivable, omnipotent, supernatural organism, a "higher unseen power" transcending and dwarfing all individuals. Man, they say, is a mere social cog or atom, whose duty is to revere this power and to sacrifice every·

thing in its behalf. Above all, they say, no such cog has the right to think for himself; every man must accept the decrees of Society's leaders, he must accept them because that is the voice of Society, whether he understands it or not. Fully as much as Tertullian, Communism demands faith from its followers and subjects, "faith" in the literal, religious sense of the term. On every count, the conclusion is the same: Communism is not a new, rational philosophy; it is a tired, slavishly imitative heir of religion.

This is why, so far, Communism has been unable to win out in the West. Unlike the Russians, we have not been steeped enough in religion—in faith, sacrifice, humility and, therefore, in servility. We are still too rational, too this-worldly, and too individualistic to submit to naked tyranny. We are still being protected by the fading remnants of our Enlightenment heritage.

But we will not be so for long if the New Right has its way.

Philosophically, the New Right holds the same fundamental ideas as the New Left—its religious zeal is merely a variant of irrationalism and the demand for self-sacrifice—and therefore it has to lead to the same result in practice: dictatorship. Nor is this merely my theoretical deduction. The New Rightists themselves announce it openly. While claiming to be the defenders of Americanism, their distinctive political agenda is pure statism.

The outstanding example of this fact is their insistence that the state prohibit abortion even in the first trimester of pregnancy. A woman, in this view, has no right to her own body or even, the most consistent New Rightists add, to her own life; instead, she should be made to sacrifice at the behest of the state, to sacrifice her desires, her life goals, and even her existence in the name of a mass of protoplasm which is at most a potential human being, not an actual one. "Abortion," says Paul Weyrich, Executive Director of the Committee for the Survival of a Free Congress, "is wrong in all cases. I believe that if you have to choose between new life and existing life, you should choose new life. The person who has had an opportunity to live at least has been given that gift by God and should make way for a new life on earth."[12]

Another example: men and women, the New Right tells us, should not be free to conduct their sexual or romantic lives in private, in accordance with their own choice and values; the law should prohibit any sexual practices condemned by religion. And: children, we are told, should be indoctrinated with state-mandated religion at school. For instance, biology texts should be rewritten under government tutelage to present the Book of Genesis as a scientific theory on a par with or even superior to the theory of evolution. And, of course, the ritual of prayer must be forced down the children's throats. Is this not, contrary to the Constitution, a state establishment of religion, and of a controversial, intellectual viewpoint? Not at all, says Jack Kemp. "If a prayer is said aloud," he explains, "it need be no more than a general acknowledgment of the existence, power, authority, and love of God, the Creator."[13] That's all—nothing controversial or indoctrinating about that!

And: when the students finally do leave school, after all the indoctrination, can they then be trusted to deal with intellectual matters responsibly? No, says the New Right. Adults should not be free to write, to publish, or to read, according to their own judgment; literature should be censored by the state according to a religious standard of what is fitting as against obscene.

Is this a movement in behalf of Americanism and individual rights? Is it a movement consistent with the principles of the Constitution?

"The Constitution established freedom *for* religion," says Mr. Kemp, "not from it"—a sentiment which is shared by President Reagan and by the whole New Right.[14] What then becomes of intellectual freedom? Are meetings such as this evening's deprived of Constitutional protection, since the viewpoint I am propounding certainly does not come under "freedom *for* religion"? And what happens when one religious sect concludes that the statements of another are subversive of true religion? Who decides which, if either, should be struck down by the standard of "freedom *for* religion, not from it"? Can you predict the fate of free thought, and of "life, liberty, and the pursuit of happiness," if Mr. Kemp and associates ever get their hands fully on the courts and the Congress?

What we are seeing is the medievalism of the Puritans all over again, but without their excuse of ignorance. We are seeing it on the part of modern Americans, who live not before the founding fathers' heroic experiment in liberty, but after it.

The New Right is not the voice of Americanism. It is the voice of thought control attempting to take over in this country and pervert and undo the actual American revolution.

But, you may say, aren't the New Rightists at least champions of property rights and capitalism, as against the economic statism of the liberals? They are not. Capitalism is the separation of state and economics, a condition that none of our current politicians or pressure groups even dreams of advocating. The New Right, like all the rest on the political scene today, accepts the welfare-state mixed economy created by the New Deal and its heirs; our conservatives now merely haggle on the system's fringes about a particular regulation or handout they happen to dislike. In this matter, the New Right is moved solely by the power of tradition. These men do not want to achieve any change of *basic* course, but merely to slow down the march to socialism by freezing the economic status quo. And even in regard to this highly limited goal, they are disarmed and useless.

If you want to know why, I refer you to the published first drafts of the [1986] pastoral letter of the U.S. Catholic bishops, men who are much more consistent and philosophical than anyone in the New Right. The bishops recommend a giant step in the direction of socialism. They ask for a vast new government presence in our economic life, overseeing a vast new redistribution of wealth in order to aid the poor, at home and abroad. They ask for it on a single basic ground: consistency with the teachings of Christianity.

Some of you may wonder here: "But if the bishops are concerned with the poor, why don't they praise and recommend capitalism, the great historical engine of productivity, which makes everyone richer?" If you think about it, however, you will see that, valid as this point may be, the bishops cannot accept it.

Can they praise the profit motive—while extolling selflessness? Can they commend the passion to own material property—while declaring that worldly possessions are not important? Can they urge men to practice the virtues of productiveness and long-range planning—while upholding as the human model the lilies of the field? Can they celebrate the self-assertive risk taking of the entrepreneur—while teaching that the meek shall inherit the earth? Can they glorify and liberate the creative ingenuity of the human mind, which is the real source of material wealth—while elevating faith above reason? The answers are obvious. Regardless of the unthinking pretenses of the New Right, no religion, by its nature, can appeal to or admire the capitalist system; not if the religion is true to itself. Nor can any religion liberate man's power to create new wealth. If, therefore, the faithful are concerned about poverty—as the Bible demands they be—they have no alternative but to counsel a redistribution of whatever wealth already happens to have been produced. The goods, they have to say, are here. How did they get here? God, they reply, has seen to that; now let men make sure that His largesse is distributed fairly. Or, as the bishops put it: "The goods of this earth are common property and . . . men and women are summoned to faithful stewardship rather than to selfish appropriation or exploitation of what was destined for all."[15]

For further details on this point, I refer you to the bishops' letter; given their premises, their argument is unanswerable. If, as the New Right claims, there is scriptural warrant for state control of men's sexual activities, then there is surely much more such warrant for state control of men's economic activities. The idea of the Bible (or the "Protestant ethic") as the base of capitalism is ludicrous, both logically and historically.

Economically, as in all other respects, the New Right is leading us, admittedly or not, to the same end as its liberal opponents. By virtue of the movement's essential premises, it is supporting and abetting the triumph of statism in this country— and, therefore, of Communism in the world at large. When a free nation betrays its own heritage, it has no heart left, no conviction by means of which to stand up to foreign aggressors.

There was a flaw in the intellectual foundations of America from the start: the attempt to combine the Enlightenment approach in politics with the Judeo-Christian ethics. For a while, the latter element was on the defensive, muted by the eighteenth-century spirit, so that America could gain a foothold, grow to maturity, and become great. But only for a while. Thanks to Immanuel Kant, as I have discussed in my book *The Ominous Parallels*, the base of religion—faith and self-sacrifice—was reestablished at the turn of the nineteenth century. Thereafter, all of modern philosophy embraced collectivism, in the form of socialism, Fascism, Communism, welfare statism. By now, the distinctive ideas at the base of America have been largely forgotten or swept aside. They will not be brought back by an appeal to religion.

What then is the solution? It is not atheism as such—and I say this even though as an Objectivist I am an atheist. "Atheism" is a negative; it means not believing in God—which leaves wide open what you do believe in. It is futile to crusade merely for a negative; the Communists, too, call themselves atheists. Nor is the answer "secular humanism," about which we often hear today. This term is used so loosely that it is practically contentless; it is compatible with a wide range of conflicting viewpoints, including, again, Communism. To combat the doctrines that are destroying our country, out-of-context terms and ideas such as these are useless. What we need is an integrated, consistent philosophy in every branch, and especially in the two most important ones: epistemology and ethics. We need a philosophy of reason and of rational self-interest, a philosophy that would once again release the power of man's mind and the energy inherent in his pursuit of happiness. Nothing less will save America or individual rights.

There are many good people in the world who accept religion, and many of them hold some good ideas on social questions. I do not dispute that. But their religion is not the solution to our problem; it *is* the problem. Do I say therefore that there should only be "freedom for atheism"? No, I am not Mr. Kemp. Of course, religions must be left free; no philosophic viewpoint, right or wrong, should be interfered with by the state. I do say, however, that it is time for patriots to take a stand—to name publicly what America does depend on, and why that is *not* Judaism or Christianity.

There are men today who advocate freedom and who recognize what ideas lie at its base, but who then counsel "practicality." It is too late, they say, to educate people philosophically; we must appeal to what they already believe; we must pretend to endorse religion on strategic grounds, even if privately we don't.

This is a counsel of intellectual dishonesty and of utter impracticality. It is too late indeed, far too late for a strategy of deception which by its nature has to backfire and always has, because it consists of affirming and supporting the very ideas that have to be uprooted and replaced. It is time to tell people the unvarnished truth: to stand up for man's mind and this earth, and against any version of mysticism or religion. It is time to tell people: "You must choose between unreason and America. You cannot have both. Take your pick."

If there is to be any chance for the future, this is the only chance there is.

NOTES

1. Quoted in *Conservative Digest*, Sept. 1980.
2. From a symposium on "Sex and God in American Politics," *Policy Review*, Summer 1984.

3. Quoted in *The New York Times*, Aug. 8, 1985.
4. *The New York Times*, Dec. 25, 1985 & Jan. 5, 1986.
5. "What the Catholic Church Teaches About Socialism, Communism, and Marxism," The Catholic Study Council, Washington, DC.
6. *The New York Times*, Feb. 2, 1986, Sept. 11, 1984, & May 17, 1985.
7. From *Reason the Only Oracle of Man* (Bennington: 1784), p. 457.
8. *The Examiners Examined: Being a Defence of the Age of Reason* (New York: 1794), pp. 9-10. *An Enquiry Relative to the Moral and Political Improvement of the Human Species* (London: 1826), p. 35. *Principles of Nature* (New York: 1801), from Ch. I and Ch. XXII.
9. *Writings*, Ed. by A. E. Bergh (Washington, DC: 1903), vol. 6, p. 258.
10. *A Sermon Preach'd . . . May 30th, 1739* (Boston: 1739), p. 40.
11. *A Sermon Preached in Long-Meadow at the Publick Fast* (Springfield: 1788).
12. From "Sex and God in American Politics," *op. cit.*
13. *Ibid.*
14. "Jack Kemp at Liberty Baptist," *Policy Review*, Spring 1984.
15. *Catholic Social Teaching and the U.S. Economy* (First Draft); in *Origins, NC documentary service*, vol. 14, no. 22/23, Nov. 15, 1984, p. 344.

Part Two:
Culture

10

The Intellectual Bankruptcy of Our Age
by Ayn Rand

*This is the first of Ayn Rand's lectures at the Ford
Hall Forum. It was delivered on March 26, 1961.*

I am speaking here today on the assumption that I am
addressing an audience consisting predominantly of "liberals"—that is: of my antagonists. Therefore, I must begin by
explaining why I chose to do it.

The briefest explanation is to tell you that in the 1930s I
envied the "liberals" for the fact that their leaders entered
political campaigns armed not with worn-out bromides, but with
intellectual arguments. I disagreed with everything they said,
but I would have fought to the death for the *method* by which
they said it: for an *intellectual* approach to political problems.

Today, I have no cause to envy the "liberals" any longer.

For many decades, the "liberals" had been the representatives
of the intellect in America, if not in the content of their ideas,
then at least in form, method, and professed epistemology. They
claimed that their views were based on reason, logic, science;
and even though they were glorifying collectivism, they projected a manner of confident, distinguished intellectuality—
while most of the so-called "conservatives," allegedly devoted to
the defense of individualism and capitalism, went about apologetically projecting such a cracker-barrel sort of folksiness that
Li'l Abner would have found it embarrassing; the monument to
which may still be seen in the corridors of the New York Stock
Exchange, in a costly display of statistical charts and models
proudly entitled: THE PEOPLE'S CAPITALISM.

Today, the two camps are moving closer and merging. Just as
the Republican and Democratic parties are becoming indistin-

guishable, so are their respective intellectual spokesmen. And while the "conservatives" are lumbering toward the Middle Ages, in quest of a philosophical base for their views—the "liberals," always the avant-garde, have outdistanced them and are now galloping, on the same quest, toward India of the fifth century B.C., the original source of Zen Buddhism.

What social or political group today is the home of those who are and still wish to be the men of the intellect? None. The intellectuals—in the strict, literal sense of the word, as distinguished from the mystics and the neo-mystics—are now homeless refugees, left behind by a silent collapse they have not had the courage to identify. They are the displaced persons of our culture, who are afraid to discover that they have been displaced by the monster whom they themselves had released: by the primordial proponents of brute force.

As an advocate of reason, freedom, individualism, and capitalism, I seek to address myself to the men of the intellect—wherever such may still be found—and I believe that more of them may be found among the former "liberals" than among the present "conservatives." I may be wrong; I am willing to find out.

The terms "liberal" and "conservative" are two of the emptiest sounds in today's political vocabulary: they have become rubber words that can be stretched to fit any meaning anyone cares to give them—words that can be used safely by any speaker who wants to be misunderstood in the greatest number of ways by the greatest number of people. Yet at the same time, everyone seems to understand these two words in some foggy, sub-verbal manner, as if they were the code signals of a dark, secret guilt, hiding an issue no one cares to face.

When an entire culture is guilty of evasion on so enormous a scale, the first thing to do, if one does not choose to be an evader, is to identify the issue that people are afraid to see. What is it that the terms "liberal" and "conservative" have now come to hide?

Well, observe a curious sequence in our intellectual trends. In the popular, political usage of today, the term "liberal" is generally understood to mean an advocate of greater government control over the country's economy, or, loosely, an advocate of socialism—while the term "conservative" is generally understood to mean an opponent of government controls, or an advocate of capitalism. But this was not the original, historical meaning of the two terms, or their use in the nineteenth century. Originally, the term "liberal" meant an advocate of individual rights, of political freedom, of laissez-faire capitalism, and an opponent of the authoritarian state—while the term "conservative" meant an advocate of the state's authority, of tradition, of the established political order, of the status quo, and an opponent of individual rights. It has been observed many times that the term "liberal" today means the opposite of its nineteenth-century meaning. This would not have been too disastrous intellectually if the two terms had been merely reversed and had exchanged their original meanings. But what *is* significant—ominously significant—is the fact that certain groups are now attempting to switch the term *"conservative"* back to its nineteenth-century meaning, to palm it off on the public by imperceptible degrees, never bringing the issue fully into the open, hoping that people will gradually come to believe that a "conservative" is an advocate of authority, but of *traditional* authority. If semantic corruption becomes accepted on that wide a scale, if the political switch pulled on us becomes a choice between *twentieth-century* statist "liberals" and *nineteenth-century* statist "conservatives," what political system will be silently obliterated by that switch? What political system is being destroyed by stealth, without letting people discover that it *is* being destroyed? *Capitalism.*

It is the very scale and virulence of the evasion that should make every rational person pause and consider the issue. Those who do, will discover that the historical, political, and economic case for capitalism has never been refuted—and that the only way the statists can hope to win is by never allowing it to be discussed.

This is the issue hidden under the foggy sloppiness of today's political terms. Most people are not consciously aware of it; what they *do* sense, however, is that they haven't a leg to stand on as far as their political views are concerned, whether they're "liberals" or "conservatives"—that they have no philosophical base, no moral justification, no principles to uphold, no policy to offer.

Observe the intellectual *disintegration* of today's political discussions, the shrinking of issues and debates to the level of single, isolated, superficial concretes, with no context, with no reference to any fundamental principles, no mention of basic issues, no proofs, no arguments, nothing but arbitrary assertions of "for" or "against." As an example, observe the level on which the last presidential campaign was fought [Kennedy vs. Nixon in 1960]. Did the candidates discuss foreign policy? No—just the fate of Quemoy and Matsu [two islands between China and Taiwan]. Did they discuss socialized medicine? No—just the cost and the procedure of medical aid to the aged. Did they discuss government control of education? No—just who should pay the teachers' salaries: the federal government or the states.

What most people are evading today is the realization that under the lip service they are paying to an anti-totalitarian crusade, they have accepted all the basic premises of a totalitarian philosophy—and the rest is only a matter of time and degree. They do not know how they came to accept it—and most of them *do not want* to accept it—but they see no alternative and they are too frightened, too bitterly discouraged to seek it.

Whose job is it to offer an alternative? Who provides a country with ideas, with knowledge, with political theories? The intellectuals. But it is the intellectuals who have brought us to this state—and are now deserting under fire; that is, giving up the task of intellectual leadership at a time when they are needed most.

When intellectual disintegration reaches such absurd extremes as, on one side, the claim of some "conservatives" that the United States of America was the product of *tradition worship*, and, on the other side, the use of a political designation such as "a *totalitarian liberal*"—it is time to stop and to realize that there are no intellectual sides any longer, no philosophical camps and no political theories, nothing but an undifferentiated mob of trembling statists who haggle only over how fast or how slowly we are to collapse into a totalitarian dictatorship, whose gang will do the dictating, and who will be sacrificed to whom.

It is the "non-totalitarian liberals" and the "non-traditional conservatives" that I seek to address. Both are homeless refugees today, because neither had a firm philosophical foundation under his political home. Those homes were jerry-built astride a deadly fissure; the fissure has opened wide and has swallowed all the cheap little platform planks. Let them go—and let us start rebuilding the foundations.

The fissure had many philosophical names: soul *versus* body—mind *versus* heart—liberty *versus* equality—the practical *versus* the moral. But all of these false dichotomies are merely secondary consequences derived by the mystics from one real, basic issue: reason *versus* mysticism—or, in political terms, reason and freedom *versus* faith and force.

Let me define my terms: reason is the faculty which perceives, identifies, and integrates the material provided by man's senses; mysticism is the claim to some non-sensory, non-rational, non-definable, supernatural means of knowledge.

Only three brief periods of history were culturally dominated by a philosophy of reason: ancient Greece, the Renaissance, the nineteenth century. These three periods were the source of mankind's greatest progress in all fields of intellectual achievement—and the eras of greatest political freedom. The rest of human history was dominated by mysticism of one kind or another; that is, by the belief that man's mind is impotent, that reason is futile or evil or both, and that man must be guided by some irrational "instinct" or feeling or intuition or revelation, by some form of blind, unreasoning *faith.* All the centuries dominated by mysticism were the eras of political tyranny and slavery, of rule by brute force—from the primitive barbarism of the jungle—to the pharaohs of Egypt—to the emperors of Rome—to the feudalism of the Dark and Middle Ages—to the absolute monarchies of Europe—to the modern dictatorships of Soviet Russia, Nazi Germany, and all their lesser carbon copies.

The Industrial Revolution, the United States of America, and the politico-economic system of capitalism were the product and result of the intellectual liberation achieved by the Renaissance and of a predominantly Aristotelian philosophical influence, which lasted, in spite of a Platonist counterrevolution, through the centuries known as the Age of Reason and the Age of Enlightenment. With so illustrious a start, how did the United States descend to its present level of intellectual bankruptcy?

I want to recommend to your attention a very interesting book, which provides the material, the historical evidence, for the answer to that question. I hasten to state that the conclusions I have drawn are my own, not the author's, that I disagree with the author's viewpoint and I believe that he would probably disagree with mine. But the book is a remarkable, scholarly, well-documented record of the history of America's intellectual life. One may disagree with a writer's interpretation of the facts, but *first* one must know the facts—and in this respect, the book is of enormous value. This book is *The Decline of American Liberalism* by Professor Arthur A. Ekirch, Jr.

Professor Ekirch himself is a "liberal"—though not of the totalitarian variety. He offers no solution for the present state of liberalism and no explanation of its decline. His thesis is only that liberalism *is* declining and that our culture is moving toward "an increasingly illiberal future."

Let me give you Professor Ekirch's definition of liberalism:

> Perhaps it is best if we think of liberalism not as a well-defined political or economic system, but as a collection of ideas or principles which go to make up an attitude or 'habit of mind.' But within this liberal climate of opinion, however broadly or narrowly it may be defined, it is necessary to include the concept of limited representative government and the widest possible freedom of the individual—both intellectually and economically.

Professor Ekirch is an historian and has given an accurate description. But what a philosopher would observe is that that description holds a clue to the disaster which has wrecked Western civilization and its intellectuals. Observe that the "liberals"—in the nineteenth century as well as today—held "a collection of ideas or principles" which had never been translated into a "well-defined political or economic system." This means that they held certain values and goals, with no knowledge of how to implement them in reality, with no understanding of what *practical* actions would achieve or defeat their goals. With so vulnerable an intellectual equipment, could they be a match for the primordial forces of totalitarian mysticism? They could not and were not. It is *they*, the intellectuals, who betrayed their own liberal ideals, defeated their own goals, paved the way for their own destroyers—and did not know it, until it was too late.

They did not know that the political and economic system they had never defined—the *only* system that could achieve a limited representative government, as well as the intellectual and economic freedom of the individual—the *ideal* system—was *laissez-faire capitalism*.

The guilt of the intellectuals, in the nineteenth century, was that they never discovered capitalism—and they have not discovered it to this day.

If you want to know the philosophical and psychological *causes* of the intellectuals' treason against capitalism, I will refer you to the title essay of my book *For the New Intellectual*. In the brief space of today's discussion, I have to confine myself to a mere indication of the nature and the consequences of that treason.

The fundamental principle of capitalism is *the separation of*

State and Economics—that is: the liberation of men's economic activities, of production and trade, from any form of intervention, coercion, compulsion, regulation, or control by the government. *This* is the essence of capitalism, which is implicit in its theory and in the operation of a free market—but this is not the way most of its advocates saw it, and it is not the way it was translated into practice. The term "laissez-faire capitalism," which one has to use today in order to be understood, is actually a redundancy: only an economy of total "laissez faire" is capitalism; anything else is a "mixed economy," that is, a mixture, in varying degrees, of freedom and controls, of voluntary choice and government compulsion, of individualism and collectivism.

A full, perfect system of capitalism has never yet existed in history. Various degrees of government intervention and control remained in all the mixed, semi-free economies of the nineteenth century, undercutting, hampering, distorting, and ultimately destroying the operations of a free market. But during the nineteenth century, mankind came close to economic freedom, for the first and only time in history. Observe the results. Observe also that the degree of a country's freedom from government control was the degree of its progress. America was the freest and achieved the most.

When two opposite principles are operating in any issue, the scientific approach to their evaluation is to study their respective performances, trace their consequences in full, precise detail, and *then* pronounce judgment on their respective merits. In the case of a mixed economy, the first duty of any thinker or scholar is to study the historical record and to discover which developments were caused by the free enterprise of private individuals, by free production and trade in a free market—and which developments were caused by government intervention into the economy. It might shock you to hear that no such study has ever been made. To my knowledge, no book dealing with this issue is available. If one wants to study this question, one has to gather information from random passages and references in books on other subjects, or from the unstated implications of known but unanalyzed facts.

Those who undertake such a study will discover that all the economic evils popularly ascribed to capitalism were caused, necessitated, and made possible not by private enterprise, not by free trade on a free market, but by government intervention into the economy, by government controls, favors, subsidies, franchises, and special privileges.

The villains were not the private businessmen who made fortunes by *productive ability* and free trade, but the bureaucrats and their friends, the men who made fortunes by *political pull* and government favor. Yet it is the private businessmen, the victims, who took the blame, while the bureaucrats and their intellectual spokesmen used their own guilt as an argument for the extension of their power. Those of you who have read *Atlas Shrugged* will recognize the difference between a businessman such as Hank Rearden, the representative of capitalism, and a businessman such as Orren Boyle, the typical product of a mixed economy. If you want an historical example, consider the career of James Jerome Hill, who built the Great Northern Railroad without a penny of federal help, who was responsible, practically single-handedly, for the development of the entire American Northwest, and who was persecuted by the government all his life, under the Sherman Act, for allegedly being a monopolist. Consider it, then compare it to the career of the famous California businessmen known as "The Big Four," who built the Central Pacific Railroad on federal subsidies, causing disastrous consequences and dislocations in the country's economy, and who held a thirty-year monopoly on railroad transportation in California, by means of special privileges granted by the state legislature which made it *legally* impossible for any competing railroad to exist in the state.

The difference between these two types of business career has never been identified in the generally accepted view of capitalism. By imperceptible degrees—first, through the default of capitalism's alleged defenders, then through the deliberate misrepresentations and falsifications of its enemies—the gradual rewriting of our economic history has brought us to the stage where people believe that all the economic evils of the last two centuries were caused by the free-enterprise element, the so-called "private sector," of our mixed economy, while the economic progress of these two centuries was the result of the government's actions and interventions. People are now told that America's spectacular industrial achievements, unmatched in any period of history or in any part of the globe, were due not to the productive genius of free men, but to the special privileges handed to them by a paternalistic government. The fact that much more autocratic governments, with much wider privilege-dispensing powers and policies, did not achieve the same results anywhere else on earth is blanked out by the proponents of this theory.

The only counterpart of this theory's grotesque inversion and monstrous injustice is the mystics' doctrine that man must give credit to God for all his virtues, but must place the blame for all his sins upon himself. Incidentally, the philosophical motive and purpose in both these instances is the same.

If you want a contemporary demonstration of the respective merits and performances of a free economy and of a controlled economy—a demonstration that comes as close to an historical laboratory experiment as one could hope to see—take a look at the condition of *West* Germany and of *East* Germany.

No politico-economic system in history had proved its value so eloquently or had benefited mankind so greatly as capitalism—and none has ever been attacked so savagely and blindly. Why did the majority of the intellectuals turn against capitalism from the start? Why did their victims, the businessmen, bear their attacks in silence? The cause of it is that primordial evil which, to this day, men are afraid to challenge: *the morality of altruism.*

Altruism has been men's ruling moral code through most of mankind's history. It has had many forms and variations, but its essence has always remained the same: altruism holds that man has no right to exist for his own sake, that service to others is the only justification of his existence, and that *self-sacrifice* is his highest moral duty, virtue, and value.

The philosophical conflict which, since the Renaissance, has been tearing Western civilization and which has reached its ultimate climax in our age is the conflict between capitalism and the altruist morality. Capitalism and altruism are philosophical opposites; they cannot coexist in the same man or in the same society.

The moral code which is implicit in capitalism had never been formulated explicitly. The basic premise of that code is that man—every man—is an end in himself, not the means to the ends of others, that man must exist for his own sake, neither sacrificing himself to others nor sacrificing others to himself, and that men must deal with one another as traders, by voluntary choice to mutual benefit. This, in essence, is the moral premise on which the United States of America was based: the principle of man's right to his own life, to his own liberty, to the pursuit of his own happiness.

This is what the philosophers and the intellectuals of the nineteenth century did not and could not choose to identify, so long as they remained committed to the mystics' morality of altruism. If the good, the virtuous, the morally ideal is suffering and self-sacrifice—then, by that standard, capitalism had to be damned as evil. Capitalism does not tell men to suffer, but to pursue enjoyment and achievement, here, on earth—capitalism does not tell men to serve and sacrifice, but to produce and profit—capitalism does not preach passivity, humility, resignation, but independence, self-confidence, self-reliance—and, above all, capitalism does not permit anyone to expect or demand, to give or to take the *unearned.* In all human relationships—private or public, spiritual or material, social or political or economic or *moral*—capitalism requires that men be guided by a principle which is the antithesis of altruism: the principle of *justice.*

So long as the intellectuals of the nineteenth century held altruism as their moral code, they had to evade the actual nature and meaning of capitalism—and thus come gradually to lose and to betray all of their initial goals and ideals.

There were two crucial errors—or evasions—in the liberals' view of capitalism, from which all the rest of their debacle proceeded. One was their attitude toward the businessman; the other, their attitude toward the use of physical force.

Since wealth, throughout all the centuries of stagnation preceding the birth of capitalism, had been gained by conquest, by physical force, by political power, the intellectuals took it as their axiom that wealth can be acquired only by force—and refused to break up their mental package deal, to differentiate between a businessman and a feudal baron.

I quote from my book *For the New Intellectual:* "Evading the difference between production and looting, they called the businessman a robber. Evading the difference between freedom and compulsion, they called him a slave driver. Evading the difference between reward and terror, they called him an exploiter. Evading the difference between paychecks and guns, they called him an autocrat. Evading the difference between trade and force, they called him a tyrant. The most crucial issue they had to evade was the difference between the *earned* and the *unearned.*"

The intellectuals refused to identify the fact that the source of industrial wealth is man's mind, that the fortunes made in a free economy are the product of intelligence, of ability. This led them to the modern version of the ancient soul-body dichotomy: to the contradiction of upholding the freedom of the mind, while denying it to the most active exponents of creative intelligence, the businessmen—the contradiction of promising to liberate man's mind by enslaving his body. It led them to regard the businessman as a "vulgar materialist" or a brute or a Babbitt [this is a reference to Sinclair Lewis's novel], as some sort of inferior species born to serve them—and to regard themselves as some sort of elite born to rule him, to control his life, and dispose of his product. The shabby monument to this premise was the idea of divorcing production from distribution, of assuming the right to distribute that which one has not produced. The only way to implement an idea of that kind, the next step in their moral descent, was the intellectuals' alliance with the thug, with the advocate of rule by brute force: the totalitarian collectivist.

The intellectuals' second error—their attitude toward the use of force—is a corollary of the first. So long as they refused to identify the nature of free trade and of a social system based on voluntary, uncoerced, unforced, non-sacrificial relationships among men, so long as the moral cannibalism of the altruist code permitted them to believe that it is virtuous and right to sacrifice some men for the sake of others—the intellectuals had to embrace the political creed of *collectivism*, the dream of establishing a perfect altruist society at the point of a gun. They projected a society where all would be sacrificed to that conveniently undefinable idol "the public good," with themselves in the role of judges of *what* that "good" might be and of *who* would be "the public" at any given moment—an ideal society to be achieved by means of physical force; that is, by means of the political power of the state, by means of a totalitarian dictatorship.

The rest is history—the shameful, sordid, ugly history of the intellectual development of the last hundred and fifty years.

In the realm of political theory, the switch from the liberalism of the nineteenth century to the collectivism of the twentieth was accomplished when people began to accept the Marxist view of the nature of government—the view that a government is and has to be the agent of the economic interests of some class or another, and that the sole political issue is: which class will seize control of the government to *force* its own interests on all other groups or classes. Thus capitalism came to be regarded as an economic system in which government coercion is used for the benefit of the businessmen, the employers, or the rich in general. This served as a justification for the "liberals," the socialists, or any other collectivists when they proposed to use government coercion for the benefit of the workers, the employees, or the poor in general. And thus the existence, the possibility, the historical record, and even the theory of a noncoercive society were wiped out of people's minds and out of public discussion.

In the early years of American capitalism, the government's intervention into the country's economy was minimal; the government's role was predominantly confined to its proper function: that of a policeman and arbiter charged with the task of protecting the individual citizen's rights and property. (The most notorious exception to that rule existed only in the agrarian, non-industrial, *non-capitalist* states of the South, where the state governments upheld the institution of slavery.) The attempts to obtain special economic privileges from the government were begun by businessmen, not by workers, but by businessmen who shared the intellectuals' view of the state as an instrument of "positive" power, serving "the public good," and who invoked it to claim that the public good demanded canals or railroads or subsidies or protective tariffs. It is not the great industrialists of America, not men like J. J. Hill, who ran to government for special favors, but random adventurers with political pull or, later, those pretentious types, indoctrinated by the intellectuals, who dreamed of statism as a "manifest destiny."

It was not the businessmen or the industrialists or the workers or the labor unions that began the revolt against freedom, the demand for greater and greater government power and, ultimately, for the return to an absolute, totalitarian state; it was the intellectuals. For a detailed history of the steps by which the intellectuals of Germany led it toward totalitarianism, culminating in the establishment of the Nazi dictatorship, I will refer you to a brilliant book entitled *Omnipotent Government* by Professor Ludwig von Mises. For a detailed history of the intellectuals' role in America, I will refer you to *The Decline of American Liberalism* by Professor Arthur A. Ekirch, Jr., which I mentioned earlier.

Professor Ekirch shares many of the errors of the "liberals." He seems to regard capitalism as a system of government coercion for the benefit of the rich; he seems to ascribe America's progress to government intervention into the economy; he does not question the government's right to initiate the use of physical force for an alleged "good purpose"; he certainly does not challenge the morality of altruism. But he is too honest and conscientious an observer not to be disturbed by certain symptoms of the totalitarian spirit in the history of the "liberals"—and he offers the evidence, without identifying its full, philosophical implications.

For example, he offers the following quotation from *The Promise of American Life* by Herbert Croly, a book published in 1909, which attacked the theory of laissez faire and had an enormous influence on the so-called progressives of the time—on Theodore Roosevelt, among others:

> The Promise of American Life is to be fulfilled—not merely by a maximum amount of economic freedom, but by a certain measure of discipline; not merely by the abundant satisfaction of individual desires, but by a large measure of individual subordination and self-denial. . . . The automatic fulfillment of the American national Promise is to be abandoned, if at all, precisely because the traditional American confidence in individual freedom has resulted in a morally and socially undesirable distribution of wealth.

If you doubt the role of altruism in the destruction of capitalism, you may observe it in that quotation. And if you doubt the hatred of collectivists for the men of ability, observe it in the following passage from the same book by Croly: "The national government must step in and discriminate; but it must discriminate, not on behalf of liberty and the special individual, but on behalf of equality and the average man."

If you have been ascribing the policy of imperialism to the "selfish" individualistic ideology of capitalism and to its "greed" for conquests, here is a quotation from *Ideals and Self-Interest in America's Foreign Relations* by R. E. Osgood: "The spirit of imperialism was an exaltation of duty above rights, of collective welfare above individual self-interest, the heroic values as opposed to materialism, action instead of logic, the natural impulse rather than the pallid intellect."

If you have accepted the Marxist doctrine that capitalism leads to wars, read Professor Ekirch's account of how Woodrow Wilson, the "liberal" reformer, pushed the United States into World War I. "He seemed to feel that the United States had a mission to spread its institutions—which he conceived as liberal and democratic—to the more benighted areas of the world." It was not the "selfish capitalists," or the "tycoons of big business," or the "greedy munitions-makers" who helped Wilson to whip up a reluctant, peace-loving nation into the hysteria of a military crusade—it was the *altruistic* "liberals" of the magazine *The New Republic* edited by that same Herbert Croly. What sort of arguments did they use? Here is a sample from Croly: "The American nation needs the tonic of a serious moral adventure."

If you still wonder about the singular recklessness with which alleged humanitarians treat such issues as force, violence, expropriation, enslavement, bloodshed—perhaps the following passage from Professor Ekirch's book will give you some clue to their motives: "Stuart Chase rushed into print late in 1932 with a popular work on economics entitled *A New Deal*. 'Why,' Chase asked with real envy at the close of the book, 'should Russia have all the fun of remaking a world?' "

Apparently, Mr. Stuart Chase objects to the "tyranny of words," but *not* to the tyranny of men.

The record speaks for itself. Starting out as advocates of limited representative government, the "liberals" end as champions of unlimited, totalitarian dictatorship. Starting out as defenders of individual rights, they end as apologists for the bloody slaughterhouse of Soviet Russia. Starting out as apostles of human welfare, who beg for a few temporary controls to relieve the emergency of people's poverty, they end with J. K. Galbraith, who demands controls for the sake of controls and a permanent cut of everybody's income, not because people are too *poor,* but because they are too *affluent.* Starting out as brave champions of freedom, they end crawling on their stomachs to Moscow, with Bertrand Russell, pleading: "Give me slavery, but please don't give me death." Starting out as advocates of reason, confident of man's power to achieve well-being and fulfillment on earth, they end hunched in the darkest corners of the oldest cellar, muttering that reason is impotent, and fumbling through musty pages for the occult guidance of Zen Buddhism.

Such is the end result of the altruist morality.

Now I will ask you to consider the following. The intellectual trend that has brought us to this state—the mysticism-collectivism-altruism axis—has been gaining momentum since the nineteenth century, has been winning victory after victory, and is, at present, our dominant cultural power. If truth and reality were on its side, if it represented the right philosophy for men to live by, one would expect to see a gradual improvement in the state of the world with every successive victory, one would expect an atmosphere of growing confidence, liberation, energy, vitality, and joy of living. Is this what we have seen in the past decades? Is this what we see around us today? Today, in the moment of their almost total triumph, the voices of the mystic-collectivist-altruist axis are rising in a single wail of despair, proclaiming that existence on earth is evil, that futility is the essence of life, that disaster is man's metaphysical destiny, that man is a miserable failure depraved by nature and unfit to exist. This was not the way that the reason-individualism-capitalism axis greeted *its* triumphs in the nineteenth century—and this was not the view of man or the sense of life that it brought to mankind.

I quote from my book *For the New Intellectual*: "The professional businessman and the professional intellectual came into existence together, as brothers born of the Industrial Revolution. Both are the sons of capitalism—and if they perish, they will perish together. The tragic irony will be that they will have destroyed each other; and the major share of the guilt will belong to the intellectual."

Those of you who may still be "liberals," in the original sense of that word, and who may have abandoned everything except loyalty to reason—now is the time to check your premises. If you do, you will find that the ideal society had once been almost within men's reach. It was the intellectuals who destroyed it— and who committed suicide in the process—but the future belongs to a new type of intellectual, a new radical: the fighter for *capitalism*.

11

Our Cultural Value-Deprivation
by Ayn Rand

*This lecture was delivered at the Ford Hall Forum
on April 10, 1966, and published in* The Objectivist,
April 1966.

In the years 1951 to 1954, a group of scientists at McGill
University conducted a series of experiments that attracted a
great deal of attention, led to many further inquiries, and became famous under the general title of "sensory deprivation."

The experiments consisted of observing the behavior of a man
in conditions of isolation which eliminated or significantly reduced the sensations of sight, hearing, and touch. The subject
was placed in a small, semi-sound-proofed cubicle, he wore trans-
lucent goggles which admitted only a diffuse light, he wore
heavy gloves and cardboard cuffs over his hands, and he lay in
bed for two to three days, with a minimum of motion.

The results varied from subject to subject, but certain general
observations could be made: the subjects found it exceedingly
difficult or impossible to concentrate, to maintain a systematic
process of thought; they lost their sense of time, they felt disori-
ented, dissociated from reality, unable to tell the difference between sleeping and waking; many subjects experienced hallucinations. Most of them spoke of feeling as if they were losing
control of their consciousness. These effects disappeared shortly
after the termination of the experiments.

The scientists pursuing these inquiries state emphatically that
no theoretical conclusions can yet be drawn from these and
other, similar experiments, because they involve too many variables, as well as undefined differences in the psychological
character of the subjects, which led to significant differences in

their reactions. But certain general indications can be observed: the experiments seem to indicate that man's consciousness requires constant activity, a constant stream of changing sensory stimuli, and that monotony or insufficient stimulation impairs its efficiency.

Even though man ignores and, to a large extent, shuts out the messages of his senses when he is concentrating on some specific intellectual task—his senses *are* his contact with reality, that contact is not stagnant, but is maintained by a constant active process, and when that process is slowed down artificially to subnormal levels, his mind slows down as well.

Man's consciousness is his least known and most abused vital organ. Most people believe that consciousness as such is some sort of indeterminate faculty which has no *nature*, no specific identity, and, therefore, no requirements, no needs, no rules for being properly or improperly used. The simplest example of this belief is people's willingness to lie or cheat, to fake reality on the premise that "I'm the only one who'll know" or "It's only in my mind"—without any concern for what this does to one's mind, what complex, untraceable, disastrous impairments it produces, what crippling damage may result.

The loss of control over one's consciousness is the most terrifying of human experiences: a consciousness that doubts its own efficacy is in a monstrously intolerable state. Yet men abuse, subvert, and starve their consciousness in a manner they would not dream of applying to their hair, toenails, or stomachs. They know that these things have a specific identity and specific requirements, and if one wishes to preserve them, one must comb one's hair, trim one's toenails, and refrain from swallowing rat poison. But one's mind? Aw, it needs nothing and can swallow anything. Or so most people believe. And they go on believing it while they toss in agony on a psychologist's couch, screaming that their mind keeps them in a state of chronic terror for no reason whatever.

One valuable aspect of the sensory-deprivation experiments is that they call attention to and dramatize a fact which neither laymen *nor* psychologists are willing fully to accept: the fact that man's consciousness possesses a specific nature with specific *cognitive* needs, that it is *not* infinitely malleable and cannot be twisted, like a piece of putty, to fit any private evasions or any public "conditioning."

If sensory deprivation has such serious consequences, what

are the consequences of "*conceptual* deprivation"? This is a question untouched by psychologists, so far, since the majority of today's psychologists do not recognize the significance of the fact that man's consciousness requires a *conceptual* mode of functioning—that *thinking* is the process of cognition appropriate to man. The ravages of "conceptual deprivation" can be observed all around us. Two interacting aspects of this issue must be distinguished: the primary cause is individual, but the contributory cause is social.

The choice to think or not is volitional. If an individual's choice is predominantly negative, the result is his self-arrested mental development, a self-made cognitive malnutrition, a stagnant, eroded, impoverished, anxiety-ridden inner life. A social environment can neither force a man to think nor prevent him from thinking. But a social environment can offer incentives or impediments; it can make the exercise of one's rational faculty easier or harder; it can encourage thinking and penalize evasion or vice versa. Today, our social environment is ruled by evasion—by entrenched, institutionalized evasion—while reason is an outcast and almost an outlaw.

The brashly aggressive irrationality and anti-rationality of today's culture leaves an individual in an intellectual desert. He is deprived of conceptual stimulation and communication; he is unable to understand people or to be understood. He is locked in the equivalent of an experimental cubicle—only that cubicle is the size of a continent—where he is given the sensory stimulation of screeching, screaming, twisting, jostling throngs, but is cut off from ideas: the sounds are unintelligible, the motions incomprehensible, the pressures unpredictable. In such conditions, only the toughest intellectual giants will preserve the unimpaired efficiency of their mind, at the price of an excruciating effort. The rest will give up—usually, in college—and will collapse into hysterical panic (the "activists") or into sluggish lethargy (the consensus-followers); and some will suffer from conceptual hallucinations (the existentialists).

The subject of "conceptual deprivation" is too vast to cover in one lecture and can merely be indicated. What I want to discuss today is one particular aspect of it: the question of *value-deprivation.*

A value is that which one acts to gain and/or keep. Values are the motivating power of man's actions and a *necessity* of his survival, psychologically as well as physically.

Man's values control his subconscious emotional mechanism, which functions like a computer adding up his desires, his experiences, his fulfillments and frustrations—like a sensitive guardian watching and constantly assessing his relationship to reality. The key question which this computer is programmed to answer is: What is *possible* to me?

There is a certain similarity between the issue of sensory perception and the issue of values. Discussing "The Cognitive Consequences of Early Sensory Deprivation," Dr. Jerome S. Bruner writes: "One may suggest that one of the prime sources of anxiety is a state in which one's conception or perception of the environment with which one must deal does not 'fit' or predict that environment in a manner that makes action possible." [*Sensory Deprivation*, a symposium at Harvard Medical School, edited by Philip Solomon et al., Cambridge: Harvard University Press, 1961.] If severe and prolonged enough, the absence of a normal, active flow of sensory stimuli may disintegrate the complex organization and the interdependent functions of man's consciousness.

Man's emotional mechanism works as the barometer of the efficacy or impotence of his actions. If severe and prolonged enough, the absence of a normal, active flow of *value experiences* may disintegrate and paralyze man's consciousness—by telling him that no action is possible.

The form in which man experiences the reality of his values is *pleasure*.

[An essay from *The Virtue of Selfishness* on "The Psychology of Pleasure" states,] "Pleasure, for man, is not a luxury, but a profound psychological need. Pleasure (in the widest sense of the term) is a metaphysical concomitant of life, the reward and consequence of successful action—just as pain is the insignia of failure, destruction, death. . . . The state of enjoyment gives [man] a direct experience of his own efficacy, of his competence to deal with the facts of reality, to achieve his values, to live. . . . As pleasure emotionally entails a sense of efficacy, so pain emotionally entails a sense of impotence. In letting man experience, in his own person, the sense that *life* is a value and that *he* is a value, pleasure serves as the emotional fuel of man's existence."

Where—in today's culture—can a man find any values or any meaningful pleasure?

If a man holds a rational, or even semi-rational, view of life, where can he find any confirmation of it, any inspiring or encouraging phenomena?

A chronic lack of pleasure, of any enjoyable, rewarding or stimulating experiences, produces a slow, gradual, day-by-day erosion of man's emotional vitality, which he may ignore or repress, but which is recorded by the relentless computer of his subconscious mechanism that registers an ebbing flow, then a trickle, then a few last drops of fuel—until the day when his inner motor stops and he wonders desperately why he has no desire to go on, unable to find any definable cause of his hopeless, chronic sense of exhaustion.

Yes, there are a few giants of spiritual self-sufficiency who can withstand even this. But this is too much to ask or to expect of most people, who are unable to generate and to maintain their own emotional fuel—their love of life—in the midst of a dead planet or a dead culture. And it is not an accident that *this* is the kind of agony—death by value-strangulation—that a culture dominated by alleged humanitarians imposes on the millions of men who need its help.

A peculiarity of certain types of asphyxiation—such as death from carbon monoxide—is that the victims do not notice it: the fumes leave them no awareness of their need of fresh air. The specific symptom of value-deprivation is a gradual lowering of one's expectations. We have already absorbed so much of our cultural fumes that we take the constant pressure of irrationality, injustice, corruption and hooligan tactics for granted, as if nothing better could be expected of life. It is only in the privacy of their own mind that men scream in protest at times—and promptly stifle the scream as "unrealistic" or "impractical." The man to whom values have no reality any longer—the man or the society that regards the pursuit of values, of *the good*, as impractical—is finished psychologically.

If, subconsciously, incoherently, inarticulately, men are still struggling for a breath of fresh air—where would they find it in today's cultural atmosphere?

The foundation of any culture, the source responsible for all of its manifestations, is its philosophy. What does modern philosophy offer us? Virtually the only point of agreement among today's leading philosophers is that there is no such thing as philosophy—and that this knowledge constitutes their claim to the title of philosophers. With a hysterical virulence, strange in advocates of skepticism, they insist that there can be no valid philosophical *systems* (i.e., there can be no integrated, consistent, comprehensive view of existence)—that there are no answers to fundamental questions—there is no such thing as truth—there is no such thing as reason, and the battle is only over what should replace it: "linguistic games" or unbridled feelings?

An excellent summary of the state of modern philosophy was offered in *Time* (January 7, 1966).

> Philosophy dead? It often seems so. In a world of war and change, of principles armed with bombs and technology searching for principles, the alarming thing is not what philosophers say but what they fail to say. When reason is overturned, blind passions are rampant, and urgent questions mount, men turn for guidance to . . . almost anyone except their traditional guide, the philosopher. . . . Contemporary philosophy looks inward at its own problems rather than outward at men, and philosophizes about philosophy, not about life.

And further:

> For both movements [the analytic and the existentialist], a question such as 'What is truth?' becomes impossible to answer. The logical positivist would say that a particular statement of fact can be declared true or false by empirical evidence; anything else is meaningless. A language philosopher would content himself with analyzing all the ways the word true can be used. The existentialist would emphasize what is true for a person in a particular situation.

What, then, are modern philosophers busy doing? "Laymen glancing at the June 10, 1965, issue of the *Journal of Philosophy* will find a brace of learned analysts discussing whether the sentence 'There are brown things and there are cows' is best expressed by the formula $(\exists x)\ Exw \cdot (\exists x)\ Exy$ or by $(\exists x)\ Bx \cdot (\exists x)\ Cx$."

If, in spite of this, someone might still hope to find something of value in modern philosophy, he will be told off explicitly.

> A great many of his colleagues in the U.S. today would agree with Donald Kalish, chairman of the philosophy department at U.C.L.A., who says: "There is no system of philosophy to spin out. There are no ethical truths, there are just clarifications of particular ethical problems. Take advantage of these clarifications and work out your own existence. You are mistaken to think anyone ever had the answers. There are no answers. Be brave and face up to it."

This means that to look for *ethical truths* (for moral principles or values) is to be a coward—and that bravery consists of dispensing with ethics, truth, values, and of acting like a drunken driver or like the mobs that riot in the streets of the cities throughout the world.

If men seek guidance, the very motive that draws them to philosophy—the desire to understand—makes them give it up. And along with philosophy a man gives up the ambitious eagerness of his mind, the quest for knowledge, the cleanliness of certainty. He shrinks the range of his vision, lowers his expectations and his eyes, and moves on, watching the small square of his immediate steps, never raising his head again. He had looked for intellectual values; the emotion of contempt and revulsion was all he found.

If anyone attempts to turn from philosophy to religion, he will find the situation still worse. When religious leaders form a new movement under a slogan such as "God is dead," there is no lower place to go in terms of cynical obfuscation.

"Theologian Calls 'God-Talk' Irrelevant," announces a headline in *The New York Times* of November 21, 1965. What sort of talk *is* relevant is not made clear in the accompanying story, which is closer to double-talk than to any other linguistic category—as may be judged from the following quotations: "Even if there once was a God, they say, He is no longer part of human experience, and hence 'God-talk' is both meaningless and irrelevant in the contemporary situation." And: "The function of religion is not to overcome the realities of evil, hopelessness, and anguish with an apocalyptic vision, but to equip people to live with these problems and to share them through the religious community."

Does this mean: not to oppose, not to resist, but to *share* "evil, hopelessness and anguish"? Your guess is as good as mine.

From a report on a television discussion in Denver, Colorado, I gather that one member of this movement has made its goal and meaning a little clearer. "God," he said, "is a process of creative social intercourse."

This, I submit, is obscene. I, who am an atheist, am shocked by so brazen an attempt to rob religion of whatever dignity and philosophical intention it might once have possessed. I am shocked by so cynically enormous a degree of contempt for the intelligence and the sensibility of people, specifically of those intended to be taken in by the switch.

Now, if men give up all abstract speculation and turn to the immediate conditions of their existence—to the realm of *politics*—what values or moral inspiration will they find?

There is a popular saying that alcohol and gasoline don't mix. Morality and cynicism are as deadly a mixture. But a political system that mixes freedom and controls will try to mix anything—with the same kind of results on the dark roads of men's spirit.

On the one hand, we are drenched in the slick, stale, sticky platitudes of altruism, an overripe altruism running amok, pouring money, blood, and slogans about global welfare, which everyone drips and no one hears any longer, since monotony—in moral, as well as sensory, deprivation—deadens perception. On the other hand, we all know and say and read in the same newspapers that all these welfare projects are merely a cynical power game, the game of buying votes with public funds, of paying off "election debts" to pressure groups, and of *creating* new pressure groups to pay off—since the sole purpose of political power, people tacitly believe, is to keep oneself in power, and the sole recourse of the citizens is to gang up on one another and maneuver for who'll get sacrificed to whom.

The first makes the second possible: altruism gives people an excuse to put up with it. Altruism serves as the veneer—a fading, cracking, peeling veneer—to hide from themselves the terror of their actual belief: that there *are no* moral principles, that morality is impotent to affect the course of their existence, that they are blind brutes caught in a charnel house and doomed to destruction.

No one believes the political proclamations of our day; no one opposes them. There is no public policy, no ideology, no goals, no convictions, no moral fire, no crusading spirit—nothing but the quiet panic of clinging to the *status quo*, with the dread of looking back to check the start of the road, with terror of looking ahead to check its end, and with a leadership whose range of vision is shrinking down to the public poll the day after tomorrow's television appearance.

Promises? "Don't remind us of promises, that was yesterday, it's too late." Results? "Don't expect results, it's too soon." Costs? "Don't think in terms of old-fashioned economics—the more we spend, the richer we'll get." Principles? "Don't think in terms of old-fashioned labels—we've got a consensus." The future? "Don't think."

Whatever public images President Johnson may project, a

moral crusader is not one of them. This lends special significance—
and a typical whiff of today's cultural atmosphere—to a column
entitled "President Johnson's Dreams" by James Reston, in *The
New York Times* (February 25, 1966).

> Though his reach may exceed his grasp, it has to be said for him
> that he is a yearner after great ideals. . . . He makes the New Deal
> seem like a grudging handout. . . . Nothing is beyond his aspira-
> tions. Roosevelt's Vice President, Henry Wallace, was condemned
> as a visionary because he wanted to give every Hottentot a quart
> of milk. Humphrey came back talking as if he wanted to send
> them all to college, and the President's message in New York was
> that the Four Freedoms can never be secure in America if they
> are violated elsewhere in the world. This is not mere speech-
> making to Lyndon Johnson. . . . He remains a believer in an unbe-
> lieving and cynical world. . . . He is out to eliminate poverty in
> America. Without any doubt, he feels he can bring adequate
> education to the multitude, and his confidence goes beyond the
> boundaries of the nation. Never mind that the British and the
> French let him know this week that they were reducing their
> commitments in the world; he sees a combination of American
> power and generosity dealing somehow with the problem. Has
> Malthus become as great a menace as Marx? Are the death rate
> and the birth rate too high? He has programs for them all . . . He
> looked troubled and sounded harried in New York, and no won-
> der, for he is bearing all the dreams and lost causes of the century.

Ask yourself: what is the moral and intellectual state of a
nation that gives a blank check on its wealth, its work, its
efforts, its lives to a "yearner" and "dreamer," to spend on *lost
causes*?

Can anyone feel morally inspired to live and work for such a
purpose?

Can anyone preserve any values by looking at anything today?
If a man who earns his living hears constant denunciations of
his "selfish greed" and then, as a moral example, is offered the
spectacle of the War on Poverty—which fills the newspapers
with allegations of political favoritism, intrigues, maneuvering,
corruption among its "selfless" administrators—what will happen to his sense of honesty? If a young man struggles sixteen
hours a day to work his way through school, and then has to pay
taxes to help the dropouts from the dropout programs—what
will happen to his ambition? If a man saves for years to build a
home, which is then seized by the profiteers of Urban Renewal

because *their* profits are "in the public interest," but *his* are not—what will happen to his sense of justice? If a miserable little private holdup man is hauled off to jail, but when the government forces men into a gang big enough to be called a union and they hold up New York City, they get away with it—what will happen to the public's respect for the law?

Can anyone wish to give his life to defend the rights of South Vietnam—when the rights of Poland, Latvia, Lithuania, Estonia, Czechoslovakia, Yugoslavia, Albania, East Germany, North Korea, Katanga, Cuba, and *Hungary* were *not* defended? Can anyone wish to uphold the honor of our treaty obligations in South Vietnam when it was *not* upheld on the construction site of the wall in Berlin? Can anyone acquire intellectual integrity by observing that it is the *collectivists* who take a moral stand against the draft, in defense of *individual rights*—while the so-called "conservatives" insist that young men must be drafted and sent to die in jungle swamps, in order that the South Vietnamese may hold a "democratic" election and vote themselves into communism, if they so choose?

The next time you hear about a crazed gang of juvenile delinquents, don't look for such explanations as "slum childhood," "economic underprivilege," or "parental neglect." Look at the moral atmosphere of the country, at the example set by their elders and by their public leaders.

Today, the very motive that arouses men's interest in politics—their sense of responsibility—makes them give it up. And along with politics a man gives up his good will toward people, his benevolence, his openness, his fairness. He withdraws into the small, tight, windowless cellar of his range-of-the-moment concerns, shrinking from any human contact, convinced that the rule of the game is to kill or be killed and that the only action possible to him is to defend himself against every passerby. He had looked for social values; the emotion of contempt and revulsion was all he found.

In the decadent eras of history, in the periods when human hopes and values were collapsing, there was, as a rule, one realm to which men could turn for support, to preserve their image of man, their vision of life's better possibilities, and their courage. That realm was art.

Let us take a look at the art of our age.

While preparing this discussion, I picked up at random the Sunday Book Review section of *The New York Times* of March

20, 1966. I shall quote from the three leading reviews of current fiction.

1. "In his new book, it is as if [the author] has taken hold of his flaws, weaknesses, errors, and indulgences, and instead of dealing strictly with them, has made them the subject of his esthetic intention. The scatology has hit the fan. When homosexual camp has become a cliché, he tries to make it new by poking it at the reader from every direction. . . . There are floating neon images of decay, corruption, putrefaction, illness." This is not a negative review, but an admiringly reproachful one: the reviewer does not like this particular novel, but he extols the author's talent and urges him to do better. As he puts it: "Give us this day our daily horror, agreed; but carry through on your promises."

2. The second review is of the same order: respectfully admiring toward the author, but critical of the particular novel under discussion. "It's hard, bright, and as cold as a block of ice. Gratuitous evil, upholstered innocence, and insane social arrangements condemn [the author's] characters to frightful violence. They must do or be done to. Under sentence, they move inexorably toward futility and destruction. . . . Three people are murdered during a wave of private crime in the West Indies. One of the murderers earns $100,000. The chief engineer of the bizarre electro-chemical derangement of two of the prey collects a lifetime of compensation for a lousy childhood. The victims burn up, get shot or pushed down a thousand-foot ravine. It's a total dark victory. One can infer positive values only by their absence. The author's own attitude is as antimoral as a tombstone."

3. The third review is enthusiastic about a novel which it describes as "remarkable as a rare instance of pornography sublimed to purest art." The content of the novel is indicated as follows: "The story gradually opens out into a Daedalian maze of perverse relationships—a clandestine society of sinister formality and elegance where the primary bond is mutual complicity in dedication to the pleasures of sadism and masochism. [The heroine] is initiated into this world by her lover, who one day takes her to a secluded mansion where she is trained through the discipline of chains and whip to be totally submissive to the men who are her masters. . . . During her subsequent prog-

ress, she is subjected to every sort of sexual debasement and torture, only to be returned in the penultimate stage of her education to a still more brutal institution, a 'gynaceum' where she not only endures the cruelest torments but begins to fulfill the sadistic lesbian underside of her own nature." The theme of this book, according to the reviewer, is: "a perversion of the Christian mystery of exaltation through debasement, of the extremity of suffering transformed into an ultimate victory over the limitations of being."

If one turns from that muck to the visual arts, one finds the same sewer in somewhat different forms. To the extent that they communicate anything at all, the visual arts are ruled by a single principle: distortion. Distortion of perspective, of space, of shape, of color, and, above all, of the human figure. We are surrounded by images of distorted, dismembered, disintegrated human bodies—such as might be drawn by a retarded five-year-old—and they pursue us everywhere: on subway ads, in fashion magazines, in TV commercials, or suspended on chains over our heads in fashionable concert halls.

There is also the nonrepresentational—or Rorschach—school of art, consisting of blobs, swirls, and smears which are and aren't, which are anything you might want them to be provided you stare at them long enough, keeping your eyes and mind out of focus. Provided also you forget that the Rorschach test was devised to detect mental illness.

If one were to look for the purpose of that sort of stuff, the kindest thing to say would be that the purpose is to take in the suckers and provide a field day for pretentious mediocrities. But if one looked deeper, one would find something much worse: the attempt to make you doubt the evidence of your senses and the sanity of your mind.

Art is a selective re-creation of reality according to an artist's metaphysical value judgments. Observe what image of man, of life and of reality modern art infects people with—particularly the young whose first access to a broad view of existence and first source of values lie in the realm of art.

Today, the very motive that draws a man to art—the quest for enjoyment—makes him run from it for his life. He runs to the gray, sunless, meaningless drudgery of his daily routine, with nothing to relieve it, nothing to expect or to enjoy. And he soon stops asking the tortured question: "Is there anything to see tonight? Is there anything to read?" Along with art, he gives up his vision of values and forgets that he had ever hoped to find or to achieve them.

He had looked for inspiration. Contempt and revulsion were not the only emotions he found, but also horror, indignation, and such a degree of boredom and loathing that anything is preferable to it—including the brutalizing emptiness of an existence devoid of any longing for values.

If you wonder what is wrong with people today, consider the fact that no laboratory experiment could ever reproduce so thorough a state of value-deprivation.

The consequences take many forms. Here is some of the evidence.

A survey in *The New York Times* (March 21, 1966) quotes some observers who estimate that forty to fifty percent of college students are drug addicts, then adds:

> Actually, no one knows, even approximately, how many students take drugs. But everyone agrees that the number is rising, that it has been for several years and that no one is quite sure what to do about it. . . .
>
> The drug takers are majoring in the humanities or social sciences, with more in English than any other subject. There are fewer consistent users in the sciences or in the professional schools. . . .
>
> [The drug takers] are vaguely leftist, disenchanted with American policies in Vietnam, agitated because there are Negro ghettos and bored with conventional politics. They do not join the Peace Corps, which, a student at Penn State said, "is for Boy Scouts."
>
> Their fathers, more often than not, are professional men or white-collar executives. They are not deprived. A California psychiatrist says that the children of television writers in Hollywood use drugs more than any other group. . . .
>
> The LSD users speak of dissolving the ego, meeting the naked self, finding a truly religious experience, and being so terribly honest with themselves that they know that all about them is sham. . . .
>
> Why do they increasingly drop out of school and join the LSD cult, there to contemplate nature, induce periodic insanity, and pursue a philosophy that is a curious mélange of Zen, Aldous Huxley, existentialism, and leftover Orientalism? Dr. John D. Walmer, director of the mental health clinic at Penn State, suggests that "for people who are chronically unhappy drugs bring some relief from a world without purpose." George H. Gaffney,

deputy commissioner of narcotics, says students take drugs because "of the growing disrespect for authority, because some professors just don't care to set any kind of moral influence and because of the growing beatnik influence." Dr. Harvey Powleson, director of the psychiatric clinic at the Berkeley campus of the University of California, notes "a connection toward mystical movements in general." . . .

A boy at San Francisco State may have spoken for his generation when he said he smoked marijuana and used LSD "because there is just no reason not to." He was absolutely sure that this was so.

Who—in today's culture—would have given him any valid reason to think otherwise?

Here is another aspect of the same phenomenon (*The New York Times*, December 29, 1964):

The number of adolescent suicides and suicide attempts is a source of alarm to an increasing number of educators, doctors, and parents. Princeton added a second full-time psychiatrist to its health services this fall; other schools are expanding existing services; at Columbia University the number of students seeking professional help has tripled in the last ten years. . . .

Surprisingly, Cornell doctors found that the student-patient who achieved the highest marks was the one most likely to do away with himself. Nonsuicidal students, on the other hand, were often doing poorly in their academic work. The bright students too often demanded far more of themselves than either their professors or the university.

Is it a matter of what the bright students demanded of themselves—or of life? A much more likely explanation is that the better the student, the more of today's intellectual poison he had absorbed; being intelligent, he saw too clearly what sort of existence awaited him and, being too young to find an antidote, he could not stand the prospect.

When a culture is dedicated to the destruction of values—of *all* values, of values as such—men's psychological destruction has to follow.

We hear it said that this is merely a period of transition, confusion, and growth, and that the leaders of today's intellectual trends are groping for new values. But here is what makes their motives suspect. When the scientists of the Renaissance concluded that certain pseudo-sciences of the Middle Ages were invalid, they did not attempt to take them over and ride on their prestige; the chemists did not call themselves alchemists, the astronomers did not call themselves astrologers. But modern philosophers proclaim themselves to be philosophers while struggling to invalidate the essence of philosophy: the study of the fundamental, universal principles of existence. When men like Auguste Comte or Karl Marx decided to substitute society for God, they had the good grace not to call themselves theologians. When the esthetic innovators of the nineteenth century created a new literary form, they called it a "novel," not an "anti-poem" —unlike the pretentious mediocrities of today who write "anti-novels." When decorative artists began to design textiles and linoleums, they did not hang them up in frames on walls or entitle them "a representation of pure emotion."

The exponents of modern movements do not seek to convert you to *their* values—they haven't any—but to destroy *yours*. Nihilism and destruction are the almost *explicit* goals of today's trends—and the horror is that these trends move on, unopposed.

Who is to blame? All those who are afraid to speak. All those who are still able to know better, but who are willing to temporize, to compromise, and thus to sanction an evil of that magnitude. All those intellectual leaders who are afraid to break with today's culture, while knowing that it has rotted to the core— who are afraid to check, challenge, and reject its basic premises, while knowing that they are seeing the ultimate results—who are afraid to step out of the "mainstream," while knowing that it is running with blood—who cringe, evade, and back away from the advance of screeching, bearded, drugged barbarians.

Now you may logically want to ask me the question: What is the solution and the antidote? But to this question, I have given an answer—at length—elsewhere. The answer lies outside today's cultural "mainstream." Its name is Objectivism.

12

Global Balkanization
by Ayn Rand

*This lecture was delivered at the Ford Hall Forum
on April 10, 1977.*

Have you ever wondered about the process of the collapse of a civilization? Not the *cause* of the collapse—the ultimate cause is always philosophical—but the *process*, the specific means by which the accumulated knowledge and achievements of centuries vanish from the earth?

The possibility of the collapse of Western civilization is not easy to imagine or to believe. Most people do not quite believe it—in spite of all the horror movies about the end of the world in a nuclear blast. But of course the world has never been destroyed by a sudden catastrophe. Man-made catastrophes of that size are not sudden; they are the result of a long, slow, gradual process, which can be observed in advance.

Let me remind you—as I have said many times before—that there is no such thing as historical determinism. The world does not have to continue moving toward disaster. But unless men change their philosophical direction—which they still have time to do—the collapse will come. And if you want to know the specific process that will bring it about, that process—the beginning of the end—is visible today.

In *The New York Times* of January 18, 1976, under the title "Europe's Restive Tribes," columnist C. L. Sulzberger is crying out in anxious bewilderment against a phenomenon he cannot understand: "It is distressing to return from Africa and find the cultivated old continent of Europe subsiding into its own form of tribalism just as new African governments make concerted

115

efforts to curb the power of tribes and subordinate them to the greater concept of the nation-state."

By "tribalism," Mr. Sulzberger means the separatist movements spreading throughout Europe. "Indeed," he declares,

> it is a peculiar phenomenon of contemporary times that so many lands which had formerly been powerful and important seem obsessed with reducing the remnants of their own strength ... *There is no logical reason* that a Scotland which was proud to be considered part of the British Empire's heart when the sun never set on it, from Calcutta to Capetown, is now increasingly eager to disengage from what is left of that grand tradition on an offshore European island. [Emphasis added.]

Oh yes, there *is* a very logical reason why Great Britain is falling apart, but Mr. Sulzberger does not see it—just as he does not see what was grand about that old tradition. He is the *Times'* columnist specializing in European affairs, and, like a conscientious reporter, he is disturbed by something which he senses to be profoundly wrong—but, tending to be a liberal, he is unable to explain it.

He keeps coming back to the subject again and again. On July 3, 1976, in a column entitled "The Split Nationality Syndrome," he writes: "The present era's most paradoxical feature is the conflict between movements seeking to unify great geographical blocs into federations or confederations, and movements seeking to disintegrate into still smaller pieces the component nations trying to get together."

He offers an impressive list of examples. In France there is a Corsican autonomy movement, and similar movements of French Basques, of French Bretons, and of French inhabitants of the Jura belt west of Switzerland. "Britain is now obsessed with what is awkwardly called 'devolution.' This means watered-down autonomy and is designed to satisfy Welsh, but above all Scottish, nationalists." Belgium remains split "by an apparently insoluble language dispute between French-speaking Walloons and Dutch-speaking Flemish." Spain is facing demands for local independence "in Catalonia and the northern Basque country. . . . German-speaking inhabitants of Italy's Alto Adige yearn to leave Rome and submit to Vienna. There is a tiny British–Danish argument . . . over the status of the Faroe Islanders. . . . In Yugoslavia there are continuing disputes between Serbs and Croats . . . There is also unresolved ferment among Macedonians . . . some of whom, on occasion, revive old dreams of their own state including Greek Salonika and part of Bulgaria."

Please remember that these tribes and subtribes, which most of the world has never heard of—since they have achieved no distinction to hear about—are struggling to secede from whatever country they are in and to form their own separate, sovereign, independent nations on their two-by-four stretches of the earth's crust.

I must make one correction. These tribes did achieve a certain kind of distinction: a history of endless, bloody warfare.

Coming back to Mr. Sulzberger: Africa, he points out, is torn apart by tribalism (in spite of the local governments' efforts), and most of Africa's recent wars were derived "from tribal causes." He concludes by observing: "The schizophrenic impulses splitting Europe threaten actually to atomize Africa—and all in the name of progress and unity."

In a column entitled "Western Schizophrenia" (December 22, 1976), Mr. Sulzberger cries: "The West is not drawing closer together; it is coming apart. This is less complicated but perhaps more distressing in North America than in Europe." For myself, I will add: and more disgusting.

Mr. Sulzberger continues: "Canada is apparently getting ready to tear itself asunder for emotional if illogical reasons which, on a massive scale, resemble the language dispute that continually splits Belgium . . ." He predicts the possibility of a formal separation between French-speaking Quebec and the rest of Canada, and comments sadly and helplessly: "Whatever happens, it is hard to foresee much good for the West ensuing." Which is certainly true.

Now what are the nature and the causes of modern tribalism?

Philosophically, tribalism is the product of irrationalism and collectivism. It is a logical consequence of modern philosophy. If men accept the notion that reason is not valid, what is to guide them and how are they to live? Obviously, they will seek to join some group—any group—which claims the ability to lead them and to provide some sort of knowledge acquired by some sort of unspecified means. If men accept the notion that the individual is helpless, intellectually and morally, that he has no mind and no rights, that he is nothing, but the group is all, and his only moral significance lies in selfless service to the group—they will be pulled obediently to join a group. But which group? Well, if you believe that you have no mind and no moral value, you cannot have the confidence to make choices—so the only thing for you to do is to join an *unchosen* group, the group into which you were born, the group to which you were predestined to belong by the sovereign, omnipotent, omniscient power of your body chemistry.

This, of course, is racism. But if your group is small enough, it will not be called "racism": it will be called "*ethnicity*."

For over half a century, modern liberals have been observing the fact that their ideas are achieving the opposite of their professed goals: instead of "liberation," communism has brought the blood-drenched dictatorship of Soviet Russia—instead of "prosperity," socialism has brought starvation to China, and Cuba, and India (and Russia)—instead of "brotherhood," the welfare state has brought the crumbling stagnation and the fierce, "elitist" power struggle of Great Britain, and Sweden, and many other, less obvious victims—instead of "peace," the spread of international altruism has brought about two world wars, an unceasing procession of local wars, and the suspending of a nuclear bomb over the heads of mankind. Yet this record does not prompt the liberals to check their premises or to glance, for contrast, at the record of the social system the last remnants of which they are so ferociously destroying.

Now we are seeing another demonstration of the fact that their professed goals are *not* the motive of today's liberals. We are seeing a special kind of intellectual cover-up—a cover-up so dirty and so low that it makes Watergate look like a childish caper.

Observe that ever since World War II, racism has been regarded as a vicious falsehood and a great evil, which it certainly is. It is not the root of all social evils—the root is collectivism—but, as I have written before (in *The Virtue of Selfishness*), "Racism is the lowest, most crudely primitive form of collectivism." One would think that Hitler had given a sufficient demonstration of racism's evil. Yet today's intellectuals, particularly the liberals, are supporting and propagating the most virulent form of racism on earth: tribalism.

The cover-up that makes it possible lies in a single word: *ethnicity*.

"Ethnicity" is an anti-concept, used as a disguise for the word "racism"—and it has no clearly definable meaning. But you can get a lead to its meaning if you hunt through a dictionary. The following are the results of my hunt through *The Random House College Dictionary* (1960), a book intended for young people.

I found no such term as "ethnicity." But I found "ethnic," which is defined as follows: "pertaining or peculiar to a population, esp. to a speech group, loosely also to a race." Under "ethnic group," the definition given as sociological usage reads: "a group of people, racially or historically related, having a common and distinctive culture, as an Italian or Chinese colony in a large American city."

I looked up the word "culture." The definition given as sociological usage reads: "the sum total of ways of living built up by a group of human beings, which is transmitted from one generation to another." I looked up also the word "tribe." The definition reads: "1. any aggregate of people united by ties of descent from a common ancestor, community of customs, and traditions, adherence to the same leaders, etc. 2. a local division of a primitive or barbarous people."

The meaning of the sum of these definitions is fairly clear: the term "ethnicity" stresses the traditional, rather than the physiological characteristics of a group, such as language—but physiology, i.e., *race*, is involved and mentioned in all but one of these definitions. So the advocacy of "ethnicity," means *racism plus tradition*—i.e., racism plus conformity—i.e., racism plus staleness.

The acceptance of the achievements of an individual by other individuals does not represent "ethnicity": it represents a cultural division of labor in a free market; it represents a conscious, individual choice on the part of all the men involved; the achievements may be scientific or technological or industrial or intellectual or esthetic—and the sum of such accepted achievements constitutes a free, civilized nation's *culture*. Tradition has nothing to do with it; tradition is being challenged and blasted daily in a free, civilized society: its citizens accept ideas and products because they are true and/or good—*not* because they are old *or* because their ancestors accepted them. In such a society, concretes change, but what remains immutable—by individual conviction, not by tradition—are those philosophical principles which correspond to reality, i.e., which are true.

The "old" and the "ancestral" are the standards of *tradition*, which supersedes reality, the standards of value of those who accept and practice "ethnicity." Culture, in the modern sociologists' view, is not a sum of achievements, but of "ways of living

... transmitted from one generation to another." This means: concrete, specific ways of living. Can you—who are still the children of the United States of America—imagine the utter horror of a way of living that does not change from generation to generation? Yet this is what the advocates of ethnicity are advocating.

Is such a way of living compatible with reason? It is not. Is it compatible with independence or individuality? It is not. Is it compatible with progress? Obviously not. Is it compatible with capitalism? Don't be funny. What century are we talking about? We are dealing with a phenomenon that is rising out of prehistorical ages.

Atavistic remnants and echoes of those ages have always existed in the backwaters of civilized countries, particularly in Europe, among the old, the tired, the timid, and those who gave up before they started. Such people are the carriers of "ethnicity." The "ways of living" they transmit from generation to generation consist in: folk songs, folk dances, special ways of cooking food, traditional costumes, and folk festivals. Although the professional "ethnics" would (and did) fight wars over the differences between *their* songs and those of their neighbors, there are no significant differences between them; all folk art is essentially similar and excruciatingly boring: if you've seen one set of people clapping their hands while jumping up and down, you've seen them all.

Now observe the nature of those traditional ethnic "achievements": all of them belong to the *perceptual level of man's consciousness*. All of them are ways of dealing with or manipulating the concrete, the immediately given, the directly perceivable. All of them are manifestations of the *preconceptual* stage of human development.

I quote from one of my articles: "The concrete-bound, anti-conceptual mentality can cope only with men who are bound by the same concretes—by the same kind of 'finite' world. To this mentality, it means a world in which men do not have to deal with abstract principles: principles are replaced by memorized rules of behavior, which are accepted uncritically as the given. What is 'finite' in such a world is not its extension, but the degree of mental effort required of its inhabitants. When they say 'finite,' they mean 'perceptual.' " (This is from "The Missing Link" in [*Philosophy: Who Needs It*]. That article deals with the psycho-epistemological roots of modern tribalism.)

In the same article I said: "John Dewey's theory of Progressive education (which has dominated the schools for close to half a century), established a method of crippling a child's conceptual faculty and replacing cognition with 'social adjustment.' It was and is a systematic attempt to manufacture tribal mentalities."

A symptom of the tribal mentality's self-arrested, perceptual level of development may be observed in the tribalists' position on *language*.

Language is a conceptual tool—a code of visual-auditory symbols that denote concepts. To a person who understands the function of language, it makes no difference what sounds are chosen to name things, provided these sounds refer to clearly defined aspects of reality. But to a tribalist, language is a mystic heritage, a string of sounds handed down from his ancestors and memorized, not understood. To him the importance lies in the perceptual concrete, the *sound* of a word, not its meaning. He would kill and die for the privilege of printing on every postage stamp the word "postage" for the English-speaking and the word "postes" for the French-speaking citizens of his bilingual Canada. Since most of the ethnic languages are not full languages, but merely dialects or local corruptions of a country's language, the distinctions which the tribalists fight for are not even as big as that.

But, of course, it is not for their language that the tribalists are fighting: they are fighting to protect their level of awareness, their mental passivity, their obedience to the tribe, and their desire to ignore the existence of outsiders.

The learning of another language expands one's abstract capacity and vision. Personally, I speak four—or rather three-and-a-half—languages: English, French, Russian, and the half is German, which I can read but not speak. I found this knowledge extremely helpful when I began writing: it gave me a wider range and choice of concepts; it showed me four different styles of expression; it made me grasp the nature of languages as such, apart from any set of concretes.

(Speaking of concretes, I would say that every civilized language has its own inimitable power and beauty, but the one I love is English—the language of my choice, not of my birth. English is the most eloquent, the most precise, the most economical, and, therefore, the most powerful. English fits me best—but I would be able to express *my* identity in any Western language.)

The tribalists clamor that their language preserves their "ethnic identity." But there is no such thing. Conformity to a racist tradition does not constitute a human identity. Just as racism provides a pseudo-self-esteem for men who have not earned an authentic one, so their hysterical loyalty to their own dialect serves a similar function: it provides a pretense at "collective self-esteem," an illusion of safety for the confused, frightened, precarious state of a tribalist's stagnant consciousness.

The proclaimed desire to preserve one's language and/or its literary works, if any, is a cover-up. In a free, or even semi-free country, no one is forbidden to speak any language he chooses with those who wish to speak it. But he cannot *force* it on others. A country has to have only *one* official language if men are to understand one another—and it makes no difference which language it is, since men live by the *meaning*, not the sound, of words. It is eminently fair that a country's official language should be the language of the majority. As to literary works, their survival does not depend on political enforcement.

But to the tribalists, language is not a tool of thought and communication. Language to them is a symbol of tribal status and power—the power to *force* their dialect on all outsiders. This appeals not even to the tribal leaders, but to the sick, touchy vanity of the tribal rank and file.

In this connection, I want to mention a hypothesis of mine, which is only a hypothesis because I have given no special study to the subject of bilingual countries, i.e., countries that have *two* official languages. But I have observed the fact that bilingual countries tend to be culturally impoverished by comparison to the major countries whose language they share in part. Bilingual countries do not produce many great, first-rate achievements in any intellectual line of endeavor, whether in science, philosophy, literature, or art. Consider the record of Belgium (which is French-speaking in part) as against the record of France—or the record of Switzerland (a trilingual country) as against the record of France, of Germany, of Italy—or the record of Canada as against the record of the United States.

The cause of the poor records may lie in the comparative territorial smallness of those countries—but this does not apply to Canada versus the United States. The cause may lie in the fact that the best, most talented citizens of the bilingual countries tend to emigrate to the major countries—but this still leaves the question: Why do they?

My hypothesis is as follows: the policy of bilingual rule (which spares some citizens the necessity to learn another language) is a concession to, and a perpetuation of, a strong ethnic-tribalist element within a country. It is an element of anti-intellectuality, conformity, and stagnation. The best minds would run from such countries: they would sense, if not know it consciously, that tribalism leaves them no chance.

But quite apart from this particular hypothesis, there can be no doubt that the spread of tribalism is an enormously anti-intellectual evil. If, as I said, some elements of "ethnicity" did remain in the backyards of civilized countries and stayed harmless for centuries, why the sudden epidemic of their rebirth? Irrationalism and collectivism—the philosophical notions of the prehistorical eras—had to be implemented in practice, in *political* action, before they could engulf the greatest scientific-technological achievements mankind had ever reached. The political cause of tribalism's rebirth is the *mixed economy*—the transitional stage of the formerly civilized countries of the West on their way to the political level from which the rest of the world has never emerged: the level of permanent tribal warfare.

As I wrote in my article on "Racism" (in *The Virtue of Selfishness*): "The growth of racism in a 'mixed economy' keeps step with the growth of government controls. A 'mixed economy' disintegrates a country into an institutionalized civil war of pressure groups, each fighting for legislative favors and special privileges at the expense of one another."

When a country begins to use such expressions as "seeking a bigger share of the pie," it is accepting a tenet of pure collectivism: the notion that the goods produced in a country do not belong to the producers, but belong to everybody, and that the government is the distributor. If so, what chance does an individual have of getting a slice of that pie? No chance at all, not even a few crumbs. An individual becomes "fair game" for every sort of organized predator. Thus people are pushed to surrender their independence in exchange for tribal protection.

The government of a mixed economy *manufactures* pressure groups—and, specifically, *manufactures* "ethnicity." The profiteers are those group leaders who discover suddenly that they can exploit the helplessness, the fear, the frustration of their "ethnic" brothers, organize them into a group, present demands to the government—and deliver the vote. The result is political jobs, subsidies, influence, and prestige for the *leaders* of the ethnic groups.

This does not improve the lot of the group's rank and file. It makes no difference to the hard-pressed unemployed of any race or color what quota of jobs, college admissions, and Washington appointments were handed out to the political manipulators from their particular race or color. But the ugly farce goes on, with the help and approval of the intellectuals, who write about "minority victories."

Here is a sample of the goal of such victories. In *The New York Times* of January 17, 1977, a news story was headlined as follows: "Hispanic Groups Say They Are Inequitably Treated in Support for Arts." At a hearing on the subject, New York State Senator Robert Garcia declared: "What we are really talking about is dollars and whether we are receiving a fair share of the revenues generated in this state." The purpose of the demands for state dollars was "to assure the growth of 'non-mainstream art forms.' " This means: art forms which people do not care to see or to support. The recommendations reached at the hearing included the demand that "at least twenty-five percent of the money goes to Hispanic arts."

This, ladies and gentlemen, is what your tax money is being spent on: the new profiteers of altruism are not the poor, the sick, or the unemployed, but ethnic females swishing their skirts in old Spanish dances which were not too good even when they were new.

This is a typical example of the motives and the vested interests behind the growth, the pushing, and the touting of "ethnicity."

An interesting article was published in the British magazine *Encounter* (February 1975). It is entitled "The Universalisation of Ethnicity" and is written by Nathan Glazer, a well-known American sociologist. It is quite revealing of the modern intellectuals' attitude toward the spread of ethnicity—more revealing in what Mr. Glazer does *not* say than in what he does.

He observes: "The overwhelming majority of people . . . are born into a religion, rather than adopt it, just as they are born into an ethnic group. In this respect both are similar. They are both groups by 'ascription' rather than 'achievement.' They are groups in which one's status is immediately given by birth rather than gained by some activities in one's life."

This is eminently—and horribly—true. There is a great deal to be said about the horrifying approach of a world dominated by people who prefer "ascription" to "achievement," and who seek a physiologically determined, automatically given status rather than a status they have to earn. Mr. Glazer does not say it; he merely reports.

He is disturbed by the relationship of "ethnic group" to "*caste*," but treats it merely as a problem of definitions. But, of course, castes are inherent in the notion of ethnicity—castes of superiors and inferiors, determined by birth, enforced and perpetuated by law, dividing people into "aristocrats," "commoners," etc., down to "untouchables."

Mr. Glazer makes a true and profoundly important statement: "The United States is perhaps unique among the states of the world in using the term 'nation' to refer not to an ethnic group but to all who choose to become Americans." But he draws no conclusions from it. Yet it is extremely significant that the United States was the archenemy and the destroyer of ethnicity, that it abolished castes and any sort of inherited titles, that it granted no recognition to groups as such, that it recognized only the right of the individual to *choose* the associations he wished to join. Freedom of association is the opposite of ethnicity.

Mr. Glazer does not raise the question of the original American philosophy and the relationship of its destruction to the rise of ethnicity. The focus of his interest lies elsewhere. He writes: "The Socialist hope for a trans-national class struggle, based on class identification, never came to pass. Instead, it has been replaced by national and ethnic conflicts." And: "In most countries national interests and ethnic interests seem to dominate over class interests." Mr. Glazer is baffled by this development. He offers some tentative explanations with which he himself is not satisfied, such as: "The trends of modernisation, even while they do destroy some bases of distinctive culture and distinctive identity, create a need for a *new kind of identity* related to the old, intimate type of village or tribal association." A modern, technological society, which includes nuclear bombs and space travel—to be run by villages or by tribal associations?

Mr. Glazer himself tends to dismiss theories of this sort, and admits that he cannot find an explanation. "This is the heart of the darkness. Why *didn't* the major lines of conflict within societies become class conflicts rather than ethnic conflicts? . . . In most developing countries Marxism remains the ideology of the students and often of the ruling group—but *ethnicity* is the focus around which identity and loyalty have been shaped." Mr. Glazer comes closer to an answer when he observes that ethnicity has "an irrational appeal," but he takes it no further. He says instead:

It would seem that the rallying cries that mobilise the classes have, in recent decades, had less power than the rallying cries that mobilise the races, tribes, religions, language-users—in short, the Ethnic Groups. Perhaps the epidemic of ethnic conflicts reflects the fact that leaders and organisers believe they can get a more potent response by appealing to *ethnicity* than they can by appealing to Class Interest.

True, leaders and organizers do believe this—but why? The answer to Mr. Glazer's questions lies in the fact that Marxism is an *intellectual* construct; it is false, but it is an *abstract* theory— and *it is too abstract for the tribalists' concrete-bound, perceptual mentalities.* It requires a significantly high level of abstraction to grasp the reality of "an *international* working class"—a level beyond the power of a consciousness that understands its own village, but has trouble treating the nearest town as fully real. No, the level of men's intelligence has not deteriorated from natural causes; it has been pushed down, retarded, stultified by modern anti-intellectual education and modern irrationalist philosophy.

Mr. Glazer does not see or is not concerned with any part of this answer. It is obvious that he is disturbed by the spread of ethnicity, but he tries to hope for the best—and this leads him, in conclusion, to a truly unspeakable statement. After proposing some sort of solution in the form of "either guaranteed shares for each group, or guaranteed rights for each individual and each group," he continues: "The United States in the past seemed to find the approach in terms of 'guaranteed rights' more congenial than the approach in terms of guaranteed shares; but recently Americans have begun to take individual rights less seriously, and to take group shares more seriously." After I recovered from feeling sick at my stomach, I asked myself: What Americans has Mr. Glazer been observing or associating with? I do not know—but his statement is libel against an entire nation. His statement means that Americans are willing to sell their rights for money—for a "share of the pie."

In his last paragraph Mr. Glazer observes that there was a time when "the problems of Ethnicity, as a source of conflict within nations and between nations, have generally appeared as simply a left-over, an embarrassment from the past. It is my conviction they must now be placed at the very centre of our concern for the human condition."

He is right to fear such a prospect.

There is no surer way to infect mankind with hatred—brute, blind, virulent hatred—than by splitting it into ethnic groups or tribes. If a man believes that his own character is determined at birth in some unknown, ineffable way, and that the characters of all strangers are determined in the same way—then no communication, no understanding, no persuasion is possible among them, only mutual fear, suspicion, and hatred. Tribal or ethnic rule has existed, at some time, in every part of the world, and, in some country, in every period of mankind's history. The record of hatred is always the same. The worst kinds of atrocities were perpetrated during ethnic (including religious) wars. A recent grand-scale example of it was Nazi Germany.

Warfare—permanent warfare—is the hallmark of tribal existence. A tribe—with its rules, dogmas, traditions, and arrested mental development—is not a productive organization. Tribes subsist on the edge of starvation, at the mercy of natural disasters, less successfully than herds of animals. War against other, momentarily luckier tribes, in the hope of looting some meager hoard, is their chronic emergency means of survival. The inculcation of hatred for other tribes is a necessary tool of tribal rulers, who need scapegoats to blame for the misery of their own subjects.

There is no tyranny worse than ethnic rule—since it is an unchosen serfdom one is asked to accept as a value, and since it applies primarily to one's mind. A man of self-esteem will not accept the notion that the content of his mind is determined by his muscles, i.e., by his own body. But by the bodies of an unspecified string of ancestors? Determinism by the means of production is preferable; it is equally false, but less offensive to human dignity. Marxism is corrupt, but clean compared to the stale, rank, musty odor of ethnicity.

As to the stagnation under tribal rule—take a look at the Balkans. At the start of this century, the Balkans were regarded as the disgrace of Europe. Six or eight tribes, plus a number of subtribes with unpronounceable names, were crowded on the Balkan peninsula, engaging in endless wars among themselves or being conquered by stronger neighbors or practicing violence for the sake of violence over some microscopic language differences. "Balkanization"—the breakup of larger nations into ethnic tribes— was used as a pejorative term by the European intellectuals of the time. Those same intellectuals were pathetically proud when they managed, after World War I, to glue most of the Balkan tribes together into two larger countries: Czechoslovakia and Yugoslavia. But the tribes never vanished; they have been popping up in minor explosions all along, and a major one is possible at any time.

In the light of tribalism's historical record, it is ludicrous to compromise with it, to hope for the best or to expect some sort of fair "group shares." Nothing can be expected from tribalism except brutality and war. But this time, it is not with bows and arrows that the tribes will be armed, but with nuclear bombs.

As a tiny preview of what tribalism would mean in a modern, technological civilization, a story in *The New York Times* of January 23, 1977, reports that the French-speaking Canadians of Quebec had demanded the use of French in all official dealings, including at airports, but "a federal court upheld a ban by the federal Ministry of Transport on the use of French for landings at Montreal's two international airports. (English is the language accepted at airports in every nation of the world.)"

Let me remind you of the recent terrible collision of two planes in the Canary Islands. Although all the personnel involved spoke English perfectly, the investigations seem to indicate that the collision was caused by linguistic misunderstandings. But what is that to the Canadians of Quebec, or to Idi Amin of Uganda, or to any other ethnic tribalists who might demand that *their* language be spoken by every plane pilot in the world? Incidentally, that collision took place because the small airport was overcrowded with planes that could not land at a nearby major airport: the major airport had been bombed by ethnic terrorists who were seeking the independence of the Canary Islands from Spain.

How long would the achievements of a technological civilization last under this sort of tribal management?

Some people ask whether local groups or provinces have the right to secede from the country of which they are a part. The answer is: on ethnic grounds, no. Ethnicity is not a valid consideration, morally or politically, and does not endow anyone with any special rights. As to other than ethnic grounds, remember that rights belong only to individuals and that there is no such thing as "group rights." If a province wants to secede from a dictatorship, or even from a mixed economy, in order to establish a free country—it has the right to do so. But if a local gang, ethnic or otherwise, wants to secede in order to establish its own government controls, it does not have that right. No group has the right to violate the rights of the individuals who happen to live in the same locality. A wish—individual or collective—is not a right.

Is there a way to avoid the rebirth of global tribalism and the approach of another Dark Ages? Yes, there is, but only one way—through the rebirth of the antagonist that has demonstrated its power to relegate ethnicity to a peaceful dump: capitalism.

Observe the paradoxes built up about capitalism. It has been called a system of selfishness (which, in *my* sense of the term, it *is*)—yet it is the only system that drew men to unite on a large scale into great countries, and peacefully to cooperate across national boundaries, while all the collectivist, internationalist, One-World systems are splitting the world into Balkanized tribes.

Capitalism has been called a system of greed—yet it is the system that raised the standard of living of its poorest citizens to heights no collectivist system has ever begun to equal, and no tribal gang can conceive of.

Capitalism has been called nationalistic—yet it is the only system that banished ethnicity, and made it possible, in the United States, for men of various, formerly antagonistic nationalities to live together in peace.

Capitalism has been called cruel—yet it brought such hope, progress and general good will that the young people of today, who have not seen it, find it hard to believe.

As to pride, dignity, self-confidence, self-esteem—these are characteristics that mark a man for martyrdom in a tribal society and under any social system except capitalism.

If you want an example of what had once been the spirit of America—a spirit which would be impossible today, but which we must now struggle to bring to a rebirth—I will quote from an old poem that represents the opposite of the abject self-abasement of ethnicity. It is a poem called "The Westerner" by Badger Clark.

He begins with "My fathers sleep on the Eastern plain and each one sleeps alone"—he acknowledges his respect for his forefathers, then says:

But I lean on no dead kin.
My name is mine for fame or scorn,
And the world began when I was born,
And the world is mine to win.

13

How to Read (and Not to Write)
by Ayn Rand

This article was published in The Ayn Rand Letter, *September 25, 1972.*

" He was doling his sentences out with cautious slowness, balancing himself between word and intonation to hit the right degree of semi-clarity. He wanted her to understand, but he did not want her to understand fully, explicitly, down to the root—since the essence of that modern language, which he had learned to speak expertly, was never to let oneself or others understand anything down to the root." [*Atlas Shrugged.*]

Today, this is the dominant method of communication in public speaking and writing, particularly on the subject of politics. A recent editorial in *The New York Times* is a valuable specimen of that method—an unusually clear example of the art of unclarity.

"The Fourth of July is a good time to remind ourselves that there is urgent necessity for the nation's intellectual and political leaders to provide moral guidance at a time when so many people feel that the nation has lost its way," said the *Times*, concluding an editorial, on July 4, 1972.

This statement is incontrovertibly true, and one would be tempted to say "amen"—but the rest of the editorial is a remarkable example of the reasons why the nation has lost its way (though not in the sense the editorial intended).

The most important issue confronting us today, the editorial declares, is "how to prevent powerful special interests from frustrating the democratic process." No definitions are given, but the context suggests that "special interests" means pressure groups. This is not exactly a fundamental issue, but this is what the editorial regards as an urgent problem. To solve a problem, one must identify and correct or eliminate its causes; therefore, one would expect the editorial writer to mention what caused the emergence of pressure groups. But he does not. He treats the subject as if pressure groups were facts of nature or irreducible primaries.

It is interesting to wonder what went on in that writer's mind in the space between two paragraphs—because the editorial continues by attacking those who might name the unnamed causes he did not find it necessary to mention:

> That issue is so difficult to solve because all the clear, simple extremes are unworkable. Given modern industrial technologies, this country cannot go back to the highly atomistic, competitive model of the early nineteenth century—even if it were willing to accept the workings of the marketplace as the arbiter of all social values and outcomes. But the experience of totalitarian and democratic societies alike suggests that mere substitution of the power of big government for that of big business and the marketplace is no solution.

As an exercise in intellectual precision, see how many things you can list as wrong in that one little paragraph. I shall indicate some of them (omitting the paragraph's first sentence, which I shall take up later).

If a euphemism is an inoffensive way of identifying an offensive fact, then "highly atomistic, competitive model" is an anti-euphemism, i.e., an offensive way of identifying an inoffensive (or great and noble) fact—in this case, capitalism. "Competitive" is a definition by nonessentials; "atomistic" is worse. Capitalism involves competition as one of its proper consequences, not as its essential or defining attribute. "Atomistic" is usually intended to imply "scattered, broken up, disintegrated." Capitalism is the system that made productive cooperation possible among men, on a large scale—a *voluntary* cooperation that raised everyone's standard of living—as the nineteenth century has demonstrated. So "atomistic" is an anti-euphemism, standing for "free, independent, individualistic." If the editorial's sentence were intended to be fully understood, it would read: "this country cannot go back to the free, individualistic, private-property system of capitalism."

Now why would "modern industrial technologies" make a return to capitalism impossible? No answer is given. It is fashionable to treat technology as a dark mystery, as a kind of black magic beyond the layman's power to understand—so the phrase is just thrown in, as an ineffable threat. But observe that modern industrial technology is a product of capitalism and, today, of the private sector of the U.S. economy, which is still the freest economy on earth—observe the abysmal failure of the world's most controlled economy, Soviet Russia, to approach America's technological achievements—observe the correlation, in all the mixed economies, between the degree of a country's freedom and the degree of its technological development—and you will have grounds to suspect that that phrase was thrown in to prevent you from realizing that modern industrial technology (if it is to survive) makes statism, not capitalism, impossible.

The clause "even if it [this country] were willing to accept the workings of the marketplace as the arbiter of all social values and outcomes" is an attack on a straw man. No advocate of capitalism ever held the workings of the marketplace as the arbiter of *all* social values and outcomes—only of the *economic* ones, i.e., those pertaining to production and trade. In a free marketplace, these values and outcomes are determined by a free, general, "democratic" vote—by the sales, purchases, and choices of every individual. And—as one indication of the fact that, under capitalism, there are social values outside the power of the marketplace—each individual votes only on those matters which he is qualified to judge: on his own preferences, interests, and needs. The paramount social value he has no power to encroach upon is: the rights of others. He cannot substitute his vote and judgment for theirs; he cannot declare himself to be "the voice of the people" and leave the people disenfranchised.

Is this what our country would be unwilling to accept?

The last sentence of the quoted paragraph resorts to the shabby old gimmick of equating opposites by substituting nonessentials for their essential characteristics. In this case, the defacing acid, obliterating differences, is the attribute of "bigness." If a reader is to be made to feel that businessmen and dictators are interchangeably equal villains, he must be pushed to forget that a *big* productive genius, e.g., Henry Ford, Sr., and a *big* killer, e.g., Stalin, are not the same thing—and that the difference between a totalitarian and a free society does not consist in substituting Stalin for Henry Ford, Sr. (For a discussion of the difference between economic and political power, see "America's Persecuted Minority: Big Business" in my book *Capitalism: The Unknown Ideal.*)

When the baser kind of politician resorts to that gimmick, he is counting on the ugliest emotion of lesser people—envy—and if they confuse "bigness" with "greatness," it serves his purpose. But why would a reputable newspaper do it?

The editorial's next paragraph gives a clue to the answer: "The crucial task facing the United States and other democratic societies is to find workable answers between the extremes—to limit concentrations of corporate power without undermining the efficiency of business; to permit the market to allocate resources insofar as possible—but also to use adequate resources to achieve socially desirable purposes in response to the democratically exercised choices of the society."

Who is to *permit* the market to allocate resources? Whose resources? What are "socially desirable purposes"? Who desires them—and at whose expense? Since the greatest, the fundamental, factor ("resource") of production is human intelligence, is it to be disposed of by the "choices of the society"?

No explicit answers are given. But observe the workings of the unnamed in the above quotation. The two "extremes" are capitalism (i.e., freedom) and totalitarianism (i.e., dictatorship). The "workable answers" are to be sought in the middle, in a combination of these two. Observe the method suggested. Business efficiency must not be undermined (which is an implicit admission that this efficiency depends on freedom)—but government must control the development and limit the growth of business. The market must be kept free "insofar as possible" —but if "society" desires some particular "purpose," freedom becomes impossible. Which of the two "extremes" is violated and which is given priority in this suggested method?

So it turns out that the editorial writer is advocating the very thing which he falsely ascribed to capitalism: he is suggesting that the marketplace *should be made* "the arbiter of all social values and outcomes"—not, however, the clean, *economic* marketplace, but the corrupt, *political* one. (An intrusion of political power, i.e, of force, into the market is corrupt and corrupting, since it introduces an opportunity for legalized looting.) He is using the word "democratic" in its original meaning, i.e., unlimited majority rule, and he is urging us to accept a social system in which one's work, one's property, one's mind, and one's life are at the mercy of any gang that may muster the vote of a majority at any moment for any purpose.

If *this* is a society's system, no power on earth can prevent men from ganging up on one another in self-defense—i.e., from forming *pressure groups*.

"There is no magic formula for reconciling those aims," the editorial continues. "Instead, this nation and all others can only seek to diffuse power by such measures as more effectively employing the antitrust laws . . ." etc.

After raising so momentous a problem as the attempt to mix freedom and dictatorship (an attempt which has brought us where we are today)—after demonstrating (between the lines) that these two extremes cannot mix and that there is, indeed, no magic formula for reconciling opposites or for having your cake and eating it, too—the editorial proceeds to suggest such remedies as: the miserably false, decrepit notion of persecutions by antitrust laws; a "sense of mission" in regulatory agencies; "new types of regulatory institutions" on the order of "public-interest crusaders" with an " 'ombudsman' role both within and outside government" (i.e., the most vicious of pressure groups: quasi-governmental private groups); the abolition of "the illegal financing of political campaigns by great corporations or labor unions"; etc., etc. (with not a word about how to "diffuse" the other power in that mixture, the power of the government).

This is offered as *moral* guidance for a nation that has lost its way.

If I were using that editorial for an actual test of reading comprehension, I would give A + to anyone who would discover why the word "moral" is introduced at the conclusion of a piece that does not discuss morality. If you look past the modern verbiage, you will find, smuggled between the lines, the thing which the editorial writer wants you "to understand, but not to understand fully, explicitly, down to the root": *altruism*. It is not any practical considerations, not "modern industrial technologies," or "the workings of the marketplace," or economics, or politics, or reality, that make it impossible for us to return to capitalism—to freedom, progress, abundance—it is the altruist moral code, which the editorial is struggling to preserve in the form of "socially desirable purposes" that supersede individual rights. The "workable answer" it exhorts us to seek, is how to combine capitalism with the creed of self-sacrifice. Brother, it can't be done. I have been saying it for years. You may take it now from the horse's mouth—from an editorial written, apparently, in the horse's unguarded moment.

It is futile to bemoan this country's moral decadence or blame politicians for the "credibility gap" if this is the kind of guidance the nation is given by its intellectual leaders. Credibility? It is almost a miracle that the nation has managed to preserve some unconquerable element of decency and common sense, instead of collapsing altogether into a sewer of amoral, anti-intellectual cynicism and skepticism under a cultural barrage of that kind.

Politicians are not the cause of a culture's trend, only its consequence. They get their notions from the cultural atmosphere, particularly from newspapers, magazines, and TV commentaries; they speak as these media teach them to speak. Who teaches the media?

And now we come down to the root: of all our institutions, it is the universities that are primarily responsible for this country losing its way—and of all the university departments, it is the departments of philosophy.

If you want to see what makes things such as that editorial possible, you will find the hoofprints of Pragmatism in two key sentences: "That issue is so difficult to solve because all the clear, simple extremes are unworkable," and: "There is no magic formula for reconciling those aims."

By "clear, simple extremes," modern intellectuals mean any rational theory, any consistent system, any conceptual integration, any precise definition, any firm principle. Pragmatists do not mean that no such theory, system, or principle has yet been discovered (and that we should look for one), but that none is possible. Epistemologically, their dogmatic agnosticism holds, as an absolute, that *a principle is false because it is a principle*—that conceptual integration (i.e., thinking) is impractical or "simplistic" —that an idea which is clear and simple is necessarily "extreme and unworkable." Along with Kant, their philosophic forefather, the pragmatists claim, in effect: "If you perceive it, it cannot be real," and: "If you conceive of it, it cannot be true."

What, then, is left to man? The sensation, the wish, the whim, the range, and the concrete of the moment. Since no solution to any problem is possible, anyone's suggestion, guess, or edict is as valid as anyone else's—provided it is narrow enough.

To give you an example: if a building were threatened with collapse and you declared that the crumbling foundation has to be rebuilt, a pragmatist would answer that your solution is too abstract, extreme, unprovable, and that immediate priority must be given to the need of putting ornaments on the balcony railings, because it would make the tenants feel better.

There was a time when a man would not utter arguments of this sort, for fear of being rightly considered a fool. Today, Pragmatism has not merely given him permission to do it and liberated him from the necessity of thought, but has elevated his mental default into an intellectual virtue, has given him the right to dismiss thinkers (or construction engineers) as naive, and has endowed him with that typically modern quality: the arrogance of the concrete-bound, who takes pride in not seeing the forest fire, or the forest, or the trees, while he is studying one inch of bark on a rotted tree stump.

Like all of Kant's progeny, modern philosophy has a single goal: the defeat of reason. The degree to which such philosophers succeed is the degree to which men and nations lose their way in a deepening night of insolvable problems.

The human products of that philosophy—on all levels of today's society—are the crude skeptics and another, more offensive breed: the professional "seeker of truth" who hopes to God he'll never find it.

If you meet one of those (and they are ubiquitous), you will find the answer to his problems—and to the dilemmas of modern philosophy—in another passage from *Atlas Shrugged*: "Do you cry that you find no answers? By what means did you hope to find them? You reject your tool of perception—your mind—then complain that the universe is a mystery. You discard your key, then wail that all doors are locked against you. You start out in pursuit of the irrational, then damn existence for making no sense."

14

The Lessons of Vietnam
by Ayn Rand

*This article was written in May 1975, a few weeks
after the fall of South Vietnam to the Communists.
Because* The Ayn Rand Letter *was behind schedule at the time, the article was published in the
issues dated August 26 and September 9, 1974.*

The televised scenes of South Vietnam's sudden collapse at
Da Nang seemed oddly familliar to me; they had a faded,
distant quality of déjà vu. The scenes of people in hopeless
flight, the panic, the despair, the frantic struggle for a foothold
on the last plane or ship leaving a doomed land, with everything
left behind and nothing ahead—people running into a void outside history, as if squeezed off the face of the earth—I had seen
it all before. It took me a moment and a shock of sadness to
realize where I had seen it: this was the Russian population
fleeing before the advance of the Red Army in the civil war of
1918–21.

The newscaster's voice said that fleeing South Vietnamese
soldiers had seized control of an American rescue ship and had
proceeded to rob, rape, and murder refugees, their own countrymen. I felt indignation, disgust, disappointment—and, again, a
faint touch of familiarity. The shock was more painful, this
time, when I realized that *this* was an example of the ignominious amorality of the so-called political right.

Let me hasten to say that individual brutes exist in any army
and cannot be taken as representative of an entire people; that
the atrocities committed by those particular South Vietnamese
would not even be reported if and when committed by the
North Vietnamese, since such atrocities represent the official,

ideological policy of North Vietnam; that South Vietnam does
not represent the political right or the political anything. Grant-
ing all this, it is still true that if a group of soldiers attack their
own countrymen in the midst of a national disaster, it means
that attackers and victims have no values in common, not even
the solidarity of primitive tribalism, that they have nothing to
uphold or defend militarily, that they do not know what they
are fighting for. And, in today's world, there is no one to tell
them.

I was in my early teens during the Russian civil war. I lived
in a small town that changed hands many times. (See *We the
Living;* that part of the story is autobiographical.) When it was
occupied by the White Army, I almost longed for the return of
the Red Army, and vice versa. There was not much difference
between them in practice, but there was in theory. The Red
Army stood for totalitarian dictatorship and rule by terror. The
White Army stood for nothing; repeat: *nothing.* In answer to the
monstrous evil they were fighting, the Whites found nothing
better to proclaim than the dustiest, smelliest bromides of the
time: we must fight, they said, for Holy Mother Russia, for
faith and tradition.

I wondered, even in those years, which is morally worse:
evil—or the appeasement of evil, the cowardly evasion that
leaves an evil unnamed, unanswered and unchallenged. I was
inclined to think that the second is worse, because it makes the
first possible. I am certain of it today. But in the years of my
adolescence, I did not know how rare a virtue intellectual integrity (i.e., the *non-evasion* of reality) actually is. So I kept waiting
for some person or group among the Whites to come out with a
real political manifesto that would explain and proclaim *why*
one must fight against communism and *what* one might fight for.
I knew even then that the "what" was freedom, *individual* freedom, and (a concept alien to Russia) *individual rights.*

I knew that man is *not* a slave of the state; I knew that man's
right to his own life (and, therefore, to freedom) has to be
upheld with as great and proud a sense of moral righteousness
as any idea could ever deserve; I knew that nothing less would
do—and that without such a stand the anti-Reds were doomed.
But I thought that this was self-evident, that the whole civilized
world knew it, and that there surely existed some minds able to
communicate this knowledge to Russia, which was perishing for
lack of it. I waited through the years of the civil war. Nothing
resembling that manifesto was ever uttered by anyone.

In a passive, indifferent way, the majority of the Russian people were behind the White Army: they were not *for* the Whites, but merely *against* the Reds; they feared the Reds' atrocities. I knew that the Reds' deepest atrocity was intellectual, that the thing which had to be fought—and *defeated*—was their *ideas*. But no one answered them. The country's passivity turned to hopeless lethargy as people gave up. The Reds had an incentive, the promise of nationwide looting; they had the leadership and the semi-discipline of a criminal gang; they had an allegedly intellectual program and an allegedly moral justification. The Whites had icons. The Reds won.

I learned a great deal in the years since. I learned that the concept of individual rights is far, far from self-evident, that most of the world does not grasp it, that the United States grasped it only for a brief historical moment and is now in the process of losing the memory. I learned that the civilized world is being destroyed by its dominant schools of philosophy—by irrationalism, altruism, collectivism—and, specifically, that altruism is the tear gas that defeats resistance, by reducing men to crying and vomiting.

The hardest thing to learn (the most difficult one to believe) was the fact that the so-called political rightists in this country—the alleged defenders of freedom (i.e., of capitalism)—were as vague, as empty, and as futile as the leaders of the White Army (more shamefully so, since they had a much, much greater knowledge to evade). For years the intellectual posture of America's political leaders has been a long, pleading, appeasing, self-abasing whine of apology for this country's greatness—an apology addressed to every advocate or perpetrator of collectivism's horrors and failures anywhere on earth.

But even American politicians had some sort of stature when compared to their intellectual mentors, those (to me, still incredible) bipeds who—unable to find a moral justification for man's life and happiness—attempted to defend freedom on the grounds of altruism (of the "public good"), or on the grounds of faith in the supernatural, or on the grounds of brushing the issue aside and proclaiming that morality is irrelevant to economics (i.e., to man's life and livelihood).

(At a certain point in recent years, I realized with astonishment that the kind of voice and manifesto I had been waiting for was my own. No, this is not a boast; it is an admission of a sort I don't like to make: a complaint. [I don't like self-pity.] I did not want, intend, or expect to be the only philosophical defender of man's rights, in the country of man's rights. But if I am, I am. And, dear reader, if I am giving you the kind of intellectual ammunition [and inspiration] I had so desperately waited to hear in my youth, I'm glad. I can say that I know how you feel.)

No country could stand for long on the kind of moral erosion that the altruists and amoralists of the right had done their best to aid and abet. The war in Vietnam was the result and dramatization of that erosion. The military collapse of South Vietnam was preceded by the philosophical collapse of the United States some decades earlier.

It was a shameful war—not for the reasons which leftists and sundry friends of North Vietnam are proclaiming, but for the exactly opposite reasons: shameful because it was a war which the U.S. had no *selfish* reason to fight, because it served no national interest, because we had nothing to gain from it, because the lives and the heroism of thousands of American soldiers (and the billions of American wealth) were sacrificed in pure compliance with the ethics of altruism, i.e., selflessly and senselessly.

In compliance with epistemological irrationalism, it was a war and a non-war at the same time. It was a modern monstrosity called a "no win" war, in which the American forces were not permitted to act, but only to react: they were to "contain" the enemy, but not to beat him.

In compliance with modern politics, the war was allegedly intended to save South Vietnam from communism, but the proclaimed purpose of the war was not to protect freedom or individual rights, it was not to establish capitalism or any particular social system—it was to uphold the South Vietnamese right to "national self-determination," i.e., the right to vote themselves into any sort of system (including communism, as American propagandists kept proclaiming).

The right to vote is a *consequence*, not a primary cause, of a free social system—and its value depends on the constitutional structure implementing and strictly delimiting the voters' power; unlimited majority rule is an instance of the principle of tyranny. Outside the context of a free society, who would want to die for the right to vote? Yet *that* is what the American soldiers were asked to die for—not even for their own vote, but to secure that privilege for the South Vietnamese, who had no other rights and no knowledge of rights or freedom.

Picking up the liberals' discarded old slogan of World War I days—"the self-determination of nations"—the American conservatives were trying to hide the American system, *capitalism*, under some sort of collectivistic cover. And it is not capitalism that most of them were (and are) advocating, it was a mixed economy. Who would want to die for a mixed economy?

In compliance with a Hegelian sort of "A is non-A" metaphysics, both sides kept contradicting their professed beliefs. Soviet Russia, who regards men as the property and fodder of the state, did not send soldiers to North Vietnam (she could not trust them to fight, so she sent only military supplies). The United States, whose foundation is the supremacy of man's right to life, sent soldiers to die in South Vietnam. Soviet Russia, the philosophical apostle of materialism, won the war in Vietnam by spiritual, i.e., moral-intellectual, means: the North Vietnamese and the Vietcong were thoroughly indoctrinated with the notion of the righteousness of their cause. The United States—whose modern leadership scorns materialism and professes to be moved by purely spiritual beliefs (mystical-religious on the right, tribalist and anti-industrial on the left)—abstained from proclaiming any moral principles or any principles whatever, and relied on an abundance of material supplies to fight the war, an abundance of planes, bombs, and guns in the hands of men who had no idea of why they should use them.

The savagely primitive farmers of North Vietnam had an incentive, the promise of looting the richer, industrialized South; they had the leadership and the semi-discipline of a criminal gang; they had an allegedly intellectual program, Marxism, and an allegedly moral justification: altruism, the sacrifice of all to some "higher" cause. The South Vietnamese had nothing but some mixed-economy echoes of the same altruism. The North Vietnamese won.

As a rule, there is an ugly period of gloating among the winners and of bitter buck-passing among the losers following a war. But I do not know of a historical precedent for the spectacle displayed by American intellectuals: an explosion of gloating over America's "defeat," of proclaiming America's "weakness," of denouncing America's "guilt," of glorifying and glamorizing the enemy, of pelting America with insults, accusations, humiliations—like an orgy of spitting at their own country's face.

When a national catastrophe, such as the U.S. involvement in Vietnam, has no generally known reason and no clearly perceivable cause, one may find leads to some contributory causes by observing who profits from the catastrophe. The intellectuals are the profiteers on the Vietnam war. They are of so miserably small a stature that it would be impossible to suspect them of causing the disaster. They are not lions, but jackals. (The lion who avenged himself for too long a neglect was philosophy, which left the U.S. vulnerable to the jackals.) What are the suspicious paw prints of a scavenger pack?

Observe the double-standard switch of the anti-concept of "isolationism." The same intellectual groups (and even some of the same aging individuals) who coined that anti-concept in World War II—and used it to denounce any patriotic opponent of America's self-immolation—the same groups who screamed that it was our duty to save the world (when the enemy was Germany or Italy or fascism) are now rabid isolationists who denounce any U.S. concern with countries fighting for freedom, when the enemy is communism and Soviet Russia.

The catch phrase of these new isolationists is a shabby little equivocation to the effect that "other countries are not ours to lose"—e.g., we did not lose South Vietnam (or China, or Hungary, or Czechoslovakia) because it was not ours to lose—i.e., the fate of other countries is none of our business. This means: other countries are not ours to judge, to deal with, to trade with, or to help. (Unless it is help with no strings attached, i.e., help without moral judgment, political appraisal, or even humanitarian concern about the results—as demanded by Laos, when it threw out a U.S. aid agency, but wanted the U.S. money turned over to the Laotian government.)

The purpose of this new isolationism is to play on the American people's legitimate weariness, confusion, and anger over Vietnam in the hope of making the U.S. government afraid to become involved in another foreign war of any kind. This would paralyze the U.S. in the conduct of any foreign policy not agreeable to Soviet Russia. The first intended victim of the new isolationism will probably be Israel—if the "antiwar" efforts of the new isolationists succeed. (Israel and Taiwan are the two countries that need and deserve U.S. help—not in the name of international altruism, but by reason of actual U.S. national interests in the Mediterranean and the Pacific.)

To oppose the spread of communism is a worthy goal. But one cannot oppose it in jungle villages while surrendering civilized countries—and one cannot oppose it by hiding from the world

the nature and the moral meaning of communism's only opposite and enemy: capitalism. To use America's phony involvement in Vietnam as a scarecrow to keep us away from the real,
the essential centers of the fight against communism—*this* is the
current gimmick or policy of the neo-isolationists.

Observe the frame-up staged against America's military power.

One of the methods used by statists to destroy capitalism
consists in establishing controls that tie a given industry hand
and foot, making it unable to solve its problems, then declaring
that freedom has failed and stronger controls are necessary. A
similar frame-up is now being perpetrated against America's
military power. It is claimed that the U.S. forces were defeated—
in a war they had never been allowed to fight. They were defeated, it is claimed, two years after their withdrawal from
Vietnam. The ignominious collapse of the South Vietnamese
when left on their own is being acclaimed as an American
military failure.

There is no doubt that America's entire involvement in Vietnam is a failure unworthy of a great power. It is a *moral* failure,
a diplomatic failure, a political failure, a philosophical failure—
the failure of American politicians and of their intellectual
advisers. But to regard it as a *military* failure is worse than
outrageous when you consider the heroic performance of Americans in a war they should never have had to fight. If there are
men or groups with a vested interest in creating an impression
of America's *military weakness*, use your own judgment as to
their nature and goals.

Now observe the moral bankruptcy of the "humanitarians."
After decades of ever louder protestations of compassionate concern with every possible form of suffering—the suffering of the
poor, the young, the old, the female, the black, the brown, the
Indian, the sick, the weak, the illiterate, the retarded, the criminal, the psychotic—after such a barrage of pleas and threats, of
saccharine and blood, that one could be tempted, in protest, to
hate babies and kittens, the altruists have suddenly shut up
before an unprecedented atrocity of historic scale: the murder
of a city, the evacuation of Phnom Penh.

A horde of savages that would make Attila look civilized by
comparison has given the world a perfect concretization of three
abstractions which civilized men have taken with too foggy a
tolerance: collectivism, which regards individual lives as of no
value—the rule of force, which implements the whims of the

subhuman—ecology as a social principle, which condemns cities, culture, industry, technology, the intellect, and advocates men's return to "nature," to the state of grunting subanimals digging the soil with their bare hands.

Since the Khmer Rouge are peasants who feel hatred for cities, the inhabitants of Phnom Penh—its entire population without exceptions—were ordered to march out of the city and to go on marching until they reached uninhabited countryside, where they were to start farming on their own, without knowledge, tools, or seed. This order applied to everyone: young and old, rich and poor, men, women, and children, the well and the ill, even the crippled and, according to a news report, even the hospital patients who had just had their legs amputated. Everyone was ordered to *walk*. They walked.

This is all we know. There have been no further reports on the fate of that evacuation. After a few shocked remarks, there were no protests from our media or from those liberal altruists who cry over the victims of "*relative* poverty" in America. The liberals had been minimizing or ridiculing the conservatives' fear that a "blood bath" would follow a communist victory. If human suffering concerned them at all, one would expect the altruists to scream their heads off against an atrocity which is worse than a blood bath: a mass execution by long-drawn-out torture. But the altruists have shut their traps. So have the altruists of Europe. There has been no significant protest from the hundreds of world organizations devoted to the relief of suffering, including that contemptible citadel of global hypocrisy, the U.N.

The best commentary on Phnom Penh, of those I have read, was "Get Out of Town" by William Safire, a conservative (*The New York Times*, May 12, 1975).

> In all human history nothing has taken place quite like the emptying of Phnom Penh. Sennacherib destroyed Babylon, the Romans sacked Carthage, and Hitler's bombers leveled Guernica, but in every case the attacker was destroying a particular city, not the idea of a city itself. . . . A city is civilization; civilization is diversity and creativity, which needs personal freedom; Communism is by its nature anti-city, anti-civilization, anti-freedom. The Khmer Rouge understand this; too many Americans do not.

To go from the horrendous to the grotesque, consider the Mayaguez incident. I hasten to say that were it not for the proper and highly *moral* action taken by President Ford, the consequences of that incident could have been more horrendous than Phnom Penh. That a small band of those same Cambodian savages dared seize an unarmed American ship was such an affront to America (and to civilization) that the collapse of international law would have followed if President Ford had not acted as he did. [President Ford used air, sea, and ground forces to free the ship.] To borrow Senator Goldwater's very appropriate phrase, every "half-assed nation" would have felt free to attack the U.S.—which would have meant world rule by terrorist gangs.

We shall never know whether the seizure of the Mayaguez was a deliberate provocation to test what the global communist scum could get away with—or the spontaneous feat of a local gang drunk with power and acting more royalist than their kings. But this does not concern us: in either case, when a foreign country initiates the use of armed force against us, it is our moral obligation to answer by force—as promptly and unequivocally as is necessary to make it clear that the matter is nonnegotiable.

Believe it or not, some American intellectuals (and some politicians) objected to President Ford's action. Mr. Anthony Lewis went so far as to declare it was America that was "a bully among nations, acting without consultation, without concern for facts or principle." [The *Times*, May 19, 1975] *His* principle (and filthy accusations) rests on the fact that "we allowed less than a day and a half for a response from the untried and isolated government of a shattered country." After which, he struggles to prove that part of the U.S. bombing of a Cambodian airport "could only have been punitive in purpose." (I hope so.)

This is international altruism gone wild. It demands that the U.S. give up self-defense in order to make allowances for an "untried government." (This means, I suppose, that we should wait until that government has gained experience in attacking us.) If those Cambodian brutes were so ignorant as to permit themselves an attack on a U.S. ship, the more reason to use force in answer, in order to teach them caution in the future; force is the only language that totalitarian brutes understand.

An interesting appraisal of the Mayaguez incident was given by C. L. Sulzberger, a liberal, who hailed President Ford's action in a column entitled "Just What the Doctor Ordered." [The *Times*, May 17, 1975] Since Mr. Sulzberger's columns deal mainly with the reactions of other countries to U.S. foreign policy, his enthusiasm in this instance is significant, revealing, and almost pathetic: it shows the extent of the dismal, gray hopelessness previously conveyed by our international diplomacy. "Small as the incident may later seem in history, a polluting stain is being erased from the previous American image of lassitude, uncertainty, and pessimism. This is a matter of world ideological concern as well as strategic balances because too many democracies are sick. . . . Now a new vibrancy creeps into the picture."

Mr. Sulzberger explains:

> The internationally renowned 'American tempo' and productivity still lag and the work ethic with its emphasis on speed and efficiency—whether prompted by puritanism or by the capitalistic profit motive—has certainly undergone visible and withering change. In this uncertain age American flabbiness is . . . harmful to the United States.

In the absence of American leadership, Mr. Sulzberger concludes, many Western countries were left adrift. "Now Gerald Ford seems to have put an end to that sad phase. Abruptly he has shown Americans and the world that he knows how to get where he wishes to go. Hopefully, he also possesses a good sense of direction."

Nobody respects an altruist, neither in private life nor in international affairs. An altruist is a person who keeps sacrificing himself and his values, which means: sacrificing his friends to his enemies, his allies to his antagonists, his interests to any cry for help, his strength to anyone's weakness, his convictions to anyone's wishes, the truth to any lie, the good to any evil. How would you tell an altruist's treacherously unpredictable policy from that of a cowardly milquetoast? And what difference would it make to his victims? A man practicing such a policy would be mistrusted and despised by everyone, including the profiteers on his "generosity"—yet *this* is the policy which the U.S. has come as close to practicing as any nation ever could. And if foreign countries are now cheering the sight of a giant, the U.S., standing up to a flea, Cambodia, it is the (momentary) defeat of altruism that they are cheering unknowingly, it is America's liberation from altruism's *flabbiness*, it is America's declaration to all the fleas of the world that the world is not to perish as a meal for fleas.

The American people's reaction to the Mayaguez incident was a great—and tragic—demonstration of America's sense of life. Great, because when the news broke out, the letters and wires received at the White House ran—ten to one—in support of President Ford's intention to use military force against Cambodia. The American people—battered by disillusionment over a senseless war and by vicious pro-enemy, antiwar propaganda—could have had an excuse to fear and oppose the potential risk of another war in the same geographical area. But they did not. They understood the principle involved; they were willing to fight, but not to accept an affront. (Which, incidentally, is the only way to avoid a war, but not many leaders said so.) This grasp of principles, when the chips are down, this proudly rebellious independence in the face of lies and threats, is what defeats the calculations of the manipulators, foreign or domestic, who attempt to con the American people.

The tragedy lies in the fact that these American characteristics can come into play *only* when the chips are down. A sense of life cannot foresee or prevent a catastrophe; it cannot save people from moving toward a disaster by single, gradual steps. Foresight and prevention are the task of conscious thought and knowledge, i.e., of political philosophy. In regard to a nation, they are the task of the intellectuals.

Just as Russia collapsed through the philosophical bankruptcy of its anticommunists, so did China—so did every rebellion against communist rule, in Hungary, in Czechoslovakia, in Poland—so did, does, and will every attempt to hold out a mixed economy (and/or *socialism!*) as an alternative to communism worth fighting and dying for. The greatest intellectual crime today is that of the alleged "rightists" in this country: with reason, reality, and (potentially) an overwhelming majority of the American people on their side, they are afraid to assume the responsibility of a *moral* crusade for America's values—i.e., for capitalism (with everything this necessitates). Observe the extent to which the tear gas of altruism is making them squirm. But unless men are brave enough to ventilate this country's moral atmosphere, they have no chance. For a nation, as for a man, a Declaration of Independence implies a declaration of self-esteem. Neither can stand without the other.

Much as I admire President Ford's conduct in the Mayaguez incident, there are many aspects of his policies with which I do not agree. The relevant one here is his appeal to leave Vietnam behind us and to avoid "recriminations" over that war. The lessons of Vietnam, he claims, have been learned. Have they?

What—and *who*—got us into that war? Why? For what reason and purpose? How did a war advocated and begun by the liberals (mainly by Presidents Kennedy and Johnson) become the conservatives' war? Isn't a moral obscenity such as a "no win" war unconstitutional—as a violation of the soldiers' right to life—since it turns soldiers into cannon fodder?

These are just a few of the questions to which the country has no clear answers. The Vietnam war is one of the most disastrous foreign-policy failures in U.S. history. We spent two years investigating everything connected with seven burglars sent by a bunch of politicians to bug the headquarters of another bunch of politicians. What was *that* compared to the enormity of Vietnam? We kept hearing, and are still hearing, that Watergate represented a threat to our rights, our freedom, our social system, and our Constitution. What was Vietnam?

Shouldn't there be an investigation of the U.S. involvement in Vietnam, wider, deeper, and more thorough than the investigation of Watergate—with nationally televised Congressional hearings, with dozens of famous witnesses, with daily headlines, editorials, debates, etc.? The purpose? To discover the causes in order to avoid the recurrence (or the continuation) of the policies that led to Vietnam.

Such an investigation would not be likely to uncover any crimes other than intellectual ones—but try to imagine the magnitude of those! Intellectual crimes cannot—and need not—be punished by law: the only punishment required is exposure. But who would conduct such an inquiry? Who would be able to ask the right questions, and integrate the answers, and point out the contradictions, and hammer at the evasions, and bring out the fundamental issues? Obviously, this is not a task for politicians, it is a task for theoretical thinkers, for intellectuals, for philosophers. But today *they* are the men who were responsible for the kind of thinking that was responsible for our involvement in Vietnam.

This is the reason why no such investigation can or will be held today. And *this* is the all-inclusive lesson to be learned from Vietnam.

15

The Sanction of the Victims
by Ayn Rand

This is Ayn Rand's last piece of writing. She delivered the lecture in New Orleans on November 21, 1981, before an audience of businessmen attending seminars sponsored by the National Committee for Monetary Reform. She was planning to give it again at the Ford Hall Forum; I delivered it there in her stead on April 25, 1982, some six weeks after her death. It was published in The Objectivist Forum, *April 1982.*

Since the subject of these seminars is investment, I must start by stating that I am not an economist and have no purely economic advice to give you. But what I am anxious to discuss with you are the preconditions that make it possible for you to gain and to *keep* the money which you can then invest.

I shall start by asking a question on a borrowed premise: *What human occupation is the most useful socially?*

The borrowed premise is the concept of social usefulness. It is not part of my philosophy to evaluate things by a *social* standard. But this is the predominant standard of value today. And sometimes it can be very enlightening to adopt the enemy's standard. So let us borrow the notion of "social" concern for just a little while—just long enough to answer the question: What human occupation is the most useful socially?

Since man's basic tool of survival is his mind, the most crucially important occupation is the discovery of knowledge—i.e., the occupation of *scientists*. But scientists are not concerned with society, with social issues or with other men. Scientists are, essentially, loners; they pursue knowledge for the sake of knowledge. A great many scientific—and technological—facts were known before the Industrial Revolution, and did not affect human existence. The steam engine, for instance, was known in ancient Greece. But knowledge of that sort remained an exclusive concern that lived and died with scientists—and, for century after century, had no connection to the lives of the rest of mankind.

Now, suppose that a group of men decided to make it their job to bring the *results* of the achievements of science within the reach of men—to apply scientific knowledge to the improvement of man's life on earth. Wouldn't such men be the greatest social benefactors (as they have been since the Industrial Revolution)? Shouldn't the socially concerned humanitarians, those who hold social usefulness as their highest value, regard such men as heroes?

If I say: No, such men are not regarded as heroes today—they are the most hated, blamed, denounced men in the humanitarians' society—would you believe me? Or would you think that I'm inventing some sort of irrational fiction? And would you say that something is wrong—terribly wrong—in such a society?

But this isn't all; there is something much worse. It isn't merely the fact that these heroic men are the victims of an unspeakable injustice: it is the fact that they are first to perpetrate that injustice against themselves—that they adopt a public "stance" of perpetual apology and universal appeasement, proclaiming themselves guilty of an unspecified evil, begging the forgiveness of every two-bit intellectual, every unskilled laborer, every unemployed politician. No, this is not fiction. That country is the United States of America today. That self-destroying group of men is *you*, the American businessmen.

When I say "you," I mean the group as a whole—I accept the tenet that present company is excepted. However, if any of you find a shoe that fits, wear it with my compliments.

Karl Marx predicted that capitalism would commit suicide. The American businessmen are carrying out that prediction. In destroying themselves, they are destroying capitalism, of which they are the symbol and product—and America, which is the greatest and freest example of capitalism mankind has ever reached. There is no outside power that can destroy such men and such a country. Only an inner power can do it: the power of morality. More specifically: the power of a contemptibly evil idea accepted as a moral principle—altruism.

Remember that "altruism" does not mean kindness or consideration for other men. Altruism is a moral theory which preaches that man must sacrifice himself for others, that he must place the interest of others *above* his own, that he must live for the sake of others.

Altruism is a monstrous notion. It is the morality of cannibals devouring one another. It is a theory of profound hatred for man, for reason, for achievement, for any form of human success or happiness on earth.

Altruism is incompatible with capitalism—and with businessmen. Businessmen are a cheerful, benevolent, optimistic, predominantly American phenomenon. The essence of their job is the constant struggle to *improve* human life, to satisfy human needs and desires—*not* to practice resignation, surrender, and worship of suffering. And *here* is the profound gulf between businessmen and altruism: businessmen do not sacrifice themselves to others—if they did, they would be out of business in a few months or days—they *profit*, they grow *rich*, they are rewarded, as they should be. *This* is what the altruists, the collectivists and other sundry "humanitarians" hate the businessmen for: that they pursue a personal goal and succeed at it. Do not fool yourself by thinking that altruists are motivated by compassion for the suffering: they are motivated by hatred for the successful.

The evidence is all around us, but one small example sticks in my mind as extremely eloquent. In the early 1930s an assistant of Jane Addams, the famous social worker, went on a visit to Soviet Russia and wrote a book about her experience. The sentence I remember is: "How wonderful it was to see everybody equally shabby!" If you think you should try to appease the altruists, *this* is what you are appeasing.

The great tragedy of capitalism and of America is the fact that most businessmen *have* accepted the morality of altruism and are trying to live up to it—which means that they are doomed before they start.

Another, contributory evil is the philosophical root of altruism, which is: mysticism—the belief in the supernatural, which preaches contempt for matter, for wealth, well-being, or happiness on earth. The mystics are constantly crying appeals for your pity, your compassion, your help to the less fortunate—yet they are condemning you for all the qualities of character that make you able to help them.

Evil theories have to rely on evil means in order to hold their victims. Altruism and collectivism cannot appeal to human virtues—they have to appeal to human weaknesses. And where there are not enough weaknesses, they have to manufacture them. It is in the nature of altruists and collectivists that the more they need a person or a group, the more they denounce their victims, induce guilt, and struggle never to let the victims discover their own importance and acquire self-esteem. The businessmen are needed most by the so-called "humanitarians" —because the businessmen produce the sustenance the "humanitarians" are unable to produce. Doctors come next in the hierarchy of being needed—and observe the hostility, the denunciations, and the attempts to enslave the doctors in today's society.

Most businessmen today have accepted the feeling of guilt induced in them by the altruists. They are accused of anything and everything; for instance, the ecologists denounce businessmen's refusal to sacrifice themselves to the snail darter and the furbish lousewort.

But *the businessmen's actual guilt* is their treason against themselves, which is also their treason against their country. The statement that aroused such fury among the collectivists— "What's good for General Motors is good for the country"—was true. And the reverse is also true: What's bad for industry is bad for the country.

I am here to ask you a question on my own—not on *borrowed*— premises: What are you doing to the advocates of capitalism, particularly the young?

Appeasement is a betrayal not only of one's own values, but of all those who share one's values. If—for whatever misguided reason—businessmen are indifferent to and ignorant of philosophy, particularly moral and political philosophy, it would be better if they kept silent rather than spread the horrible advertisements that make us cringe with embarrassment. By "us" I mean advocates of capitalism. Mobil Oil ran ads in the *New York Times* which stated the following (I quote from memory): "Of the expression free, private, responsible enterprise, we strike out 'free' and 'private' as nonessential." One of the big industries advertises on television that they are full of "people working for people," and some other big company announces on television that its goal is "ideas that help people." (I do not know what the ghastly P.R. men who come up with these slogans wanted us to think: that the companies worked "for free," or that they traded with people rather than with animals?)

The worst of the bunch is some new group in Washington, D.C., called something like "Committee for the American Way," which puts out a television commercial showing some ugly, commonplace people of all kinds, each proclaiming that he likes a different type of music ("I like rock 'n roll." "And I like jazz." "And I like Beethoven" etc.)—ending on a voice declaring: "*This* is the American way—with every man entitled to have and express his own opinion."

I, who come from Soviet Russia, can assure you that debates and differences of *that* kind were and are permitted in Soviet Russia. What about political or philosophical issues? Why didn't those upholders of the American Way show people disagreeing about nuclear weapons? Or about abortion? Or about "affirmative action"? If that committee stands for the American Way—there is no such Way any longer.

Observe also that in today's proliferation of pressure groups, the lowest sort of unskilled laborer is regarded as "the public," and presents claims to society in the name of "the public interest," and is encouraged to assert his "right" to a livelihood—but the businessmen, the intelligent, the creative, the successful men who make the laborer's livelihood possible, have no rights, and no (legitimate) interests, are not entitled to *their* livelihood (their profits), and are not part of "the public."

Every kind of ethnic group is enormously sensitive to any slight. If one made a derogatory remark about the Kurds of Iran, dozens of voices would leap to their defense. But no one speaks out for businessmen, when they are attacked and insulted by everyone as a matter of routine.

What causes this overwhelming injustice? The businessmen's own policies: their betrayal of their own values, their appeasement of enemies, their compromises—all of which add up to an air of moral cowardice. Add to it the fact that businessmen are creating and supporting their own destroyers.

The sources and centers of today's philosophical corruption are the universities. Businessmen are both contemptuous of and superstitiously frightened by the subject of philosophy. There is a vicious circle involved here: businessmen have good ground to despise philosophy as it is taught today, but it is taught that way because businessmen abandoned the intellect to the lowest rungs of the unemployables. All the conditions and ideas necessary to turn men into abjectly helpless serfs of dictatorship, rule the institutes of today's higher education as a tight monopoly, with very few and rare exceptions. Hatred of reason and worship of blind emotions, hatred of the individual and worship of the collective, hatred of success and worship of self-sacrifice—these are the fundamental notions that dominate today's universities. These notions condition (and paralyze) the minds of the young.

If you want to discover how a country's philosophy determines its history, I urge you to read *The Ominous Parallels* by Leonard Peikoff [Mentor, 1983]. This brilliant book presents the philosophical similarities between the state of America's culture today and the state of Germany's culture in the Weimar Republic in the years preceding the rise of Nazism.

It is the businessmen's money that supports American universities—not merely in the form of taxes and government handouts, but much worse: in the form of voluntary, private contributions, donations, endowments, etc. In preparation for this lecture, I tried to do some research on the nature and amounts of such contributions. I had to give it up: it is too complex and *too vast* a field for the efforts of one person. To untangle it now would require a major research project and, probably, years of work. All I can say is that millions and millions and millions of dollars are being donated to universities by big business enterprises every year, and that the donors have no idea of what their money is being spent on or whom it is supporting. What is certain is only the fact that some of the worst anti-business, anti-capitalism propaganda has been financed by businessmen in such projects.

Money is a great power—because in a free or even a semi-free society, it is a frozen form of productive energy. And, therefore, the spending of money is a grave responsibility. Contrary to the altruists and the advocates of the so-called "academic freedom," it is a moral crime to give money to support ideas with which you disagree; it means: ideas which you consider wrong, false, evil. It is a moral crime to give money to support your own destroyers. Yet that is what businessmen are doing with such reckless irresponsibility.

On the faculties of most colleges and universities, the advocates of reason, individualism and capitalism are a very small minority, often represented by a feeble specimen of window dressing. But the valiant minority of authentic fighters is struggling against overwhelming odds and growing, very slowly. The hardships, the injustices, and the persecutions suffered by these young advocates of reason and capitalism are too terrible a story to be told briefly. These are the young people whom business-men should support. Or, if businessmen are too ignorant of academic issues, they should leave academic matters alone. But to support irrationalists, nihilists, socialists, and communists—who form an impenetrable barrier against the young advocates of capitalism, denying them jobs, recognition, or a mere hearing—is an unforgivable outrage on the part of irresponsible business-men who imagine that it is morally safe to give money to institu-tions of higher learning.

The lasting influence of the universities is caused by the fact that most people question the truth or falsehood of philosophical ideas only in their youth, and whatever they learn in college marks them for life. If they are given intellectual poison, as they are today, they carry it into their professions, particularly in the humanities. Observe the lifeless grayness, the boring mediocrity of today's culture—the empty pretentiousness and mawkish sen-timentality of today's stage, screen, and television writing. There are no serious dramas any longer—and such few as attempt to be serious are of a leftist-collectivist persuasion.

On this subject, I can speak from personal experience. For several years, a distinguished producer in Hollywood has been attempting to make a television mini-series or a movie of my novel *Atlas Shrugged*. He was stopped on two counts: (1) he could not find a writer able to write a Romantic drama, even though there are many good writers in Hollywood; and (2) he could not raise the money for his project.

Allow me to say, even though I do not like to say it, that if there existed a novel of the same value and popularity as *Atlas Shrugged*, but written to glorify collectivism (which would be a contradiction in terms), it would have been produced on the screen long ago.

But I do not believe in giving up—and so, in answer to many questions, I chose this occasion to make a very special announce-ment:

I am writing a nine-hour teleplay for *Atlas Shrugged*.

I intend to produce the mini-series myself.

There is a strong possibility I will be looking for outside financing to produce the *Atlas Shrugged* series. [Miss Rand died a few months later, before completing the teleplay.]

In conclusion, let me touch briefly on another question often asked me: What do I think of President Reagan? The best answer to give would be: But I don't think of him—and the more I see, the less I think. I did not vote for him (or for anyone else) and events seem to justify me. The appalling disgrace of his administration is his connection with the so-called "Moral Majority" and sundry other TV religionists, who are struggling— apparently with his approval—to take us back to the Middle Ages, via the unconstitutional union of religion and politics.

The threat to the future of capitalism is the fact that Reagan might fail so badly that he will become another ghost, like Herbert Hoover, to be invoked as an example of capitalism's failure for another fifty years.

Observe Reagan's futile attempts to arouse the country by some sort of inspirational appeal. He is right in thinking that the country needs an inspirational element. But he will not find it in the God-Family-Tradition swamp.

The greatest inspirational leadership this country could ever find rests in the hands of the most typically American group: the businessmen. But they could provide it only if they acquired philosophical self-defense and self-esteem.

Here is what young Americans have to say about it.

I quote from the May 15, 1980 issue of *The Intellectual Activist*, a newsletter published by Peter Schwartz:

> Feminists threaten to publicize the names of psychologists who hold their convention in a state which has not yet endorsed the Equal Rights Amendment. Unionists protest political functions that serve lettuce not approved by Cesar Chavez. Yet businessmen are willing not simply to tolerate denunciations of free enterprise, but to financially sponsor them.

And: I quote from an article by M. Northrup Buechner, "The Root of Terrorism," in the October 1981 issue of *The Objectivist Forum*, published by Harry Binswanger:

> Imagine the effect if [some] prominent businessmen ... were to defend publicly their right to their own lives. Imagine the earthshaking social reverberations if they were to assert their moral right to their own profits, not because those profits are necessary for economic progress or the elimination of poverty (which are purely collectivist justifications), but because a living being has the right to live and progress and do the best he can for his life for the time he has on this earth.

I recommend both these publications very highly. You may write to *The Intellectual Activist* at: [Box 582, Murray Hill Station, New York, NY 10156]—and to *The Objectivist Forum* at: Box 5311, New York, NY 10150. [*The Objectivist Forum* ceased publication in December 1987.]

As for me, I will close with a quotation which is probably familiar to you—and I will say that the battle for capitalism will be won when we find a president capable of saying it:

"The world you desired can be won, it exists, it is real, it is possible, it's yours.

"But to win it requires your total dedication and a total break with the world of your past, with the doctrine that man is a sacrificial animal who exists for the pleasure of others. Fight for the value of your person. Fight for the virtue of your pride. Fight for the essence of that which is man: for his sovereign rational mind. Fight with the radiant certainty and the absolute rectitude of knowing that yours is the Morality of Life and that yours is the battle for any achievement, any value, any grandeur, any goodness, any joy that has ever existed on this earth."

16

Through Your Most Grievous Fault
by Ayn Rand

*This was one of Ayn Rand's newspaper columns. It
appeared in the* Los Angeles Times *on August 19,
1962, two weeks after Marilyn Monroe's death.*

The death of Marilyn Monroe shocked people with an impact different from their reaction to the death of any other movie star or public figure. All over the world, people felt a peculiar sense of personal involvement and of protest, like a universal cry of "Oh, no!"

They felt that her death had some special significance, almost like a warning which they could not decipher—and they felt a nameless apprehension, the sense that something terribly wrong was involved.

They were right to feel it.

Marilyn Monroe on the screen was an image of pure, innocent, childlike joy in living. She projected the sense of a person born and reared in some radiant utopia untouched by suffering, unable to conceive of ugliness or evil, facing life with the confidence, the benevolence, and the joyous self-flaunting of a child or a kitten who is happy to display its own attractiveness as the best gift it can offer the world, and who expects to be admired for it, not hurt.

In real life, Marilyn Monroe's probable suicide—or worse: a death that might have been an accident, suggesting that, to her, the difference did not matter—was a declaration that we live in a world which made it impossible for her kind of spirit, and for the things she represented, to survive.

If there ever was a victim of society, Marilyn Monroe was that victim—of a society that professes dedication to the relief of the suffering, but kills the joyous.

None of the objects of the humanitarians' tender solicitude, the juvenile delinquents, could have had so sordid and horrifying a childhood as did Marilyn Monroe.

To survive it and to preserve the kind of spirit she projected on the screen—the radiantly benevolent sense of life, which cannot be faked—was an almost inconceivable psychological achievement that required a heroism of the highest order. Whatever scars her past had left were insignificant by comparison.

She preserved her vision of life through a nightmare struggle, fighting her way to the top. What broke her was the discovery, at the top, of as sordid an evil as the one she had left behind—worse, perhaps, because incomprehensible. She had expected to reach the sunlight; she found, instead, a limitless swamp of malice.

It was a malice of a very special kind. If you want to see her groping struggle to understand it, read the magnificent article in [the August 17, 1962] issue of *Life* magazine. It is not actually an article, it is a verbatim transcript of her own words—and the most tragically revealing document published in many years. It is a cry for help, which came too late to be answered.

"When you're famous, you kind of run into human nature in a raw kind of way," she said. "It stirs up envy, fame does. People you run into feel that, well, who is she—who does she think she is, Marilyn Monroe? They feel fame gives them some kind of privilege to walk up to you and say anything to you, you know, of any kind of nature—and it won't hurt your feelings—like it's happening to your clothing. . . . I don't understand why people aren't a little more generous with each other. I don't like to say this, but I'm afraid there is a lot of envy in this business."

"Envy" is the only name she could find for the monstrous thing she faced, but it was much worse than envy: it was the profound hatred of life, of success and of all human values, felt by a certain kind of mediocrity—the kind who feels pleasure on hearing about a stranger's misfortune. It was hatred of the good for being the good—hatred of ability, of beauty, of honesty, of earnestness, of achievement and, above all, of human joy.

Read the *Life* article to see how it worked and what it did to her:

An eager child, who was rebuked for her eagerness—"Sometimes the [foster] families used to worry because I used to laugh so loud and so gay; I guess they felt it was hysterical."

A spectacularly successful star, whose employers kept repeating: "Remember you're not a star," in a determined effort, apparently, not to let her discover her own importance.

A brilliantly talented actress, who was told by the alleged authorities, by Hollywood, by the press, that she could not act.

An actress, dedicated to her art with passionate earnestness— "When I was five—I think that's when I started wanting to be an actress—I loved to play. I didn't like the world around me because it was kind of grim—but I loved to play house and it was like you could make your own boundaries"—who went through hell to make her own boundaries, to offer people the sunlit universe of her own vision—"It's almost having certain kinds of secrets for yourself that you'll let the whole world in on only for a moment, when you're acting"—but who was ridiculed for her desire to play serious parts.

A woman, the only one, who was able to project the glowingly innocent sexuality of a being from some planet uncorrupted by guilt—who found herself regarded and ballyhooed as a vulgar symbol of obscenity—and who still had the courage to declare: "We are all born sexual creatures, thank God, but it's a pity so many people despise and crush this natural gift."

A happy child who was offering her achievement to the world, with the pride of an authentic greatness and of a kitten depositing a hunting trophy at your feet—who found herself answered by concerted efforts to negate, to degrade, to ridicule, to insult, to destroy her achievement—who was unable to conceive that it was her best she was punished for, not her worst—who could only sense, in helpless terror, that she was facing some unspeakable kind of evil.

How long do you think a human being could stand it?

That hatred of values has always existed in some people, in any age or culture. But a hundred years ago, they would have been expected to hide it. Today, it is all around us; it is the style and fashion of our century.

Where would a sinking spirit find relief from it?

The evil of a cultural atmosphere is made by all those who share it. Anyone who has ever felt resentment against the good for being the good and has given voice to it, is the murderer of Marilyn Monroe.

17

Apollo 11
by Ayn Rand

This article was published in The Objectivist, *September 1969.*

"No matter what discomforts and expenses you had to bear to come here," said a NASA guide to a group of guests, at the conclusion of a tour of the Space Center on Cape Kennedy, on July 15, 1969, "there will be seven minutes tomorrow morning that will make you feel it was worth it."

It was.

The tour had been arranged for the guests invited by NASA to attend the launching of Apollo 11. As far as I was able to find out, the guests—apart from government officials and foreign dignitaries—were mainly scientists, industrialists, and a few intellectuals who had been selected to represent the American people and culture on this occasion. If this was the standard of selection, I am happy and proud that I was one of these guests.

The NASA tour guide was a slight, stocky, middle-aged man who wore glasses and spoke—through a microphone, at the front of the bus—in the mild, gentle, patient manner of a schoolteacher. He reminded me of television's Mr. Peepers—until he took off his glasses and I took a closer look at his face: he had unusual, intensely intelligent eyes.

The Space Center is an enormous place that looks like an untouched wilderness cut, incongruously, by a net of clean, new, paved roads: stretches of wild, subtropical growth, an eagle's nest in a dead tree, an alligator in a stagnant moat—and, scattered at random, in the distance, a few vertical shafts rising from the jungle, slender structures of a shape peculiar to the technology of space, which do not belong to the age of the jungle or even fully to ours.

The discomfort was an inhuman, brain-melting heat. The sky was a sunless spread of glaring white, and the physical objects seemed to glare so that the mere sensation of sight became an effort. We kept plunging into an oven, when the bus stopped and we ran to modern, air-conditioned buildings that looked quietly unobtrusive and militarily efficient, then plunging back into the air-conditioned bus as into a pool. Our guide kept talking and explaining, patiently, courteously, conscientiously, but his heart was not in it, and neither was ours, even though the things he showed us would have been fascinating at any other time. The reason was not the heat; it was as if nothing could register on us, as if we were out of focus, or, rather, focused too intently and irresistibly on the event of the following day.

It was the guide who identified it, when he announced: "And now we'll show you what you *really* want to see"—and we were driven to the site of Apollo 11.

The "VIP's" tumbled out of the bus like tourists and rushed to photograph one another, with the giant rocket a few hundred yards away in the background. But some just stood and looked.

I felt a kind of awe, but it was a purely theoretical awe; I had to remind myself: "This is it," in order to experience any emotion. Visually it was just another rocket, the kind you can see in any science-fiction movie or on any toy counter: a tall, slender shape of dead, powdery white against the white glare of the sky and the steel lacing of the service tower. There were sharp black lines encircling the white body at intervals—and our guide explained matter-of-factly that these marked the stages that would be burned off in tomorrow's firings. This made the meaning of the rocket more real for an instant. But the fact that the lunar module, as he told us, was already installed inside the small, slanted part way on top of the rocket, just under the still smaller, barely visible spacecraft itself, would not become fully real; it seemed too small, too far away from us, and, simultaneously, too close: I could not quite integrate it with the parched stubble of grass under our feet, with its wholesomely usual touches of litter, with the psychedelic colors of the shirts on the tourists snapping pictures.

Tomorrow, our guide explained, we would be sitting on bleachers three miles away; he warned us that the sound of the blast would reach us some seconds later than the sight, and assured us that it would be loud, but not unbearable.

I do not know that guide's actual work at the Space Center, and I do not know by what imperceptible signs he gave me the impression that he was a man in love with his work. It was only that concluding remark of his, later, at the end of the tour, that confirmed my impression. In a certain way, he set, for me, the tone of the entire occasion: the sense of what lay under the surface of the seemingly commonplace activities.

My husband and I were staying in Titusville, a tiny frontier settlement—the frontier of science—built and inhabited predominantly by the Space Center's employees. It was just like any small town, perhaps a little newer and cleaner—except that ten miles away, across the bluish spread of the Indian River, one could see the foggy, bluish, rectangular shape of the Space Center's largest structure, the Vehicle Assembly Building, and, a little farther away, two faint vertical shafts: Apollo 11 and its service tower. No matter what one looked at in that town, one could not really see anything else.

I noticed only that Titusville had many churches, too many, and that they had incredible, modernistic forms. Architecturally, they reminded me of the more extreme types of Hollywood drive-ins: a huge, cone-shaped roof, with practically no walls to support it—or an erratic conglomeration of triangles, like a coral bush gone wild—or a fairy-tale candy-house, with S-shaped windows dripping at random like gobs of frosting. I may be mistaken about this, but I had the impression that here, on the doorstep of the future, religion felt out of place and this was the way it was trying to be modern.

Since all the motels of Titusville were crowded beyond capacity, we had rented a room in a private home: as their contribution to the great event, many of the local homeowners had volunteered to help their chamber of commerce with the unprecedented flood of visitors. Our room was in the home of an engineer employed at the Space Center. It was a nice, gracious family, and one might have said a typical small-town family, except for one thing: a quality of cheerful openness, directness, almost innocence—the benevolent, unself-consciously self-confident quality of those who live in the clean, strict, reality-oriented atmosphere of science.

On the morning of July 16, we got up at 3 A.M. in order to reach the NASA Guest Center by 6 A.M., a distance that a car traveled normally in ten minutes. (Special buses were to pick up the guests at that Center, for the trip to the launching.) But Titusville was being engulfed by such a flood of cars that even the police traffic department could not predict whether one would be able to move through the streets that morning. We reached the Guest Center long before sunrise, thanks to the courtesy of our hostess, who drove us there through twisting back streets.

On the shore of the Indian River, we saw cars, trucks, trailers filling every foot of space on both sides of the drive, in the vacant lots, on the lawns, on the river's sloping embankment. There were tents perched at the edge of the water; there were men and children sleeping on the roofs of station wagons, in the twisted positions of exhaustion; I saw a half-naked man asleep in a hammock strung between a car and a tree. These people had come from all over the country to watch the launching across the river, miles away. (We heard later that the same patient, cheerful human flood had spread through all the small communities around Cape Kennedy that night, and that it numbered one million persons.) I could not understand why these people would have such an intense desire to witness just a few brief moments; some hours later, I understood it.

It was still dark as we drove along the river. The sky and the water were a solid spread of dark blue that seemed soft, cold, and empty. But, framed by the motionless black leaves of the trees on the embankment, two things marked off the identity of the sky and the earth: far above in the sky, there was a single, large star; and on earth, far across the river, two enormous sheaves of white light stood shooting motionlessly into the empty darkness from two tiny upright shafts of crystal that looked like glowing icicles; they were Apollo 11 and its service tower.

It was dark when a caravan of buses set out at 7 A.M. on the journey to the Space Center. The light came slowly, beyond the steam-veiled windows, as we moved laboriously through back streets and back roads. No one asked any questions; there was a kind of tense solemnity about that journey, as if we were caught in the backwash of the enormous discipline of an enormous purpose and were now carried along on the power of an invisible authority.

It was full daylight—a broiling, dusty, hazy daylight—when we stepped out of the buses. The launch site looked big and empty like a desert; the bleachers, made of crude, dried planks, seemed small, precariously fragile and irrelevant, like a hasty footnote. Three miles away, the shaft of Apollo 11 looked a dusty white again, like a tired cigarette planted upright.

The worst part of the trip was that last hour and a quarter, which we spent sitting on wooden planks in the sun. There was a crowd of seven thousand people filling the stands, there was the cool, clear, courteous voice of a loudspeaker rasping into sound every few minutes, keeping us informed of the progress of the countdown (and announcing, somewhat dutifully, the arrival of some prominent government personage, which did not seem worth the effort of turning one's head to see), but all of it seemed unreal. The full reality was only the vast empty space, above and below, and the tired white cigarette in the distance.

The sun was rolling up and straight at our faces, like a white ball wrapped in dirty cotton. But beyond the haze, the sky was clear—which meant that we would be able to see the whole of the launching, including the firing of the second and third stages.

Let me warn you that television does not give any idea of what we saw. Later, I saw that launching again on color television, and it did not resemble the original.

The loudspeaker began counting the minutes when there were only five left. When I heard: "Three-quarters of a minute," I was up, standing on the wooden bench, and do not remember hearing the rest.

It began with a large patch of bright, yellow-orange flame shooting sideways from under the base of the rocket. It looked like a normal kind of flame and I felt an instant's shock of anxiety, as if this were a building on fire. In the next instant the flame and the rocket were hidden by such a sweep of dark red fire that the anxiety vanished: this was not part of any normal experience and could not be integrated with anything. The dark red fire parted into two gigantic wings, as if a hydrant were shooting streams of fire outward and up, toward the zenith— and between the two wings, against a pitch-black sky, the rocket rose slowly, so slowly that it seemed to hang still in the air, a pale cylinder with a blinding oval of white light at the bottom, like an upturned candle with its flame directed at the earth. Then I became aware that this was happening in total silence, because I heard the cries of birds winging frantically away from the flames. The rocket was rising faster, slanting a little, its tense white flame leaving a long, thin spiral of bluish smoke behind it. It had risen into the open blue sky, and the dark red fire had turned into enormous billows of brown smoke, when the sound reached us: it was a long, violent crack, not a rolling sound, but specifically a cracking, grinding sound, as if space were breaking apart, but it seemed irrelevant and unimportant, because it was a sound from the past and the rocket was long since speeding safely out of its reach—though it was strange to realize that only a few seconds had passed. I found myself waving to the rocket involuntarily, I heard people applauding and joined them, grasping our common motive; it was impossible to watch passively, one had to express, by some physical action, a feeling that was not triumph, but more: the feeling that that white object's unobstructed streak of motion was the only thing that mattered in the universe. The rocket was almost above our heads when a sudden flare of yellow-gold fire seemed to envelop it—I felt a stab of anxiety, the thought that something had gone wrong, then heard a burst of applause and realized that this was the firing of the second stage. When the loud, space-cracking sound reached us, the fire had turned into a small puff of white vapor floating away. At the firing of the third stage, the rocket was barely visible; it seemed to be shrinking and descending; there was a brief spark, a white puff of vapor, a distant crack—and when the white puff dissolved, the rocket was gone.

These were the seven minutes.

What did one feel afterward? An abnormal, tense overconcentration on the commonplace necessities of the immediate moment, such as stumbling over patches of rough gravel, running to find the appropriate guest bus. One had to overconcentrate, because one knew that one did not give a damn about anything, because one had no mind and no motivation left for any immediate action. How do you descend from a state of pure exaltation?

What we had seen, in naked essentials—but in reality, not in a work of art—was the concretized abstraction of man's greatness.

The meaning of the sight lay in the fact that when those dark red wings of fire flared open, one knew that one was not looking at a normal occurrence, but at a cataclysm which, if unleashed by nature, would have wiped man out of existence—and one knew also that this cataclysm was planned, unleashed, and *controlled* by man, that this unimaginable power was ruled by *his* power and, obediently serving his purpose, was making way for a slender, rising craft. One knew that this spectacle was not the product of inanimate nature, like some aurora borealis, or of chance, or of luck, that it was unmistakably human—with "human," for once, meaning *grandeur*—that a purpose and a long, sustained, disciplined effort had gone to achieve this series of moments, and that man was succeeding, succeeding, succeeding! For once, if only for seven minutes, the worst among those who saw it had to feel—not "How small is man by the side of the Grand Canyon!"—but "How great is man and how safe is nature when he conquers it!"

That we had seen a demonstration of man at his best, no one could doubt—this was the cause of the event's attraction and of the stunned, numbed state in which it left us. And no one could doubt that we had seen an achievement of man in his capacity as a rational being—an achievement of reason, of logic, of mathematics, of total dedication to the absolutism of reality. How many people would connect these two facts, I do not know.

The next four days were a period torn out of the world's usual context, like a breathing spell with a sweep of clean air piercing mankind's lethargic suffocation. For thirty years or longer, the newspapers had featured nothing but disasters, catastrophes, betrayals, the shrinking stature of men, the sordid mess of a collapsing civilization; their voice had become a long, sustained whine, the megaphone of failure, like the sound of an oriental bazaar where leprous beggars, of spirit or matter, compete for attention by displaying their sores. Now, for once, the newspapers were announcing a human achievement, were reporting on a human triumph, were reminding us that man still exists and functions as man.

Those four days conveyed the sense that we were watching a magnificent work of art—a play dramatizing a single theme: the efficacy of man's mind. One after another, the crucial, dangerous maneuvers of Apollo 11's fight were carried out according to plan, with what appeared to be an effortless perfection. They reached us in the form of brief, rasping sounds relayed from space to Houston and from Houston to our television screens, sounds interspersed with computerized figures, translated for us by commentators who, for once, by contagion, lost their usual manner of snide equivocation and spoke with compelling clarity.

The most confirmed evader in the worldwide audience could

not escape the fact that these sounds announced events taking place far beyond the earth's atmosphere—that while he moaned about his loneliness and "alienation" and fear of entering an unknown cocktail party, three men were floating in a fragile capsule in the unknown darkness and loneliness of space, with earth and moon suspended like little tennis balls behind and ahead of them, and with their lives suspended on the microscopic threads connecting numbers on their computer panels in consequence of the invisible connections made well in advance by man's brain—that the more effortless their performance appeared, the more it proclaimed the magnitude of the effort expended to project it and achieve it—that no feelings, wishes, urges, instincts, or lucky "conditioning," either in these three men or in all those behind them, from highest thinker to lowliest laborer who touched a bolt of that spacecraft, could have achieved this incomparable feat—that we were watching the embodied concretization of a single faculty of man: his rationality.

There was an aura of triumph about the entire mission of Apollo 11, from the perfect launch to the climax. An assurance of success was growing in the wake of the rocket through the four days of its moon-bound flight. No, not because success was guaranteed—it is never guaranteed to man—but because a progression of evidence was displaying the precondition of success: *these men know what they are doing.*

No event in contemporary history was as thrilling, here on earth, as three moments of the mission's climax: the moment when, superimposed over the image of a garishly colored imitation-module standing motionless on the television screen, there flashed the words: "Lunar module has landed"—the moment when the faint, gray shape of the actual module came shivering from the moon to the screen—and the moment when the shining white blob which was Neil Armstrong took his immortal first step. At this last, I felt one instant of unhappy fear, wondering what he would say, because he had it in his power to destroy the meaning and the glory of that moment, as the astronauts of Apollo 8 had done in their time. He did not. He made no reference to God; he did not undercut the rationality of his achievement by paying tribute to the forces of its opposite; he spoke of man. "That's one small step for a man, one giant leap for mankind." So it was.

As to my personal reaction to the entire mission of Apollo 11, I can express it best by paraphrasing a passage from *Atlas Shrugged* that kept coming back to my mind: "Why did I feel that joyous sense of confidence while watching the mission? In all of its giant course, two aspects pertaining to the inhuman were radiantly absent: the causeless and the purposeless. Every part of the mission was an embodied answer to 'Why?' and 'What for?' —like the steps of a life-course chosen by the sort of mind I worship. The mission was a moral code enacted in space."

Now, coming back to earth (as it is at present), I want to answer briefly some questions that will arise in this context. Is it proper for the government to engage in space projects? No, it is not—except insofar as space projects involve military aspects, in which case, and to that extent, it is not merely proper but mandatory. Scientific research as such, however, is not the proper province of the government.

But this is a political issue; it pertains to the money behind the lunar mission or to the method of obtaining that money, and to the project's administration; it does not affect the nature of the mission as such, it does not alter the fact that this was a superlative technological achievement.

In judging the effectiveness of the various elements involved in any large-scale undertaking of a mixed economy, one must be guided by the question: which elements were the result of coercion and which the result of freedom? It is not coercion, not the physical force or threat of a gun, that created Apollo 11. The scientists, the technologists, the engineers, the astronauts were free men acting of their own choice. The various parts of the spacecraft were produced by private industrial concerns. Of all human activities, science is the field least amenable to force: the facts of reality do not take orders. (This is one of the reasons why science perishes under dictatorships, though technology may survive for a short while.)

It is said that without the "unlimited" resources of the government, such an enormous project would not have been undertaken. No, it would not have been—*at this time.* But it would have been, when the economy was ready for it. There is a precedent for this situation. The first transcontinental railroad of the United States was built by order of the government, on government subsidies. It was hailed as a great achievement (which, in some respects, it was). But it caused economic dislocations and political evils, for the consequences of which we are paying to this day in many forms.

If the government deserves any credit for the space program, it is only to the extent that it did not act as a government, i.e., did not use coercion in regard to its participants (which it used in regard to its backers, i.e., the taxpayers). And what is relevant in this context (but is not to be taken as a justification or endorsement of a mixed economy) is the fact that of all our government programs, the space program is the cleanest and best: it, at least, has brought the American citizens a return on their forced investment, it has worked for its money, it has earned its keep, which cannot be said about any other program of the government.

There is, however, a shameful element in the ideological motivation (or the publicly alleged motivation) that gave birth to our space program: John F. Kennedy's notion of a space competition between the United States and Soviet Russia.

A competition presupposes some basic principles held in common by all the competitors, such as the rules of the game in athletics, or the functions of the free market in business. The notion of a competition between the United States and Soviet Russia in any field whatsoever is obscene: they are incommensurable entities, intellectually and morally. What would you think of a competition between a doctor and a murderer to determine who could affect the greatest number of people? Or: a competition between Thomas A. Edison and Al Capone to see who could get rich quicker?

The fundamental significance of Apollo 11's triumph is not political; it is philosophical; specifically, moral-epistemological.

The lunar landing as such was not a milestone of science, but of technology. Technology is an applied science, i.e., it translates the discoveries of theoretical science into practical application to man's life. As such, technology is not the first step in the development of a given body of knowledge, but the last; it is not the most difficult step, but it is the ultimate step, the implicit purpose, of man's quest for knowledge.

The lunar landing was not the greatest achievement of science, but its greatest visible result. The greatest achievements of science are invisible: they take place in a man's mind; they occur in the form of a connection integrating a broad range of phenomena. The astronaut of an earlier mission who remarked that his spacecraft was driven by Sir Isaac Newton understood this issue. (And if I may be permitted to amend that remark, I would say that Sir Isaac Newton was the copilot of the flight;

the pilot was Aristotle.) In this sense, the lunar landing was a first step, a beginning, in regard to the moon, but it was a last step, an end product, in regard to the earth—the end product of a long, intellectual-scientific development.

This does not diminish in any way the intellectual stature, power, or achievement of the technologists and the astronauts; it merely indicates that they were the worthy recipients of an illustrious heritage, who made full use of it by the exercise of their own individual ability. (The fact that man is the only species capable of transmitting knowledge and thus capable of progress, the fact that man can achieve a division of labor, and the fact that large numbers of men are required for a large-scale undertaking, do not mean what some creeps are suggesting: that achievement has become collective.)

I am not implying that all the men who contributed to the flight of Apollo 11 were necessarily rational in every aspect of their lives or convictions. But in their various professional capacities—each to the extent that he did contribute to the mission—they had to act on the principle of strict rationality.

The most inspiring aspect of Apollo 11's flight was that it made such abstractions as rationality, knowledge, science perceivable in direct, immediate experience. That it involved a landing on another celestial body was like a dramatist's emphasis on the dimensions of reason's power: it is not of enormous importance to most people that man lands on the moon, but that man *can* do it, is.

This was the cause of the world's response to the flight of Apollo 11.

Frustration is the leitmotif in the lives of most men, particularly today—the frustration of inarticulate desires, with no knowledge of the means to achieve them. In the sight and hearing of a crumbling world, Apollo 11 enacted the story of an audacious purpose, its execution, its triumph, and the means that achieved it—the story and the demonstration of man's highest potential. Whatever his particular ability or goal, if a man is not to give up his struggle, he needs the reminder that success is possible; if he is not to regard the human species with fear, contempt, or hatred, he needs the spiritual fuel of knowing that man the hero is possible.

This was the meaning and the unidentified motive of the millions of eager, smiling faces that looked up to the flight of Apollo 11 from all over the remnants and ruins of the civilized world. This was the meaning that people sensed, but did not know in conscious terms—and will give up or betray tomorrow. It was the job of their teachers, the intellectuals, to tell them. But it is not what they are being told.

A great event is like an explosion that blasts off pretenses and brings the hidden out to the surface, be it diamonds or muck. The flight of Apollo 11 was "a moment of truth": it revealed an abyss between the physical sciences and the humanities that has to be measured in terms of interplanetary distances. If the achievements of the physical sciences have to be watched through a telescope, the state of the humanities requires a microscope: there is no historical precedent for the smallness of stature and shabbiness of mind displayed by today's intellectuals.

In *The New York Times* of July 21, 1969, there appeared two whole pages devoted to an assortment of reactions to the lunar landing, from all kinds of prominent and semi-prominent people who represent a cross-section of our culture.

It was astonishing to see how many ways people could find to utter variants of the same bromides. Under an overwhelming air of staleness, of pettiness, of musty meanness, the collection revealed the naked essence (and spiritual consequences) of the basic premises ruling today's culture: irrationalism—altruism—collectivism.

The extent of the hatred for reason was somewhat startling. (And, psychologically, it gave the show away: one does not hate that which one honestly regards as ineffectual.) It was, however, expressed indirectly, in the form of denunciations of technology. (And since technology is the means of bringing the benefits of science to man's life, judge for yourself the motive and the sincerity of the protestations of concern with human suffering.)

"But the chief reason for assessing the significance of the moon landing negatively, even while the paeans of triumph are sung, is that this tremendous technical achievement represents a defective sense of human values, and of a sense of priorities of our technical culture." "We are betraying our moral weakness in our very triumphs in technology and economics." "How can this nation swell and stagger with technological pride when it is so weak, so wicked, so blinded and misdirected in its priorities? While we can send men to the moon or deadly missiles to Moscow or toward Mao, we can't get foodstuffs across town to starving folks in the teeming ghettos." "Are things more impor-

tant than people? I simply do not believe that a program comparable to the moon landing cannot be projected around poverty,
the war, crime, and so on." "If we show the same determination
and willingness to commit our resources, we can master the
problems of our cities just as we have mastered the challenge of
space." "In this regard, the contemporary triumphs of man's
mind—his ability to translate his dreams of grandeur into awe-
some accomplishments—are not to be equated with progress, as
defined in terms of man's primary concern with the welfare of
the masses of fellow human beings ... the power of human
intelligence which was mobilized to accomplish this feat can
also be mobilized to address itself to the ultimate acts of human
compassion." "But, the most wondrous event would be if man
could relinquish all the stains and defilements of the untamed
mind ..."

There was one entirely consistent person in that collection,
Pablo Picasso, whose statement, in full, was: "It means nothing
to me. I have no opinion about it, and I don't care." His work has
been demonstrating that for years.

The best statement was, surprisingly, that of the playwright
Eugene Ionesco, who was perceptive about the nature of his
fellow intellectuals. He said, in part:

> It's an extraordinary event of incalculable importance. The sign
> that it's so important is that most people aren't interested in it.
> They go on discussing riots and strikes and sentimental affairs.
> The perspectives opened up are enormous, and the absence of
> interest shows an astonishing lack of goodwill. I have the impres-
> sion that writers and intellectuals—men of the left—are turning
> their backs to the event.

This is an honest statement—and the only pathetic (or terrible) thing about it is the fact that the speaker has not observed
that "men of the left" are not "most people."

Now consider the exact, specific meaning of the evil revealed
in that collection: it is the *moral* significance of Apollo 11 that is
being ignored; it is the *moral stature* of the astronauts—and of all
the men behind them, and of all achievement—that is being
denied. Think of what was required to achieve that mission:
think of the unself-pitying effort; the merciless discipline; the
courage; the responsibility of relying on one's judgment; the
days, nights and years of unswerving dedication to a goal; the

tension of the unbroken maintenance of a full, clear mental focus; and the honesty (honesty means: loyalty to truth, and truth means: the recognition of reality). All these are not regarded as virtues by the altruists and are treated as of no moral significance.

Now perhaps you will grasp the infamous inversion represented by the morality of altruism.

Some people accused me of exaggeration when I said that altruism does not mean mere kindness or generosity, but the sacrifice of the best among men to the worst, the sacrifice of virtues to flaws, of ability to incompetence, of progress to stagnation—and the subordinating of all life and of all values to the claims of anyone's suffering.

You have seen it enacted in reality.

What else is the meaning of the brazen presumption of those who protest against the mission of Apollo 11, demanding that the money (which is not theirs) be spent, instead, on the relief of poverty?

This is not an old-fashioned protest against mythical tycoons who "exploit" their workers, it is not a protest against the rich, it is not a protest against idle luxury, it is not a plea for some marginal charity, for money that "no one would miss." It is a protest against science and progress, it is the impertinent demand that man's mind cease to function, that man's ability be denied the means to move forward, that achievement stop— because the poor hold a first mortgage on the lives of their betters.

By their own assessment, by demanding that the public support them, these protesters declare that they have not produced enough to support themselves—yet they present a claim on the men whose ability produced so enormous a result as Apollo 11, declaring that it was done at *their* expense, that the money behind it was taken from *them*. Led by their spiritual equivalents and spokesmen, they assert a private right to public funds, while denying the public (i.e., the rest of us) the right to any higher, better purpose.

I could remind them that without the technology they damn, there would be no means to support them. I could remind them of the pretechnological centuries when men subsisted in such poverty that they were unable to feed themselves, let alone give assistance to others. I could say that anyone who used one-hundredth of the mental effort used by the smallest of the technicians responsible for Apollo 11 would not be consigned to permanent poverty, not in a free or even semi-free society. I could say it, but I won't. It is not their practice that I challenge, but their moral premise. Poverty is not a mortgage on the labor of others—misfortune is not a mortgage on achievement—failure is not a mortgage on success—suffering is not a claim check, and its relief is not the goal of existence—man is not a sacrificial animal on anyone's altar or for anyone's cause—life is not one huge hospital.

Those who suggest that we substitute a war on poverty for the space program should ask themselves whether the premises and values that form the character of an astronaut would be satisfied by a lifetime of carrying bedpans and teaching the alphabet to the mentally retarded. The answer applies as well to the values and premises of the astronauts' admirers. Slums are not a substitute for stars.

The question we are constantly hearing today is: why are men able to reach the moon, but unable to solve their social-political problems? This question involves the abyss between the physical sciences and the humanities. The flight of Apollo 11 has made the answer obvious: because, in regard to their social problems, men reject and evade the means that made the lunar landing possible, the only means of solving any problem—reason.

In the field of technology, men cannot permit themselves the kind of mental processes that have been demonstrated by some of the reactions to Apollo 11. In technology, there are no gross irrationalities such as the conclusion that since mankind was united by its enthusiasm for the flight, it can be united by anything (as if the ability to unite were a primary, regardless of purpose or cause). There are, in technology, no evasions of such magnitude as the present chorus of slogans to the effect that Apollo 11's mission should somehow lead men to peace, goodwill, and the realization that mankind is one big family. What family? With one-third of mankind enslaved under an unspeakable rule of brute force, are we to accept the rulers as members of the family, make terms with them, and sanction the terrible fate of the victims? If so, why are the victims to be expelled from the one big human family? The speakers have no answer. But their implicit answer is: We could make it work somehow, if we *wanted* to!

In technology, men know that all the wishes and prayers in the world will not change the nature of a grain of sand.

It would not have occurred to the builders of the spacecraft to select its materials without the most minute, exhaustive study of their characteristics and properties. But, in the humanities, every sort of scheme or project is proposed and carried out without a moment's thought or study of the nature of man. No instrument was installed aboard the spacecraft without a thorough knowledge of the conditions its functions required. All kinds of impossible, contradictory demands are imposed on man in the humanities with no concern for the conditions of existence he requires. No one tore apart the circuits of the spacecraft's electric system and declared: "It will do the job if it *wants* to!" This is the standard policy in regard to man. No one chose a type of fuel for Apollo 11 because he "felt like it," or ignored the results of a test because he "didn't feel like it," or programmed a computer with a jumble of random, irrelevant nonsense he "didn't know why." These are the standard procedures and criteria accepted in the humanities. No one made a decision affecting the spacecraft by hunch, by whim, or by sudden, inexplicable "intuition." In the humanities, these methods are regarded as superior to reason. No one proposed a new design for the spacecraft, worked out in every detail, except that it had no provision for rockets or for any means of propulsion. It is the standard practice in the humanities to devise and design social systems controlling every aspect of man's life, except that no provision is made for the fact that man possesses a mind and that his mind is his means of survival. No one suggested that the flight of Apollo 11 be planned according to the rules of astrology, and its course be charted by the rules of numerology. In the humanities, man's nature is interpreted according to Freud, and his social course is prescribed by Marx.

But—the practitioners of the humanities protest—we cannot treat man as an inanimate object. The truth of the matter is that they treat man as *less* than an inanimate object, with less concern, less respect for his nature. If they gave to man's nature a small fraction of the meticulous, *rational* study that the scientists are now giving to lunar dust, we would be living in a better world. No, the specific procedures for studying man are not the same as for studying inanimate objects—but the epistemological principles are.

Nothing on earth or beyond it is closed to the power of man's reason. Yes, reason could solve human problems—but nothing else on earth or beyond it can.

This is the fundamental lesson to be learned from the triumph of Apollo 11. Let us hope that some men will learn it. But it will not be learned by most of today's intellectuals, since the core and motor of all their incredible constructs is the attempt to establish human tyranny as an escape from what they call "the tyranny" of reason and reality.

If the lesson is learned in time, the flight of Apollo 11 will be the first achievement of a great new age; if not, it will be a glorious last—not forever, but for a long, long time to come.

I want to mention one small incident, an indication of why achievement perishes under altruist-collectivist rule. One of the ugliest aspects of altruism is that it penalizes the good for being the good, and success for being success. We have seen that, too, enacted in reality.

It is obvious that one of the reasons motivating the NASA administrators to achieve a lunar landing was the desire to demonstrate the value of the space program and receive financial appropriations to continue the program's work. This was fully rational and proper for the managers of a government project: there is no honest way of obtaining public funds except by impressing the public with a project's actual results. But such a motive involves an old-fashioned kind of innocence; it comes from an implicit free-enterprise context, from the premise that rewards are to be earned by achievement, and that achievement is to be rewarded. Apparently, they had not grasped the modern notion, the basic premise of the welfare state: that rewards are divorced from achievement, that one obtains money from the government by giving nothing in return, and the more one gets, the more one should demand.

The response of Congress to Apollo 11 included some prominent voices who declared that NASA's appropriations should be cut *because* the lunar mission has succeeded.(!) The purpose of the years of scientific work is completed, they said, and "national priorities" demand that we now pour more money down the sewers of the war on poverty.

If you want to know the process that embitters, corrupts, and destroys the managers of government projects, you are seeing it in action. I hope that the NASA administrators will be able to withstand it.

As far as "national priorities" are concerned, I want to say the following: we do not have to have a mixed economy, we still have a chance to change our course and thus to survive. But if we do continue down the road of a mixed economy, then let them pour all the millions and billions they can into the space program. If the United States is to commit suicide, let it not be for the sake and support of the worst human elements, the parasites-on-principle, at home and abroad. Let it not be its only epitaph that it died paying its enemies for its own destruction. Let some of its lifeblood go to the support of achievement and the progress of science. The American flag on the moon—or on Mars, or on Jupiter—will, at least, be a worthy monument to what had once been a great country.

18

Epitaph for a Culture
by Ayn Rand

This article was published in The Ayn Rand Letter *on January 15, 1973, three-and-a-half years after the flight of Apollo 11.*

"A sense of loss pervades the space community on the day after [the] Apollo [program]. It is the bewilderment that comes from having achieved 'the impossible dream'—a frequently used phrase here—and now being left with nothing but memories and a gnawing feeling that all the effort was not really appreciated."

This is the opening paragraph of a news story in *The New York Times* (December 21, 1972), sent from Houston on December 20, the day after the splashdown of Apollo 17, which marked the end of the Apollo program. It is an interesting story in that it is written by a good reporter who, by presenting the facts, offers, inadvertently, a profound indictment of today's culture.

In regard to great events, objectivity is possible to good reporters, but neutrality is not. It is obvious that that reporter feels sympathy for the men of the Apollo program and shares their bewilderment. It is obvious also that he feels admiration for their achievements—and, at a certain point, proceeds to repress it, right there, on paper, before the reader's eyes.

The story, entitled "Meaning of Apollo: The Future Will Decide," is an attempt to answer the question: "After eleven years and an expenditure of $25 billion, after nine spaceships have flown to the moon and twelve men have walked its surface, what has it all meant?"

"It may be the greatest achievement of the century. . . . It may be a major 'turning point' in history . . . But it may never be

179

possible for the people who willed this glorious adventure to know what they have wrought. Such is the inevitable frustration of those who attempt truly great things." He is wrong on this point. Those who achieve truly great things *know* what they have achieved, which makes their social position harder to bear: it is the lack of appreciation that they are unable to understand.

The story quotes one tribute—introducing it as "Perhaps the most satisfying assessment for the four hundred thousand people who toiled on Apollo at its peak . . ."—a statement made by, of all people, Arthur Schlesinger, Jr.: "The twentieth century will be remembered, when all else about it is forgotten, as the century in which man first burst his terrestrial bonds and began the exploration of space." This seems to be a minority opinion, however, at least as far as the material quoted in the story is concerned.

"The critics of Apollo, and there have been many, believe it was an evasion of earthly responsibility. They usually share the sentiments of the late Max Born, the Nobel laureate who said, 'Space travel is a triumph of intellect, but a tragic failure of reason.' They view Apollo as America's pyramids, a folly of national vanity, or as technology's Chartres, a symbol of the machine's new dominion over man and reason."

Don't ask me what they mean by the word "reason"—ask Immanuel Kant.

"Even though there are no immediate plans for return trips to the moon or for manned voyages to the planets, who knows how the awareness of such a capability will affect man's image of himself?"

Some people seem to know—and are struggling frantically to kill that image. The reporter indicates their kind of reaction. The first photographs of the whole earth, he states, which were brought by Apollo 8, made people feel that "the earth was a small and fragile sphere." I do not personally know anyone who felt that way, but it has certainly been a stressed, pushed, well-press-agented sentiment, then and since.

Whose purpose and motives would it serve? Well, Dr. René Dubos, a microbiologist at the Rockefeller University (and an influential leader of the ecological crusade), says that this sentiment "may be Apollo's greatest contribution and could lead to a 'new theology of the earth.' It was no coincidence," he says, "that the ecology movement gathered real force at the time of Apollo."

Two paragraphs later, the story presents the three truest,

most perceptive, most philosophical—and, in regard to the essence of today's culture, most horrifying—paragraphs I have ever read in a newspaper:

> Another reason for some confusion over Apollo's significance could be that, in one sense, the program was out of step with the times. For all its vaunted technology, it was somewhat old-fashioned, a reflection of America past more than of America present.
>
> Apollo was an expression of faith in the value of scientific discovery in a time of reaction against science, even against rationality. Apollo was an act of can-do optimism, of a belief in progress, in a time of reigning pessimism.
>
> Apollo was the work of a dedicated team, pursuing a well-defined goal, in a time of bitter confusion of national purpose. Apollo was, moreover, a success rising above so much failure.

If you want to know the difference between me and many other people, it is this: the moment I grasped that such was the essence of the culture, I would be on the barricades, fighting for man's highest value: his mind—against the whole world, if necessary (as I am doing). And I would not be able fully to grasp the answer to the question: How can anyone accept such a culture in passive resignation? (Forgive me for talking about myself at this point and in this context: I have no other way to express my appraisal.)

Oddly enough, the story gives a clue to that answer. The very next paragraph is an act of repression displayed in public, the act of a mind slamming the door on a blinding vision, on itself, and on the best within it: "But these are complex contradictions better left to the historians of another time"—which is an impersonal substitute for the sentence: "Who am I to know?"

What is left after such an abdication? Within the two-and-a-half inches of newsprint concluding the story, we are offered the sight of a phenomenon much broader than the problem of that particular reporter: the birth of a hopeless longing in a human mind, of a limp, quiet, wistful aspiration and a static pain—the noninflammable ashes left by the renunciation of something man may not renounce:

> Perhaps a better measure of Apollo will come from some future Homer, who will be able to thrill generations with tales of those frail little vessels out on the black sea of space and of those men in strange white suits stepping tentatively among the boulders

and craters of the moon. . . . In those legends of Tranquility Base and Neil A. Armstrong, of the beauty of the earth as seen from space, may lie the inspiration for even greater deeds both in space and on earth.

.   If that future Homer came today, that reporter would no longer be able to hear him.

I remember wondering, at the age of about ten, why adults admired virtue and heroism in literature, yet never sought to bring them into their own lives. In this respect, I have never grown up. But I felt an enormous sadness, when I began to understand such lives.

[In my article on "Apollo 11," I wrote:] "For once, if only for seven minutes, the worst among those who saw it had to feel not 'How small is man by the side of the Grand Canyon!' but 'How great is man and how safe is nature when he conquers it!' That we had seen a demonstration of man at his best, no one could doubt . . . And no one could doubt that we had seen an achievement of man in his capacity as a rational being."

Apparently, Dr. Dubos's followers and I perceived the same implications in the same event. The difference—the death-or-life difference—lies in our respective estimates of these implications.

I have been saying for years that the goal of modern philosophy is the destruction of reason, and that today's culture is motivated by hatred of man. Now you can hear it admitted—not in esoteric academic publications, or in the tone of a shocking discovery, but in the matter-of-fact, taken-for-granted, reportorial voice of a newspaper story.

Referring to that story's three crucial paragraphs, ask yourself whether men may permit themselves to evade the conclusions that scream from between the lines. If the Apollo program was "out of step with the times," then what sort of hell is our time, and where are our steps leading us? If Apollo was "somewhat old-fashioned," then what is the meaning of today's fashions? If Apollo was "a reflection of America past more than of America present," then America past was incalculably superior to America present: it had created a better way of living, it knew some truths which we have lost and which, if we value our lives, we should rush to recover.

"Apollo was an expression of faith in the value of scientific discovery" ("faith in science" is a post-Kantian contradiction in terms: "confidence" is the proper word)—while ours is "a time of reaction against science, even against rationality." If so, then that reaction should have been blasted out of any honest mind by the blast that lifted Apollo 11—which was a spectacular proof of the power of science and rationality.

"Apollo was an act of can-do optimism, of a belief in progress" ("can-do" is a timid substitute for "self-confidence")—while ours is "a time of reigning pessimism." If so, then self-confident optimism and the conviction that progress is possible to man have been justified and validated more resoundingly than anyone could ask for. And the same event has shown us the precondition of self-confidence, optimism, and progress, like skywriting left in the wake of those rockets: rationality. There is no necessity or justification for men to suffer in stagnant hopelessness. If pessimism is reigning over our time, who enthroned it and isn't it time to stage a revolution against its reign?

"Apollo was, moreover, a success rising above so much failure." Is *this* a reason for being confused over and indifferent to Apollo's significance? *Innocent* failure makes an honest mind check its premises, seek further knowledge, and seize upon the sight of a triumphant success as upon a life line—in order to gain courage, inspiration, and a lead to the secret that made it possible.

But all these conclusions presuppose an honest (i.e., rational) mind, an authentic goodwill toward men, an unbreached dedication to the pursuit of truth, and an eager desire to discover the proper way for man to live on earth. What if a person lacks these qualifications? If he does, the result will be the mentality represented by the "critics of Apollo."

If repeated failures make some men stick blindly to the same course, and damn success as evil—while proclaiming that they are moved by love for mankind—it is their motive that must be questioned.

In various disguises, the motive has been the same throughout history: hatred of man's mind—and, therefore, of man—and, therefore, of life—and, therefore, of any success, happiness or value man may achieve in life. The motive is hatred of the good for being the good. (See my article "The Age of Envy," in [*The New Left: The Anti-Industrial Revolution*, 2nd ed.].)

The publicly visible symptom of this hatred is the desire to infect man with a *metaphysical* inferiority complex—to hold up to him a loathsome self-image, to keep him small, to keep him guilty. The invisible part of it is the desire to break man's spirit. The greatest threat to such a goal is any glimpse of man the hero, which the victims might catch. And nothing could offer mankind so direct, dramatic, and stunning an image of man the hero, on such a globally visible scale, as Apollo's feat has done.

For ages, it was religion that had done the job of keeping man small—by comparing him to the immensity of alleged supernatural powers. Its secular equivalents implemented the same intention by comparing him to the size of the Grand Canyon. When science enabled man to lift his head, when he began to gain control of the earth, and the Grand Canyon ploy wore out, the haters' contingents swooped down upon the task of minimizing his achievement by shrinking the stature of the earth—which, they declared, "was a small and fragile sphere." No, it was no coincidence that "the ecology movement gathered real force at the time of Apollo"—or that Dr. René Dubos is dreaming of a new *theology*.

Most people do not share the views of Apollo's critics. The popular reaction to Apollo 11 was a significant demonstration of the breach between the American people and the intellectuals. But in this issue, the people are helpless: they respond to Apollo's greatness, they admire it, they long for the values it represents— but they are not aware of their reasons in clear, conscious terms. They cannot express, uphold, or fight for what they know only in the form of nameless emotions, and they will give up—as the *Times* reporter gave up. A culture is made—or destroyed—by its articulate voices.

That reporter could have enlightened people—but he, too, is a victim. He said more, with deeper theoretical perceptiveness, than most newsmen do today. But without the help of philosophy, he was unable to be certain of his own convictions—so he passed the buck to future historians and bowed to the will of "our times." *Who* makes our time what it is? *Who* makes any times or any culture? Philosophers. What did they teach that reporter in college? What are they teaching today?

Suppose you heard a man make the following speech: "I ignore the great achievement I have just witnessed—because the age of achievement is past. This achievement is a feat of science— but science is futile. This achievement is a triumph of rationality—but reason is impotent. This achievement is the product of self-confidence and of man's capacity for progress—but man is a weak, evil, miserable creature, born to be depraved and helpless. This achievement is the product of a dedicated team, pursuing a well-defined goal—but voluntary cooperation is impossible to men, goals are unattainable, and definitions are superfluous (or arbitrary). This achievement is a glorious success rising above a swamp of failure, but man, by his nature, is doomed to fail—and anyone who says otherwise is a hater of mankind!" If you heard this, you would run—or you would fight. Yet this is the speech which modern philosophy has been making for well over a century—and this is the speech you have been hearing for years, from two-bit intellectuals and fifty-grand-a-year professors, who are in control of today's culture.

A culture that tolerates such leadership is doomed. That reporter's story is its appropriate epitaph. If a future historian were to say: "This was the age when men traveled to another celestial body for the first time, but their contemporaries did not acclaim their achievement—some, because they knew it was great; the rest, because greatness did not matter to them any longer"—this would be the most damning obituary on the soul of our times.

As to the men of Apollo, this would add another measure of heroism (the status of being an exception) to their heroic achievement—like a salute from a great distance, some sense of which may, perhaps, reach them in their present loneliness: they are used to great distances.

19

Assault from the Ivory Tower:
The Professors' War Against America
by Leonard Peikoff

*This lecture was delivered at the Ford Hall Forum
on April 24, 1983, and published in* The Objectivist Forum, *October–December 1983.*

Intellectuals around the world generally take a certain pride, whether deserved or not, in their own countries' achievements and traditions. When they lash out at some group, it is not their nation, but some villain allegedly threatening it, such as the rich, the Jews, or the West. This pattern is true of Canada, from which I originally came, and it is true to my knowledge of England, France, Germany, Russia, China. But it is *not* true of America. One of the most striking things I observed when I first came here was the disapproval, the resentment, even the hatred of America, of the country as such and of most things, American, which is displayed by American intellectuals; it is especially evident among professors in the humanities and social sciences, whom I came to know the best.

Typically these professors regard the American political system, capitalism, as barbaric, anachronistic, selfish. They tell their classes that the American past is a record of brutal injustice, whether to the poor, or to the Third World, or to the fish, or to the ethnic group of the moment. They describe the American people as materialistic, insensitive, racist. They seem to regard most things European or Oriental or even primitive as interesting, cultured, potentially deep, and anything characteristically American—from rugged individualism to moon landings to tap dancing to hamburgers—as junk, as superficial, vulgar, philistine. When the New Left, taught by these same professors, erupted a while back, the student rebels expressed their philosophy by desecrating the American flag—blowing their noses in it, or using it to patch the seat of their pants. I do not know another country in which *anti*-patriotism has ever on such a scale been the symbol of an ideology.

It happened here because America at root *is* an ideology. America is the only country in history created not by meaningless warfare or geographical accident, but deliberately, on the basis of certain fundamental ideas. The founding fathers explicitly championed a certain *philosophy*, which they made the basis of America's distinctive political institutions and national character, and that philosophy to some extent survives among the citizens to this day. That is why the professors I mentioned can feel at home and at peace anywhere else in the world, but not here: the fundamental ideas of the founding fathers are anathema to today's intellectuals.

The war against America mentioned in the title of my talk is not a political or anticapitalist war as such; that is merely a result, a last consequence. The war I want to discuss is deeper: it is the assault against the founding philosophy of this country that is now being conducted by our universities. This war is being conducted not only by radicals and by leftists, but also by most of the mainstream, respectable moderates on the faculties. There *are* exceptions; there are professors still carrying on some traditions from a better era. But these men are not a power in our colleges, merely a remnant of the past that has not yet fully died out.

The basic philosophic credo of the United States was eloquently stated two centuries ago by Elihu Palmer, a spokesman of the revolutionary era. "The strength of the human understanding," he wrote, "is incalculable, its keenness of discernment would ultimately penetrate into every part of nature, were it permitted to operate with uncontrolled and unqualified freedom." At last, he says, men have escaped from the mind-destroying ideas of the Middle Ages; they have grasped "the unlimited power of human reason," "reason, which is the glory of our nature." Now, he says, men should feel "an unqualified confidence" in their mental powers and energy, and they should proceed to remake the world accordingly.[1]

Such was the basic approach of the men who threw off the shackles of a despotic past and built this nation.

Now let me quote, more or less at random, from some modern college teachers. In preparation for this talk, I asked Objectivists around the country to tell me what they are being taught in college on basic issues. I received a flood of eloquent mail and clippings, for which I am very grateful, and I would like to share some of it with you.

First, an excerpt from a textbook on *The Craft of Writing* prepared by some professors of rhetoric at Berkeley:

"What do Plato's opinions, or any other writer's opinions we might choose to study, have to do with learning to write? Everything. Before anything good can come out of writing, the students must at least sense the presuppositions of the writer in his civilization. And the first presupposition is this: we do not really *know*, surely and indubitably, the answer to any important question. Other cultures know such answers, or think they do, and writing is consequently a very different experience for them. But we, collectively, do not. . . . It would be very comfortable to be able to act upon the basis of immutable truth, but it is not available to us."[2] Note here the statement of pure skepticism: truth or knowledge is not available to us—offered as a flat statement, uncontroversial, even self-evident.

Next I quote from *The Washington Post,* from a story about a symposium held at Catholic University, dealing with Galileo's intransigent defense of his beliefs against the Inquisition. At one point, a prominent Harvard astronomer made an offhand comment contrasting Galileo's attitude toward scientific beliefs with that of modern scientists. "Today in science," the professor said, "there is no 'belief' as such, only probability."

A man in the audience, visibly emotional, stood up [the story continues]. "I cannot credit it. I cannot believe you would say" that scientists do not really "believe" in the objects they study. . . . "Do you really think it's possible that [astronomical science] is all wrong?" he demanded. "Yes," said [the astronomer]. "It is possible."

We cannot, he went on, know that there are atoms or what stars are. The reporter then summarizes the astronomer's conclusion:

Scientists now cannot fail to remember that absolute reality collapsed just after the turn of the century, with Einstein. . . . Since then, one simply cannot speak of certainties, of what is real and what is not. "I cannot believe it," muttered the man in the audience as he sat down.[3]

He better believe it. This viewpoint is standard today; the latest scientific discoveries, we are told regularly, invalidate everything we thought we once knew, and prove that reality is inaccessible to our minds. If so, one might ask, what is it that scientists are studying? If we can know nothing, how did Einstein arrive at his discoveries and how do we know that they are right? And if certainty is unattainable and inconceivable, how can we decide how close we are to it, which is what a probability estimate is? But it is no use asking such questions, because the cause of modern skepticism is not Einstein or any scientific discoveries.

Now let me tell you about another incident. One Objectivist undergraduate at Columbia University wrote, for a composition course, a research paper presenting the founding fathers' view of reason. The paper was sympathetic to the founding fathers' view, though not explicitly so. The teacher several times put question marks beside phrases that bothered her (e.g., beside "facts of reality") or wrote marginal comments such as "Do you really believe this?" At the end, she summed up: "The paper is very well written. . . . It's difficult for me to see how we can write about 'reason' without the nineteenth century's sad discovery in mind—that . . . [the belief that] reason will help us get better and better meant naiveté in many senses. Let's discuss." In the discussion, the student told me, the teacher said that the nineteenth century had established the inability of reason to know reality. Freud in particular, she said, had refuted the founding fathers. "He showed that man is really an irrational creature, and that the Enlightenment idea that all our problems can be solved by reason is quite unjustified."[4]

The founding fathers, as thinkers of the Enlightenment era, championed the power of man's unaided intellect. It was on this basis, after centuries of European tyranny, that they urged the right to *liberty*, which was the right of each man to rely in action on his own mind's judgment. They upheld this right because they believed that the human mind is *reliable*—that, properly employed, it can reach a knowledge of reality and give the individual the guidance he needs to live. The individual, they held, does not have to submit blindly to any authority, whether church or state, because he has within himself a brilliant and potent cognitive tool to direct him. That tool is the power of reason, the "only oracle" he needs—"oracle" in the sense of a source of absolute, objective truth.

There is no such truth, said the antipode and destroyer of the founding fathers' legacy. I mean the philosopher Immanuel Kant. Kant is the basic cause of the modern anti-reason trend. He is the man who, two hundred years ago, launched an unprecedented attack on the power of the human mind, declared that reason is in principle incapable of knowing reality, and thereby put an end to the Enlightenment. Freud was merely one of his many heirs, as are the modern skeptics who distort Einstein's findings to rationalize their viewpoint, as are the rhetoric professors at Berkeley and all their like-minded colleagues. In countless forms, Kant's rejection of reason is at the root of our modern colleges.

Question, debate, dispute—the founding fathers urged men— because by this means you will reach answers to your questions and discover how to act. Question, debate, dispute—our Kantianized faculty urges today—not to find the answers, but to discover that there aren't any, that there is no source of truth and no guide to action, that the Enlightenment viewpoint was merely a comfortable superstition or a naiveté. Come to college, they say, and we'll cure you of that superstition for life. Which, unfortunately, they often do. "On the first day of classes," a student from Kent State University in Ohio wrote me, "my English professor said the purpose of college is to take a high-school graduate who's sure of himself and make him confused."

"Kent fulfills that objective perfectly," the writer adds, not only in its insistent pro-skepticism propaganda, but also in its very method of presenting the course material. "Its courses are a hodgepodge of random and contradictory information that can't possibly be integrated into a consistent whole, and one of the first things it teaches its students is not to bother to try. The typical Kent graduate leaves the school feeling bewildered ... vaguely pleased that his bewilderment must mean he came out of college smarter than when he went in, and vaguely displeased that his enlightened confusion hasn't made him happier than it has."[5] This is an exact description of many current graduates, and unfortunately not only in Ohio. That English professor's statement of the purpose of college was not a wisecrack; it was meant, and practiced, as a serious pedagogical principle. We have reached a variant of the inverted slogans of Orwell's *1984*: the claim to knowledge, we are being taught, betrays ignorance. Knowledge is Ignorance, but Confusion is Enlightenment. That is what you can hope to achieve after tens of thousands of dollars in tuition and four years of study and agonizing term papers—a B.C. degree, Bachelor of Confusion.

If no one can know the truth, you might ask, why are these professors bothering to pursue their subjects at all? Some claim to be attaining probability, by unspecified means. But some are more modern and more frank. Here is another teacher from Columbia, this time from the Graduate School of Business, who offers a course entitled "Individual and Collective Behavior." According to one of his students, this teacher stated in class "that psychological theories cannot be proved. He added that this was a good thing, since it provided scope for further research."[6]

Do you follow the reasoning here? If we could prove a psychological theory, that would eliminate a whole area of research; there would be no need to investigate that particular question, because we would already have established the answer. On the other hand, if we can never know, we can go on looking forever, with no ugly barriers, such as knowledge, to stand in the way. But why then look? Why is research good if we never prove anything by it? Obviously, it is an end in itself. One does research in order to get research grants from the government, in order to write papers and get promotions so that other researchers can attack one's papers and thereby get more grants to finance more research for more studies, forever; with a voluminous literature on the weirdest, most senseless subjects pouring out, which everyone must study and no one can keep up with or integrate, and with everyone agreeing that none of it proves anything—all of it a giant academic con game divorced from cognition, from human life, from reality. Such is the nature of research under the reign of skepticism.

No one, however, can be a consistent skeptic; a man devoid of all knowledge would be like a newborn baby, unable to act or function at all. Despite their viewpoint, therefore, skeptics have to find something to rely on and follow as a guide, and what most of them choose to follow ultimately is: the opinion of others, the group, society.

Kant gave this approach a complex philosophic defense. There are, he says, *two* realities. There is reality as it is in itself, which is unknowable. And there is the reality we live in and deal with, the physical world, which, he says, mankind itself creates; the physical world, he says, is created by subjective but universal mechanisms inherent in the human mind. An idea that is merely the product of an individual brain, in this view, may or may not be acceptable; but an idea universal to the mind of the *species* can necessarily be relied on, because that defines reality for us; that is what creates reality, at least our private, subjective, human reality. Under all its complexities and qualifications (and there are mountains of them) this doctrine amounts to saying: the individual's mind is helpless, but the group, mankind, is cognitively all-powerful. If mankind collectively thinks in terms of a certain idea, that is truth, not the *objective*, real truth, of course, we can't know that; but subjective, human truth, which is the only truth we can know.

The founding fathers, being champions of reason, were champions of *the individual*. Reason, they held, is an attribute of each man alone, by himself; the power of the mind means the power of the individual. With today's anti-reason trend, however, such individualism simply disappears. In our colleges today, therefore, alongside Kant's skepticism about true reality, there is also the other element of Kant, the one systematically promoted by Hegel and Marx: the exaltation of the *social*. The student gets a powerful double message: you can't know anything, there is no certainty—*and*: society knows, you must adapt to its beliefs, who are you to question the consensus?

Here is an example of the second from a psychology textbook written by a professor at the University of North Carolina. Let me preface this by saying that philosophers before Kant used to distinguish two sources of knowledge: experience (which led to empirical knowledge) and reason (rational knowledge). These two were conceived, with whatever errors, as capacities of the individual enabling him to reach truth. Now here are the new, Kantian definitions. "Empirical knowledge is the agreement in reports of repeated observations made by two or more persons. Rational knowledge is the agreement in results of problem solving by two or more persons."[7] In other words: the genus of knowledge is *agreement*; the fundamental of knowledge is a social consideration, not the relationship of your mind to reality, but to other men. The individual by himself, on a desert island, cannot learn, he is cut off from the possibility of any knowledge, because he cannot tabulate agreement or disagreement. Empirical observation is not using your eyes, but taking a Gallup poll of others' reports on *their* eyes. Rational knowledge is not achieved by your brain grasping a logical argument; it is "agreement in results of problem solving"—and if men happen not to agree, for whatever reason or lack of reason, then there is no rational knowledge. This is nothing less than public ownership of the means of cognition, which, as Ayn Rand observed, is what underlies the notion of public ownership of the means of production.

If you want to see both Kantian elements—skepticism and the worship of the social—come together, consider the field of *history* today. Here is an excerpt from a course description at the University of Indiana (Bloomington); the course is titled "Freedom and the Historian."

> History is made by the historian. Each generation of historians reinterprets the past in the light of its own historical experience and values. . . . There can be thus no one definitive history of Alexander and no one historical truth about the fall of the Roman Empire. . . . There have been as many concepts of history, as many views of historical truth, as there have been cultures.[8]

The skeptical theme here is clear—there is "no one definitive history," "no one historical truth." An old-fashioned person, even of a skeptic mentality, would react: "Well, then, let's close down the field, if we can't know the truth." But not the moderns. We can't know the real truth, they say, but we can know the subjective truth that we ourselves create. "History is made by the historian." If there is a consensus of historians, therefore, their viewpoint is valid and worth studying, for that time and culture. As in Kant, there are two realities: the real past (unknowable), and the private past each generation creates, its own subjective historical truth. Notice that in this viewpoint the historian is at once helpless and omnipotent: he can know nothing really; but on the other hand he is the creator of history, of the history that we can know, and so he is an unchallengeable authority. If any student disagrees with the fraternity of historians, therefore, he has no chance. On the one side, he hears: "Who are you to know? There are no definitive facts." On the other, he hears: "History is made by the historian. Who are you to question it?"

Observe what people allow themselves when hiding behind a group. If the author of that course description were to say: "History is made by *me*," he would be dismissed as a paranoid personality. But when he says it collectively: "History is made by *us*, by our guild, by historians," that is acceptable. This is the Kantian exaltation of the social.

There is a further development of Kant's approach beckoning here. Why, historians soon began to ask, should the social authority be universal? Why can't there be *many* groups of historians, each creating history in accordance with its own mental structure, each version being true for that group though not for the others? Why, in effect, shouldn't we be democratic and let every collective into the act? The result of this line of thinking is *pressure-group history*, a pluralization of the Kantian approach, in which every group rewrites the past according to its own predilections, and every group's views are deemed to be as valid (or invalid) as every other group's. To be progressive in history today means precisely this: it means to respect the rewriting of all the newest groups, especially if their spokesmen make no sense to you; that shows that you are open-minded, and are not trying to impose your group's private views on others. To each his own subjectivism.

Is this an exaggeration? A prominent history professor at Stanford University, Carl Degler, recently made a plea for women's history, explaining that history varies subjectively from men to women. He declared: "The real test of the success of affirmative action for women will come not by counting the number or proportion of women in a department or profession, but by the extent to which men ... are willing to accept the new and peculiar interests of women as legitimate and serious, even when those interests are *strikingly novel and perhaps even bizarre* when compared with current acceptable work in a given field."[9] [Emphasis added.]

I once heard a feminist intellectual on television declare that the central fact of the ages is rape, and that the culmination of the historical process is the discovery of the clitoral orgasm, which has finally freed women from men. This is surely an approach to history which is "strikingly novel and even bizarre," but we mustn't be chauvinistic; history is made by historians, and if a certain group begins to push a certain line, and organizes into a new pressure-unit, that line becomes true,

true for these people, as true as any other claim in a world where no one can really know anything. *This* is what I call Kantianized history.

The founding fathers, as men of the Enlightenment, were champions of dispassionate *objectivity;* any form of subjectivism, or of emotion-driven cognition, was considered reprehensible by them. The opposite is true today. If objectivity is not possible to man, as the Kantians hold, then in the end anything goes, including any kind of emotionalism; and the humanities and social sciences end up, not as academic disciplines teaching facts, but as the preserve of shifting lobbyists disseminating sheer propaganda, which is what is happening increasingly in our colleges.

History is merely one example of it. The field of *anthropology* offers another eloquent illustration. First we read, a few months ago, about the scandal of Margaret Mead. In her famous 1928 book *Coming of Age in Samoa,* Miss Mead presented an idyllic picture of life in Samoa. The natives, she claimed, were gentle, peaceful, open, devoid of jealousy, free of stress. It was Rousseau over again (the noble savage), and Miss Mead's implicit moral was: the superiority of primitive culture over competitive, repressed Western society. Now, finally, a true scholar, Derek Freeman, an anthropologist from New Zealand, has set the record straight. After years of study in Samoa, he concluded that the Samoans [I quote *The New York Times*'s summary] "have high rates of homicide and assault, and the incidence of rape in Samoa is among the highest in the world. . . . [The Samoans] live within an authority system that regularly results in psychological disturbances ranging from compulsive behaviors to hysterical illnesses and suicide. They are extremely prone to fits of jealousy." Etc. Miss Mead's claims, in sum, "are fundamentally in error and some of them preposterously false."[10]

Judging by what one can gather from the press, anthropologists had known some of this for some time, but few had wanted to challenge Miss Mead publicly. Why not? Aside from a nature-nurture controversy that became involved here, two main reasons were operative, as far as I can make out.

One was the feeling that Miss Mead's *viewpoint*—her endorsement of primitive society over Western civilization—is noble, moral, good. The second is a pervasive subjectivism, which makes a potential dissenter feel: "I can't be sure, anybody can claim to prove or disprove anything, anthropology is whatever anthropologists say, why start a fight with a saint of the field for nothing?"

Now couple this episode with another recent scandal in anthropology. Did you read about the doctoral candidate from Stanford who, while studying in Red China, found that abortions were being forcibly performed on helpless women *after* the sixth month of pregnancy (when it is a dangerous, bloody practice), and who published this news in a Taiwanese weekly complete with photographs? The Chinese were furious, though the truth of his charges is not debated; and the Stanford Anthropology Department expelled the student from Stanford for unethical conduct—in effect, so far as one can decipher the department's statements, for blowing the whistle on his host country, an allegedly unforgivable academic sin. As one radio talk-show host in New York, Barry Farber, asked rhetorically: can you imagine the Stanford Anthropology Department expelling a student for doing exactly the same thing in regard to South Africa, i.e., for publishing articles about that regime's racial crimes? Such a student would have been treated as an academic hero.

The double standard involved in the two cases is appalling. One scholar, Margaret Mead, who condemns the West, becomes a revered figure for decades, even though her factual claims are dead wrong. Another, who prints the uncontested truth about a communist dictatorship, is expelled from his discipline. Is this fairness? Is this objectivity? Or is this the complete politicization of the field? But we must remember: the Kantians declare that there is no objectivity, and that truth is whatever the group wants it to be. In the social sciences today, the teachers do not leave much doubt about what they want it to be.

I must quote one further example of today's subjectivist trend, simply to indicate to you how brazen it is becoming. A recent issue of *The National Law Journal* describes a new development in the teaching of *law* in our universities, a development sponsored by a Harvard law professor, a law professor from SUNY (Buffalo), a sociologist from the University of Pennsylvania, and many others. These men "agree that an objective legal mode of reasoning, distinguishable from the society where it is being applied and the people applying it and capable of yielding an inevitable result, does not exist; that law, by its mask of objectivity, functions chiefly to legitimize social and economic inequities in the eyes of the lower classes as a way of keeping them docile; that because democracy is a good and the law a shell, the goal is to found a government not by law but by people."[11]

This statement is a union of Kant and Marx. Let me translate it. "There is no objective legal reasoning; law pretends to be objective, but really it is an instrument of the wealthy to keep the poor docile; law, in effect, is the opiate of the masses"— these are law professors speaking, mind you—"and our goal should be a system run not by law, but by people." How are the people to govern themselves, if not by reference to an objective code of laws? How are they to settle their disputes and resolve conflicting claims? In this context, there is only one alternative to government by law: government by pressure group, i.e., by every sizable pack or tribe in the land struggling to seize control of the legislature and the courts, and then ramming its arbitrary desires down the throats of the rest, until they rebel and start ramming their desires, etc.—all of it a naked exercise in power politics, of group-eat-group, without the pretense of objectivity or justice.

One of the great achievements of Western civilization was the concept of a society in which men are *not* left helplessly at the mercy of clashing groups, but can resolve disputes fairly, as individuals, by reference to impersonal principle. This is what used to be called a government of laws and not of men. Today we have the frightening spectacle of law professors telling us that what we need is a government of men and not of laws. If this school needs a name, it should call itself "Lawyers for Gang Warfare."

You may be wondering whether things are better in the physical sciences today. They are, somewhat, but science, too, depends on philosophy. Modern science arose in an Aristotelian period, a period characterized by respect for reason and objective reality, and it cannot survive the collapse of that philosophy. One sign of this is the skepticism among scientists illustrated by the Harvard astronomer I quoted earlier. But there is another, even more ominous sign. I mean the claims made by an increasing number of physicists that modern physics is growing closer to *Oriental mysticism;* you may have heard the tributes that these scientists now lavish on works such as the *Upanishads* and the *I Ching.* In a rather mild statement, one such scientist wrote recently that there is a "curious connection between the subrational and the super-rational. Intuition, sudden flashes of insight, and even mystical experiences seem to play a role in the restructuring of science." This quote, by the way, is from a textbook written by the Head of the Astrophysics Department at the University of Colorado (Boulder).

I have said that men cannot be consistent skeptics. One way out is to turn for guidance to society. But there is another way: *old-fashioned mysticism*—the turning not to society, but to the supernatural. Although this method was hardly originated by Kant, here, too, his influence is at work today. Our minds cannot know reality, Kant said, but certain of our *feelings*—our unprovable, nonconceptual, nonrational feelings—can give us a hint as to its nature. This Kantian suggestion—that the mind is helpless, but feelings may be able to replace it as a cognitive faculty—was taken up in the nineteenth century by a whole school of Romanticists, such as Schopenhauer and Nietzsche, who admired and agreed with the essential ideas of Kant, and proceeded to unleash a flood of overt irrationalism, often including a deep admiration for Oriental mysticism. Today, this particular development has also become widespread in the West; you can see it in everything from art to psychotherapy to diet fads, and it is showing up now even in physics. If scientists do not have a rational philosophy to guide them, they, too, have to sink back ultimately into the common horde.

If you wonder what kind of physics is being produced by these mystical scientists, let me quote one paragraph from the Colorado textbook. The passage occurs in the context of an attack on the concept of reality.

> Even more disruptive to our notions of reality is the recognition that it is impossible to describe the entirety of an object at one time. Because of the finite speed of light no object has an instantaneous existence. All extended objects are fuzzy time averages. In order for an object to be totally present at a given instant of time, instantaneous communication would be required. Since that is impossible, all parts of an object exist in the past of every other part. Our present does not exist. One not only needs a clairvoyant to foretell the future but also to foretell the present.

The name of this textbook, by the way, is *The Fermenting Universe*.[12] I do not say that this book is typical of our college science, not yet. What I do say is this: it is significant, it is frightening, that such a book by an author in such a prestigious position is even possible.

As to the wider meaning of the latest scientific theorizing taken as a whole, I will leave it to an intellectual historian from SUNY (Oswego) to comment. This professor seems to agree with all the skeptical and mystical modern interpretations of science. In a lecture entitled "The Collapse of Absolutes," he sums up for his students:

> What does all this mean? Well, first of all, it means that the universe has become unintelligible.... Secondly, scientists themselves have become humble and admit that science may never be able to observe reality.... Thirdly, the physical world of Einstein has become something that even the most educated layman finds difficult to understand ... He in short finds it incomprehensible and irrational.[13]

In other words, if the college student runs to science as an escape from the humanities and the social sciences, he is learning there, too, that the mind is impotent.

Philosophy sets the standards for *every* school and department within a university. When philosophy goes bad, corrupt manifestations turn up everywhere. Visit Stanford's Graduate School of Business, for instance, and audit a course titled "Creativity in Business" offered to MBA candidates. I quote the *San Francisco Chronicle*:

> The students [in this course] learn meditation and chanting, analyze dreams, paint pictures, study *I Ching* and tarot cards.... The course reading includes *I am That* by Swami Muktananda ... *Precision Nirvana* ... *Yoga Aphorisms.* ... One woman who had been a Moonie earlier in her life was fearful after a couple of sessions that she was getting into the same sort of thing, said [the professor]. It's nothing of the kind, he added, but the heavy emphasis on developing the intuitive side of a student's mind, where creativity is expressed, can sometimes leave that impression.

There are, this professor teaches his students, two main blocks to creativity. One is fear; the other is: "the endless chattering of the mind."[14] If mysticism is the fashion among scientists, why not among our future business leaders, too?

According to *The Chronicle of Higher Education*, the Moonies and the Hare Krishnas have become a problem to the colleges. "Many administrators ... agree that religious cults have found college campuses to be among their more profitable recruiting grounds in recent years."[15] This is hardly a mystery. The colleges, by means of what they are teaching, are systematically setting the students up to be taken over. The Reverend Moon or his equivalent will be the ultimate profiteer of today's trends if these are not stopped.

Now let us switch fields and turn to the area of *sex education*. I suggest you read a text widely used in junior high and high schools, cited by the American Library Association as one of the "Best Books for Young Adults in 1978." The book claims, to impressionable teenagers, that anything in the realm of sex is acceptable as long as those who do it feel no guilt. Among other practices, the book explicitly endorses transvestism, prostitution, open marriage, sado-masochism, and bestiality. In regard to this latter, however, the book cautions the youngsters to avoid "poor hygiene, injury by the animal or to the animal, or guilt on the part of the human."[16]

If you want still more, turn to *art*—for instance, poetry—as it is taught today in our colleges. For an eloquent example, read the widely used *Norton's Introduction to Poetry,* and see what modern poems are offered to students alongside the recognized classics of the past as equally deserving of study, analysis, respect. One typical entry, which immediately precedes a poem by Blake, is entitled "Hard Rock Returns to Prison from the Hospital for the Criminal Insane." The poem begins: "Hard Rock was 'known not to take no shit / From nobody' . . ." and continues in similar vein throughout. This item can be topped only by the volume's editor, who discusses the poem reverently, explaining that it has a profound social message: "the despair of the hopeless."[17] Just as history is what historians say, so art today is supposed to be whatever the art world endorses, and this is the kind of stuff it is endorsing. After all, the modernists shrug, who is to say what's really good in art? Aren't Hard Rock's feelings just as good as Tennyson's or Milton's?

Now I want to discuss the cash value of the trends we have been considering. The base of philosophy is metaphysics and epistemology, i.e., a view of reality and of reason. The first major result of this base, its most important practical consequence, is ethics or morality, i.e., a code of values.

The founding fathers held a definite view of morality. Although they were not consistent, their distinctive ethical principle was: a man's right to the pursuit of happiness, his *own* happiness, to be achieved by his own thought and effort—which means: not an ethics of self-sacrifice, but of self-reliance and self-fulfillment—in other words, an ethics of *egoism*, or what Ayn Rand called "the virtue of selfishness." The founding fathers built this country on a twofold philosophical basis: first, on the championship of reason; then, as a result, on the principle of egoism, in the sense just indicated. The product of this combination was the idea: let us have a political system in which the individual is free to function *by* his own mind and *for* his own sake or profit. Such was the grounding of capitalism in America.

Just as our modern colleges have declared war on the first of these ideas (on reason), so they have declared war on the second. Here again they are following Kant. Kant was the greatest champion of self-sacrifice in the history of thought. He held that total selflessness is man's duty, that suffering is man's destiny in life, and that any egoistic motive, any quest for personal joy and any form of self-love, is the antonym of morality.

The Dean of Arts and Sciences at Colgate University expressed a similar viewpoint clearly in some convocation remarks he offered in 1981, attacking what he saw as an epidemic of egoism on campus. Egoism, the dean claimed, necessarily means whim-worship. Here is his definition of egoism: "serving the self, or taking care of number one . . . mindless hedonism and a concern for *me*, me *now*." Where did he get this definition? Why can't an egoist be enlightened, rational, long-range? No answer was given. The proper path for us to follow, the dean went on, was indicated by the "socially concerned" students of the sixties, with their "emphasis on duty to others" and on "the ascetic mode." We may leave aside here the actual moral character of those violent, drug-addicted rebels of the sixties so admired by the dean. The point is the choice he offers: mindless hedonism versus *asceticism*—note the word—i.e., utter self-abnegation, renunciation, sacrifice. Today's students, the dean said disapprovingly, attend college for reasons such as "to get a better job and to make more money." This, he said, is wrong. "It is . . . my hope for you that you will recognize that there is life outside the self, that we live in a world that cries out for those with visions of a community founded upon just principles. . . . and [I] wish that preoccupation with self will give way to concern for others."[18]

Professors sometimes take sides in a controversy, but deans, to my knowledge, never do. When a dean makes an ideological statement, you can be sure that it is a universally accepted bromide on campus.

Our colleges are allegedly open to all ideas, yet on the fundamental issues of philosophy we hear everywhere the same rigid, dogmatic viewpoint, just as though the faculties were living and teaching under government censorship. I visited Columbia's graduation exercises last year, and the priest who delivered the invocation declared to the assembled graduates: "The age of individual achievement has passed. When you come to Columbia, you are not to be motivated by the desire for money, or personal ambition, or success; you are here to learn to serve. And my prayer for you today is that at the end of your life you will be able to say, 'Lord, I have been an unworthy servant.' " If that priest had come out with a plug for the Communist party, it would have caused a stir; if he had upheld the superiority of Catholicism, ditto. But to state as self-evident the moral code common to both caused not a murmur of protest.

A social psychologist from Harvard, who also regards that code as self-evident, has devised a test to measure a person's level of *moral reasoning*. This test is the basis of many of the new courses in morality now being offered in schools around the country. The testers give the student a hypothetical situation and several possible responses to it. He then chooses the response that best fits his own attitude. Here is a typical example. "Your spouse is dying from a rare cancer, and doctors believe a drug recently discovered by the town pharmacist may provide a cure. The pharmacist, however, charges $2,000 for the drug (which costs only $200 to make). You can't afford the drug and can't raise the money."

Before we proceed to the answers, observe what moral lessons a student would absorb from the statement of the problem alone. Morality does not pertain to normal situations, it is not concerned with how to live, he learns, but with how to meet disaster, death, terminal cancer. The obstacle to his values, he learns, is greed, the greed of the pharmacist who is trying to exploit him by charging ten times the cost of the product. There is no mention of any effort the pharmacist might have exerted to discover the drug, no mention of any research or thought or study required of him in order to have discovered an unprecedented cure for cancer, no mention of any other costs he might have incurred, no question of any gratitude to the man who alone has created the power to save the spouse, no mention of any reason why that pharmacist, counter to every principle of self-interest, would overcharge for the drug when he would make more money in the long run by selling it in greater quantity at a lower price, as the whole history of mass production shows. All of this—in an exercise designed to teach *moral reasoning*—is omitted as irrelevant. Nor is there any explanation of why the student cannot raise money—no reference to banks, or savings, or insurance, or relatives. The case is simple: senseless greed on the part of a callous inventor, and what do you do about it?

Now comes the answer—six choices, and you must pick one; the answers are given in ascending order, the morally lowest first. The lowest is: not to steal the drug (not out of respect for property rights, that doesn't enter even on the lowest rung of the test, but out of fear of jail). The other five answers all advocate stealing the drug; they differ merely in their reasons. Here are the three *most moral* reasons, according to the test: "(4) I would steal the drug because I have a duty springing from the marriage vow I took. (5) I would steal the drug because the right to life is higher than the right to property. (6) I would steal the drug because I respect the dignity of human beings. . . . [I should] act in the best interest of mankind."[19]

Here is an eloquent example of what Ayn Rand has amply demonstrated: the creed of self-sacrifice is *not* concerned with the "dignity of human beings" or with "the best interest of mankind." This creed is the destroyer of human dignity and of mankind, because it is incompatible with the requirements of human life. It scorns—and dismisses as irrelevant—thought, effort, work, achievement, property, trade, justice, every value life requires. All of this is to be sacrificed, the altruist claims, to that which has the first right on earth: pain, pain as such, weakness, illness, suffering, regardless of its cause. This is the penalization of success for being success and the rewarding of failure for being failure; it is what Ayn Rand called the hatred of the good for being the good; and it is now being taught to our children, courtesy of a Harvard authority, as an example of high-quality moral reasoning. (As to what will happen to the weak and the sick after the able and productive have been demeaned, expropriated, and throttled, read *Atlas Shrugged,* or look at Soviet Russia.)

Did Ayn Rand exaggerate in saying that altruists wish to

sacrifice thought to pain? Let me quote from *Dental Products Report* magazine in 1982. I do not know first-hand whether this item is true; I hope not. "Some medical schools in the United States are considering major changes in the traditional curriculum requirements for premed and medical students. Harvard, for example, is considering abolishing requirements for premed science and, instead, requiring courses stressing compassion and understanding in dealing with patients."[20]

Did you hear that one? Our doctors may not study much science any longer, but they will be skilled in expressing compassion to the suffering—who will suffer permanently, without any chance of relief, because the doctors will no longer be wasting their time on science or thought. This is a perfect, fiction-like example of an altruistic curriculum change, if ever I heard one.

Now let us sum up the total philosophy advocated by today's colleges: reality has collapsed; reason is naive; achievement is unnecessary and unreal. I sometimes fantasize the ideal modern curriculum, which would capture explicitly the fundamental ideas of the modern university, and recently I found it. I found three actual courses offered at three different schools, one covering each basic branch of philosophy, the sum indicating the naked essence of the modern trend.

For metaphysics, we go to the University of Delaware (Newark) to take an interdisciplinary honors course titled: "Nothing." Subtitle: "A study of Nil, Void, Vacuum, Null, Zero, and Other Kinds of Nothingness." The description: "A lecture course exploring the varieties of nothingness from the vacuum and void of physics and astronomy to political nihilism, to the emptiness of the arts and the soul."[21] That is our metaphysical base, our view of reality: nothing.

For epistemology, we move to New York University to take a course titled "Theory of Knowledge." The description: "Various theories of knowledge are discussed, including the view that they are all inadequate and that, in fact, nobody knows anything. The consequences of skepticism are explored for thought, action, language, and emotional relations."[22]

We end up, for ethics, at Indiana (Bloomington), taking a course titled: "Social Reactions to Handicaps," the description of which reads, in part: "This course will ... explore some of the different ways in which the handicapped individual and the idea of handicap have been regarded in Western Civilization.

Figures from the past such as the fool, the madman, the blind beggar, and the witch . . . will be discussed.''[23]

There was once a time when college students studied facts, knowledge, and human greatness. Now they study nothingness, ignorance, and the fool, the madman, the blind beggar, and the witch.

If the philosophical message taught by our colleges is clear to you, the *political* views of the faculties will require very little discussion. Politics is a consequence of philosophy. The precondition of capitalism is egoism, and beneath that: the efficacy of reason. The consequence of unreason and self-sacrifice, by contrast, is this idea: the individual is helpless on his own and has no value anyway, and therefore should merge himself into the group and obey its spokesman, the state. Given today's basic ideas, in short, the collectivism and statism of the faculties are inevitable—and too obvious to need documentation.

What I do want to mention is the political end result of our current trend. In *The Ominous Parallels* I argue that the intellectuals are preparing us for a totalitarian dictatorship. This may seem like an exaggeration, so I want to offer one final quote, this one from a philosopher, Richard Rorty, long at Princeton, now at the University of Virginia. Professor Rorty, himself a thorough modern, does not shrink from spelling out the final consequences of the modern skepticism; whatever you think of him, he has the honesty to state his ideas forthrightly. There is no truth, he holds, there is no such subject as philosophy, there are no objective standards by which to evaluate or criticize social and political practices. No matter what is done to the citizens of a country, therefore, they can have no objective grounds on which to protest.

Once, Professor Rorty writes, men could criticize political dictators, at least in their own minds. They could say to the dictator: '' 'There is something within you which you are betraying. Though you embody the practices of a totalitarian society which will endure forever, there is something beyond those practices which condemns you.' '' Once, he states, we could have said that; but no longer. Now we know that there is no knowledge, no values, no standards. Now we must accept the fact ''that we have *not* once seen the Truth, and so will not, intuitively, recognize it when we see it again. This means that when the secret police come, when the torturers violate the innocent, there is nothing to be said to them.'' Professor Rorty, I must add, claims to be disturbed by this result; but he is propagating it vigorously all the same.[24]

Ladies and gentlemen, higher education today has a remarkable press. We hear over and over about the value of our colleges and universities, their importance to the nation, and our need to contribute financially to their survival and growth. In regard to many professional and scientific schools, this is true. But in regard to the arts, the humanities, the social sciences, the opposite is true. In those areas, with some rare exceptions, our colleges and universities are a national menace, and the better the university, such as Harvard and Berkeley and Columbia, the worse it is. Today's college faculties are hostile to every idea on which this country was founded, they are corrupting an entire generation of students, and they are leading the United States to slavery and destruction.

What is the solution? The only answer to a corrupt philosophy is a rational philosophy, and the only way to spread a rational philosophy is through the universities. The universities today—not the churches any longer, and not the press or TV—are the main transmitters of philosophy; they are what set the tone and direction of a culture. To those of you of college age, therefore, those who do not subscribe to Kant's philosophy, I want to say that the moral of my remarks is *not*: quit college. On the contrary, if you are considering college or are already enrolled in one, I urge you to enter or stay, stay and fight the system, by trying to gain a hearing for some other ideas, some pro-American ideas. The colleges pretend to be open to all viewpoints, even though they are not. The only hope is to make them live up to their pretense. If you give up the colleges, you give up any role in the decisive battle for the world, the intellectual battle.

I am not suggesting that you become a martyr, or enter into arguments with professors who will penalize you for your ideas. Not all of them will, however, and I am speaking within the context and limits of rational self-interest. Within that context, I say: speak up when appropriate, let your voice be heard on campus, try to stick it out and obtain your degree, come back to teach if you can get in the door and if that is the lifework you want; and if you are an alumnus, be careful what kind of academic programs you support financially. In this battle, every word, man, and penny counts.

I wish I could tell you that your college years will be a

glorious crusade. Actually, they will probably be a miserable experience. If you are a philosophically pro-American student, you have to expect every kind of smear from many of your professors. If you uphold the power of reason, you will be called a fanatic or a dogmatist. If you uphold the right to happiness, you will be called anti-social or even a fascist. If you admire Ayn Rand, you will be called a cultist. You will experience every kind of injustice, and even hatred, and you will be unbelievably bored most of the time, and often you will be alone and lonely. But if you have the courage to venture out into this kind of nightmare, you will not only be acquiring the diploma necessary for your professional future, you will also be helping to save the world, and we are all in your debt.

The young lady who typed this speech said to me at this point: "It's pretty depressing. Aren't you going to end on an inspiring note?" I wish I could think of one. Perhaps, someday, Objectivists will start a better university, which would provide a real alternative to the current scene and offer sanctuary to the kind of young minds now being tortured by the Establishment. But this project, though possible, is still far from being a reality.

To those of you in the college trenches today, therefore, I have only a bleak conclusion to offer. And even if I am an atheist, I know no better way to say it: God bless you, and God help you!

NOTES

1. *Principles of Nature* (New York: 1801); excerpted in *Ideas in America*, ed. by G.N. Grob and R. N. Beck (Free Press: 1970). pp. 81–84.
2. W.J. Brandt, R. Beloof, L. Nathan, and C.E. Selph (Prentice Hall: 1969), p. 23.
3. Philip J. Hilts, "Caught Between Faith and Fact," Sept. 26, 1982, p. H1.
4. College Composition I, F1101 Y:01, Spring, 1980. In cases such as this, to protect the privacy of students, I am citing only the course number and/or year (when known to me).
5. Fall 1969.
6. B9706, sec. 101, Spring 1982.
7. William S. Ray, *The Science of Psychology* (Macmillan: 1964), p. 5.
8. Course number H300, cross-listed as History K492, sec. 2856; date unknown.
9. "Women Approach History Differently—and Men Must Understand the Difference," *The Stanford Observer*, Oct., 1982, p. 2; reprinted from *The Chronicle of Higher Education*, Sept. 15, 1982. Emphasis added.
10. Edwin McDowell, "New Samoa Book Challenges Margaret Mead's Conclusions," Jan. 31, 1983, p. C21.
11. Ben Gerson, "Professors for the Revolution," Aug. 23, 1982, p. 10.
12. J. McKim Malville (Seabury Press: 1981), pp. 44, 18.
13. Lecture by Thomas Judd; date and course title unknown.
14. Jerry Carroll, "Over-Achievers Swarm to This Exotic Class," Feb. 17, 1983, p. 46.
15. Lawrence Biemiller, "Campuses Trying to Control Religious Cults," April 6, 1983.
16. Quoted by Diane Ravitch, "The New Right and the Schools," *American Educator*, Fall 1982, p. 13. Professor Ravitch does not give the book's title.

17. Ed. by J. Paul Hunter, 2nd ed. (Norton: 1981).
18. Founders Day Convocation remarks, Sept. 8, 1981, reprinted in *The Colgate Scene*, Oct. 1981, pp. 1–2.
19. The wording of the situation and responses is from Christy Hudgins, "Teaching Morality: A Test for the 1970s," *The Minneapolis Star*, Mar. 26, 1979, p. 3B. The author of the six-stage morality scale is Lawrence Kohlberg.
20. "Medical Schools May Stress Compassion, Practical Experience," Nov.–Dec. 1982.
21. Course no. A5 267–80, Spring 1979.
22. Philosophy V83.0083, 1981–82.
23. Course no. H200, cross-listed as Education F200; date unknown.
24. Richard Rorty, "The Fate of Philosophy," *New Republic*, Oct. 18, 1982, p. 33.

20

The American School:
Why Johnny Can't Think
by Leonard Peikoff

*This lecture was delivered at the Ford Hall Forum
on April 15, 1984, and published in* The Objectivist Forum, *October–December 1984.*

We are now a few hours from Income Tax Day in George
Orwell's year—an ominous moment, symbolically, when
we feel acutely the weight of an ever growing government, and
must begin to wonder what will happen next and how long our
liberty can last.

The answer depends on the youth of the country and on the
institutions that educate them. The best indicator of our government tomorrow is our schools today. Are our youngsters being
brought up to be free, independent, thinking men and women?
Or are they being turned into helpless, mindless pawns, who
will run into the arms of the first dictator that sounds plausible?

One does not have to be an Objectivist to be alarmed about the
state of today's schools. Virtually everybody is in a panic over
them—shocked by continuously falling SAT scores; by college
entrants unable to write, spell, paragraph, or reason; by a generation of schoolteachers so bad that even teachers-union president Albert Shanker says of them: "For the most part, you are
getting illiterate, incompetent people who cannot go into any
other field."[1]

Last November, a new academic achievement test was given
to some six hundred sixth-grade students in eight industrialized
countries. The American students, chosen to be representative
of the nation, finished dead last in mathematics, miles behind
the Japanese, and sixth out of eight in science. As to geography,
twenty percent of the Americans at one school could not find

the U.S. on a world map. The *Chicago Tribune* reported these findings under the headline: "Study hands world dunce cap to U.S. pupils."[2]

A year ago, the National Commission on Excellence in Education described the United States as "a nation at risk," pointing to what it called "a rising tide of mediocrity [in our schools] that threatens our very future as a nation and as a people."[3] These are extreme words for normally bland government commissioners, but the words are no exaggeration.

To prepare for this evening's discussion, I did some first-hand research. I spent two weeks in February visiting schools in New York City, both public and private, from kindergarten through teachers college. I deliberately chose schools with good reputations—some of which are the shining models for the rest of the country; and I let the principals guide me to their top teachers. I wanted to see the system not when it was just scraping by, starved for money and full of compromises, but at its best, when it was adequately funded, competently staffed, and proud of its activities. I got an eyeful.

My experience at one school, a famous Progressive institution, will serve to introduce my impression of the whole system. I had said that I was interested in observing how children are taught concepts, and the school obligingly directed me to three classes. The first, for nine- and ten-year-olds, was a group discussion of thirteen steps in seal-hunting, from cutting the hole in the ice at the start to sharing the blubber with others at the end. The teacher gave no indication of the purpose of this topic, but he did indicate that the class would later perform a play on seal-hunting and perhaps even computerize the steps. The next class, for thirteen-year-olds, consisted of a mock Washington hearing on the question of whether there should be an import tax on Japanese cars; students played senators, Japanese lobbyists, Lee Iacocca, and so on, and did it quite well; the teacher sat silently, observing. I never learned the name of this course or of the seal-hunting one, but finally I was to observe a meeting described to me as a class in English. At last, I thought, an academic subject. But no. The book being covered was Robert Kennedy's *Thirteen Days*, a memoir of the Cuban missile crisis of 1962; a typical topic for discussion was whether a surgical air strike against Cuba would have been better policy than a blockade.

The school, undoubtedly, would defend these classes as exercises in ethnicity or democracy or relevance, but, whatever the defense, the fact is that all these classes were utterly concrete-bound. Seal-hunting was not used to illustrate the rigors of northern life or the method of analyzing a skill into steps or *anything* at all. The issue of taxing Japanese cars was not related to a study of free trade vs. protectionism, or of the proper function of government, or of the principles of foreign policy, or of any principles. The same applies to the Cuban discussion. In all cases, a narrow concrete was taught, enacted, discussed, argued over in and of itself, i.e., as a concrete, without connection to any wider issue. This is the essence of the approach that, in various forms, is destroying all of our schools: the *anti-conceptual* approach.

Let me elaborate for a moment on the crucial philosophic point involved here.

Man's knowledge begins on the perceptual level, with the use of the five senses. This much we share with the animals. But what makes us human is what our mind does with our sense experiences. What makes us human is the *conceptual* level, which includes our capacity to abstract, to grasp common denominators, to classify, to organize our perceptual field. The conceptual level is based on the perceptual, but there are profound differences between the two—in other words, between perceiving and *thinking*. Here are some of the differences; this is not an exhaustive list, merely enough to indicate the contrast.

The perceptual level is concerned only with concretes. For example, a man goes for a casual stroll on the beach—let's make it a drunken stroll so as to numb the higher faculties and isolate the animal element—and he sees a number of concrete entities: those birds chattering over there, this wave crashing to shore, that boulder rolling downhill. He observes, moves on, sees a bit more, forgets the earlier. On the conceptual level, however, we function very differently; we integrate concretes by means of abstractions, and thereby immensely expand the amount of material we can deal with. The animal or drunk merely looks at a few birds, then forgets them; a functioning man can retain an unlimited number, by integrating them all into the *concept* "bird," and can then proceed deliberately to study the nature of birds, their anatomy, habits, and so forth.

The drunk on his walk is aware of a vast multiplicity of things. He lurches past a chaos made of waves, rocks, and countless other entities, and has no ability to make connections among them. On the conceptual level, however, we do not accept such chaos; we turn a multiplicity into a *unity* by finding the common denominators that run through all the seemingly disconnected concretes; and we thereby make them intelligible. We discover the law of gravity, for example, and grasp that by means of a single principle we can understand the falling boulder, the rising tide, and many other phenomena.

On the perceptual level, no special order is necessary. The drunk can totter from bird to rock to tree in any order he wishes and still see them all. But we cannot do that conceptually; in the realm of thought, a definite progression is required. Since we build knowledge on previous knowledge, we need to know the necessary background, or context, at each stage. For example, we cannot start calculus before we know arithmetic—or argue about tariff protection before we know the nature of government.

Finally, for this brief sketch: on the perceptual level, there is no need of logic, argument, proof; a man sees what he sees, the facts are self-evident, and no further cognitive process is required. But on the conceptual level, we do need proof. We need a method of validating our ideas; we need a guide to let us know what conclusions follow from what data. That guide is logic.

Perception as such, the sheer animal capacity, consists merely in staring at concretes, at a multiplicity of them, in no order, with no context, no proof, no understanding—and all one can know by this means is whatever he is staring at, as long as he is staring. Conception, however—the distinctively human faculty—involves the formation of abstractions that reduce the multiplicity to an intelligible unity. This process requires a definite order, a specific context at each stage, and the methodical use of logic.

Now let us apply the above to the subject of our schools. An education that trains a child's mind would be one that teaches him to make connections, to generalize, to understand the wider issues and principles involved in any topic. It would achieve this feat by presenting the material to him in a calculated, conceptually proper order, with the necessary context, and with the proof that validates each stage. This would be an education that teaches a child to think.

The complete opposite—the most perverse aberration imaginable—is *to take conceptual-level material and present it to the students by the method of perception.* This means taking the students through history, literature, science, and the other subjects on the exact model of that casual, unthinking, drunken walk on the beach. The effect is to exile the student to a no-man's-land of cognition, which is neither perception nor conception. What it is, in fact, is destruction, the destruction of the minds of the students and of their motivation to learn.

This is literally what our schools are doing today. Let me illustrate by indicating how various subjects are taught, in the best schools, by the best teachers. You can then judge for yourself why Johnny can't think.

I went to an eighth grade class on Western European history in a highly regarded, non-Progressive school with a university affiliation. The subject that day was: why does human history constantly change? This is an excellent question, which really belongs to the philosophy of history. What factors, the teacher was asking, move history and explain men's past actions? Here are the answers he listed on the board: competition among classes for land, money, power, or trade routes; disasters and catastrophes (such as wars and plagues); the personality of leaders; innovations, technology, new discoveries (potatoes and coffee were included here); and developments in the rest of the world, which interacts with a given region. At this point, time ran out. But think of what else could qualify as causes in this kind of approach. What about an era's press or media of communication? Is that a factor in history? What about people's psychology, including their sexual proclivities? What about their art or their geography? What about the weather?

Do you see the hodgepodge the students are being given? History, they are told, is moved by power struggles and diseases and potatoes and wars and chance personalities. Who can make sense out of such a chaos? Here is a random multiplicity thrown at a youngster without any attempt to conceptualize it—to reduce it to an intelligible unity, to trace the operation of principles. This is perceptual-level history, history as nothing but a torrent of unrelated, disintegrated concretes.

The American Revolution, to take a specific example, was once taught in the schools on the conceptual level. The Revolution's manifold aspects were identified, then united and explained by a principle: the commitment of the colonists to individual rights and their consequent resolve to throw off the tyrant's yoke. This was a lesson students could understand and find relevant in today's world. But now the same event is ascribed to a whole list of alleged causes. The students are given ten (or fifty) causes of the Revolution, including the big land-owners' desire to preserve their estates, the Southern planters' desire for a cancellation of their English debts, the Bostonians' opposition to tea taxes, the Western land speculators' need to expand past the Appalachians, etc. No one can retain such a list longer than is required to pass the exam; it must be memorized, then regurgitated, then happily and thoroughly forgotten. That is all one can do with unrelated concretes.

If the students were taught by avowed Marxists—if they were told that history reflects the clash between the factors of production and the modes of ownership—it would be dead wrong, but it would still be a principle, an integrating generalization, and it would be much less harmful to the students' ability to think; they might still be open to argument on the subject. But to teach them an unconceptualized hash is to imply that history is a tale told by an idiot, without wider meaning, or relevance to the present. This approach destroys the possibility of the students thinking or caring at all about the field.

I cannot resist adding that the State Education Department of New York has found a way, believe it or not, to make the teaching of history still worse. You might think that, in history at least, the necessary *order* of presenting the material is self-evident. Since each era grows out of the preceding, the obvious way to teach events is as they happened, i.e., chronologically. But not according to a new proposal. In order "to put greater emphasis on sociological, political, and economic issues," a New York State proposal recommends that historical material be organized for the students according to six master topics picked out of the blue from the pop ethos: "ecology, human needs, human rights, cultural interaction, the global system of economic interdependence, and the future." In this approach, an event from a later period can easily be taught (in connection with one master topic) first, long before the developments from an earlier period that actually led to it. As a more traditional professor from Columbia has noted: "The whole thing would be wildly out of chronological order. The [Russian] purge trials of the 1930s would be taught before the revolutions of 1905 and 1917. It is all fragmented and there is no way that this curriculum relates one part of a historical period to another, which is what you want kids to be able to do."[4] But the modern educators don't seem to care about that. They *want* "fragments," i.e., concretes, without context, logic, or any other demands of a conceptual progression.

I do not know what became of this New York proposal. The fact that it was announced to the press and discussed seriously is revealing enough.

Given the way history is now being taught, it is not surprising that huge chunks of it promptly get forgotten by the students or simply are never taken in. The result is many adolescents' shocking ignorance of the most elementary historical, or current, facts. One man wrote a column recently in *The Washington Post* recounting his conversations with today's teenagers. He found high-school graduates who did not know anything about World War II, including what happened at Pearl Harbor, or what country the United States was fighting in the Pacific. "Who won?" one college student asked him. At one point, the writer and a girl who was a junior at the University of Southern California were watching television coverage of Poland after martial law had been imposed; the set showed political prisoners being put into a cage. The girl could not understand it.

" 'Why don't they just leave and come to LA.?' " she asked.

"I explained that they were not allowed to leave."

" 'They're not?' " she said. " 'Why not?' "

"I explained that in totalitarian states citizens usually could not emigrate."

" 'They can't?' " she said. " 'Since when? Is that something new?' "[5]

Now let us make a big jump—from history to *reading*. Let us look at the method of teaching reading that is used by most American schools in some form: the Look-Say method (as against Phonics).

The method of Phonics, the old-fashioned approach, first teaches a child the sound of individual letters; then it teaches him to read words by combining these sounds. Each letter thus represents an abstraction subsuming countless instances. Once a child knows that *p* sounds "puh," for instance, that becomes a principle; he grasps that every *p* he meets sounds the same way. When he has learned a few dozen such abstractions, he has acquired the knowledge necessary to decipher virtually any new word he encounters. Thus the gigantic multiplicity of the English vocabulary is reduced to a handful of symbols. This is the conceptual method of learning to read.

Modern educators object to it. Phonics, they say (among many such charges), is unreal. I quote from one such mentality: "There is little value in pronouncing the letter *p* in isolation; it is almost impossible to do this—a vowel of some sort almost inevitably follows the pronunciation of any consonant."[6] This means: when you pronounce the sound of *p*—"puh"—you have to utter the vowel sound "uh"; so you haven't isolated the pure consonant; so Phonics is artificial. But why can't you isolate *in your mind*, focusing only on the consonant sound, ignoring the accompanying vowel for purposes of analysis—just as men focus on a red table's color but ignore its shape in order to reach the concept "red"? Why does this writer rule out selective attention and analysis, which are the very essence of human cognition? Because these involve an act of abstraction; they represent a conceptual process, precisely the process that modern educators oppose.

Their favored method, Look-Say, dispenses with abstractions. Look-Say forces a child to learn the sounds of whole words without knowing the sounds of the individual letters or syllables. This makes every word a new concrete to be grasped only by perceptual means, such as trying to remember its distinctive shape on the page, or some special picture the teacher has associated with it. Which amounts to heaping on the student a vast multiplicity of concretes and saying: stare at these and memorize them. (You may not be surprised to discover that this method was invented, as far as I can tell, by an eighteenth-century German professor who was a follower of Rousseau, the passionate opponent of reason.)

There is a colossal Big Lie involved in the Look-Say propaganda. Its advocates crusade *against* the overuse of memory; they decry Phonics because, they say, it requires a boring memorization of all the sounds of the alphabet. Their solution is to replace such brief, simple memorization with the task of memorizing the sound of every word in the language. In fact, if one wishes to save children from the drudgery of endless memorization, only the teaching of abstractions will do it—in any field.

No one can learn to read by the Look-Say method. It is too anti-human. Our schools today, therefore, are busy teaching a new skill: guessing. They offer the children some memorized shapes and pictures to start, throw in a little Phonics (thanks to immense parental pressure), count on the parents secretly teaching their children something at home about reading—and then, given this stew of haphazard clues, they concentrate their efforts on teaching the children assorted methods of *guessing* what a given word might be.

Here is a Look-Say expert describing a child's *proper* mental processes when trying to determine the last word of the sentence, "They make belts out of plastic." The child must not, of course, try to sound out the letters. Here is what should go on in his brain instead:

"Well, it isn't leather, because that begins with *l*. My mother has a straw belt, but it isn't straw either. It looks like a root. I'll divide it between *s* and *t*. There couldn't be more than two syllables because there are only two vowels. Let's see—*p, l, a, s*. One vowel and it's not at the end of the syllable . . ." This goes on a while longer, and the child finally comes up with: "Oh, sure, plastic! I'm surprised I didn't think of that right away because so many things are made of plastic." The expert comments: "Just described is a child who was not about to carry out a letter-by-letter analysis of plastic if it wasn't necessary, which is exactly right."[7]

Can you imagine reading *War and Peace* by this method? You would die of old age before you reached the third chapter.

I must add that the Look-Say educators demand that children—I quote another devotee—"receive praise for a good guess even though it is not completely accurate. For example, if a child reads 'I like to eat carrots' as 'I like to eat cake,' praise should be given for supplying a word that makes sense and follows at least some of the phonic cues."[8]

How would you like to see, at the head of our army, a general with this kind of schooling? He receives a telegram from the president during a crisis ordering him to "reject nuclear option," proceeds to make a good guess, and reads it as "release nuclear option." Linguistically, the two are as close as "carrots" and "cake."

The result of the Look-Say method is a widespread "reading neurosis" among children, a flat inability to read, which never existed in the days of Phonics (and also a bizarre inability to spell). In 1975, for example, 35 percent of fourth-graders, 37 percent of eighth-graders, and 23 percent of twelfth-graders could not read simple printed instructions. The U.S. literacy rate, it has been estimated, is now about equal to that of Burma or Albania, and by all signs is still dropping. Do you see why angry parents are suing school systems for a new crime: educational malpractice?

Now let us look at another aspect of English studies: the teaching of *grammar*. This subject brings out even more clearly the modern educators' contempt for concepts.

Grammar is the study of how to combine words—i.e., concepts— into sentences. The basic rules of grammar—such as the need of subject and predicate, or the relation of nouns and verbs—are inherent in the nature of concepts and apply to every language; they define the principles necessary to use concepts intelligibly. Grammar, therefore, is an indispensable subject; it is a science based entirely on facts—and not a very difficult science, either.

Our leading educators, however, see no relation between concepts and facts. The reason they present material from subjects such as history without conceptualizing it, is precisely that they regard concepts as mental constructs without relation to reality. Concepts, they hold, are not a device of cognition, but a mere human convention, a ritual unrelated to knowledge or reality, to be performed according to arbitrary social fiat. It follows that grammar is a set of pointless rules, decreed by society for no objectively defensible reason.

I quote from a book on linguistics written for English teachers by a modern professor: "Because we know that language is arbitrary and changing, a teacher's attitude toward nonstandard usage should be one of acceptance. . . . One level of language is not 'better' than another; this is why the term *nonstandard* is preferable to *substandard* in describing such usage as 'He don't do it,' 'Was you there?' A person who uses terms such as these will probably be penalized in terms of social and educational advancement in our society, however, and it is for this reason that the teacher helps children work toward, and eventually achieve, standard usage, perhaps as a 'second' language."[9] In short, there is no "correct" or "incorrect" any more, not in any aspect of language; there is only the senseless prejudice of society.

I saw the results of this approach in the classroom. I watched an excellent public-school teacher trying to explain the possessive forms of nouns. She gave a clear statement of the rules, with striking examples and frequent repetition; she was dynamic, she was colorful, she was teaching her heart out. But it was futile. This teacher was not a philosopher of language, and she could not combat the idea, implicit in the textbook and in all the years of the students' earlier schooling, that grammar is purposeless. The students seemed to be impervious to instruction and incapable of attention, even when the teacher would blow a shrieking police whistle to shock them momentarily into silence. To them, the subject was nothing but senseless rules: the apostrophe goes here in this case, there in that one. Here was a whole science reduced to disintegrated concretes that had to be blindly memorized—just like the ten causes of the American Revolution, or the ten shapes of the last Look-Say session.

You might wonder how one teaches *composition*—the methods of expressing one's thoughts clearly and eloquently in writing— given today's philosophy of grammar and of concepts. I will answer by reading excerpts from a recent manifesto.

"We affirm the students' right to their own patterns and varieties of language—the dialects of their nurture or whatever dialects in which they find their own identity and style. . . . The claim that any one dialect is unacceptable amounts to an attempt of one social group to exert its dominance over another." If so, why does anyone need English teachers?

Who issued this manifesto? Was it some ignorant, hotheaded teenagers drunk on the notion of student power? No. It was the National Council of Teachers of English.[10]

If you want a hint as to the basic philosophy operative here, I will mention that the editor of *College English,* one of the major journals of the profession, objects to "an industrial society [that] will continue to want from us—or someone else—composition, verbal manners, discipline in problem solving, and docile rationality."[11] Note how explicit this is. The climax of *his* "enemies list" is "rationality."

Despite today's subjectivism, some rules of composition are still being taught. Certain of these are valid enough, having been carried over from a better past. But some are horrifying. Here is an exercise in how to write topic sentences. The students are given two possible sentences with which to start a paragraph, then are asked to choose which would make a good opening and which a bad one. Here is one such pair:

1. Cooking is my favorite hobby.
2. It really isn't hard to stir-fry Chinese vegetables.

The correct answer? Number 1 is bad. It is too abstract. (!) Students should not write about so enormous a subject as an entire hobby. They should focus only on one concrete under it, such as Chinese vegetables.

Here is another pair:

1. There is too much pollution in the world.
2. We have begun to fight pollution in our own neighborhood.

Of course, Number 1 is inadmissible. Students must not think about world problems—that is too vague—only about the dinky concretes in their own backyard.[12]

This sort of exercise has been consciously designed to *teach* students to be concrete-bound. How are children with such an upbringing ever to deal with or think about problems that transcend Chinese vegetables and their own neighborhood? The implicit answer, absorbed by the students unavoidably, is: "You don't have to worry about things like that; society or the president will take care of you; all you have to do is adapt."

Before we leave English, I want to mention what has been happening to the teaching of *literature* in our schools as a consequence of the attitude toward concepts that we have been discussing. First, there has been the disappearance from the schools of the classics in favor of cheap current novels. The language and themes of the classics are too difficult for today's students to grasp; one does not teach Shakespeare to savages, or to civilized children being turned into savages. Then, there is the continuous decline even of today's debased standards. I quote from two English teachers: "Years ago we used to hear that *Julius Caesar* was too difficult for ninth-graders; now we are told that *Lord of the Flies* is too hard for the general run of tenth-graders." Then, there is the final result, now increasingly common: the disappearance of literature of any kind and its replacement by what are called "media classes." These are classes, in one book's apt description, that "teach television, newspapers, car-repair magazines, and movies."[13]

I will pass up all the obvious comments on this frightening descent. I have just one question about it: why should these graduates of TV and car-repair magazines care if the great books of the past are burned by government edict—when they can't read them anyway?

Turning to the teaching of *science* in our schools, I want to mention an instructive book written by two professors at Purdue University; titled *Creative Sciencing*, it tells science teachers how to teach their subject properly. To learn science, the book declares, students must engage in "hands-on science activities." They must perform a series of concrete "experiments," such as designing a bug catcher, collecting pictures of objects that begin with a *c*, going on field trips to the local factory, or finding polluters in the community. (These examples are taken from the book.) There is no necessary order to these activities. The children are encouraged to interact with the classroom materials "in their own way," as the mood strikes them. They are not to be inhibited by a teacher-imposed structure or by the logic of the subject.[14]

You may wonder whether students taught in this manner will ever learn the abstract concepts and principles of science, the natural laws and explanatory theories that have been painstakingly discovered across the centuries—the knowledge that makes us civilized men rather than jungle primitives.

The answer has been given by F. James Rutherford, chief education officer of the American Association for the Advancement of Science. "We're too serious," he declared. "We insist on all the abstract stuff. We need to relax and let the children learn their own neighborhood." This statement was made at a meeting of experts brought together by a large foundation to discover what ails science teaching.[15]

Today's education, I have said, reduces children to the status of animals, without the ability to know or predict the future. Animals, however, can rely on brute instinct to guide them. Children cannot; brought up this way, they soon begin to feel helpless—to feel that everything is changing and that they can count on nothing.

The above is not merely my polemic. The science teachers are working deliberately to create this state of mind. The teachers are openly skeptical themselves, having been given a similar upbringing, and they insist to their students that everything is changing, that factual information is continuously becoming outdated, and that there are things much more important in class—in *science* class—than truth. It is hard to believe how brazen these people have become. "When preparing performance objectives," the *Creative Sciencing* book says, "you may wish to consider the fact that we don't demand accuracy in art or creative writing, but we have permitted ourselves to require accuracy in science. We may be paying a high price in lost interest, enthusiasm, vitality, and creativity in science because of this requirement of accuracy."[16]

Our students should not have to be concerned about factual accuracy. They need have no idea whether gases expand or contract under pressure, or whether typhus germs cause or cure disease—but this will leave them free to be "vital" and "creative."

But, you may ask, what if a student comes out in class with a wrong answer to a factual question? You are old-fashioned. There is no such answer, and besides it would be bad for the student's psychology if there were: "How many times will a student try to respond to a question if continually told that his or her answers are wrong? Wrong answers should be reserved for quiz shows on television."[17]

What then is the point in having a teacher at all?—since there are no wrong answers, and since adults must not be "authoritarian," and since, as John Dewey has proclaimed, students do not learn by listening or by reading, but only by "doing." This brings me to an extremely important issue, one that is much wider than science teaching.

My overriding impression of today's schools, derived from every class I visited, is that teachers no longer teach. They no longer deliver prepared material while the students listen attentively and take notes. Instead, what one encounters everywhere is *group-talking*, i.e., class participation and class discussion. Most of the teachers I saw were enthusiastic professionals, excellent at what they do. But they conceive their role primarily as bull-session moderators. Some of the teachers obviously had a concealed lesson in mind, which they were bootlegging to the students—in the guise of asking leading questions or making brief, purposeful side comments. But the point is that the lesson had to be bootlegged. The official purpose of the class was for the pupils to speak more or less continuously—at any rate, well over half the time.

I asked one group of high-school students if their teachers ever delivered *lectures* in class. "Oh no!" they cried incredulously, as though I had come from another planet or a barbaric past. "No one does that anymore."

All the arguments offered to defend this anti-teaching approach are senseless.

"Students," I have heard it said, "should develop initiative; they should discover knowledge on their own, not be spoon-fed by the teachers." Then why should they go to school at all? Schooling is a process in which an expert is paid to impart his superior knowledge to ignorant beginners. How can this involve shelving the expert and leaving the ignorant to shift for themselves? What would you think of a doctor who told a patient to cure himself because the doctor opposed spoon-feeding?

"Students," I have heard, "should be creative, not merely passive and receptive." How can they be creative before they know anything? Creativity does not arise in a void; it can develop only *after* one has mastered the current cognitive context. A creative ignoramus is a contradiction in terms.

"We teach the method of thought," I have heard, "rather than the content." This is the most senseless claim of all. Let us leave aside the obvious fact that method cannot exist apart from some content. The more important point here is that *thought* is precisely what cannot be taught by the discussion approach. If you want to teach thought, you must first put up a sign at the front of the class: "Children should be seen and not heard." To be exact: they may be heard as an adjunct of the lesson, if the teacher wishes to probe their knowledge, or answer a question of clarification, or assess their motivation to learn, or entertain a brief comment. But the dominant presence and voice must be that of the teacher, the cognitive expert, who should be feeding the material to the class in a highly purposeful fashion, carefully balancing concretes and abstractions, preparing for and then drawing and then interrelating generalizations, identifying the evidence at each point, etc. These are the processes that must first be absorbed year after year by the student in relation to a whole series of different contents. In the end, such training will jell in his mind into a knowledge of how to think—which he can then apply on his own, without any teacher. But he can never even begin to grasp these processes in the chaotic hullabaloo of a perpetual class discussion with equally ignorant peers.

Have you seen the [1984] television debates among the Democrats seeking to be president? Do you regard these spectacles of arbitrary assertion, constant subject-switching, absurd concrete-boundedness, and brazen *ad hominem* as examples of thinking? This is exactly the pattern that is being inculcated as thinking today by the class-discussion method.

An educator with any inkling of the requirements of a conceptual consciousness would never dream of running a school this way. But an educator contemptuous of concepts, and therefore of knowledge, would see no objection to it.

In the class discussions I saw, the students were regularly asked to state their own opinion. They were asked it in regard to issues about which they had no idea *how* to have an opinion, since they had no knowledge of the relevant facts or principles, and no knowledge of the methods of logical argument. Most of the time the students were honest; they had no opinion, in the sense of a sincere, even if mistaken, conviction on the question at hand. But they knew that they were expected to "express themselves." Time and again, therefore, I heard the following: "I like (or dislike) X." "Why?" "Because I do. That's my opinion." Whereupon the teacher would nod and say "very interesting" or "good point." Everybody's point, it seemed, was good, as good as everybody else's, and reasons were simply irrelevant. The conclusion being fostered in the minds of the class was: "It's all arbitrary; anything goes and no one really knows." The result is not only the spread of subjectivism, but of a self-righteous subjectivism, which cannot even imagine what objectivity would consist of.

Project a dozen years of this kind of daily processing. One study of American students notes that they "generally offered superficial comments ... and consultants observed that they seemed 'genuinely puzzled at requests to explain or defend their points of view.' "[18] What else could anyone expect?

Now let me quote from a *New York Times* news story.

> "I like [Senator Gary Hart's] ideas," said Darla Doyle, a Tampa homemaker. "He's a good man. His ideas are fresher than Mondale's are. I like the way he comes across."
> A reporter asked Mrs. Doyle to identify the ideas that appealed to her. "That's an unfair question," she said, asking for a moment to consider her answer. Then she replied, "He wants to talk with Russia."

The headline of this story is: "Hart's Fans Can't Say Why They Are."[19]

According to John Dewey, students are bored by lectures, but motivated to learn by collective "doing." Not the ones I saw. Virtually every class was in continuous turmoil, created by students waving their hands to speak, dropping books, giggling, calling out remarks, whispering asides, yawning, fidgeting, shifting, shuffling. The dominant emotion was a painful boredom, which is the sign of minds being mercilessly starved and stunted. Perhaps this explains the magic influence of the bell. The instant it rang, everywhere I went, the room was empty, as though helpless victims were running for their lives from a dread plague. And so in a sense they were.

Ladies and gentlemen, our schools are failing in every subject and on a fundamental level. They are failing methodically, as a matter of philosophic principle. The anti-conceptual epistemology that grips them comes from John Dewey and from all his fellow irrationalists, who dominate twentieth-century American culture, such as linguistic analysts, psychoanalysts, and neo-Existentialists. And behind all these, as I argued in *The Ominous Parallels*, stands a century of German philosophy inaugurated by history's greatest villain: Immanuel Kant, the first man to dedicate his life and his system to the destruction of reason.

Epistemological corruption is not the only cause of today's educational fiasco. There are many other contributing factors, such as the teachers unions, and the senseless requirements of the teachers colleges, and the government bureaucracies (local and federal). But epistemology is the *basic* cause, without reference to which none of the others can be intelligently analyzed or remedied.

Now let me recount for you two last experiences, which bear on the political implications of today's educational trend.

One occurred at the most prestigious teacher-training institution in the country, Teachers College of Columbia University.

In my first class there, chosen at random, the professor made the following pronouncement to a group of sixty future teachers: "The evil of the West is not primarily its economic exploitation of the Third World, but its ideological exploitation. The crime of the West was to impose upon the communal culture of Africa the concept of the individual." I thought I had heard everything, but this shocked me. I looked around. The future teachers were dutifully taking it down; there were no objections.

Despite their talk about "self-expression," today's educators have to inculcate collectivism. Man's organ of individuality is his mind; deprived of it, he is nothing, and can do nothing but huddle in a group as his only hope of survival.

The second experience occurred in a class of juniors and seniors at a high school for the academically gifted. The students had just returned from a visit to the United Nations, where they had met with an official of the Russian delegation, and they were eager to discuss their reactions. The class obviously disliked the Russian, feeling that his answers to their questions about life in Russia had been evasions or lies. But soon someone remarked that we Americans are accustomed to believing what our government says, while the Russians naturally believe theirs. "So how do I know?" he concluded. "Maybe everything is a lie."

"What is truth?" asked one boy, seemingly quite sincere; the class laughed, as though this were obviously unanswerable.

"Neither side is good," said another student. "Both countries lie all the time. But the issue is the percentage. What we need to know is how much they lie—is it 99 percent for one, for example, and 82 percent for the other?"

After a lot more of this, including some pretty weak arguments in favor of America by a small patriotic faction, one boy summed up the emerging consensus. "We can never know who is lying or telling the truth," he said. "The only thing we can know is bare fact. For example, we can know that a Korean airliner was shot down by the Russians [in 1983]. But as to the Russians' story of the cause vs. our story, that is mere opinion."

To which one girl replied in all seriousness: "But we can't even know that—none of us saw the plane shot down."

This class discussion was the climax of my tour. I felt as though I were witnessing the condensed essence of a perceptual-level schooling. "Thought," these students were saying, "is helpless, principles are nonexistent, truth is unknowable, and there is, therefore, no way to choose between the United States of America and the bloodiest dictatorship in history, not unless we have seen the blood with our own eyes."

These youngsters represent the future of our country. They are the children of the best and the brightest, who will become the businessmen, the artists, and the political leaders of tomorrow. Does this kind of generation have the strength—the intellectual strength, the strength of conviction—necessary to uphold the American heritage in an era dominated by incipient Big Brothers at home and missile-rattling enemies abroad?

It is not the students' fault, and they do not fully believe the awful things they say, not yet. The ones I saw, at every school except for Columbia—and here I want to register some positive impressions—were extremely likable. For the most part, they struck me as clean-cut, well-mannered, exuberant, intelligent, innocent. They were not like the typical college student one meets, who is already hardening into a brash cynic or skeptic. These youngsters, despite all their doubts and scars, still seemed eager to discover some answers, albeit sporadically. They were still clinging to vestiges of the idea that man's mind can understand reality and make sense of the world.

They are still open to reason—if someone would teach it to them.

Nor is it basically the teachers' fault. The ones I saw were not like the college professors I know, who reek of stale malice and delight in wrecking their students' minds. The teachers seemed to take their jobs seriously; they genuinely liked their classes and wanted to educate them. But given the direction of their own training, they were unable to do it.

There is a whole generation of children who still want to learn, and a profession much of which wants to help them, to say nothing of a country that devoutly wishes both groups well. Everything anyone would need to save the world is there, it is waiting, and all that is required to activate it is . . . what?

Merit pay? First we need a definition of merit, i.e., of the purpose of teaching. More classes in the use of computers? We have enough children who know FORTRAN but not English. Compulsory community service? (A recommendation of the Carnegie Commission.) Prayer in the schools? (President Reagan's idea of a solution.)

All these are the equivalent of sticking Band-Aids on (or in the last two cases knives into) a dying man. The only real solution, which is a precondition of any other reform, is a philosophic change in our culture. We need a philosophy that will teach our colleges—and thereby our schoolteachers, and thus finally our youngsters—an abiding respect, a respect for reason, for man's mind, for the conceptual level of consciousness. That is why I subscribe to the philosophy of Ayn Rand. Hers is the only such philosophy in America today. It could be the wonder cure that would revive a generation.

The National Committee on Excellence in Education declared, "If an unfriendly foreign power had attempted to impose on America the mediocre educational performance that exists today, we might well have viewed it as an act of war."[20] Intellectually speaking, however, we *are* under the yoke of a foreign power. We are under the yoke of Kant, Hegel, Marx, and all their disciples. What we need now is another Declaration of Independence—not political independence from England this time, but philosophical independence from Germany.

To achieve it would be a monumental job, which would take many decades. As part of the job, I want to recommend one specific step to improve our schools: close down the teachers colleges.

There is no rational purpose to these institutions (and so they do little but disseminate poisonous ideas). Teaching is not a skill acquired through years of classes; it is not improved by the study of "psychology" or "methodology" or any of the rest of the stuff the schools of education offer. Teaching requires only the obvious: motivation, common sense, experience, a few good books or courses on technique, and, above all, a knowledge of the material being taught. Teachers must be masters of their subject; this—not a degree in education—is what school boards should demand as a condition of employment.

This one change would dramatically improve the schools. If experts in subject matter were setting the terms in the classroom, some significant content would have to reach the students, even given today's dominant philosophy. In addition, the basket cases who know only the Newspeak of their education professors would be out of a job, which would be another big improvement.

This reform, of course, would be resisted to the end by today's educational establishment, and could hardly be achieved nationally without a philosophic change in the country. But it gives us a starting point to rally around that pertains specifically to the field of education. If you are a parent or a teacher or merely a concerned taxpayer, you can start the battle for quality in education by demanding loudly—even in today's corrupt climate—that the teachers your school employs know what they are talking about, and then talk about it.

"If a nation expects to be ignorant and free . . ." wrote Thomas Jefferson, "it expects what never was and never will be."[21]

Let us fight to make our schools once again bastions of *knowledge*. Then no dictator can rise among us by counting, like Big Brother in *1984*, on the enshrinement of ignorance.

And then we may once again have a human future ahead of us.

___

NOTES

1. Quoted in *USA Today*, Aug. 12, 1983.
2. Dec. 12, 1983.
3. Quoted in *The New York Times*, Apr. 27, 1983.
4. *The New York Times*, Apr. 18, 1983; the professor is Hazel Hertzberg.
5. Benjamin J. Stein, "The Cheerful Ignorance of the Young in L.A.," Oct. 3, 1983.
6. Pose Lamb, *Linguistics in Proper Perspective* (Charles E. Merrill: 1977, 2nd ed.), p. 29.
7. Dolores Durkin, *Strategies for Identifying Words*, p. 83; quoted in Rudolf Flesch, *Why Johnny Still Can't Read* (Harper Colophon: 1983), p. 81.
8. Dixie Lee Spiegel, in *Reading Teacher*, April 1978; quoted in Flesch, *op. cit.*, p. 24.

9. Lamb, *op. cit.*, p. 19.

10. From *Students' Right to Their Own Language*, Conference on College Composition and Communication, Fall, 1974; quoted in Arn and Charlene Tibbetts, *What's Happening to American English?* (Scribner's: 1978), p. 118.

11. See *College English*, Feb. 1976, p. 631; quoted in Tibbetts, *op. cit.*, p. 119.

12. *Basic English Skills Practice Book*, Orange Level (McDougal, Littell), p. 17.

13. Tibbetts, *op. cit.*, pp. 80, 76.

14. Alfred De Vito & Gerald H. Krockover, *Creative Sciencing* (Little, Brown: 1980), pp. 15, 70, 74, 19.

15. Quoted in *The New York Times*, Jan, 31, 1984.

16. *Op. cit.*, p. 33.

17. *Ibid.*, p. 38.

18. "Are Your Kids Learning to Think?" *Changing Times*, Dec. 1983; quoting the National Assessment of Educational Progress.

19. Mar. 9, 1984.

20. Quoted in *The New York Times*, Apr. 27, 1983.

21. *The Jeffersonian Cyclopedia*, "Freedom and Education," p. 274.

Part Three:
Politics

21

Representation Without Authorization
by Ayn Rand

This article was published in The Ayn Rand Letter,
July 17, 1972.

The theory of representative government rests on the principle that man is a rational being, i.e., that he is able to perceive the facts of reality, to evaluate them, to form rational judgments, to make his own choices, and to bear responsibility for the course of his life.

Politically, this principle is implemented by a man's right to choose his own agents, i.e., those whom he authorizes to represent him in the government of his country. To represent him, in this context, means to represent his views in terms of political principles. Thus the government of a free country derives its "just powers from the consent of the governed." (For the basis of this discussion, see "Man's Rights" and "The Nature of Government" in *Capitalism: the Unknown Ideal.*)

As a corroboration of the link between man's rational faculty and a representative form of government, observe that those who are demonstrably (or physiologically) incapable of rational judgment cannot exercise the right to vote. (Voting is a derivative, not a fundamental, right; it is derived from the right to life, as a political implementation of the requirements of a rational being's survival.) Children do not vote because they have not acquired the knowledge necessary to form a rational judgment on political issues; neither do the feeble-minded or the insane, who have lost or never developed their rational faculty. (The possession of a rational faculty does not guarantee that a man will use it, only that he is *able* to use it and is, therefore, responsible for his actions.)

233

The mentally unprepared or incapacitated are unable personally to exercise their rights—e.g., the right to acquire property or to assume contractual obligations—and the protection of their rights is delegated to their parents or to legally appointed guardians, who act in their name. The right to vote, however, is nontransferable. The father of twelve minors does not acquire the right to cast twelve votes in addition to his own; neither does the keeper of an insane asylum.

Philosophically, the theory of representative government is in profound conflict with the dominant schools of modern philosophy, which deny the efficacy or existence of reason and of volition. Dictatorship and determinism are reciprocally reinforcing corollaries: if one seeks to enslave men, one has to destroy their reliance on the validity of their own judgments and choices—if one believes that reason and volition are impotent, one has to accept the rule of force.

Ever since Kant, the dominant method of modern philosophers has been to fight issues not by open intellectual presentation, but by *corruption*—the corruption into its opposite of any concept which they dared not oppose explicitly. Just as Kant corrupted the concept "reason" to mean a mystic faculty pertaining to another dimension, so his theoretical and practical descendants have been employing his technique on an ever growing scale and shrinking subjects. Thus "freedom," in today's jargon, means obedience to a totalitarian ruler—"security" is dependence on the whims of the government—"individuality" is conformity to the life-style of a pack—a *Putsch* to seize dictatorial power is a "War of Liberation"—the "Right to Life" is the right of the unborn to sacrifice the living—and "love of this earth" consists in making it impossible for men to live on it.

It is fairly easy to corrupt the concept of representative government in a country that has had no experience of it: people are offered the flattering paraphernalia of ballot boxes, but only one party to vote for. It is more difficult in a country whose history began with free elections. For half a century (or longer), the collectivist intellectuals have been corrupting our two major political parties to make them merge into one by making them indistinguishable—while the commentators ignored the country's discontent and pretended that no opposition existed. But this did not work: instead of merging, both parties are now breaking up into irreconcilable factions. In the meantime, the collectivists have come out with a new corruption of the concept of political representation, more grotesque than the rest of their notions.

It is expressed in the demand that various statistical quotas be imposed on this country, in order to "represent" various kinds of people.

It has never been made clear what the term "represent" means in this context. Represent—where and by whom? At first, the demands were voiced in regard to private or semiprivate activities, but in fields vulnerable to political pressure—e.g., the demands for racial quotas in the student enrollment and on the faculties of schools, or in the employment practices of government-controlled industries, such as television. Then the demands grew louder and more directly political, seeking "representation" in Cabinet posts and even on the Supreme Court. The [1972] rules for the Democratic party's choice of convention delegates implemented these demands and brought them straight into the field of political elections.

It is, therefore, time to examine the meaning of the quota doctrine.

The notion of racial quotas is so obviously an expression of racism that no lengthy discussion is necessary. If a young man is barred from a school or a job because the quota for his particular race has been filled, he is barred by reason of his race. Telling him that those admitted are his "representatives" is adding insult to injury. To demand such quotas in the name of fighting racial discrimination is an obscene mockery.

But observe that the demands for "representation" by quotas are not confined to minorities and are not made exclusively on the grounds of race. The same demands are presented on behalf of a majority: women—on the grounds of age: the young—and on the grounds of economics: the poor.

Now observe the common denominator of these groups. The basis of their grouping and of the quotas they advocate is not intellectual, but *physiological*. (In the case of poverty, it is physical: an absence of material means.)

This is the sort of doctrine with which today's intellectuals, particularly the academic crowd, would feel profoundly at home—most of them emotionally and subconsciously, and a few of them with full, conscious awareness of all the implications.

This doctrine—a product of determinism—assumes that physiology is the determining factor in human life and that the interests of all the members of a given physiological group are

identical. Yet it is obvious that an intelligent, efficient career
woman has more interests in common with men than with a
sloppy housewife who joins Women's Lib and refuses to cook
her husband's dinner. A successful, self-made black businessman has more interests in common with white businessmen
than with a black mugger. A rational young student seeking
knowledge has more interests in common with old professors
than with drugged young "Jesus freaks."

The quota doctrine assumes that all members of a given physiological group are identical and interchangeable—not merely in
the eyes of other people, but in their own eyes and minds.
Assuming a total merging of the self with the group, the doctrine
holds that it makes no difference to a man whether *he* or his
"representative" is admitted to a school, gets a job, or makes a
decision. This particular notion is widely believed by the student activists, who clamor for participation in running universities and other institutions, declaring: "We want to have a say
about the things that affect our lives"—the "say" consisting in
casting one vote out of thousands for some little campus politician, while surrendering the only "say" they have the right to
demand: the say about their own lives.

It is obvious why the quota doctrine appeals to modern intellectuals: it eliminates the responsibility of thought, judgment,
and choice. Just follow your group leaders, it advises, they are
physiologically predestined to protect you and take care of you.
To most of them, this promises the comfort of lethargy, and to a
few—a road to power.

If and to the extent that the quota doctrine is taken seriously,
it can lead to the abolition of actual political elections, which
would be replaced by a system guaranteeing that every sort of
group—except one—will be "represented" in the government.
There are already suggestions for labor "representation," and
special demands by groups laying the groundwork for welfare
recipients' "representation," for "gay representation," for the
"representation" of the fetus, etc. The one kind of group to be
excepted and excluded is a group brought together by *ideas*.
There is to be no *ideological* representation—or differentiation.

(A precedent for this sort of electoral policy is offered by
Soviet Russia. Ethnic, or physiological, diversity is welcomed
and fostered in Russia [unless some group displeases the author-
ities]. The Soviet Union is broken up into a number of racially
different states, each with its own language, folk songs, com-

memorative postage stamps, and U.N. representation. This flatters the enslaved and is of no danger to the rulers. But ideological diversity is not to be mentioned or dreamed about, under penalty of death.)

As one more example of the connection between reason and freedom, observe that the quota doctrine relegates people to the status of children or of the mentally incompetent, with appointed guardians in place of genuine representatives. No individual choice, no personal authorization to represent him, is required on the part of the citizen—physiology provides the authorization.

The advantages to the leaders of the pressure-group racket are obvious. As to the followers, they would have to reach that hopeless, brutalized state in which people accept as flattery the assertion that the pharaoh's pyramids or the palaces of Versailles, of Berchtesgaden, of the Kremlin are erected to "represent" *their,* the people's, glory.

I do not believe that the collectivists can get away with it in America. But any suggestion of the quota doctrine is too much for this country—and, today, we are hearing and seeing more than a suggestion. The introduction of that doctrine into the Democratic party's rules of delegate selection is not merely a future and potential, but a present and actual, violation of a citizen's individual rights.

The violation lies in the *statistical* method of apportioning the quotas. They are apportioned not on the basis of a given organization's membership, but on the basis of the number of persons of a certain physiological type who live in a given district or in the country at large. Thus fifty percent of a delegation "represents" women (*all* women), ten percent "represents" blacks (*all* blacks), etc. This means that an individual woman or an individual black—who has never heard of these delegates, may not agree with their views, may not even be a Democrat—is counted as one of the delegate's constituents, without voting, consent, or authorization on her or his part.

An individual's right to choose his own representatives or agents is recognized in the material realm, but, apparently, not in the ideological one. If some stranger sold you the Brooklyn Bridge or the Empire State Building, he would be arrested for fraud, because he had no authorization to act as agent for the owners of the bridge or the building. Yet the quota advocates regard you as a unit of meat and appoint themselves your "representatives" in so vast, complex and controversial a field as political elections.

No organization has the right to speak for or to act in the name of anyone but its own members. No organization may be taken as an agent for an individual without his personal knowledge and consent.

If "taxation without representation is slavery," then representation without authorization is slavery embellished with fraud.

22

To Dream the Noncommercial Dream
by Ayn Rand

This article was published in The Ayn Rand Letter,
January 1, 1973.

Have you ever wondered about the mentality of those who advocate government financing of intellectual and artistic pursuits, in the name of intellectual independence and creative freedom?

Their goal, they claim, is to liberate men's mind from material concerns or economic pressures. The necessity to earn a living in a free marketplace, they claim, is demeaning and corrupting. In their language, the word "commercial" is a pejorative term, an antonym of "intellectual." Only the security of government support, they claim, can release the full power of the intellect.

The contradictions in this viewpoint are so obvious that it seems impossible for anyone to miss seeing them. Nothing is less secure than a position of dependence on the arbitrary power of politicians dispensing favors. The fate of thinkers, scientists, and artists whose livelihood depends on the government—any government in any age, at the courts of absolute monarchs or in modern dictatorships or in mixed economies—is too well-known to leave anyone in "idealistic" doubt. So are the fear, the intrigues, the rigid censorship, and the abject bootlicking in which and with which the recipients of governmental favors have to live moment by precarious moment. How can today's intellectuals fail to know it?

Some of them are motivated by powerlust and long for political careers in the roles of manipulators or "powers behind the thrones." But these, as a rule, advocate some form of government control over the intellectual professions, in the hope of maneuvering themselves or their cliques into the posts of professional "czars"; they do not plead for economic security and do not talk too much about intellectual freedom. What is the motive of those who do? What prompts the rank and file of the intellectual professions, who are loudly, touchily, belligerently championing such things as the First Amendment, civil liberties, academic freedom, etc., and, simultaneously, are pleading with the government for financial support? What can they hope for?

A significant answer may be found in a very enlightening article which appeared in *The New York Times* (July 29, 1972): "Another Channel" by Lester Markel, the retired Sunday Editor of the *Times*.

The article discusses the current troubles of public television: the chronic and growing financial plight of this noncommercial venture. The issue has aroused the intellectuals' angrily anxious concern ever since President Nixon vetoed a bill appropriating 65 million dollars for public television, which Congress had passed.

"The government has been engaged in an unholy crusade against public television," the article declares. "[The Administration's] attacks aroused neither the general public nor the Congress because of the feeling that public television is a dispensable institution. It isn't, but it has not shown that it isn't."

What makes public television *indispensable*? Mr. Markel does not say; he merely indicates that its purpose is "to fill the large gaps left by commercial television." What gaps? "It can reach an audience commercial television considers economically unfeasible." What audience? Mr. Markel states only that it is (either actually or potentially) an "audience of ten or fifteen million listeners" and that they are very "intent." What does this audience want? "In the cultural and entertainment areas [public television] can do much imaginative and experimental work."

But it is "the area of public affairs" that Mr. Markel regards as most important. "Genuine democracy depends ultimately on an informed opinion; American opinion is insufficiently or wrongly informed; this means that those whose duty it is to enlighten the citizenry are not doing their jobs." In the news area, commercial television "shirks the assignment because the undertaking is unprofitable; entertainment pays off, information doesn't. And public television has failed to fill the gap; it has not provided public affairs programming of consequence and immediacy."

If "information doesn't pay off," it means that the public doesn't want to listen to it. If so, then what will be accomplished by broadcasts which people do not hear? Will "genuine democracy" be served by the "informed opinion" of ten or fifteen million people, i.e., less than ten percent of a population of two hundred ten million whose taxes have to pay for it? No answer is given, except for the statement (at the end of the article) that "the size of informed minority can be significantly increased—and that would be a long forward stride in the democratic process."

"In general, the shortcoming of public television can be attributed to lack of independence, of money, of inspiration and of perspective. The first two lacks can be remedied only if the government, executive and Congress, are pressured into action by public demand." What public? The ten or fifteen million? Do they represent or *are* they the public? No answer is given, but, in the context of today's pressure-group demands, the answer is obvious.

"That demand will not come unless public television supplies the two other ingredients—imagination and balance." And then, astonishingly, Mr. Markel proceeds to list the present flaws of public television, more correctly and succinctly than its enemies have done.

> For the most part, public television caters to the elite and preaches to the converted. In the effort to be different, programs have often been only eccentric or ineffectively experimental; they have been marked by an amateur rather than a professional touch.... Moreover and most seriously, the attacks on the score of bias have been justified in numerous instances; for example, many of the programs of station WNET [in New York City] have had a distinctly leftist coloration.... The sledding for public television has been made harder also because of clashes and power duels in the system, notably between left- and right-wing outfits and over the issue of central versus local power.

All this is eminently true; it has always been true of any government-sponsored "cultural" establishment. It is not a matter of personalities: a man of integrity and impeccable taste will not preserve either in such an establishment. It is not the free market, but government patronage that corrupts. The corruption is inherent in the status of a privileged political elite—i.e., an elite selected by favor and maintained by force. If a member of that elite has no particular convictions, his performance will be bad; if he has, it will be worse. His convictions, his vanity, and his quest for "prestige" will blend inextricably into a driving motive to ram *his* ideas down the throats of the country and of his disarmed opponents, who are forced to pay for his support. Thus, whether for "idealistic" or for the lowest kinds of motives, the "power duels" among the members of the elite will continue.

As to the quality of their work, a "professional touch" is achieved by the element of *objectivity*—by objective standards of value, of performance, of taste—which is a necessity for an artist seeking the voluntary support of an audience. Men liberated from that necessity and guided by whims can be nothing but amateurs.

On the basis of his own observations, one would expect Mr. Markel to conclude that public television is a useless, hopeless, and evil institution. But he springs another surprise on his readers.

"If public TV is to have a future," he declares, "it must evolve a new philosophy and a new approach. It must clear its head and clean its house." What philosophy, what approach, what is to be cleared or cleaned and in what way, is not indicated, beyond the statement that "the coverage of public affairs must be greatly improved," and the advice to emulate the B.B.C. And on the basis of these floating platitudes, Mr. Markel comes out with the one paragraph for which all the rest serves merely as verbal window dressing:

"In such ways public TV can win popular support and so achieve both independence and economic relief (the two are linked). As long as it is dependent for funding on Congress, and therefore on politics, public TV will not be free. *The only solution is an excise tax, possibly a levy on sets as in Britain.*" [Emphasis added.]

Get this straight: public TV is to be liberated from politics by the nonpolitical (!) means of a tax imposed on the people for the exclusive benefit, use, and disposal of the men in public TV.

Even the welfare recipients who stage demonstrations have more decency than that: they, at least, present demands to Congress—they do not seek a direct lien on their neighbors' pockets.

Congress is a body of representatives chosen by the people; if public TV is *public,* on whom should its funding—and its control—depend if not on the public's representatives? Yet it is Congress that Mr. Markel's proposal seeks to bypass.

Yes, Congress is a fluid, flexible institution, unpredictable in its policies, subject to the fluctuating views of the electorate—as it has to be, in a free country (where its power is limited by a Constitution), or in the sort of "genuine democracy" that liberals of Mr. Markel's kind are constantly touting. Yes, to depend on the switching moods of momentary majorities is as precarious as to build on quicksand—which is one of the reasons why intellectual pursuits must be kept outside the reach of government power. Yes, "independence and economic relief [i.e., the security of one's financial means] are linked," and there can be no independence when the means to achieve one's goals depend, not on mutual trade, but on unilateral favor—which is one of the reasons why independence is the corollary of a free economy and cannot be achieved anywhere else.

But Mr. Markel wants to eat his cake and have it, too. He advocates public service without public responsibility; a blank check on public funds without public accounting; the "security" of a public income without public control.

Who, in such a setup, would determine the policies of public TV? Who would choose its managers and performers, the recipients of public money? Who would judge the value of its programs—and by what standard? Who would establish what is "imagination" and "balance"? Who would determine what is biased and what is not—what is informative and what is not—what sort of information is needed by the public and what sort is not—what is "imaginative" and what is "eccentric"—and whether a symbolic study of space, time, and sex in the subconscious of a fruit fly is effectively or ineffectively "experimental"?

If, under the vague control of a loose, haphazard, too easily tolerant Congressional supervision, public TV has done as badly as it has—and as Mr. Markel describes—what can lead one to expect that it would turn into an assembly of genius, of great thinkers, unbiased commentators, and brilliantly original artists, if unlimited funds were placed at its disposal, with no supervision, no rules, no strings attached? No group of people has so great a faith in the power of money as those who are socialistically inclined.

It is useless to raise moral questions in regard to a moral obscen-

ity such as the proposal to *force* people to support public TV—
which means: to take from people, by force, the money they had
to work for, and give it to sundry intellectual connivers in
exchange for a nebulous non-product which people cannot use,
would not want to use, and would hate if they tried it (but
which is allegedly desired by ten million college hippies who do
not propose to pay for anything they desire). Consider the issue
of pay-TV (for which only those who want it, would pay): the
same types of mentalities who oppose pay-TV, for fear that it
might eventually deprive the poor of the free commercial programs they now enjoy, do not hesitate to support the imposition
of a tax on the television sets of the poor, in order to make them
pay for programs they would not see.

In my [article in *Philosophy: Who Needs It*] on "The Establishing of an Establishment," which discussed government grants to
the social sciences, I wrote: "The origin of an aristocracy is the
king's power to confer on a chosen individual the privilege of
receiving an unearned income from the involuntary servitude of
the inhabitants of a given district. Now, the same policy is
operating in the United States—only the privileges are granted
not in perpetuity, but in a lump sum for a limited time, and the
involuntary servitude is imposed not on a group of serfs in a
specific territory, but on all the citizens of the country."

I overestimated the moral stature and underestimated the
ambition of modern intellectuals. Their goal is not the position
of a temporary elite, but the establishment of a full-fledged
aristocracy in perpetuity (with the succession determined not
by birth, but by self-perpetuating professional guilds)—an aristocracy which, once established, would no longer be subject to
public choice, approval, or control, an aristocracy independent
of the government, except for the government's obligation to
send out internal revenue agents to collect from the country at
large the private tax imposed by the aristocrats.

This is the secret dream of those advocates of "genuine democracy" who regard the free market as insecure and the necessity to earn a living as an impediment, who long for liberation
from material concerns, and who are not afraid to exchange the
"tyranny" of a private employer for the terrible chains of a
government's control. *They* do not intend to be under government control; *they* would be exempt; the government would
guarantee their income, collect it, deliver it, and ask no questions; they *would* achieve liberation from material concerns, by

the only means it can ever be attempted: by the slave labor of others.

There is a limit to everything, even to the human capacity for evasion. No man could face others and declare that he intends to force them to support him for no reason whatever, just because he wants it, for his own "selfish" sake. He needs to justify his intention, not merely in their eyes, but, above all, in his own. There is only one doctrine that can pass for a justification: *altruism*.

Observe that such men are impassioned advocates of altruistic ideals, of collectivism, brother love, social service, and self-sacrificial dedication to the good of others. They are not hypocrites; in their own way, they are "sincere"; they have to be. They *need* to believe that their work serves others, whether those others like it or not, and that the good of others is their only motivation; they do believe it—passionately, fiercely, militantly—in the sense in which a *belief* is distinguishable from a *conviction*: in the form of an emotion impervious to reality.

It makes no difference whether they embraced altruism as a means to their ulterior motives or the motives grew out of their altruistic creed. The two elements are mutually reinforcing, and neither is given a conscious identification in their minds. The same lack of self-esteem that would make a man accept and *desire* the position of being supported by the forced labor of others, would make him accept, and regard as noble, the doctrine demanding his self-immolation.

In this special sense, the advocates of every vicious, irrational doctrine are "sincere" and believe what they preach, though their belief is somewhat different and deeper than the faith they demand of their victims (if "depth," in this case, is to be measured by distance from reality). The victims are commanded to believe and to take the blame if they permit their faith to be shaken by facts that contradict it. The leaders are free (up to a point) to face the facts of their own performance, to lie, to cheat, to rob, to kill—so long as they hold, as an inviolate absolute, the belief that they are the vehicles of a higher truth which justifies, somehow, any action they might commit; this grants them the kind of malleable, non-absolute reality which is their basic goal.

For the victims of altruism, doubt is paralyzed by guilt; for the leaders, altruism removes the necessity of doubt, i.e., of thought.

In the case of some liberals' clamor for public TV, nothing more may be involved than some hack's desire to see his epic produced at public expense. But that hack's psychology—his belief—is part of a continuum that leads to Robespierre or Hitler or Stalin.

Let me give you an illustration of such belief. When Khrushchev visited the United States in 1959, he was interviewed on various television news programs, usually through the voice of a translator; but on one occasion his answers were broadcast in Russian (with the English translation following). He was asked about the grounds of his faith in the ultimate triumph of world communism. And suddenly this cynical old brute—this Big Boss, feared by the whole world, known in Russia as "the Butcher of the Ukraine" for the mass slaughter that raised him to prominence— began to recite the credo of dialectic materialism in the exact words and tone in which I had heard it recited at exams, in my college days, by students at the University of Leningrad. He had the same uninflected, monotonous tone of a memorized lesson, the same automatic progression of sounds rather than meaning, the same earnest, dutiful, desperate hope that the sacred formulas would come out correctly. But in the face and eyes of a large television closeup, there was a shade more intensity than in the faces of the poor little college robots, more superstitious awe, and less comprehension: it was the face of a man performing a magic ritual on which his life depends. This man, I thought, believes it; he is compelled to believe it; he does not know what it means—but he knows that if this string of sounds were taken away from him, he would be left to face something more frightening than death.

Such is the nature, the pattern, and the ultimate exponent of those who have faith—and a vested interest—in altruism.

23

Tax Credits for Education
by Ayn Rand

This article was published in The Ayn Rand Letter,
March 13, 1972.

Politically, the goal of today's dominant trend is statism. Philosophically, the goal is the obliteration of reason; psychologically, it is the erosion of ambition.

The political goal presupposes the two others. The human characteristic required by statism is *docility*, which is the product of hopelessness and intellectual stagnation. Thinking men cannot be ruled; ambitious men do not stagnate.

"Ambition" means the systematic pursuit of achievement and of constant improvement in respect to one's goal. Like the word "selfishness," and for the same reasons, the word "ambition" has been perverted to mean only the pursuit of dubious or evil goals, such as the pursuit of power; this left no concept to designate the pursuit of actual values. But "ambition" as such is a neutral concept: the evaluation of a given ambition as moral or immoral depends on the nature of the goal. A great scientist or a great artist is the most passionately ambitious of men. A demagogue seeking political power is ambitious. So is a social climber seeking "prestige." So is a modest laborer who works conscientiously to acquire a home of his own. The common denominator is the drive to improve the conditions of one's existence, however broadly or narrowly conceived. ("Improvement" is a moral term and depends on one's standard of values. An ambition guided by an irrational standard does not, *in fact*, lead to improvement, but to self-destruction.)

An economic "freeze" is intended to paralyze ambition (and its root: the active mind). A freeze is an order not to act, not to grow, not to improve. It is a demand to sacrifice one's future. But—since an essential characteristic of life is motion—when men do not move forward, they move back; the demand to stop cannot stop and becomes a demand to sacrifice one's present.

The Nixon Administration did not even take the trouble to delay or disguise this process. After all the mawkish pleas to "hold the line" against inflation—to forgo, "temporarily," higher profits or higher wages or a higher standard of living—the Administration is now proposing *higher taxes*. This means that our standard of living is not to stand still, but to collapse under a huge new tax burden, a so-called "value-added tax" (which is a complex form of national sales tax).

To add insult to injury, this tax is intended to finance not some sudden national emergency, but *public education*.

Of all the government undertakings, none has failed so disastrously as public education. The scope, the depth, and the evidence of this failure are observable all around us. To name three of its obvious symptoms: drug addiction among the young (which is an attempt to escape the unbearable state of a mind unable to cope with existence)—functional illiteracy (the inability of the average high-school or college graduate to speak English, i.e., to speak or write coherently)—student violence (which means that students have not learned what savages know to some minimal extent: the impracticality and immorality of resorting to physical force).

In the face of such evidence, one would expect the government's performance in the field of education to be questioned, at the least. Instead, the government is demanding more money—at a time of national economic crisis—to continue spreading the wreckage wider and wider. (Observe, incidentally, the consistency with which moral principles work out in politics: when need, not achievement, is the standard of value, success at a given assignment is penalized, and failure rewarded. For example, NASA's success in landing a man on the moon was followed by cuts in Congressional appropriations for the space program; the growing failures of the educational establishment are followed by the appropriation of larger and larger sums.)

There is, however, a practical alternative. If the countless individuals who are eager to "do something" in politics, and the countless groups who profess concern over the growth of statism, really wish to accomplish something of value, the coming debate on the new tax to support education offers them a chance.

(It is also a chance for any honest politician, of either party, who seeks a worthy issue to crusade for at election time.) It is an opportunity to unite many people of different viewpoints in an ad hoc movement for a specifically defined goal.

The goal is: *tax credits for education.*

The idea is not entirely new. (I was advocating it ten years ago.) Different versions of it were periodically proposed in Congress, but were defeated in committee. (In 1964, one of the proposal's notable supporters was Senator Ribicoff.) The evidence of the desperate need for such a program has never been as clear as it is at present.

The essentials of the idea (in *my* version) are as follows: an individual citizen would be given tax credits for the money he spends on education, whether his own education, his children's, or any person's he wants to put through a bona fide school of his own choice (including primary, secondary, and higher education).

The upper limits of what he may spend on any one person would be equal to what it costs the government to provide a student with a comparable education (if there is a computer big enough to calculate it, including all the costs involved, local, state, and federal, the government loans, scholarships, subsidies, etc.).

If a young person's parents are too poor to pay for his education or to pay income taxes, and if he cannot find a private sponsor to finance him, the public schools would still be available to him, as they are at present—with the likelihood that these schools would be greatly improved by the relief of the pressure of overcrowding, and by the influence of a broad variety of private schools.

I want to stress that I am *not* an advocate of public (i.e., government-operated) schools, that I am *not* an advocate of the income tax, and that I am *not* an advocate of the government's "right" to expropriate a citizen's money or to control his spending through tax incentives. None of these phenomena would exist in a free economy. But we are living in a disastrously mixed economy, which cannot be freed overnight. And in today's context, the above proposal would be a step in the right direction, a measure to avert an immediate catastrophe.

It would accomplish the following: instead of becoming a crushing new tax burden at a time when the country is staggering under the present one, the costs of education would be borne directly by those who now pay them indirectly—by individual citizens. (The public schools would remain in existence and would be financed out of general tax revenues.) Parents would still have to pay for education, but they would have a choice: either to send their children to free public schools and pay their taxes in full—or to pay tuition to a private school, with money saved from their taxes.

It would give private schools a chance to survive (which they do not have at present). It would bring their tuition fees within the reach of the majority of people (today, only the well-to-do can afford them). It would break up the government's stranglehold, decentralize education, and open it to competition—as well as to a free marketplace of ideas.

It would eliminate the huge educational bureaucracy of the government (which is now growing with the speed of a terminal cancer) and reduce it to a reasonable size. The amount of money this would save is literally inconceivable to the average citizen. To give just one example: it was estimated that the Job Corps [a federal training program] spent $9,210 to $13,000 per year per enrollee; at some camps, the figure reached $22,000, and even $39,205. At private residential schools giving vocational training, the costs ranged from $2,300 to $2,600 per student per year. (Shirley Scheibla, *Poverty Is Where the Money Is,* New Rochelle, N.Y.: Arlington House, 1968.)

Let the schoolteachers and college professors remember these figures. Theirs is one of the lowest paid professions today, yet most of them are supporters of the status quo. Let them realize that it is not the poverty of their students, but the enrichment of the bureaucracy, that is responsible for their plight—and what a competitive market would do in regard to the financial value of their services.

At present, the biggest spender of government funds, the largest recipient of tax money in the national budget, is not the Department of Defense, but the Department of Health, Education and Welfare. It is clear why the government must hold a monopoly on national defense. But no one—except a full-fledged communist or fascist—would advocate a government monopoly on education. Yet such a monopoly is what we are, *in fact,* approaching—and *taxation* is the main cause of the trend.

Private universities are being ground out of existence between two modern disasters, both products of government policies: the erosion of private contributions (eaten away by taxes), and rising costs (brought about by inflation, which is caused by government spending). State universities with nominal or free tuition are another factor destroying the chances of the private universities' survival. No private concern can compete with a government institution for any length of time, and the injustice involved is obvious: it is a competition in which one contestant has unlimited funds, part of them taken from the other, and in which one contestant is forced to obey the rules arbitrarily set by the other. If any private schools survive, they will survive in name only (which is the typical policy of a fascist state): they are all but hog-tied by the government already. The current attempts to assist private universities with federal funds will complete the job. If "the power to tax is the power to destroy," the power to disburse government funds is the power to rule.

Now consider the nature of today's tax policies in regard to the educational needs of young people.

While millions of dollars are being spent by the government on attempts to educate young people most of whom have no ability and/or no desire to get an education, what happens to the young man who has both? If he is poor, he has to work his way through school—a terrible process that takes eight years or longer for a four-year course, consuming his youth and becoming progressively harder, in view of rising costs and shrinking opportunities of employment. (Scholarships are a drop in the bucket, nor are they always granted fairly.) Yet out of his meager income, he has to pay taxes—not only the hidden ones in the cost of everything he buys, but income taxes as well. Thus while he is allowed no deductions for the costs of his own education, he is paying for the *free* education of the youths enrolled in government projects.

To seek education in such circumstances requires an unusual strength of character, an unusual independence, ambition, and long-range vision. The young people who do it are, potentially, the best of the nation; they are its future; they do not need help, only a fair chance, which they are denied. Many of them are broken by the struggle and driven to give up. But wherever they go, their taxes still pay for the education and "rehabilitation" efforts which allegedly strive (but fail) to develop in stuporous hippies the qualities of character which they, the victims, had once possessed.

If a young man does not, or cannot afford to, go to college, but goes to work instead, to earn his living, he will soon discover—if he is an actively interested, conscientious, ambitious worker—

that he needs education to rise to a better job. The tax laws allow him deductions only if the schooling is demanded by his employer as a condition of keeping his job—*not* if he seeks special training on his own initiative. What does this do to his self-confidence or his sense of control over his own future? Yet in the government's job-training programs, the lethargic recipients are not merely given free training, but are *paid* for attending the courses. It is inequities of this kind that make Mr. Nixon's exhortations to "self-reliance" sound so ludicrously and cruelly hypocritical.

All over the country, self-respecting and self-supporting young couples are carrying a double financial burden: paying constantly rising taxes for the support of schools to which they cannot in conscience send their own children. The private revival of Montessori schools demonstrates the plight of conscientious young parents on a nationwide scale. Aware of the ravages of Progressive education in public schools, such parents send their children to private schools (or join to build such schools), which few of them can afford. It is a heavy sacrifice for most of them, at a time when they are struggling to achieve some degree of professional and financial security. They are given no tax relief for such expenses, which places private schools outside the reach of the hard-working, respectable lower middle class.

The same injustice is perpetrated against the parents who send their children to parochial schools. As you surely know, I am *not* an advocate of religion or of religious education, but the double burden of a forced necessity to pay for the support of secular schools is a violation of the parents' right to religious freedom. The parochial schools are collapsing financially, for the same reasons and under the same pressures as the private universities—and the current controversy over the support of parochial schools illustrates the nature of the issue. On the one hand, it is certainly improper and unconstitutional to use public funds for the support of religious schools. On the other hand, it is unjust that the children of religious taxpayers are denied the special advantages granted to the children of nonreligious ones. You may take it as a general rule: whenever an issue leads to an unresolvable conflict, you will find, at its root, the violation of someone's rights.

These are only a few of the problems that tax credits for education would solve.

The opposition to such a program would be horrendous and

would come from an entrenched pressure group: the educational establishment. But this is the time to raise the question of a "conflict of interests." Public officials who have connections with private sources of income that involve government matters—as, for instance, with a company seeking government contracts—are regarded as suspect, unless they break the connection. By the same token, a bureaucrat whose source of income is a government job (an unnecessary job, more often than not) should be regarded as suspect when and if he opposes a program that threatens the source of his income.

Some people would oppose the program on the grounds that it will foster the development of different educational theories and methods in the various private schools. The answer to them is that that precisely is one of the program's goals—that differences, not regimented uniformity, are essential to the progress of a free country—and that equality before the law, *not* egalitarianism, is one of this country's fundamental principles.

Let us take the educational establishment at their word and hold them to it: that their goal is to provide education, *not* to control the intellectual life of this country.

24

Antitrust: The Rule of Unreason
by Ayn Rand

*This is one of Ayn Rand's earliest discussions of the
evils of antitrust legislation. It was published in*
The Objectivist Newsletter, *February 1962.*

It is a grave error to suppose that a dictatorship rules a nation
by means of strict, rigid laws which are obeyed and enforced
with rigorous, military precision. Such a rule would be evil, but
almost bearable; men could endure the harshest edicts, provided these edicts were known, specific, and stable; it is not the
known that breaks men's spirits, but the unpredictable. A dictatorship has to be capricious; it has to rule by means of the
unexpected, the incomprehensible, the wantonly irrational; it
has to deal not in death, but in *sudden* death; a state of chronic
uncertainty is what men are psychologically unable to bear.

The American businessmen have had to live in that state for
seventy years. They were condemned to it by that judicial version of the doctrine of original sin which presumes men to be
guilty with little or no chance to be proved innocent and which
is known as the antitrust laws.

No business-hating collectivist could have gotten away with
creating so perfect an instrument for the destruction of capitalism and the delivery of businessmen into the total power of the
government. It took the so-called "conservatives," the alleged
defenders of capitalism, to create the antitrust laws. And it
takes the intellectual superficiality of today's "conservatives" to
continue supporting these laws, in spite of their meaning, record, and results.

The alleged purpose of the antitrust laws was to protect competition; that purpose was based on the socialistic fallacy that a

free, unregulated market will inevitably lead to the establishment of coercive monopolies. But, in fact, no coercive monopoly
has ever been or ever can be established by means of free trade
on a free market. Every coercive monopoly was created by government intervention into the economy: by special privileges,
such as franchises or subsidies, which closed the entry of competitors into a given field, by legislative action. (For a full
demonstration of this fact, I refer you to the works of the best
economists.) The antitrust laws were the classic example of a
moral inversion prevalent in the history of capitalism: an example of the victims, the businessmen, taking the blame for the
evils caused by the government, and the government using its
own guilt as a justification for acquiring wider powers, on the
pretext of "correcting" the evils.

Since *"free* competition *enforced* by law" is a grotesque contradiction in terms, antitrust grew into a haphazard accumulation
of non-objective laws so vague, complex, contradictory, and inconsistent that any business practice can now be construed as
illegal, and by complying with one law a businessman opens
himself to prosecution under several others. No two jurists can
agree on the meaning and application of these laws. No one can
give an exact definition of what constitutes "restraint of trade"
or "intent to monopolize" or any of the other, similar "crimes."
No one can tell what the law forbids or permits one to do. The
interpretation is left entirely up to the courts. "The courts in
the United States have been engaged ever since 1890 in deciding
case by case exactly what the law proscribes. No broad definition can really unlock the meaning of the statute." [A.D. Neale,
The Antitrust Laws of the U.S.A., Cambridge University Press,
1960, p. 13.]

Thus a businessman has no way of knowing in advance whether
the action he takes is legal or illegal, whether he is guilty or
innocent. Yet he has to act; he has to run his business.

Retroactive law—which means: a law that punishes a man for
an action which was not legally defined as a crime at the time
he committed it—is a form of persecution practiced only in
dictatorships and forbidden by every civilized legal code. It is
not supposed to exist in the United States and it is not applied
to anyone—except to businessmen. A case in which a man cannot know until he is convicted whether the action he took in the
past was legal or illegal is certainly a case of retroactive law.

At first, antitrust was merely a potential club, a "big stick" over businessmen's heads, but it soon became actual. From their hesitant, sluggish beginnings in a few vaguely semi-plausible cases, antitrust prosecutions accelerated by a progression of logical steps to such judicial decisions as: that established businesses have to share with any newcomer the facilities it had taken them years to create, if the lack of such facilities imposes a real hardship on the would-be competitor (*Associated Press* case, 1945)—that business concerns have no right to pool their patents and that the penalty for such pools is either the compulsory licensing of their patents to any and all comers or the outright confiscation of the patents; and if a businessman, who is a member of such a pool, sues a competitor who has infringed his patent, the competitor not only wins the case, but collects treble damages from the man whose patent he had infringed (*Kobe* v. *Dempsey Pump Company,* 1952)—that if a would-be competitor's efficiency is so low that he is unable even to pay a royalty on the patents owned by stronger companies, he is entitled to such patents royalty-free (*General Electric* case, 1948)—that business concerns must not merely make a gift of their patents to any rival, but must also *teach* him how to use these patents (*I.C.I. and duPont* case, 1952)—that a business concern must not anticipate increases in the demand for its product and must not be prepared to meet them by expanding its capacity "before others entered the field," because this might *discourage* newcomers (*ALCOA* case, 1945).

Is the basic line clear? Do you observe the nature of the principle that dictated the decisions in these cases?

A. D. Neale identifies it as follows: "There is an element of pure 'underdoggery' in the law; an element of throwing the weight of the enforcement authorities into the scale on the side of the weaker parties, which has *little* to do with the economic control of monopoly." [p. 461]

I identify it as: the penalizing of ability for being ability, the penalizing of success for being success, and the sacrifice of productive genius to the demands of envious mediocrity.

Who were the profiteers of antitrust? Many businessmen supported it from the start: some innocently, some not. These last were the kind who seek to rise not by free trade and productive ability, but by *political favor and pull,* which means: not by merit, but by *force.* They are the typical products of a "mixed economy" and their numbers multiply as the economy grows more "mixed."

The other group of profiteers was the bureaucrats and the statists. As the trend toward statism grew, the statists found an invaluable instrument for the persecution and the eventual enslavement of businessmen. Observe that the most outrageous antitrust cases date from the 1940s. Power in a statist sense means *arbitrary* power. An *objective* law protects a country's freedom; only a *non-objective* law can give a statist the chance he seeks: a chance to impose *his* arbitrary will—*his* policies, *his* decisions, *his* interpretations, *his* enforcement, *his* punishment or favor—on disarmed, defenseless victims. He does not have to exercise his power too frequently or too openly; he merely has to have it and let his victims know that he has it; fear will do the rest.

In the light of this, consider the *new* phase of antitrust enforcement. In February of 1961, in Philadelphia, seven businessmen, representing some of America's greatest industrial concerns, were sentenced to jail in the "Electrical Conspiracy" case. This case involved twenty-nine companies manufacturing electrical equipment. The charge against them was that they had made secret agreements to fix prices and rig bids. But without such agreements, the larger companies could have set their prices so low that the smaller ones would have been unable to match them and would have gone out of business, whereupon the larger companies would have faced prosecution, under these same antitrust laws, for "intent to monopolize."

It is evil enough to impose ruinous fines under laws which the victims have no way to comply with, laws which everyone concedes to be non-objective, contradictory, and undefinable. It is obscene, under such laws, to impose jail sentences on men of distinguished achievement, outstanding ability, and unimpeachable moral character, who had spent their lives on so responsible a task as industrial production.

But *this*, perhaps, is the clue to the purpose of that disgraceful verdict. It created in the public's mind the impression that industrial production is some sort of sinister underworld activity and that businessmen, by their nature and profession, are to be treated as criminals.

Such was the obvious implication of the disgusting howling that went on in the press. The same humanitarians who rush to the defense of any homicidal dipsomaniac did not hesitate to release all of their repressed hatred and malice on seven silent, defenseless men whose profession was *business*. That the leftist press would enjoy it is understandable and, at least, consistent. But what is one to think of the alleged "conservative" press? Take a look at the February 17, 1961, issue of *Time* magazine; with its story about the verdict, *Time* published photographs of six of the victims—six faces with intelligence and determination as their common characteristic—and under them, the caption: "A drama that U.S. business will long remember to its shame."

The same humanitarians of the press who clamor that penitentiaries are a useless, vengeful form of cruelty to juvenile switchblade killers questing for "kicks" and that these sensitive victims of society should be "given a chance" and should be sent to garden rest homes for rehabilitation—these same humanitarians have remained silent while a bill is proposed in Congress to the effect that an executive convicted of an antitrust violation may not, thereafter, be given employment by any business concern and is thus to be deprived of the right to earn a living.

No, all this is not the result of a communist conspiracy. It is the result of something much harder to fight: the result of a culture's cynical, goal-less disintegration, which can benefit no one but the communists and the random little powerlusters of the moment, who fish in muddy waters.

It is futile to wonder about the policies or the intentions of the present [Kennedy] administration. Whether the whole administration or any one of its members is consciously dedicated to the destruction of American business does not matter. What matters is that if any of them *are*, they have the machinery to accomplish it and no opposition: a culture without goals, values, or political principles can offer no opposition to anything.

Intentionally or not, the purpose achieved by those jail sentences is: intimidation—or, more precisely: terrorization. The antitrust laws give the government the power to prosecute and convict any business concern in the country any time it chooses. The threat of sudden destruction, of unpredictable retaliation for unnamed offenses, is a much more potent means of enslavement than explicit dictatorial laws. It demands more than mere obedience; it leaves men no policy save one: *to please* the authorities; to please—blindly, uncritically, without standards or principles; to please—in any issue, matter, or circumstance, for fear of an unknowable, unprovable vengeance. Anyone possessing such a stranglehold on businessmen possesses a stranglehold on the wealth and the material resources of the country, which means: a stranglehold on the country.

Businessmen are already helpless and almost silenced. It is only the intellectuals who still have a chance to be heard. That is why I suggest to you the following test: if you hear an alleged "conservative" who quibbles bravely over taxes, budgets, or school aid, but supports the antitrust laws—you may be sure that he is futile as a fighter for capitalism. To combat petty larceny as a crucial danger, at a time when murder is being committed, is to sanction the murder.

What should we do? We should demand a reexamination and revision of the entire issue of antitrust. We should challenge its philosophical, political, economic and *moral* base. We should have a Civil Liberties Union—for businessmen. The repeal of the antitrust laws should be our ultimate goal; it will require a long intellectual and political struggle, but, in the meantime and as a first step, we should urge that the jail-penalty provisions of these laws be abolished.

Businessmen are the one group that distinguishes capitalism and the American way of life from the totalitarian statism that is swallowing the rest of the world. All the other social groups—workers, professional men, scientists, soldiers—exist under dictatorships, even though they exist in chains, in terror, in misery and in progressive self-destruction. *But there is no such group as businessmen under a dictatorship.* Their place is taken by armed thugs: by bureaucrats and commissars. So if you want to fight for freedom, you must begin by fighting for its unrewarded, unrecognized, unacknowledged, yet best representatives—the American businessmen.

25

The Pull Peddlers
by Ayn Rand

Ayn Rand regarded a country's domestic policy (and the philosophy underlying it) as decisive for its future and as the source of its foreign policy. Accordingly, she wrote relatively little about foreign policy as such. This discussion of foreign aid is one of her few articles on the area, published in The Objectivist Newsletter, *September 1962.*

America's foreign policy is so grotesquely irrational that most people believe there must be some sensible purpose behind it. The extent of the irrationality acts as its own protection: like the technique of the "Big Lie," it makes people assume that so blatant an evil could not possibly be as evil as it appears to them and, therefore, that *somebody* must understand its meaning, even though they themselves do not.

The sickening generalities and contradictions cited in justification of the foreign aid program fall roughly into two categories which are offered to us simultaneously: the "idealistic" and the "practical," or mush and fear.

The "idealistic" arguments consist of appeals to altruism and swim out of focus in a fog of floating abstractions about our duty to support the "underdeveloped" nations of the entire globe, who are starving and will perish without our selfless help.

The "practical" arguments consist of appeals to fear and emit a different sort of fog, to the effect that our own selfish interest requires that we go bankrupt buying the favor of the "underdeveloped" nations, who, otherwise, will become a dangerous threat to us.

It is useless to point out to the advocates of our foreign policy that it's either-or: either the "underdeveloped" nations are so weak that they are doomed without our help, in which case they cannot become a threat to us—or they are so strong that with some other assistance they can develop to the point of endangering us, in which case we should not drain our economic power to help the growth of potential enemies who are that powerful.

It is useless to discuss the contradiction between these two assertions, because neither of them is true. Their proponents are impervious to facts, to logic, and to the mounting evidence that after two decades of global altruism, our foreign policy is achieving the exact opposite of its alleged goals: it is wrecking our economy—it is reducing us internationally to the position of an impotent failure who has nothing but a series of compromises, retreats, defeats, and betrayals on his record—and, instead of bringing progress to the world, it is bringing the bloody chaos of tribal warfare and delivering one helpless nation after another into the power of communism.

When a society insists on pursuing a suicidal course, one may be sure that the alleged reasons and proclaimed slogans are mere rationalizations. The question is only: what is it that these rationalizations are hiding?

Observe that there is no consistent pattern in the erratic chaos of our foreign aid. And although in the long run it leads to the benefit of Soviet Russia, Russia is not its direct, immediate beneficiary. There is no consistent winner, only a consistent loser: the United States.

In the face of such a spectacle, some people give up the attempt to understand; others imagine that some omnipotent conspiracy is destroying America, that the rationalizations are hiding some malevolent, fantastically powerful giant.

The truth is worse than that: the truth is that the rationalizations are hiding nothing—that there is nothing at the bottom of the fog but a nest of scurrying cockroaches.

I submit in evidence an article in the editorial section of *The New York Times* of July 15, 1962, entitled: "Role of Foreign Lobbies."

A "non-diplomatic corps" of foreign agents has bloomed in recent years [in Washington]. . . . Lobbying in Congress to obtain—or prevent—the passage of legislation of interest to their foreign clients, seeking to pressure the Administration into adopting certain political or economic policies, or attempting to mold public opinion through a myriad of methods and techniques, this legion of special agents has become an elusive shadow for operating in Washington and the width and the length of the land.

"Lobbying" is the activity of attempting to influence legislation by privately influencing the legislators. It is the result and creation of a "mixed economy"—of government by pressure groups. Its methods range from mere social courtesies and cocktail-party or luncheon "friendships" to favors, threats, bribes, blackmail.

All lobbyists, whether serving foreign or domestic interests, are required—by laws passed in the last three decades—to register with the government. The registrations have been growing at such a rate—with the foreign lobbyists outnumbering the domestic ones—that legislators are beginning to be alarmed. The Senate Foreign Relations Committee has announced that it is preparing an investigation of these foreign agents' activities.

The *New York Times* article describes foreign lobbying as follows:

> The theory behind this whole enterprise is that for a fee or a retainer and often for hundreds of thousands of dollars in advertising, publicity and expense money, a foreign Government or a foreign economic or political interest *can purchase a favorable legislation in the United States Congress, a friendly policy of the Administration* or a positive image in the eyes of the American public opinion, leading in turn to *profitable political or economic advantage.* [Emphasis added.]

Who are these lobbyists? Men with political pull—with "access" to influential Washington figures—American men hired by foreign interests. The article mentions that most of these men are "Washington lawyers" or "New York public relations firms."

Russia is one of these foreign interests and is served by registered lobbyists in Washington, but she is merely cashing in on the situation, like the others. The success of her conspiracy in this country is the result, not the cause, of our self-destruction; she is winning by default. The cause is much deeper than that.

The issue of lobbies has attracted attention recently through the struggle of foreign lobbyists to obtain sugar quotas from the American government. "Their efforts," states the article, "were centered on Representative Harold D. Cooley, Democrat of North Carolina, chairman of the House Committee on Agriculture, who at least until this year held almost the complete power in the distribution of quotas. It has never been too clear what criteria Mr. Cooley used in allocating these quotas, and, by the same token, it is impossible to determine what was the actual effect of the lobbyists' entreaties on him.

"But in offering their services to foreign governments or sugar growers' associations, these representatives were, in effect, offering for sale their real or alleged friendship with Mr. Cooley."

This is the core and essence of the issue of lobbying—and of our foreign aid—and of a "mixed economy."

The trouble is not that "it has never been too clear what criteria Mr. Cooley used in allocating these quotas"—but that it has never been and never can be too clear what criteria he was expected to use by the legislation that granted him these powers. No criteria can ever be defined in this context; such is the nature of non-objective law and of all economic legislation.

So long as a concept such as "the public interest" (or the "social" or "national" or "international" interest) is regarded as a valid principle to guide legislation—lobbies and pressure groups will necessarily continue to exist. Since there is no such entity as *"the public,"* since the public is merely a number of individuals, the idea that "the public interest" supersedes private interests and rights can have but one meaning: that the interests and rights of some individuals take precedence over the interests and rights of others.

If so, then all men and all private groups have to fight to the death for the privilege of being regarded as "the public." The government's policy has to swing like an erratic pendulum from group to group, hitting some and favoring others, at the whim of any given moment—and so grotesque a profession as lobbying (selling "influence") becomes a full-time job. If parasitism, favoritism, corruption, and greed for the unearned did not exist, a "mixed economy" would bring them into existence.

Since there is no rational justification for the sacrifice of some men to others, there is no objective criterion by which such a sacrifice can be guided in practice. All "public interest" legislation (and any distribution of money taken by force from some men for the unearned benefit of others) comes down ultimately to the grant of an undefined, undefinable, nonobjective, arbitrary power to some government officials.

The worst aspect of it is not that such a power can be used dishonestly, but that *it cannot be used honestly*. The wisest man in the world, with the purest integrity, cannot find a criterion for the just, equitable, rational application of an unjust, inequitable, irrational principle. The best that an honest official can do is to accept no material bribe for his arbitrary decision; but this does not make his decision and its consequences more just or less calamitous.

A man of clear-cut convictions is impervious to anyone's influence. But when clear-cut convictions are impossible, personal influences take over. When a man's mind is trapped in the foggy labyrinth of the non-objective, that has no exits and no solutions, he will welcome any quasi-persuasive, semi-plausible argument. Lacking certainty, he will follow anyone's facsimile thereof. He is the natural prey of social "manipulators," of propaganda salesmen, of lobbyists.

When any argument is as inconclusive as any other, the subjective, emotional, or "human" element becomes decisive. A harried legislator may conclude, consciously or subconsciously, that the friendly man who smiled at him at the cocktail party last week was a good person who would not deceive him and whose opinion can be trusted safely. It is by considerations such as these that officials may dispose of your money, your effort, and your future.

Although cases of actual corruption do undoubtedly exist among legislators and government officials, they are not a major motivating factor in today's situation. It is significant that in such cases as have been publicly exposed, the bribes were almost pathetically small. Men who held the power to dispose of millions of dollars sold their favors for a thousand-dollar rug or a fur coat or a refrigerator.

The truth, most likely, is that they did not regard it as bribery or as a betrayal of their public trust; they did not think that their particular decision could matter one way or another, in the kind of causeless choices they had to make, in the absence of any criteria, in the midst of the general orgy of tossing away an apparently ownerless wealth. Men who would not sell out their country for a million dollars are selling it out for somebody's smile and a vacation trip to Florida. "It is of such pennies and smiles that the destruction of your country is made."

The general public is helplessly bewildered. The "intellectuals" do not care to look at our foreign policy too closely. They feel guilt; they sense that their own worn-out ideologies, which they dare not challenge, are the cause of the consequences which they dare not face. The more they evade, the greater their eagerness to grasp at any fashionable straw or rationalization and to uphold it with glassy-eyed aggressiveness. The threadbare cloak of altruism serves to cover it up and to sanction the evasions by a fading aura of moral righteousness. The exhausted cynicism of a bankrupt culture, of a society without values, principles, convictions, or intellectual standards, does the rest: it leaves a vacuum for anyone to take over and use.

The motive power behind the suicidal bleeding of the greatest country in the world is not an altruistic fervor or a collectivist crusade any longer, but the manipulations of little lawyers and public relations men pulling the mental strings of lifeless automatons.

These—the lobbyists in the pay of foreign interests, the men who could not hope to get, in any other circumstances, the money they are getting now—are the real and only profiteers on the global sacrifice, as their ilk has always been at the close of every altruistic movement in history. It is not the "underdeveloped" nations or the "underprivileged" masses or the starving children of jungle villages who benefit from America's self-immolation—it is only the men who are too small to start such movements and small enough to cash in at the end.

It is not any "lofty ideal" that the altruism-collectivism doctrine accomplishes or can ever accomplish. Its end-of-trail is as follows: "A local railroad had gone bankrupt in North Dakota, abandoning the region to the fate of a blighted area, the local banker had committed suicide, first killing his wife and children—a freight train had been taken off the schedule in Tennessee, leaving a local factory without transportation at a day's notice, the factory owner's son had quit college and was now in jail, awaiting execution for a murder committed with a gang of raiders—a way station had been closed in Kansas, and the station agent, who had wanted to be a scientist, had given up his studies and become a dishwasher—that he, James Taggart, might sit in a private barroom and pay for the alcohol pouring down Orren Boyle's throat, for the waiter who sponged Boyle's garments when he spilled his drink over his chest, for the carpet burned by the cigarettes of an ex-pimp from Chile who did not want to take the trouble of reaching for an ashtray across a distance of three feet." [*Atlas Shrugged*]

26

About a Woman President
by Ayn Rand

*This piece, an answer to letters from readers, was
published in the issue of* The Objectivist *dated
December 1968, although the piece was actually
written in January 1969.*

About a year ago, in the issue of January 1968, *McCall's*
published an article-interview with sixteen prominent
women (myself included) who had been asked to answer the
question: What would I do if I were president of the United
States? The first paragraph of my answer read: "I would not
want to be president and would not vote for a woman president.
A woman cannot reasonably want to be a commander-in-chief. I
prefer to answer the question by outlining what a rational man
would do if *he* were president."

Thereafter, I received many letters from students of Objectivism, asking me the reasons of that particular paragraph.

I was counting on the readers of my novels to understand my
reasons. I grant you, however, that the issue is not self-evident
and that it is not easy to conceptualize. For illustrative material, I
suggest that you study the basic motivation of the heroines in my
novels, particularly Dagny Taggart.

I do not think that a rational woman can want to be president.
Observe that I did not say she would be unable to do the job; I
said that she could not *want* it. It is not a matter of her ability,
but of her *values.*

It is not an issue of feminine "inferiority," intellectually or
morally; women are not inferior to men in ability or intelligence; besides, it would not take much to do a better job than
some of our recent presidents have done. It is certainly not an

267

issue of the popular notion that women are motivated predominantly by their emotions rather than by reason—which is plain nonsense. It is not an issue of the false dichotomy of marriage versus career, with the corollary notion that "a woman's place is in the home"; whether married or single, women need and should have careers, for the same reasons as men. Women may properly rise as high as their ability and ambition will carry them; in politics, they may reach the ranks of congresswomen, senators, judges, or any similar rank they choose.

But when it comes to the post of president, do not look at the issue primarily from a somewhat altruistic or social viewpoint— i.e., do not ask: "Could she do the job and would it be good for the country?" Conceivably, she could and it would—but *what would it do to her?*

The issue is primarily psychological. It involves a woman's fundamental view of life, of herself and of her basic values. For a woman *qua* woman, the essence of femininity is hero worship— the desire to look up to man. "To look up" does not mean dependence, obedience, or anything implying inferiority. It means an intense kind of admiration; and admiration is an emotion that can be experienced only by a person of strong character and independent value judgments. A "clinging vine" type of woman is not an admirer, but an exploiter of men. Hero worship is a demanding virtue: a woman has to be worthy of it and of the hero she worships. Intellectually and morally, i.e., as a human being, she has to be his equal; then the object of her worship is specifically his *masculinity,* not any human virtue she might lack.

This does not mean that a feminine woman feels or projects hero worship for any and every individual man; as human beings, many of them may, in fact, be her inferiors. Her worship is an abstract emotion for the *metaphysical* concept of masculinity as such—which she experiences fully and concretely only for the man she loves, but which colors her attitude toward all men. This does not mean that there is a romantic or sexual intention in her attitude toward all men; quite the contrary: the higher her view of masculinity, the more severely demanding her standards. It means that she never loses the awareness of her own sexual identity and theirs. It means that a properly feminine woman does not treat men as if she were their pal, sister, mother—or *leader.*

Now consider the meaning of the presidency: in all his professional relationships, within the entire sphere of his work, the president is the *highest authority;* he is the "chief executive," the "commander-in-chief." Even in a fully free country, with an unbreached constitutional division of powers, a president is the final authority who sets the terms, the goals, the policies of every job in the executive branch of the government. In the performance of his duties, a president does not deal with equals, but only with inferiors (not inferiors as persons, but in respect to the hierarchy of their positions, their work, and their responsibilities).

This, for a rational woman, would be an unbearable situation. (And if she is *not* rational, she is unfit for the presidency or for any important position, anyway.) To act as the superior, the leader, virtually the *ruler* of all the men she deals with, would be an excruciating psychological torture. It would require a total depersonalization, an utter selflessness, and an incommunicable loneliness; she would have to suppress (or repress) every personal aspect of her own character and attitude; she could not be herself, i.e., a woman; she would have to function only as a *mind,* not as a *person,* i.e., as a thinker devoid of personal values—a dangerously artificial dichotomy which no one could sustain for long. By the nature of her duties and daily activities, she would become the most unfeminine, sexless, metaphysically inappropriate, and rationally revolting figure of all: a *matriarch.*

This would apply to the reigning queen of an absolute monarchy, but it would not apply to a woman in any field of endeavor other than politics. It does not apply, for instance, to a woman who heads a business concern; even though she is the highest authority within that concern, she deals constantly with men who are not under her orders: with customers, suppliers, competitors; she is not condemned to the solitary confinement of dealing exclusively with men who are her hierarchical inferiors (nor is her power as wide as that of a president).

It is conceivable that in some unusual historical context, in some period of extreme national emergency, it would be proper for a woman temporarily to assume the leadership of a country, in the role of president, if there were no men able to assume it. But what would this imply about the character of the men at that time? (Normally, the best and ablest among men do not necessarily have to seek the presidency, but in an extreme emergency, they would have to—as did the founding fathers.)

There is a historical precedent for the fate of a woman leader

in a period of extreme emergency: Joan of Arc—the most heroic
woman and the most tragic symbol in history. I say "tragic" not
merely because she was burned at the stake in reward for having saved her country—although that monstrous physical evil is
singularly appropriate, as a fiction-like concretization of the
spiritual tragedy of her life. Ask yourself: what power of dedication she must have possessed when she found herself as the only
one able to revive the fighting spirit of men who had given
up—and what would *she personally* have felt about it?

For a woman to seek or desire the presidency is, in fact, so
terrible a prospect of spiritual self-immolation that the woman
who would seek it is psychologically unworthy of the job.

27

The Inverted Moral Priorities
by Ayn Rand

This article was published in the issue of The Ayn
Rand Letter *dated July 15, 1974, though it was
written a few months later than this date.*

A widespread ignorance of a crucial economic issue is
apparent in most discussions of today's problems: it is
ignorance on the part of the public, evasion on the part of most
economists, and crude demagoguery on the part of certain politicians. The issue is *the function of wealth in an industrial economy.*

Most people seem to believe that wealth is primarily an object
of consumption—that the rich spend all or most of their money
on personal luxury. Even if this were true, it would be their
inalienable right—but it does not happen to be true. The percentage of income which men spend on consumption stands in
inverse ratio to the amount of their wealth. The percentage
which the rich spend on personal consumption is so small that it
is of no significance to a country's economy. The money of the
rich is invested in production; it is an indispensable part of the
stock seed that makes production possible.

Even the most primitive forms of production require an investment of time and sustenance (i.e., of unconsumed goods) to
enable men to produce. The higher a society's industrial development, the more expensive the tools required to put men to
work (and the greater the productivity of their labor). Some
years ago, it took an investment of five thousand dollars per
worker to create jobs in industry; I have no exact figures for the
present time, but the investment is now much higher. Deferred
consumption (i.e., *savings*) on a gigantic scale is required to keep
industrial production going. Savings pay for machines which

enable men to produce in a day an amount of goods they would not be able to produce by hand in a year (if at all). This enables the workers in turn to defer consumption and to save some of their income for their future needs or goals. The hallmark of an industrial society is its members' distance from a hand-to-mouth mode of living; the greater this distance, the greater men's progress.

The major part of this country's stock seed is not the fortunes of the rich (who are a small minority), but the savings of the middle class—i.e., of responsible men who have the ability to grasp the concept "future" and to deposit one dollar (or more) into a bank account. A man of this type saves money for his own future, but the bank invests his money in productive enterprises; thus, the goods he did not consume today are available to him when he needs them tomorrow—and, in the meantime, these goods serve as fuel for the country's productive process.

Except for short periods of unforeseeable emergency, a rational person cannot stand living hand-to-mouth. No matter what his income, he saves some part of it, large or small—because he knows that his life is not confined to the immediate moment, that he has to plan ahead, and that savings are his means of control over his life: savings are his badge of independence and his door to the future—if he is to have a future.

Project fully and concretely what a hand-to-mouth existence would be like. Assume that you have a job which takes care of your immediate physical needs (food, clothing, and shelter), but nothing more: you consume everything you earn. Without the possibility of saving, you would live in a state of chronic terror; terror of losing your job and terror of sudden illness. (Never mind unemployment insurance and Medicaid: insurance is a form of saving, and compulsory savings leave you at the mercy of the government.) Could you look for a better job? No—because you have no reserves to carry you a single day. Could you go to school to learn a new skill? No—because this takes savings. Could you plan to buy a car? No—this takes savings. Could you plan to buy a home of your own? No—this takes an enormous amount of savings over a long period of time. Could you plan an unusual vacation, such as a trip to Europe? No, nor any kind of vacation—a vacation takes savings. Could you go to a movie, a theater, a concert? No—this takes savings. Could you buy a book, a phonograph record, a print for your bare walls? No—these take savings. If you have a family, could you send your children through college? No—this takes a small fortune in savings. If you are single, could you get married? No—you have no way to increase your income. If you are an aspiring young writer or artist, could you hold a job, and skimp and go hungry and deny yourself everything—in order to buy time to write or paint? Forget it.

Would you care to go on living in such conditions? Since you are a person able to read, the answer is: No. Yet this is the state to which today's intellectual leaders (who are led by the egalitarians) wish to reduce you.

There is an old saying: "Time is money," which is true enough in an efficient, productive, free society. Today, the urgent thing to realize is that *money is time*. Money is the goods which *you* produced, but did not consume; what your deferred consumption buys for you is time to achieve your goals. Bear this in mind when you consider what inflation is doing to *your* savings.

Let us suppose that you have $1,000 in a savings account. If the [1974] rate of inflation is ten percent (it is actually higher), you lose $100 a year—the government is robbing you of that amount, as surely as if it took the bills out of your pocket. Are you permitted to write that loss off on your tax return? No—the government is pretending that the loss did not occur. But the bank pays you, say, 5 percent interest, i.e., $50 a year—does this make up for half of your loss? No—because the government regards bank interest as "unearned income," and taxes you on it (the amount of the tax depends on your income bracket). Are there any public voices—in this age of "social conscience" —protesting against so vicious an injustice? No.

"Stripped of its academic jargon, the welfare state is nothing more than a mechanism by which governments confiscate the wealth of the productive members of a society to support a wide variety of welfare schemes." [Alan Greenspan, "Gold and Economic Freedom," in my book *Capitalism: The Unknown Ideal*] The major part of this country's wealth belongs to the middle class. The middle class is the heart, the lifeblood, the energy source of a free, industrial economy, i.e., of capitalism; it did not and cannot exist under any other system; it is the product of upward mobility, incompatible with frozen social castes. Do not ask, therefore, for whom the bell of inflation is tolling; it tolls for *you*. It is not at the destruction of a handful of the rich that inflation is aimed (the rich are mostly in the vanguard of the destroyers), but at the middle class. It is the middle class that was wiped out in the German inflation, and the cannibalistic society that permitted it to happen got what it deserved: Hitler.

Inflation is a symptom of the terminal stage of that social disease which is a mixed economy. A mixed economy (as I have said many, many times) is an invalid, unstable, unworkable system which leads to one of two endings: either a return to freedom or a collapse into dictatorship. In the face of an approaching disaster, what is the attitude of most of our public leaders? Politics as usual, evasion as usual, moral cowardice as usual.

In view of what they hear from the experts, the people cannot be blamed for their ignorance and their helpless confusion. If an average housewife struggles with her incomprehensibly shrinking budget and sees a tycoon in a resplendent limousine, she might well think that just one of his diamond cuff links would solve all her problems. She has no way of knowing that if all the personal luxuries of all the tycoons were expropriated, it would not feed her family—and millions of other, similar families—for one week; and that the entire country would starve on the first morning of the week to follow. (This is what happened in Chile.) How would she know it if all the voices she hears are telling her that we must soak the rich?

No one tells her that higher taxes imposed on the rich (and the semi-rich) will not come out of their consumption expenditures, but out of their investment capital (i.e., their savings); that such taxes will mean less investment, i.e., less production, fewer jobs, higher prices for scarcer goods; and that by the time the rich have to lower their standard of living, hers will be gone, along with *her* savings and her husband's job—and no power in the world (no *economic* power) will be able to revive the dead industries (there will be no such power left).

Since the men who know it keep silent, they leave the field open to swarms of political demagogues, who cash in on that housewife's despair and bewilderment. They provide her with a scapegoat, the usual one, the easiest to set up: the businessman. When she hears denunciations of "windfall" profits (or "exorbitant" profits, or "unfair" profits), she does not know how to determine what this means, what the size of profits "should" be—and she does not suspect that the demagogues do not know it, either (because no one can determine it, except the free market). It merely confirms her consumption-oriented view of wealth and suggests that she is the victim of somebody's "greed"—which nurtures her ugliest emotions. No one tells her that the businessmen's *profits* are the only protection of her home, her family, her life—and that if the erosion of profits were to force businessmen out of production altogether, the only alternative would be a "nonprofit" industry run by the government; what *this* would mean to the people has been demonstrated amply and conclusively in Soviet Russia.

These are the things which the public urgently needs to know today, but is not being told. The better kinds of politicians do not indulge in business-baiting demagoguery, but they do not fight it; they are afraid to fight it; they merely struggle to appease the demagogues. So do most economists and most businessmen. What do they all fear?

The televised summit conference on inflation gave a clue to the answer. It presented a sorry spectacle of this country's intellectual leadership—and a startling dramatization of the fundamental problem: today's inverted moral priorities.

The representatives of the men who are of greatest importance to this country's production and are most needed today—the businessmen—were quiet, earnest, undemanding, and concerned (a little too selflessly) with the state of the economy as a whole.

The representatives of the men next in importance to production—organized labor—were louder and more self-assertive; but, with the exception of a few demagogues, they assumed the responsibility of concern with national problems.

The representatives of the men who contribute nothing—the welfare recipients, the professional consumerists, the nonproducers, the objects of public charity—were the loudest, the most aggressive, the most self-righteously arrogant and hostile. They made demands, displaying the kind of conventional "selfishness"—the greedy, grasping, grabbing kind—which is usually ascribed to a rich magnate in leftist cartoons. They shouted, screamed, hissed accusations and commands in the tone of conquerors delivering ultimatums to their cowed, vanquished serfs. Their message, in effect, was that the needs of the nonproducers are a first mortgage on the nation and must be met regardless of what happens to the rest of the country. How? They scorned the necessity to think of an answer. The answer was loudly implicit in their manner: Somehow.

Acting as if *need* conferred on their clients a special privilege superseding reality—as if the *needy* had rights denied to the rest of mankind—they flaunted the consumption-oriented, range-of-the-moment, hand-to-mouth mentality that sees economics in terms of hunger, not of production, seeks "fairness" in terms of equalizing the hunger; and stands ready to devour the rest of the country (*this* country, where—according to their own leaders—poverty is not absolute, but "relative").

Nobody (with a very few exceptions) answered them or protested at that conference. Why did the reputable politicians, the economists, the businessmen keep silent in the face of outrageous abuse? Why did they allow the deadly, illiterate nonsense to proliferate without opposition? Why did they listen respectfully, apologetically, "compassionately," and promise more help to egalitarian savages? There is only one power that could paralyze the country's leaders, a power more potent than the power of money, of professional knowledge, even of political force: the power of morality. *This* was what the inverted morality of altruism accomplished, *this* was the kind of moral cowardice, intellectual disintegration, professional dishonesty, and patriotic default it led to in practice, at a time of national emergency.

There is a group of economists who deserved it: the so-called "conservatives" who claim that economics has nothing to do with morality.

28

Hunger and Freedom
by Ayn Rand

This article, a follow-up to "The Inverted Moral Priorities," was published in the next issue of The Ayn Rand Letter, *dated July 29, 1974; again, it was written several months later than this date.*

I hope that my [recent articles] have helped you to see the cannibalistic nature of altruism in action and the extent to which it is devouring this country. But you have not yet heard the whole story.

At a time like the present—when this country is threatened with economic collapse under the burden of supporting millions of nonproductive citizens, and the heavier burden of the parasites-on-parasitism: the welfare-state bureaucracy—a new campaign is being sneaked up on us, softly, tentatively, but insistently: a campaign to load us with the responsibility of feeding the whole world.

No, that campaign does not mean it symbolically or allegorically or oratorically, or in the form of aspirational mush—but literally, officially, permanently, by law and by force. (I do not know which is more evil in this context: those who believe that that mush *is* an idealistic aspiration or those who cash in on it. I am inclined to say: the former.)

An interesting trial balloon was sent up in a column by Anthony Lewis, entitled "The Politics of Hunger" (*The New York Times*, October 24, 1974). It is particularly interesting (and revealing) in its implications, which the columnist, apparently, did not see and does not consider.

In its own journalistic terms, the column is honestly factual: it presents the problem clearly and offers no solution (except in murky hints). It starts with: "On the current trends of population and food production, according to international experts, by 1985 the poor countries of the world would need 85 million tons of grain a year from outside. In a year of bad harvests, the need could be 100 million tons, or even more." And: "Before the problem of moving that much food, there are the questions of how to grow it and pay for it. At today's prices, 100 million tons of cereals would cost something approaching $20 billion. Haiti and Bangladesh and the thirty other food-short countries will not have the foreign exchange to pay for it. Who will?" This, properly, is the first question to ask. (The column does not answer it.)

> That is the scale of the issues facing the World Food Conference in Rome starting Nov. 5. Public discussion of the food problem understandably tends to focus on immediate matters, such as the amount of American aid to hold off imminent mass starvation in South Asia. But the conference is meant to take a longer view, and *that means dealing with the most fundamental issues of population, resources and the wealth of nations.* [Emphasis added.]

It sure does. (No such issues were raised at that conference.)

Mr. Lewis indicates, "State Department officials preparing for the conference seem modestly hopeful of agreed progress in defining the problems"—and lists some of the points they "sketch." One such point reads: "There must be intensified international efforts to increase food production in the less developed countries, for example by scientific improvements in tropical agriculture."

"Scientific improvement" means *technology.* How would they reconcile it with the worldwide assault on science and technology by ecological crusaders, who demand a return to "unspoiled" nature? Those starving populations are certainly living in the midst of "unspoiled," untouched nature. Which fundamental goal are the world-planners going to pursue: production or ecology? And how will the scientists function in countries where science is banned, reason is a hated enemy, and the crudest mystic superstitions rule the people's lives, traditions, and rudimentary culture? What self-respecting scientist would want to work in such conditions—and why should he? Neither the column nor, I am sure, the State Department answers any of these questions.

The paragraph continues: "But for the foreseeable future there will be dependence on imports from a handful of surplus countries, primarily the U.S., Canada, Australia, Argentina, and the Common Market." Ask yourself: What do these countries (with one exception) have in common? Two paragraphs later, Mr. Lewis says that the American delegates expect another conference after the one in Rome, "a negotiating conference among the major grain-exporting countries and the big consistent importers: India, Pakistan, Bangladesh, Japan, the Soviet Union, and China." What do *these* countries (also with one exception) have in common?

The column offers some vague hints about someone's proposal to establish world grain reserves, and to agree on "who should contribute how much . . . in what would amount to an international system of national reserves." (?) There is even an indication of what is the immediate, "practical" goal behind that food conference and what sort of deadly game is being played. "Secretary Kissinger is said by his associates to see the food issue now as a crucial example of the new interdependence of nations."

The game, apparently, is to trick the Arabs into some sort of One-World Economic Order which would enable us to barter our grain for their oil (if they don't outsmart us). And *this* is the sort of lofty purpose for which somebody is willing to sell America's soul, her sovereignty, her freedom, and *your* standard of living. The alleged justification is global need, compassion, altruism. To pragmatists of this kind, altruism is the window dressing, the bait that lures the victims to slaughter.

(This is an interesting example of today's alliance between the "practical" men and the intellectuals—an alliance based on mutual contempt, with each side believing that it is using the other. The "practical" men are willing to adopt any currently fashionable ideology in exchange for some material advantage of the moment. The intellectuals are willing to support any "practical" policy that leads toward their own long-range ideological goals. In this case, the "practical" men want oil; the intellectuals want One World.)

Mr. Lewis seems to see a little further than the "practical" diplomats. He seems to take altruism seriously—and he is pressing for the logical consequences of such international schemes. His concluding paragraph states:

All of the thought on reserve mechanisms, hard as it is, *only touches the surface of the world food problem. Underneath there is the* question of money—the need for the less developed countries to have enough of it so the U.S. and others can go all-out in food production for them. Aid can hardly make a dent in that need. *In the long run there must be real transfers of purchasing power,* and that in turn raises the whole question of the oil producers and their responsibility as well as ours. [Emphasis added.]

And this in turn raises the whole question of what is purchasing power and whether it can be "transferred."

In my [article in *Philosophy: Who Needs It*] on "Egalitarianism and Inflation," I said that money cannot function as money, i.e., as a medium of exchange, unless it is backed by actual, *unconsumed* goods. Mr. Lewis's last paragraph is a nice bit of evidence to support my contention. If money does not have to be backed by goods, why do the less developed countries need it so badly? Why can't their governments print more paper currency? Why are the U.S. and others unable to go all-out in food production, without receiving any payment for it? Why doesn't the need— the desperate need—of the consumers endow them with purchasing power?

Obviously, purchasing power is an attribute of producers, not of consumers. Purchasing power is a consequence of production: it is the power of possessing goods which one can trade for other goods. A *"purchase"* is an exchange of goods (or services) for goods (or services). Any other form of transferring goods from one person to another may belong to many different categories of transactions, but it is *not a purchase.* It may be a gift, a loan, an inheritance, a handout, a fraud, a theft, a robbery, a burglary, an expropriation. In regard to services, however (omitting temporary or occasional acts of friendship, in which the payment is the friend's value), there is only one alternative to trading: unpaid services, i.e., slavery.

How can you "transfer purchasing power" to people who are unwilling or unable to produce? You can transfer your goods to them without payment—by means of one of the transactions listed above—but if you then receive from them the goods which you produced, in payment for the goods which you are now producing, this cannot be designated as a "purchase" even by the sloppiest of today's linguistic usage. And even if we all agreed so to designate it, how long would we be able to continue producing under a system of that kind? How would we accumulate the stock seed of production, i.e., unconsumed goods?

If you are sick (as I am) of hearing such accusations as "Americans represent only 6 percent of the world population, but consume 54 percent of its natural resources," ask the accusers: "How can 6 percent of the world population feed 94 percent of it?" (This is the ultimate intention of all international-feeding schemes.)

But the real question goes deeper than that. The real question lies in those "most fundamental issues of population, resources, and the wealth of nations" which Mr. Lewis mentioned, but did not discuss. *Why* are some nations wealthy and others not? *Why* do some nations produce abundance and others starve? The answer, strangely enough, is contained (implicitly) in Mr. Lewis's column—and one can see it, without any further research, if one accepts his facts as facts (which they are).

Let us go back to the two groups of countries he lists. The "handful of [grain] surplus countries [are] primarily the U.S., Canada, Australia, Argentina, and the Common Market." The "big consistent [grain] importers [are] India, Pakistan, Bangladesh, Japan, the Soviet Union, and China." The surplus countries are semi-free economies, with a century of greater freedom behind them and, in various degrees, some traditional remnants and memories of freedom. (The exception is Argentina, a semi-dictatorship in bad economic shape, but traditionally an agricultural country.) The grain importers, which live under a chronic threat of hunger, are socialist and communist dictatorships. (The exception is Japan, which, however, has never been a free country, and which is geographically unable to develop its agriculture to any significant extent.)

The relevance of two of Mr. Lewis's "fundamental issues" breaks down in the light of his own lists. "Population" and "resources" do not determine "the wealth of nations." The countries of Europe's Common Market are as densely populated as most of the countries on the hunger list. Russia has greater natural resources than the U.S., but they are untouched and unused.

It is the presence of Russia on the hunger list that blasts all modern economic theories out of the realm of serious consideration. Under the inept government of the czars and with the most primitive methods of agriculture, Russia was a major grain exporter. The unusually fertile soil of the Ukraine alone was (and is) capable of feeding the entire world. Whatever natural conditions are required for growing wheat, Russia had (and has) them in overabundance. That Russia should now be on a list of hungry, wheat-begging importers is the most damning indictment of a collectivist economy that reality can offer us.

The simple, *metaphysical* fact—which no man-made wishes or edicts can alter—is that individual freedom is the precondition of human productivity and, therefore, of abundance, and, therefore, of the wealth of nations. The history of mankind bears witness to this fact—particularly, the prosperity explosion of the nineteenth century (the century dominated by capitalism), as against the millennia of stagnant misery under every variant of "democratically" or autocratically controlled economy.

(If you hear it said that that prosperity was caused by an abundance of natural resources, which are now exhausted, remember that similar allegations and dire warnings were voiced by statists from the beginning of the Industrial Revolution, and that they were prompted by the same motives. Furthermore, at the turn of this century, there were voices claiming that all possible forms of industrial production had been discovered and we could expect nothing but general decline. This was said before the invention of the electric light bulb, the automobile, the airplane, the telephone, the telegraph, the movies, radio, television, atomic motors, spaceships, etc.)

The simple, metaphysical fact is that man by nature is not equipped to survive "in nature." His mind is his basic tool of survival, and his mind creates three life-supporting achievements: science, technology, industrial production. Without these, he cannot wrest sufficient sustenance from nature to fill his immediate, physical needs. In the pre-industrial era, population control was accomplished by starvation: a periodic famine, every twenty years, wiped out the surplus population, which the hand plows and hand looms of Europe were unable to feed. The famines were assisted by periodic wars, which tribal rulers waged in order to loot one another's precarious sustenance. The famines (and the world wars) stopped with the coming of the Industrial Revolution—and, in the nineteenth century, the population of Europe rose by over three hundred percent.

Today, as freedom vanishes from an ever larger area of the globe, famine is coming back—mass famine killing off the millions of human beings whom controlled economies are unable to feed.

In the face of a spectacle of this kind, what are we to think of those alleged humanitarians who plead with us for help and compassion, screaming that the horror of mass starvation supersedes all selfish political concerns? Does it?

If a self-respecting American industrialist were to declare that he cannot and will not help the starving because his productive capacity is not unlimited and he has no desire to descend to a Haitian's standard of living—it is easy to imagine the howls of indignation we would hear from today's intellectuals. Why are they practicing a double standard? Why do they scream that the needs of the hungry supersede our lives, freedom, future, and all values—*except* their hatred of capitalism? Why do they ask us to sacrifice everything—while they refuse to sacrifice their power lust or their mental lethargy long enough to discover the cure, *the only cure*, of global starvation?

While you consider these questions, consider also the following facts: contemporary history has demonstrated that the lives of the people, of the broad masses, have not been improved under any collectivist system, but have been reduced to hopeless misery. But there have been profiteers under every such system: the ruling bureaucracy—the parasites-on-parasitism—the wretched handful of pretentious mediocrities who, unable to compete on a free market, extort an unearned "prestige" and a luxurious living from "the sores of the poor and the blood of the rich."

These are the men who would let mankind starve, but will not relinquish their power—*these* are the men to whom the world is being sacrificed—*these*, not the poor brutes of Russia, China, or India who are perishing because the last of their meager earnings has been plundered to support the nuclear armaments of their rulers.

It is to *these rulers* that we are now asked to sacrifice the last, best hope on earth: the United States of America.

Such is the nature of altruism.

29

How *Not* to Fight Against Socialized Medicine
by Ayn Rand

In the spring of 1962, some two hundred New Jersey doctors, led by Dr. J. Bruce Henriksen, signed a resolution of protest against the Kennedy Administration's King-Anderson bill, which was the precursor of President Johnson's Medicare program. The doctors stated that they would treat the indigent aged without charge, but would not treat anyone whose medical care was financed under the Kennedy plan. The King-Anderson bill was soon afterwards defeated in Congress.

The following is a condensed version of a talk delivered on February 6, 1963 at a meeting of the Ocean County Medical Society of New Jersey, to which Dr. Henriksen and his group belonged. These remarks were published in The Objectivist Newsletter, *March 1963.*

I am happy to have this opportunity to express my admiration for Dr. Henriksen and the group of doctors who signed his resolution.

Dr. Henriksen and his group took a heroic stand. The storm of vicious denunciations unleashed against them at the time showed that they had delivered a dangerous blow to the welfare-statists. More than any other single factor, it was Dr. Henriksen's group that demonstrated to the public the real nature of the issue, prevented the passage of the King-Anderson bill and saved this country from socialized medicine—so far.

Their action was an eloquent example of the fact that only a strong, uncompromising stand—a stand of *moral* self-confidence, on clear-cut, consistent principles—can win.

But there are grave danger signs that the medical profession as a whole—like every other group today—will ignore that example and pursue the usual modern policy of caution and compromise. Such a policy is worse than futile: it assists and promotes the victory of one's own enemies. The battle is not over. The King-Anderson bill will be brought up again, and if the doctors are defeated, they will be defeated by their own hand, or rather: by their own mind.

I want, therefore, to make certain suggestions to the medical profession—on the subject of how *not* to fight against socialized medicine.

The majority of people in this country—and in the world—do not want to adopt socialism; yet it is growing. It is growing because its victims concede its basic moral premises. Without challenging these premises, one cannot win.

The strategy of the Kennedy administration, and of all welfare-statists, consists of attempts to make people accept certain intellectual "package deals," without letting them identify and differentiate the various elements—and equivocations—involved. The deadliest of such "package deals" is the attempt to make people accept the collectivist-altruist principle of self-immolation under the guise of mere kindness, generosity, or charity. It is done by hammering into people's minds the idea that *need* supersedes all rights—that the need of some men is a first mortgage on the lives of others—and that everything should be sacrificed to the undefined, undefinable grab bag known as "*the public interest.*"

Doctors have no chance to win if they concede that idea and help their enemies to propagate it.

Yet the ideological policy of most spokesmen for the medical profession—such as the A.M.A.—is as permeated by the collectivist-altruist spirit as the pronouncements of the welfare-statists. The doctors' spokesmen declare, in net effect, that selfless service to their patients is the doctors' only goal, that concern for the needy is their only motive, and that "the public interest" is the only justification of their battle.

The sole difference is this: the voices of the welfare-statists are brazenly, self-righteously overbearing—while the voices of the doctors' spokesmen are guiltily, evasively apologetic.

Whom can one expect the people to believe and to follow?

People can always sense guilt, insincerity, hypocrisy. The lack of a morally righteous tone, the absence of moral certainty, have a disastrous effect on an audience—an effect which is not improved by the triviality of the arguments over political minutiae. And the terrible thing is that the doctors' spokesmen give an impression of guilty evasiveness while *the right is on their side*. They do it by being afraid to assert their rights.

They are afraid of it because they do not believe that they possess any rights—because they have conceded the enemy's premises—because they have no moral base, no intellectual guide lines, no ideology, no defense.

Consider, for instance, the outcome of the Canadian doctors' struggle in Saskatchewan. The doctors had gone on strike [in 1962] against the full-scale socialized medicine instituted by the provincial government. They won the battle—and lost the war; in exchange for a few superficial concessions, they surrendered the principle for which they had been fighting: to permit no socialized medicine in the Western hemisphere.

They surrendered even though the overwhelming sympathy and support of the Canadian people were on their side (except for *the intellectuals* and the labor unions). They were defeated not by the power of the socialists, but by the gaping holes in their own ideological armor.

They had been fighting, properly, in the name of individual rights, against the enslavement of medicine by totalitarian-statist controls. Then, under the pressure of the usual intellectual lynching, under the hysterical, collectivist charges of "antisocial selfishness and greed," they made a shocking change in their stand. Declaring, in effect, that their rebellion was not directed against socialized medicine as such, but against the high-handed, arbitrary manner in which the government had put it over, their spokesmen began to argue that the government plan did not represent "the will of the people." The ideological kiss of death was a statement by Dr. Dalgleish, the strikers' leader, who declared that if a *plebiscite* were taken and the people voted for it, the doctors would accept socialized medicine.

Could they deserve to win after that? They could not and did not.

Consider the full meaning of Dr. Dalgleish's statement. It meant the total repudiation of individual rights and the acceptance of unlimited majority rule, of the collectivist doctrine that the people's vote may dispose of an individual in any way it pleases. Instead of a battle for the integrity of a doctor's professional judgment and practice, it became a battle over *who* should violate his integrity. Instead of a battle against the enslavement of medicine, it became a battle over *who* should enslave it. Instead of a battle for freedom, it became a battle over a choice of masters. Instead of a moral crusade, it became a petty quarrel over political technicalities.

This led to the ludicrous spectacle of the alleged individualists arguing for democratic mob rule, and the socialists righteously upholding the parliamentary form of government.

Those who doubt the power of ideas should note the fact that the doctors' surrender took place five days after Dr. Dalgleish's statement.

The text of the agreement reached between the doctors and the government contained the following horrifying sentence: "The doctors fear that if the government becomes their only source of income they are in danger of becoming servants of the state and not *servants of their patients.*" [Emphasis added.]

A more abject statement of self-abnegation could not be hoped for or extorted by the most extreme collectivist.

No self-respecting labor union would declare that its members are "*servants*" of their employers. It took so-called "conservatives" to declare that professional men—and of so responsible, so demanding, so unusually skilled a profession as medicine—are the "servants" of their patients or of anyone who pays them.

The concept of "service" has been turned into a collectivist "package deal" by means of a crude equivocation and a cruder evasion. In the language of economics, the word "service" means *work* offered for trade on a free market, to be paid for by those who choose to buy it. In a free society, men deal with one another by voluntary, uncoerced exchange, by mutual consent to mutual profit, each man pursuing his own rational self-interest, none sacrificing himself or others; and all values—whether goods or services—are *traded*, not given away.

This is the opposite of what the word "service" means in the language of altruist ethics: to an altruist, "service" means unrewarded, self-sacrificial, unilateral *giving*, while receiving nothing in return. It is this sort of selfless "service" to "society" that collectivists demand of all men.

One of the grotesque phenomena of the twentieth century is the fact that the "package deal" of "service" is most vociferously propagated by the "conservatives." Intellectually bankrupt, possessing no political philosophy, no direction, no goal, but clinging desperately to the ethics of altruism, such "conservatives" rest their case on a cheap equivocation: they proclaim that "service" to others (to one's customers or clients or patients or "consumers" in general) is the motive power and the moral justification of a free society—and evade the question of whether such "services" are or are not to be paid for.

But if "service" to the "consumers" is our primary goal, why should these masters pay us or grant us any rights? Why shouldn't they dictate the terms and conditions of our work?

If socialized medicine comes to the United States, it is such "conservatives" that the doctors would have to thank for it, as well as their own spokesmen who recklessly play with an intellectual poison of that kind.

Doctors are *not* the servants of their patients. No free man is a "servant" of those he deals with. Doctors are *traders*, like everyone else in a free society—and they should bear that title proudly, considering the crucial importance of the services they offer.

The pursuit of his own productive career is—and, morally, should be—the primary goal of a doctor's work, as it is the primary goal of any self-respecting, productive man. But there is no clash of interests among rational men in a free society, and there is no clash of interests between doctors and patients. In pursuing his own career, a doctor does have to do his best for the welfare of his patients. This relationship, however, cannot be reversed: one cannot sacrifice the doctor's interests, desires, and freedom to whatever the patients (or their politicians) might deem to be their own "welfare."

Many doctors know this, but are afraid to assert their rights, because they dare not challenge the morality of altruism, neither in the public's mind nor in their own. Others are collectivists at heart, who believe that socialized medicine is morally right and who feel guilty while opposing it. Still others are so cynically embittered that they believe that the whole country consists of fools or parasites eager to get something for nothing—that morality and justice are futile—that ideas are impotent—that the cause of freedom is doomed—and that the doctors' only chance lies in borrowing the enemy's arguments and gaining a brief span of borrowed time.

This last is usually regarded as the "practical" attitude for "conservatives."

But nobody is as naïve as a cynic, and nothing is as impractical as the attempt to win by conceding the enemy's premises. How many defeats and disasters will collectivism's victims have to witness before they become convinced of it?

In any issue, it is the most consistent of the adversaries who wins. One cannot win on the enemy's premises, because *he* is then the more consistent, and all of one's efforts serve only to propagate *his* principles.

Most people in this country are not moochers who seek the unearned, not even today. But if all their intellectual leaders *and the doctors themselves* tell them that doctors are only their "selfless servants," they will feel justified in expecting and demanding unearned services.

When a politician tells them that they are entitled to the unearned, they are wise enough to suspect his motives; but when the proposed victim, the doctor, says it too, they feel that socialization is safe.

If you are afraid of people's irrationality, you will not protect yourself by assuring them that their irrational notions are right.

The advocates of "Medicare" admit that their purpose is not help to the needy, the sick, or the aged. Their purpose is to spare people "the embarrassment" of a means test—that is, to establish the principle and precedent that some people are entitled to the unrewarded services of others, not as charity, but as a *right*.

Can you placate, conciliate, temporize, or compromise with a principle of that kind?

As doctors, what would you say if someone told you that you must not try to *cure* a deadly disease—you must give it *some* chance—you must reach a "compromise" with cancer or with coronary thrombosis or with leprosy? You would answer that it is a battle of life or death. The same is true of your political battle.

Would you follow the advice of someone who told you that you must fight tuberculosis by confining the treatment to its symptoms—that you must treat the cough, the high temperature, the loss of weight—but must refuse to consider or to touch its cause, the germs in the patient's lungs, in order not to antagonize the germs?

Do not adopt such a course in politics. The principle—and the consequences—are the same. It *is* a battle of life or death.

30

Medicine: The Death of a Profession
by Leonard Peikoff

This lecture was delivered at the Ford Hall Forum on April 14, 1985, more than twenty years after Ayn Rand's talk to the New Jersey doctors, and was published in The Objectivist Forum, *April–June 1985. I wish to acknowledge the invaluable assistance given to me in the preparation of this lecture by my brother, Dr. Michael Peikoff, who is a surgeon in Nevada.*

One day, when you are out of town on a business trip, you wake up with a cough, muscle aches, chills, and a high fever. You do not know what it is, you start to panic, but you do know one action to take: you call a doctor. He conducts a physical exam, takes a history, administers lab tests, narrows down the possibilities; within hours, he reaches a diagnosis of pneumonia and prescribes a course of treatment, including antibiotics. Soon you begin to respond, you relax, the crisis is over. Or: you are getting out of your car, you fall and break your leg. It is a disaster, but you remain calm, because you can utter one sentence to your wife: "Call the doctor." He proceeds to examine your leg for nerve and blood-vessel injury, he takes X rays, reduces the fracture, puts on a cast; the disaster has faded into a mere inconvenience, and you resume your normal life. Or: your child comes home from school with a stabbing pain in the abdomen. There is only one hope: you call the doctor. He performs an appendectomy—the child recovers.

We take all this completely for granted, as though modern drugs, modern hospitals, and modern doctors were facts of nature, which always had been there and which always will be there. Many people today take for granted not only the simpler kinds of medical intervention, but even the wonder cures and wonder treatments that the medical profession has painstakingly devised—like the latest radiation therapy for breast cancer, or the intricate delicacy of modern brain surgery, or such a breathtaking achievement as the artificial-heart implants performed by Dr. William C. DeVries. Most of us expect that the doctors will go on accomplishing such feats routinely, steadily removing pain and thus enhancing the quality of our life, while adding ever more years to its quantity.

America's medical system is the envy of the globe. The rich from every other country, when they get sick, do not head for Moscow or Stockholm or even London anymore; they come here. And in some way, despite the many public complaints against the medical profession, we all know this fact; we know how good our doctors are, and how much we depend on their knowledge, skill, and dedication. Suppose you had to go on a six-month ocean voyage with no stops in port, with ample provisions and sailors, but with only one additional profession represented on board, and you could decide which it would be. Would you ask for your lawyer to come along? your accountant? your congressman? Would you dare even to ask for your favorite movie star? Or would you say: "Bring a doctor. What if something happens?" The terror of having no answer to this question is precisely what the medical profession saves us from.

I am not saying that all doctors are perfect—they are not; or that they all have a good bedside manner—they do not; or that the profession is free from flaws—like every other group today, the medical profession has its share of errors, deficiencies, weaknesses. But these are not my subject tonight, and they do not alter two facts: that our doctors, whatever their failings, do give us the highest caliber health care in world history—and that they live a grueling existence in order to do so.

I come from a medical family, and I can tell you what a doctor's life is like. Most of them study nonstop for years in medical school and then work nonstop until they die. My own father, who was a surgeon, operated daily from 7 A.M. until noon and then made hospital rounds; from 2 to 6 P.M., he held office hours. When he came home for dinner, if he did, the phone never stopped ringing—it was nurses asking instructions, or doctors discussing emergency cases, or patients presenting symptoms. When he got the chance, usually late at night or on Sundays after rounds, he would read medical journals (or write for them), to keep abreast of the latest research. My father was not an exception. This is how most doctors, in any branch of medicine, live, and how they work.

The profession imposes not only killing hours, but also continuous tension: doctors deal all the time with *crisis*—with accidents, diseases, trauma, disaster, the imminence of death. Even when an ailment is not a mortal threat, the patient often fears that it is, and he must be reassured, nursed through the terror, even counseled psychologically by the physician. The pressure on the doctor never lets up. If he wants to escape even for the space of a single dinner on the town, chances are that he cannot: he will probably get beeped and have to rush to the emergency room just as the entrée is being served.

The doctor not only has to live and work in such a pressure cooker, he has to *think* all the time—clearly, objectively, scientifically. Medicine is a field that requires a vast body of specialized theoretical knowledge; to apply it properly to particular cases, the doctor must regularly make delicate, excruciatingly complex decisions. Medical treatment is not usually a cut-and-dried affair, involving a simple, self-evident course of action; it requires the balancing of countless variables; it requires clinical judgment. And the doctor must not only exercise such judgment— he must do it fast; typically, he has to act *now*. He cannot petition the court or his client or any employer for a postponement. He faces daily, hourly, the merciless timetable of nature itself.

What I personally admire most about doctors is the fact that they live this kind of life not out of any desire for altruistic self-sacrifice, but *selfishly*—which is the only thing that enables them to survive it. They love the field, most of them; they find the work a fascinating challenge in applied science. They are proud men, most of them, with an earned pride in their ability to observe, evaluate, act, cure. And, to their credit, they expect to be rewarded materially for their skill; they want to make a good living, which is the least men can offer them in payment for their achievements. They make that living, as a rule, by standing on their own, not as cogs in some faceless, government-subsidized enterprise, but as entrepreneurs in private practice. The doctors are among the last of the capitalist breed left in this country. They are among the last of the individualists that once populated this great nation.

If I knew nothing about today's world but the nature of our politicians and the philosophy represented by the medical profession, I would predict an inevitable, catastrophic clash between the two: between the government and the doctors. On purely theoretical grounds, I would predict the destruction of the doctors by the government, which in every field now protects and rewards the exact opposite of thought, effort, and achievement.

This catastrophe is actually taking place. It will affect your future as well as that of the doctors.

To understand what is happening in medicine today, we must go back to the beginning, which in this case is 1965, the year when Medicare and Medicaid were finally pushed through Congress by Lyndon Johnson. Medicare covers most of the medical expenses of those over sixty-five, whatever their income. Medicaid is a supplemental program for the poor of any age.

Those of us who opposed the Johnson plan argued at the time that government intervention in medicine is immoral in principle and would be disastrous in practice. No man, we claimed, has a *right* to medical care; if he cannot pay for what he needs, then he must depend on voluntary charity. Government financing of medical expenses, we argued, even if it is for only a fraction of the population, necessarily means eventual enslavement of the doctors and, as a result, a profound deterioration in the quality of medical care for everyone, including the aged and the poor.

The proponents of Medicare were unmoved by any arguments. Altruistic service to the needy, they said, is man's duty. It is degrading, they said, for the elderly to be dependent on private charity; a "means test" is incompatible with human dignity. Besides, they added, the government would not dream of asking for any control over the doctors or over their methods of patient care. All we want the state to do, they said, is pay the bills.

It is now twenty years later. Let us look at what actually happened.

The first result of the new programs should have been self-evident. Suppose we apply the same principle to nutrition. Suppose President Johnson had said: "It is unfair for you to have to pay for your own food and restaurant bills. Men have a right to eat. Washington, therefore, will pick up the tab." Can you project the results? Can you imagine the eating binges, the sudden mania for dining out, the soaring demand for baked peacock tongues and other gourmet delicacies? Do you see Lutèce and the "21" Club becoming nationally franchised and starting to outdraw McDonald's? Why not? The eaters do not have to pay for it. And the food industry, including its most sincere members, is ecstatic; now that the money is pouring from Washington into the grocery chains and the restaurants, they can give every customer the kind of luxury treatment once reserved for millionaires. Everybody is happy—except that expenditure on food becomes so great a percentage of our GNP, and the drain on the federal treasury becomes so ominous, that every other industry starts to protest and soon even the bureaucrats begin to panic.

This is what happened to medical spending in the United States. The patients covered by the new programs no longer had to pay much attention to cost—that was the whole purpose of the programs. And the health-care professionals at first were generally delighted. Now, many of them felt, the sky is the limit, and they proceeded to build hospitals, purchase equipment, and administer tests accordingly. Medical expenditures in the U.S. were 4.3% of GNP in 1952; today they are about 11% and still rising. Medicare expenditures doubled from 1974 to 1979, doubled again by 1984, and are expected to double again by 1991, at which time, according to current estimates, the Medicare program will be bankrupt. Something, the government recognized, has to be done; we are going broke because of the insatiable demand for medical care.

The government did not decide to cancel its programs and return to a free market in medicine—when are disastrous government programs ever canceled? Instead, it did what governments always do: it decided to keep the programs but impose rigid controls on them. The first step was a campaign to force hospitals not to spend much on Medicare patients, no matter what the effects on the health of those patients.

We will no longer, officials said, pay hospitals a fee for each service they render a Medicare patient. That method of payment, they said, simply encourages spending. Instead, we will pay according to a new principle, DRGs. DRGs represent the first major assault by the government against the doctors and their patients. It is not yet the strangulation of the medical profession. But it *is* the official dropping of the noose around their necks.

DRG means "diagnosis-related group." According to this approach, the government has divided all ailments into 468 possible diagnoses, and has set in advance a fixed, arbitrary fee for each: it will pay a hospital only what it claims is the *average cost* of the ailment. For example, for a Medicare patient in the Western Mountain region who is admitted to a hospital with a heart attack and finally recovers enough to go home, the government now pays the hospital exactly $5,094—no more and no less. And it pays this amount *no matter what the hospital does for the patient*, no matter how long his stay or how short, no matter how many services he requires or how few. If the patient costs the hospital more than the government payment, the hospital loses money on him. If he costs less, the hospital makes a profit.

Here is a fictional story now in process of becoming reality around the country. A man suffering from severe chest pains is taken by ambulance to the hospital. He receives certain standard tests, including a cardiogram, then is moved to the Intensive Care Unit, where his vital signs are continuously monitored. His doctor thinks that in this instance a further test, an angiogram, is urgently indicated; this test would outline the arteries of the heart and indicate if one is about to close off, an event that could be fatal. The hospital administrator protests: "An angiogram is expensive. It costs up to $1,000, about 20% of our total fee for this man, and who knows what else he's still going to cost us? You can't prove this test is necessary. Let's wait and see." The test is not given. Maybe the patient lives, maybe not. Several days later, the administrator comes to the doctor: "You've got to get this man out of the ICU. It's costing almost $800 per day, and he's been here now for five days. What with everything else, we've already spent almost the whole payment we get for him." The doctor thinks that the patient still desperately needs the specialized nursing available only in the ICU. The administrator overrules him. "There's an area of judgment here," he says. "We'll just have to take a bit of a chance on this case."

Or: the doctor decides that the patient is an excellent candidate for remedial heart surgery. A bypass operation, he thinks, would probably prolong the man's life considerably while relieving him of pain. But the man, after all, is elderly and the operation would involve a lengthy hospital stay. "Let's try a more conservative treatment first," the administrator says, "let's give him some medication and wait and see." Again, maybe the patient lives, maybe not.

Let us say that he lives and is moved to a bed in the regular ward. He still feels very weak, and the doctor does not think he is anywhere near ready to be discharged. But the $5,094 has long since been spent, and the administrator starts to wonder aloud: "Maybe this man could manage somehow at home. In any event, he's eating us alive—get him out of here." Maybe the patient will survive at home, maybe not.

Do you see the thrust of the system? If the hospital does relatively little for the patient, it makes money; if it provides an extensive range of services, it loses heavily. The best case from its viewpoint is for the patient to die right after admission: the hospital still gets the full fee. The worst case is for him to survive with complications and require a lengthy stay—which is why some hospitals are refusing to admit patients they fear will linger on too long.

I do not mean to suggest that our hospitals are now callously withholding urgently needed treatment from Medicare patients. Today's hospitals and doctors do have integrity; most are continuing to do their best for the patient. The point is that they have to do it within the DRG constraints. The issue is not simply: treat the patient or let him die. The issue is: treat him how? At what cost? With what range of services, specialists, and equipment? With what degree of safety or of risk? This is the area where there is enormous room for alternatives in the quality of medical treatment. And this is the area that is now in the process of being slashed across the board for Medicare patients, the very people singled out by the liberals in the 1960s as needing better medical care.

To revert to our nutrition analogy: it is as though the government socialized eating out, paying restaurants only what it computed to be the average cost per meal. There would then be a powerful incentive for restaurants to cut corners in every imaginable way—to serve only the cheapest foods in the smallest amounts in the cheesiest settings. What do you think would happen to the nation's eaters—*and its chefs*—under such a setup? How long could the chefs preserve their dedication to preparing haute cuisine, when the restaurant owners, in self-preservation, were forced to fight them at every step and to demand junk food instead?

There is now a new and deadly pressure on the doctors, which continuously threatens the independence and integrity of their medical judgment: the pressure to cave in to arbitrary DRG economies, while blanking out the effects on the patient.

In some places, hospitals are offering special financial incentives to the physician whose expenditure per patient averages out to be relatively low. For example, the hospital might subsidize such a doctor's office rent or purchase new equipment for him. On the other hand, a doctor who insists on quality care for his Medicare patients and thereby drives up costs is likely to incur the hospital's displeasure. In the extreme case, the doctor risks being denied staff privileges, which means cutting off his major source of livelihood. Thanks to DRGs, a new conflict is in the offing, just starting to take shape: the patient *vs.* the hospital. To put it another way, the conflict is: doctors *vs.* hospitals—doctors fighting a rearguard action to maintain standards against hospitals that are forced by the government to become cost-cutting ogres. How would you like to practice a profession in which half your mind is devoted to healing the patient, while the other half is trying to appease a hospital administrator who himself is trying to appease some official in Washington?

Medicare patients are not a small group. Because of their age, they constitute a significant part of most doctors' practice. Medicare patients now make up about fifty percent of all hospital admissions in the U.S.

The defenders of DRGs answer all criticisms by saying that costs simply must be cut. Even under complete capitalism, they say, doctors could not give unlimited treatment to every patient. This is true, but it ignores two crucial facts. (1) It is *because* of government programs that medical prices have soared to the point of being out of reach for masses of patients. This was not true in the days of private medicine. The average American a generation ago could afford quality, in medicine as in every other area of life, without courting bankruptcy. (2) Even if a patient could not afford it, at least, in the pre-welfare-state era, he was told the truth: as a rule, he was told about the treatment options available, and it was up to him, in consultation with his doctor, to weigh the possibilities and decide how to cut costs. But under the present system, the hospital not only has to cut services drastically—it is to its interest to conceal this fact from the patient. If he or his family ever learns that the angiogram he is not going to have, or the heart surgery, would make all the difference to the outcome of his case, he would immediately protest, insist on the service, even threaten to launch a malpractice suit. The system is rigged to squeezing every drop of quality out of medical care, so long as the patient does not understand what is happening. The patient does not know medicine; he relies on the doctor's integrity to tell him what services are available and necessary in his case—yet, increasingly, the hospitals must try to batter down that integrity. They must try to make the doctor keep silent and not tell the patient the full truth.

The Medicare patient is no longer a free man to be accorded dignity and respect, but a puppet on the dole, to be manipulated accordingly—while the doctor is being transformed from a sovereign professional into a mere appendage and accessory, a helpless tool in a government-orchestrated campaign of shoddy quality and deception.

The government's takeover of medical practice is not confined to public patients; it is starting to extend into the private sector as well. This brings me to the HMOs, which are now mushrooming all over the country.

HMO means "health-maintenance organization." It could also have been called BBM, for "bargain-basement medicine." In this setup, a group of doctors, perhaps with their own hospital, offers prepaid, all-inclusive medical care at a cheap rate. For a fixed payment in advance, a payment substantially less than a regular doctor would charge, the patient is guaranteed virtually complete coverage of his medical costs, no matter what they are. The principle here is the same as that of the DRG system: if the patient's costs exceed his payment, the HMO loses money on him; if not, it makes a profit.

Although HMOs are privately owned, the spread of these organizations is wholly caused by government. There were very few HMOs in the days of private medicine. As part of the government's campaign to lower the cost of medical care, however, Washington has decided to throw its immense weight behind HMOs, even going so far as to advertise nationally on their behalf and to give them direct financial subsidies.

How do HMOs achieve their low rates? In essence, by the DRG method—the method of curtailing services. In this case, however, the cuts in quality are more sweeping, inasmuch as the HMO embraces every aspect of medical care, not merely hospital costs. As a rule, HMO doctors do not have personal patients, nor does the patient have a choice of doctors or even necessarily see the same one twice—that is too expensive. The patient sees whoever is on duty when he shows up; the doctor gives up the luxury of following a case from beginning to end. Nor does the doctor have much time to spend with a given patient—HMOs are generally understaffed to save money; typically, there are long waiting lines of patients. Further, the doctor must obtain prior authorization of any significant expenditure from a highly cost-conscious administrator. The doctor may detect a possible abdominal tumor and request a CAT scan—in effect, an exquisitely detailed, 3-D X ray. But if the administrator says to him: "It costs a lot. I don't think it's necessary," the doctor is helpless. Or he may find that the patient has an aneurysm, a weakening of an artery that is like a time bomb waiting to go off, and he may want to operate to remove it. But the administrator can reply: "These cases often go years without rupturing. Let's wait awhile." Like the doctor under DRGs, the HMO doctor ultimately has to obey: he either keeps his costs within the dictated parameters, or he is out of work.

The kind of doctor who is willing or eager to practice medicine under these conditions represents a new breed, new at least in quantity. There is a generation of utterly unambitious young doctors growing up today, especially conspicuous in the HMOs, doctors who are the opposite of the old-fashioned physician in private practice—doctors who want to *escape* the responsibility of independent thought and judgment, and who are prepared to abandon the prospect of a large income or a private practice in order to achieve this end. These doctors do not mind the forfeit of their professional autonomy to the HMO administrator. They do not object to practicing cut-rate medicine with faceless patients on an assembly-line basis, so long as they themselves can escape blame for any bad results and cover their own tracks. These are the new bureaucratic doctors, the MDs with the mentality, and the fundamental indifference to their job, of the typical post-office clerk.

I hasten to add that there *are* better doctors in the HMOs (and that some HMOs are better than others). As a rule, however, these better doctors are mercilessly exploited. Being conscientious, they put in longer hours than necessary, trying to make up for the chronic understaffing. They do not give in meekly to arbitrary decrees on cost, but fight the administrator when they feel their own judgment is right. Increasingly, their professional life becomes a series of such fights, which makes them the heavies, hard to get along with and guilty of costing the HMO money—while their lesser colleagues capitulate to the system, do as they are told, and take things easy. Time after time, the better men step in to bail out such colleagues, struggling to correct their errors, clean up their messes, rescue their patients. At a certain point, however, the better doctors get fed up.

An HMO doctor in California, a qualified internist and a highly conscientious woman, told me the following story. "I was looking through a pile of cardiograms one day," she said, "and I saw one that was clearly abnormal. I knew that the man should be taken by ambulance to the emergency room for retesting and possible hospitalization. Then I thought: it's late Friday afternoon, and it's going to take an hour and a half, and I'm not being paid for the extra work, and who will know if I wait until Monday? I was tempted for a minute to drop the whole thing and go home, but then the remnants of my conscience made me get up wearily and telephone the patient. This sort of thing," she concluded, "happens all the time and not just to me, and often the doctor does simply look the other way." Do you see what happens under a system in which the doctor is penalized for his virtue or, at the least, is deprived of any incentive, spiritual or material, including pride in his judgment and payment for his work? Would you like your cardiogram to be in a pile on this new breed's desk? Yours is next—all of ours are.

The debased standards inherent in government medicine are now spreading to the whole of medical practice in the United States. The new medicine is not restricted to Medicare patients or to HMO members; it is soon going to engulf private doctors as well, even when they see their own private, paying patients. There are many reasons for this. The most obvious is the pressure from the health-insurance companies, such as Blue Cross and Blue Shield. Hospitals now are charging higher rates to private patients in order to recoup their losses from Medicare cases. As a result, the private insurance companies are demanding that a DRG-type system be imposed uniformly, on all patients. They want private insurance policies from now on to pay only according to arbitrary, preset rates, just as Medicare does now, which would put the total of medicine in this country—all patients, all doctors, all ailments—into the same category as the heart-attack patient we discussed earlier. His fate would become everyone's, and the standards of American medicine would simply collapse.

If this demand of the insurance companies surprises you, remember that there are no truly private health-insurance companies in the U.S. today. What we have in this field is a government-protected, government-regulated cartel. And what the cartel wants is not more freedom, but more money through government favors, including stiffer government controls over medical costs.

The end of the Medicare road is complete socialized medicine.

Now you can see the absurdity of the claim that state payment of medical bills will not affect the freedom of physicians or the quality of patient care. State funding necessarily affects and corrupts every private service. Communism, in fact, is essentially nothing more than state funding. The Soviets pretty much leave doctors and everyone else free to dream or fantasize within their own skulls; all the government does is fund everything, i.e., take over the physical means of every citizen's existence. The enslavement of the country, and thus the collapse of all standards, follows as a matter of course.

Now let me backtrack to answer an objection. I have been maintaining that the cause of our soaring health-care costs is government funding of medical care. Many observers, however, claim that the cause is the rapid advances in medical technology, such as CAT scanners or the latest, most sophisticated disease-detecting instruments, the magnetic resonance imaging or MRI machines. These people want to limit such technology or even abolish it.

Technology by itself does *not* drive up costs; it generally reduces costs as it improves the quality of life. The normal pattern, exemplified by the automobile and computer industries, is that a new invention is expensive at first, so that only a few can afford it. But inventors and businessmen persevere, aiming for the profits that come from a mass market. Eventually, they discover cheaper and better methods of production. Gradually, costs come down until the general population can afford to buy. No one is bankrupted, everyone gains.

The source of today's national bankruptcy in the field of medicine is not technology, but technology injected into the field by government decree, apart from supply and demand. State-of-the-art medical treatment—including new inventions or procedures that are still prohibitively expensive, such as liver transplants and long-term kidney dialyses—is now being financed by the government for the total population in the name of egalitarianism. The result is the unbelievable expenditures, far beyond most people's capacity to afford, which are made routinely in our hospitals. These expenditures are particularly evident in regard to the terminally ill, who almost always fall under the umbrella of some government-supported insurance program. It has been estimated that 1% of our GNP is now spent on the *dying* in their last *weeks* of life. Or: *one-half* of a man's lifetime medical expenses occur now in the last *six months* of his life.

In a free society, you personally would have to make a choice: do you want to defer consumption, cancel vacations, forgo pleasures year after year, so as to extend your life in the ICU by a few months at the end? If you do, no one would interfere under capitalism. You could hoard your cash and then have a glorious spree in the hospital as you die. I would not care to do this. It does not bother me that some billionaire can live months longer than I by using machinery that I cannot begin to afford. I would rather be able to make ends meet, enjoy my life, and die a bit sooner. But in a free society, you are not bound by my decision; each man makes and finances his own choice. The moral principle here is clear-cut: a man has a right to act to sustain his life, but no right to loot others in the process. If he cannot afford some science-fiction cure, he must learn to accept the facts of reality and make the best of it.

In a free society, the few who could afford costly discoveries would, by the normal mechanism, help to bring the costs down. Gradually, more and more of us could afford more and more of the new technology, and there would be no health-cost crisis at all. Everyone would benefit, no one would be crushed. The terminally ill would not be robbing everyone else of his life, as is happening now, thanks to government intervention; the elderly would not be devouring the substance of the young.

You may wonder if I have now covered, at least in essence, the ways in which government is wrecking the practice of medicine. I have barely scratched the surface. For example, I have not even mentioned the formal introduction of the principle of collectivism into medical practice—of committee-medicine as against individual judgment. This is exemplified by the flourishing PROs in our hospitals, the Professional Review Organizations, which act to oversee and strengthen the various DRG controls.

PROs are committees of doctors and nurses established by the government to monitor the treatment of Medicare patients, and especially to cut its cost—committees with substantial power to enforce their arbitrary judgments on any dissenting doctor. These committees are the equivalent in the Medicare system of the HMO administrators, and have potentially the same kind of all-encompassing power to forbid hospital stays (along with the associated tests and surgical procedures), even when the admitting doctor thinks they are required.

Nor have I yet mentioned CONs, or Certificates of Need. Since the government regards anything new in the field of medicine as potentially expensive, a hospital today is prohibited from growing in any respect, whether we speak of more beds or new technology, unless the administrator can prove "need" to some official. Since "need" in this context is undefined and unprovable, the operative criterion is not "need" at all, but pull, political pull. Under this program, the government [in 1984] denied Sloan-Kettering, the famous New York cancer hospital, permission to purchase an MRI machine, because another New York hospital already had one. Later, the government backed down in the face of the resulting public uproar. But what about the hospitals that do not enjoy such fame or contacts, and that are inexplicably denied the right to acquire a crucial diagnostic tool? So far, the freeze on them is only partly effective. Doctors are still allowed to purchase new equipment for their own offices, which hospital patients now often use. But the government is fighting to close this loophole; it is on the verge of decreeing that private doctors in their own offices out of their own funds cannot purchase new equipment without a government certificate of "need." Here again you can see how *your* care will be affected, even if you are not a Medicare patient. If your doctor or hospital is not allowed to have the equipment, you cannot benefit from it either. It isn't there. It doesn't exist.

Nor have I mentioned the hundreds of other government interventions in medicine. In the space of a year, state legislatures alone recently enacted almost three hundred pieces of health-cost containment legislation. One hospital in New York now reports to ninety-nine separate regulatory agencies.

And I have not yet touched on what is perhaps the worst crisis in the field of medicine today, the one most demoralizing to the doctors: the *malpractice* crisis. This crisis illustrates dramatically, in yet another form, the lethal effects of government intervention in the field of medicine.

Medical malpractice suits have trebled in the past decade. There are now [1985] about sixteen lawsuits for every hundred doctors. In addition, awards to plaintiffs average around $330,000 and are steadily climbing. The effect of this situation on physicians is unspeakable. First, I have been told, there is fear, chronic fear, the terror of the next attorney's letter in the mail. Then there is the agony of drawn-out legal harassment, including endless depositions and a protracted trial. There is the exhaustion of feeling that one lives in a malevolent universe, in which every patient is a potential enemy. Always, there is the looming specter: a career-destroying verdict. And whatever the verdict, win or lose, there is the fact that *all* the doctors, innocent and guilty alike, are paying for it. They are paying for the exorbitant awards in the form of unbelievable insurance premiums—over $100,000 per year per physician in some places.

In response to this situation, doctors are forced to engage wholesale in "defensive medicine," i.e., the performing of unnecessary tests or procedures solely in order to build a legal record and thereby prevent the patient from suing later. For example, I heard about the case of a man falling and bumping his head slightly. Since there was no evidence of any head injury, there was no basis, in the doctor's judgment, to order an expensive series of skull X rays. But if he does not order it, he takes a chance: if months or even years later, the man should develop mysterious headaches, the doctor might be sued. He might be charged retroactively with negligence, since he omitted a test that might have shown something that might have enabled him to prevent the headaches. So the doctor has no choice; he has to order the tests to protect himself. By a conservative estimate, defensive medicine now accounts for *one-third* of all health-care costs.

Since the medical profession did not suddenly turn evil or irresponsible in the last several years, we must ask what is the cause of the soaring lawsuits. The most immediately apparent answer lies in the law, which has now lost any pretense at rationality. The standards of liability are corrupt. Negligence, in any rational sense of the term, is no longer the legal standard. Today's standard demands of the doctor not responsible care, but omniscience and omnipotence.

For example, if a doctor prescribes a drug that is safe by every known test, and years later it is discovered to have side effects undreamed of at the time, the doctor can be sued. Was he negligent? No, merely not omniscient. If he treats a patient with less than the most expensive technology, whether the patient can afford it or not, he can be sued. "You open yourself to a malpractice suit," says an attorney in the field, "if you even give the *appearance* of letting financial considerations conflict with good patient care."[1] Or: if a baby has a birth defect that can be ascribed to the trauma of labor, the obstetrician can be sued for *not* having done a Caesarian, even though there were no advance indications in favor of one—because, as one obstetrician puts it, people assume "that anything less [than perfection] is due to negligence."[2] This last statement actually reveals the operative principle of the law today, not of some crackpot left-wing radical, but of the *law*: the patient is entitled to have whatever he wishes, regardless of cost or means; it makes no difference what doctors know, or whether the money exists; the patient's desire is an absolute, the doctor is a mere serf expected to provide all comers with an undefined "perfect care" somehow.

Do you see where this idea comes from? It is the basic principle that underlies and gave birth to Medicare. "You the patient," Washington said in the 1960s, "need do nothing to *earn* your medical care or your cures. From now on you need merely *wish*, and the all-powerful government will do the rest for you." Well, now we see the result. We see the rise of a generation of patients (and lawyers) who believe it, who expect treatment and cures as a matter of right, simply because they wish it, and who storm into court when their wish is frustrated.

The government not only inculcates such an attitude, but makes it seem financially feasible as well, because Washington has poured so much money into the field of medicine for so long. How else could anyone afford the defensive tests, or the inflated medical prices necessary to help pay for the incredible malpractice awards? They could not have been afforded in a free-market context. In the days of private medicine, there was no malpractice crisis; there was neither the public psychology nor the irresponsible funding that it requires. But now, thanks to government, there is both. And there is also a large enough corps of unscrupulous lawyers who are delighted to cash in on the disaster, lawyers who are eager to extort every penny they can from conscientious, bewildered, and in most cases utterly innocent doctors—while grabbing off huge contingency fees for themselves in the process.

The only solution to the malpractice crisis is a rational definition of "malpractice," which would restrict the concept severely, to cases of demonstrable negligence or irresponsibility, within the context of objective definitions of these terms, taking into account the knowledge and the money available at the time. But this approach is impossible until the government gets its standards and its cash out of the medical business altogether.

We are all kept alive by the work of man's mind—the individual minds that still retain the autonomy necessary to think and to judge. In medicine, above all, the mind must be left free. Medical treatment, as I have said, involves countless variables and options that must be taken into account, weighed, and summed up by the doctor's mind and subconscious. Your life depends on the private, inner essence of the doctor's function: it depends on the input that enters his brain, and on the processing such input receives from him.

What is being thrust now into the equation? It is not only objective medical facts any longer. Today, in one form or another, the following also has to enter that brain: "The DRG administrator will raise hell if I operate, but the malpractice attorney will have a field day if I don't—and my rival down the street, who heads the local PRO, favors a CAT scan in these cases, I can't afford to antagonize him, but the CON boys disagree and they won't authorize a CAT scanner for our hospital —and besides the FDA prohibits the drug I should be prescribing, even though it is widely used in Europe, and the IRS might not allow the patient a tax deduction for it, anyhow, and I can't get a specialist's advice because the latest Medicare rules prohibit a consultation with this diagnosis, and maybe I shouldn't even take this patient, he's so sick—after all, some doctors are manipulating their slate of patients, they accept only the healthiest ones, so their average costs are coming in lower than mine, and it looks bad for my staff privileges . . ." Would you like your case to be treated this way—by a doctor who takes into account your objective medical needs *and* the contradictory, unintelligible demands of ninety-nine different government agencies and lawyer squads? If you were a doctor, could you comply with all of it? Could you plan for or work around or deal with the unknowable? But how could you not? Those agencies and squads are real, and they are rapidly gaining total power over you and your mind and your patients.

In this kind of nightmare world, if and when it takes hold fully, thought is helpless; no one can decide by rational means what to do. A doctor either obeys the loudest authority; or he tries to sneak by unnoticed, bootlegging some good health care occasionally; or he gives up and quits the field.

Now you can understand why Objectivism holds that mind and force are opposites—and why innovation always disappears in totalitarian countries—and why doctors and patients alike are going to perish under socialized medicine if its invasion of this nation is not reversed.

Conservatives sometimes observe that government, by freezing medical fees, is destroying the doctors' financial incentive to practice. This is true enough, but my point is different. With or without incentive, the doctors are being placed in a position where they literally cannot function—where they cannot think, judge, know what to do, or act on their conclusions. Increasingly, for a man who is conscientious, today's government is making the practice of medicine impossible.

The doctors know it, and many have decided what to do about it. In preparation for this talk, I spoke to or heard from physicians around the country. I wanted to learn their view of the state of their profession. From New York to California, from Minnesota to Florida, the response was almost always the same: "I'm getting out of medicine." "I can't take it any more." "I'm putting every cent I can into my pension plan. In five years, I'll retire."

Such is the reward our country is now offering to its doctors, in payment for their life-saving dedication, effort, and achievements.

As to talented newcomers rising to replace the men who quit, I want to point out that medical-school enrollments are dropping. Bright students today, says the president of the Mount Sinai School of Medicine, are "discouraged by the perception of growing government regulation of medicine."[3] Note that it is bright students about whom he speaks. The other kind will always be in ample supply.

Any government program has beneficiaries who fight to keep the program going. Who is benefiting from the destruction of the doctors? It is not the poor. A generation ago, the poor in this country received excellent care through private charity, comparatively much better care than they are going to get now under the DRG and HMO approaches. The beneficiary is not the poor, but only one subgroup among them: those who do not want to admit that they are charity cases, those who want to pretend that they are entitled to medical handouts as a matter of right. In other words, the beneficiary is the dishonest poor, who want righteously to collect the unearned and consider it an affront even to have to say "Thank you." There is a second beneficiary: the new 9-to-5, civil-servant doctor, the kind who once existed only on the fringes of medicine, but who now basks in the limelight of being a physician and healer, because his betters are being frozen out. And there is one more kind of beneficiary: the medical bureaucrats, lobbyists, legislators, and the malpractice lawyers—in short, all the force-wielders now slithering out of their holes, gorging themselves on unearned jobs, money, fame, and/or power, by virtue of having sunk their fangs into the body of the medical profession.

Altruism, as Ayn Rand has demonstrated, does not mean kindness or benevolence; it means that man is a sacrificial animal; it means that some men are to be sacrificed to others. Our country today is a textbook illustration of her point. The competent doctors, along with their self-supporting patients, are being sacrificed—to the parasites, the incompetents, and the brutes. This is how altruism always works. This is how it has to work, by its nature.

The doctors resent today's situation passionately. Many of them are ready to quit, but not to fight for their field—at least, not to fight in the manner that would be necessary, if they were to have a chance of winning. In part, this is because the doctors are frightened; they sense that if they speak out too loudly, they may be subject to government reprisals. Most of all, however, the doctors feel guilty. Their own professional motivation—the personal, selfish love of their field and of their mind's ability to function—*is* noble, but they do not know it.

For ages they have had it pounded into them that it is wrong to have a personal motivation, wrong to enjoy the material rewards of their labor, wrong to assert their own individual rights. They have been told over and over that, no matter what their own private desires, they *should* want to sacrifice themselves to society. And so they are torn now by a moral conflict and silenced by despair. They do not know what to say if they quit, or how to protest their enslavement. They do not know that selfishness, the rational selfishness they embody and practice, is the essence of virtue. They do not know that they are *not* servants of their patients, but, to quote Ayn Rand, "*traders*, like everyone else in a free society—and they should bear that title proudly, considering the crucial importance of the services they offer." If the doctors could hear just this much and learn to speak out against their jailers, there would still be a chance; but only if they speak out as a matter of solemn justice, upholding a moral principle, the first moral principle: self-preservation.

Thereafter, in practical terms, they—and all of us—could advocate the only solution to today's crisis: removing its primary cause. This means: closing down Medicare. Reducing Medicare's budget is not the answer—that will simply tighten the DRG noose. The program itself must be abolished. In principle, the method is simple: phase it out in stages. Let the government continue to pay, on a sliding scale, for those who are already too old to save for their final years, but give clear notice to the younger generations that there is a cutoff age, and that they must begin now to make their own provision for their later medical costs.

Is there still time for such a step? The most I can answer is: in ten years, there won't be—that is how fast things are moving. In ten years, perhaps even in five, our medical system will have been dismantled. Most of the best doctors will have retired or gone on strike, and the government will be so entrenched in the field that nothing will get rid of it.

If you are my age, you may sneak by with the rest of your lifespan, relying on the remnants of private medicine that still exist. But if you are in your teens, twenties, thirties, then you are too young to count on such a hope. To you in particular, I want to conclude by saying: find out what is going on in this field—don't take my word for it—and then act, let people know the situation, in whatever way is open to you. Above all, talk to your doctor. If you agree with the Declaration of Independence, tell him that he, too, comes under it; that he, too, is a human being with a right to life; and that you want to help protect his freedom, and his income, on purely selfish grounds.

If you are looking for a crusade, there is none that is more idealistic or more practical. This one is devoted to protecting some of the greatest creators in the history of this country. It is also literally a matter of life and death—*your* life, and that of anyone you love. Don't let it go without a fight.

NOTES

1. Arthur R. Chenen, "Prospective Payment Can Put You in Court," *Medical Economics*, July 9, 1984.
2. Allan Rosenfield, quoted in Susan Squire, "The Doctors' Dilemma," *New York*, March 18, 1985.
3. James F. Glenn, quoted in "Professional Schools' Enrollment Off," *The New York Times*, Feb. 10, 1985.

31

Libertarianism: The Perversion of Liberty
by Peter Schwartz

The following is a highly condensed version of an article published in The Intellectual Activist, *May–June and December 1985.*

The Libertarian movement has acquired an unwarranted reputation. It has come under attack in various quarters for holding the value of liberty as an absolute. It has been condemned by conservatives for elevating liberty above tradition and authority, and by liberals for elevating liberty above equality and humanitarianism.

Both camps are mistaken. Libertarianism deserves only one fundamental criticism: it does *not* value liberty. If it were ever successful, it would destroy the remnants of freedom that still exist in this country far faster than any of the more explicit enemies of liberty.

Libertarianism has no philosophy. To put this more accurately: it renounces the need for any intellectual basis for its beliefs. The volumes of scholarly material defending Libertarianism are self-admittedly pointless, since the true Libertarian position is that no defense is necessary. Murray Rothbard, widely viewed as the father of the movement, expresses this clearly in presenting his central argument for liberty.

"Should virtuous action (however we define it) be compelled, or should it be left up to the free and voluntary choice of the individual?" he asks. And he answers: "To be virtuous in any meaningful sense, a man's actions must be free. . . . The point is more forceful: no action *can be* virtuous unless it is freely chosen." Freedom, therefore, is a prerequisite of any virtue, and thus can be validated with no knowledge of virtue at all. Morality, in other words, is irrelevant to the issue of liberty. "Freedom is necessary to, and integral with, the achievement of *any* of man's ends," Rothbard insists. [Last emphasis added.]¹

How can a man identify the requirements of virtue without first knowing what virtue *is*? Yet Rothbard does not ask why the very concept of virtue is necessary, what it consists of, or how it is justified. Without understanding anything about the nature of virtue, he proceeds to declare that liberty is its sine qua non. His reasoning is an effort to subvert—indeed, to *invert*—the logical hierarchy of ethics and politics by claiming that one need know nothing about the first in order to establish the principles of the second.

But since the fundamental question of ethics is how to define the good, it is ethics itself which must determine the propriety or impropriety of force. If, for example, the good is—as many believe—a world that heeds God's will, then it is virtuous to prevent, by force if necessary, the distribution of pornography or the drinking of alcohol or the preaching of atheism. If prayer is a duty one is obliged to perform—if the act of praying is intrinsically good, regardless of one's knowledge or rational interests—why *shouldn't* one be compelled to go through the motions of prayer, if that is supposed to bring greater glory to God? How many "sinners" throughout history have been tortured and killed in order to save their souls and thereby please God? Of what logical relevance is the victim's lack of consent, if one accepts this concept of the good?

One cannot exhort people to have faith in a being beyond their comprehension, and then insist that freedom—which means the right to act on the judgment of one's mind—is a prerequisite of virtue. A moral code that urges man to surrender his mind to a higher authority is irreconcilable with the principle that man ought to live his life guided by his own thinking. If obedience is a virtue, freedom of thought and action cannot be a right.

Most secular codes of morality are also in conflict with the principle of freedom. If the good is an egalitarian society, for example, then it is virtuous to expropriate the wealth of the rich and give it to the poor. If the good is that which gives the greatest pleasure to the greatest number, then it is virtuous to kill off some minority of "undesirables," if the majority so wishes. If the good is the melding of the individual's "unreal self" into the collective, organic whole of humanity, then it is virtuous to establish a totalitarian state.

The evil of the initiation of force lies in the fact that force is the negation of the mind. It makes the victim act not by the guidance of his independent perception, but by the dictates of a gun. Only if *reason* is a virtue, therefore, can force be a vice. But to uphold reason as a virtue requires a specific code of morality. It requires a morality the standard of which is man's life, and which recognizes that human survival depends on human rationality. With that as an ethical base, one can demonstrate that the initiation of physical force is anti-life and thus immoral. In this approach, liberty is indeed a prerequisite of virtue.

But if reason is *not* a moral value, if virtue is based on dogmatically asserted duties or on subjectively asserted desires, then human understanding of right and wrong is irrelevant—is, in fact, an obstacle—to morality. In this view, there are no grounds for barring force in human relations, and more: force becomes *indispensable* in obtaining compliance with unprovable moral imperatives. Without reason, no resolution of disagreements can take place, except by resort to fists and bullets.

In defiance of all fact, Libertarianism declares that there is no need for any concept such as individual rights, there is no need for any code of ethics, there is no need for any philosophical ideas at all—other than the Libertarian axiom that no matter how irrational one's values, "liberty" is the prerequisite of achieving them.

This fatuous reasoning brings even Marxism and Nazism under the Libertarian umbrella. After all, the values of a liberated proletariat or of a purified Aryan race cannot really be achieved— the Libertarian would have to argue—except through uncoerced action. Marxists and Nazis need not repudiate their philosophies— they merely have to call for the factory owners to hand over their property to the state, for the book publishers to accept the views of the Minister of Propaganda, for the Jews to march into the gas chambers . . . *voluntarily!* If the Hitlers and the Stalins want to implant the virtue of absolute submission to the state— Rothbard would tell them—they must persuade the people to submit willingly. In other words, only when political freedom reigns can the goals of barbarians be realized.

There is nothing un-Libertarian about the basic moral tenets of dictatorship. The ethical values—the ends—of Soviet Russia and Nazi Germany (as of anyone else) are perfectly consistent with Libertarianism; it is only their coercive *means* that, allegedly, aren't.

Libertarianism is a version of moral subjectivism. It is the view that all values are equally valid, and therefore equally irrelevant to the issue of political liberty. Consequently, all of ethics must be expunged from Libertarian doctrine. There must be no hint of any position being taken in regard to moral values.

For example, a statement on racial discrimination in the 1978 Libertarian Party platform said: "We condemn bigotry as irrational and repugnant."[2] It was subsequently eliminated for being incompatible with Libertarianism. "Such a moralism simply has no business in a Libertarian platform," a former state party chairman explains. "Bigotry does not contradict basic Libertarian principle. . . . To condemn it is to make an ethical value judgment, not a Libertarian political statement."[3]

A second section in the platform, on health care, proposed to condemn government restrictions on scientific research, particularly "attempts to suppress recombinant DNA research, which has opened the way for increased supply of medically useful human proteins, such as insulin, and shows promise of revealing the nature of hereditary diseases, the structure of bacteria and viruses, and the nature of the immune response."[4] This statement, too, was found to be unacceptable because "scientific research and improvement of medical technology are values that simply have no place in the Libertarian Party platform. . . . What about those Libertarians who don't value recombinant DNA research?"[5]

A leading Libertarian writer and speaker, Walter Block, states this antipathy toward moral principles even more baldly. He asks whether Libertarianism "must be honest and truthful," and whether it ought to involve not just a "disembodied ideology" but some "animating ideal or spirit to give the movement a sense of purpose." And he answers with an unequivocal no. "There must *not* be more to our Libertarian movement than its disembodied ideology—its nonaggression principle. Any sort of additional 'animating ideal' or 'spirit' will only needlessly, and *unjustly*, force true Libertarians to leave; although they may agree with the noninitiation of force, they may not be in tune with this undefined, ineffable 'spirit.' " As to the issue of honesty: "Lying violates no Libertarian principle. . . . You don't *owe* [anyone] the truth unless he's paid you for it."[6]

Block is correct: Libertarianism is incompatible with values *as such*. If no morality is unacceptable to Libertarianism, then no morality can be acceptable, either. There can be no endorsement of scientific progress, or of honesty; there can be no criticism of irrationality. What Block fails to grasp, however, is that once ethics is abandoned, *all* values become groundless and must be repudiated—including the value of liberty. Libertarianism cannot argue, for instance, that socialized medicine destroys medical care—why is health necessarily a value? It cannot condemn the public school system for making true education impossible— why should education be a value? It cannot claim that price controls destroy an economy's productivity—why is production or prosperity a value? Does justice demand that the individual be free? What about those Libertarians who believe that justice is heartless and that mercy is morally superior? Is coercion wrong because it interferes with people's pursuit of happiness? What about those Libertarians who regard happiness as a vice? Is liberty to be upheld because it is allegedly the means of achieving whatever it is one happens to value? What about the Libertarian who preaches a life of suffering and frustration, who considers the *renunciation*, rather than the achievement, of values to be a virtue?

If Libertarianism were consistent in its avowed rejection of the realm of morality, if it stopped smuggling in implicit value judgments to give its statements a deceptive veneer of coherence, it could say *nothing* in favor of liberty.

This contempt for ideas extends far beyond the field of ethics. It is not only moral principles that Libertarianism repudiates, but all philosophic ideas. Murray Rothbard claims to hold a philosophy but predictably regards it, too, as inconsequential. He writes:

> As a political theory, Libertarianism is a coalition of adherents from all manner of philosophic (or nonphilosophic) positions, including emotivism, hedonism, Kantian a priorism, and many others. My own position grounds Libertarianism on a natural rights theory embedded in a wider system of Aristotelian-Lockean natural law and a realist ontology and metaphysics. But although those of us taking this position believe that *only it* provides a satisfactory groundwork and basis for individual liberty, this is an argument within the Libertarian camp about the proper basis and grounding of Libertarianism rather than about the doctrine itself. [Emphasis added.][7]

This reflects Rothbard's utter scorn for ideas—even his own. If he claims to believe that only an Aristotelian system can "ground" Libertarianism, how can he call the adherents of "emotivism, hedonism, and Kantian a priorism" members of the same camp? If these proponents are presenting false arguments based on false premises, why does he not see this as undercutting his own case for liberty? If an investment adviser tells people to buy gold because he believes that the price will rise and they will get rich, while a devout Hindu, who believes that wealth is evil, tells people to buy gold because he believes the price will plummet and they will become impoverished, the two advisers are *not* reaching the same conclusion, even though both say: "Buy gold." And neither are the Aristotelian and the Kantian, even though both may proclaim the words: "Liberty is good." Only a total disregard for the context and the meaning of concepts could allow anyone to equate the two viewpoints.

Rothbard is saying simultaneously that only one philosophic foundation can justify liberty—and that Libertarianism is comfortable with *any* foundation, or with no foundation. This can only mean that liberty needs no justification, and that he regards all discussion, including his own copious contributions, about its proper "grounding" as pointless pedanticism.

Imagine a pro-capitalist who joins with socialists in a demonstration against the Reagan Administration. Should he overlook, as a mere detail, the fact that he believes Reagan is too appeasing of Russia and too tolerant of social-welfare spending, while the socialists believe that Reagan is too harsh toward the Soviets and too draconian in his budget cuts? Would any sane person dismiss this disagreement as just an intra-camp argument about "grounding," but not about the crucial point itself of Reagan's undesirability? Yet this is exactly the attitude taken by Libertarians toward the question of the desirability of liberty.

In logic, there is no way to comprehend the meaning of the principle of the noninitiation of force without a philosophical foundation. And there is no way to apply the principle in a political context without formulating a code of *rights*, particularly property rights. Without such a base, liberty could mean anything from socialism, which offers "freedom" from the law of supply and demand, to Zen Buddhism, which offers "freedom" from the law of noncontradiction.

But a code of rights cannot be established except by reference to a code of ethics. Rights pertain to freedom of action in a social context, and one cannot know how man should act as a member of society before knowing how man should act as man. Ethics itself, moreover, is the product of a view of man and of reality. In other words, to arrive at a proper understanding and an objective validation of liberty, philosophy is inescapable. One has to begin with a view of reality as comprehensible, and of man as a rational being who relies upon reason as his sole means of valid knowledge and as his basic tool of survival. One must then identify man's life as the proper standard of value, and morality as the principles defining the actions necessary to maintain man's life. Since life is sustained through thought and action, one then concludes that the individual must have the *right* to think and to act, and to keep the product of that thinking and acting—which means: the right to life, liberty, and property. Because the initiation of force is the means by which a mind is paralyzed, such force is evil. Because force is the means by which one's rights are violated, it must be outlawed. Thus the conclusion that liberty is a fundamental social good.

Without such a philosophic base, the concept of liberty cannot be defended. At the core of Libertarianism, however, is the denial of this basic connection. Libertarians display nothing but disdain for fundamental ideas. They disparage the very *idea* of a fundamental idea. Libertarianism wishes to espouse an end product: liberty—while remaining oblivious to its source: philosophy. It sees no logical, ordered structure of ideas, but only a haphazard smorgasbord of notions, and feels entitled to help itself to any one, at any time, in any sequence, as the mood strikes.

What must this imply about the effort to achieve liberty in practice? If liberty poses no threat to the dominant ideas of our culture today, where is the resistance to it emanating from? If the ideal of freedom is so devoid of intellectual content and controversy—if it is compatible with all philosophies and all values—if it is, as Rothbard puts it, "necessary to, and integral with, the achievement of any of man's ends"—what *ideas* do people need to be convinced of in order for the ideal of liberty to gain wide acceptance? The Libertarian answer has to be: none.

According to the basic premise of Libertarianism, no ideological education is possible. Can Libertarians persuade people of the truth of some particular philosophy? One philosophy is as good as any other. Can they point out the errors of various philosophies? Even false philosophies are compatible with liberty. Can they show how certain moral values are in conflict with liberty? None are. But if wrong ideas are not the problem, and correct ideas are not the solution, what explains our steady drift toward statism, and what could reverse it?

The answer indicates the next development in Libertarian thinking: its version of the Marxist theory of class struggle.

"American society is divided into a government-oppressed class and a government-privileged class, and is ruled by a power elite," says the Libertarian Party Radical Caucus.[8] Therefore,

> A Libertarian *class analysis* is the key theoretical tool, the one indispensable method of unraveling complex strategic and tactical questions. Crucial to any Libertarian theory of social change is the clear moral and political distinction to be made between those who hold state power and those who do not—between those who rule and those who are ruled.... Our Libertarian worldview comes ever more clearly into focus as we draw the line politically between two *opposing* classes with mutually exclusive relations to the state. *Which side are you on?* Do you defend the state—or do you side with the people?[9]

There is no intellectual conflict in regard to liberty, this view declares. The people are simply kept in chains by a privileged elite, which has somehow managed to take control of the coercive machinery of the state. Each group is drawn to pursue its innate "class interests." The masses for some reason are driven to seek freedom; the ruling bureaucrats, power.

What weapons do Libertarians intend to use in this type of battle, since education is pointless? The abandonment of reason necessitates the endorsement of force. In Libertarianism's pursuit of social change, therefore, it is left with only one recourse: violence.

Libertarians want to transform the present system not by force of argument, but by plain force. And some of them broadcast this openly. "The fact is that no ruling class has ever given up its power voluntarily—and any movement for radical social change which fails to realize this will never achieve its goals," says *Libertarian Vanguard*, a "radical" newspaper within the Libertarian movement. America's "present system cannot be reformed or wished away—extra-parliamentary action is, ultimately, the prospect awaiting us."[10]

The goal of Libertarians is to topple the state's power elite through armed struggle. The Libertarian battleground is not the halls of academia or the editorial pages of the newspapers, but the streets and the back alleys. The troops Libertarianism seeks are not individuals armed with convincing arguments, but a mindless horde avid to lash out against the "system" and the state with machine guns and hand grenades. The *Libertarian Vanguard* describes the makeup of this corps:

> The revolutionary potential of blacks, Chicanos, women, and gays who have been betrayed by decades of social welfare programs, which have led to nothing but misery, exploitation, and crushing inflation, is the greatest fear of the Corporate State oligarchy.... Slavery, the conquest of the West and the subsequent looting of American Indian and Mexican land rights, the historical subjugation of women, the brutal repression of lesbians and gay men—every single one of these are crimes committed on a scale so massive that it is almost unimaginable; and every single one of these crimes can be traced directly to the actions of the state. In these instances, and in others, what is involved is nothing less than the attempted systematic obliteration of an entire class formation.[11]

The Libertarian campaign for "liberty" is a war against the state, *not* against statism. It is not the ideas behind statism that Libertarians attack—there are no such ideas, they believe; the target of their attack is the state itself, even the state as defined and established by America's founding fathers. It is the state, in any form, that represents a restriction upon their "liberty," and therefore deserves to be crushed. This is the anarchism inherent in the movement.

"Libertarian principle and the dynamics of social change dictate that we be perpetual state-haters," says a former vice chairman of the Libertarian Party.[12] Not haters of slavery or of tyranny—but of the state as such.

"We seek the abolition of the Central Intelligence Agency and the Federal Bureau of Investigation," declares the platform of the Libertarian Party.[13] "We favor international negotiations toward general and complete disarmament down to police levels."[14]

"The U.S. government should unilaterally abandon all nuclear weapons," says a former editor of the *Libertarian Party News*. "The desire of some to support the U.S. nuclear buildup is based on the faulty notion that the U.S. government is on 'our side'—that it will use these weapons to defend our lives and liberty. Yet this is clearly not the case. It uses these weapons . . .

to defend *the state*. If Libertarians truly regard the state as their enemy, they cannot support its holding of nuclear weapons."[15]

The goals of achieving liberty and destroying the state are incompatible—yet Libertarians choose the latter. A properly functioning government, one whose purpose is to protect individual rights against attack, is essential to the preservation of liberty; but this is of no concern to Libertarians—*all* states are the enemy. Libertarians do not believe that by crippling the state they are helping the cause of freedom. The dissolution of the state is an end of itself. To Libertarians, whatever harms the state is categorically good; whatever helps the state is categorically bad—regardless of the effect on human liberty.

For example, when South Vietnam was conquered by North Vietnam in 1975, Murray Rothbard found it an occasion for celebration: "What is inspiring to Libertarians is to actually see the final and swift disintegration of a State. . . . None of [America's] superior might and firepower could in the end prevail against the will and determination of the mass of Vietnamese (and Cambodians) bent against seemingly impossible odds to dislodge dictatorial governments." The death of a state, he writes,

> vindicates once again the insights of the theorists of mass guerrilla warfare . . . that after a slow, patient, protracted struggle, in which the guerrilla armies (backed by the populace) whittle and wear down the massively superior firepower of the state armies (generally backed by other, imperialist governments), the final blow occurs in which the state dissolves and disintegrates with remarkable speed.[16]

It is immaterial to Rothbard that communism had triumphed and that the freedom of the South Vietnamese people had been reduced from minuscule to nonexistent. All that matters to "perpetual state-haters" is that for one brief moment they experience the exhilaration of seeing a government ground into dust. And the number one target of this hostility is the government not of some totalitarian dictatorship, but of the United States.

America has become "a new worldwide empire which has set itself up as the military guardian of the status quo—and the main enemy of every national liberation movement seeking autonomy," says the Libertarian Party Radical Caucus. "The national isolation of the American Libertarian movement can only be prolonged by an attempt to deny what is clear, by now, to people all around the globe—the fact that the United States is the main danger to peace and freedom."[17]

Libertarianism thus provides the grotesque spectacle of a movement claiming to support individual liberty—while reviling America as the world's most immoral nation. When communists issue the same vituperative charge against the U.S., they are at least honest in naming their standard of value.

According to Libertarians, America is far more contemptible than even the Soviet Union. Murray Rothbard writes,

> Taking the twentieth century as a whole, the single most warlike, most interventionist, most imperialist government has been the United States. ... Lenin and his fellow Bolsheviks adopted the theory of "peaceful coexistence" as the basic foreign policy for a communist state. The idea was this: as the first successful communist movement, Soviet Russia would serve as a beacon for and supporter of other communist parties throughout the world. But the Soviet state qua state would devote itself to peaceful relations with all the other countries, and would not attempt to export communism through interstate warfare. ... Thus, fortuitously, from a mixture of theoretical and practical grounds of their own, the Soviets arrived early at what Libertarians consider to be *the only proper and principled foreign policy.* ... Increasing conservatism under Stalin and his successors strengthened and reinforced the nonaggressive, "peaceful coexistence" policy. [Emphasis added][18]

The communist guerrilla movement that is trying to overthrow the American-backed government in El Salvador deserves unqualified moral support, says the *Libertarian Vanguard*:

> There can be no moral or political neutrality in a battle of this kind. If we must temporarily join forces with Marxist-Leninists to fight the junta and its U.S. supporters, then so be it. ... A victory for the revolution in El Salvador would be a major defeat for U.S. imperialism—the main danger to peace and liberty—right in Washington's own back yard.[19]

What emerges from Libertarianism—the alleged advocate of absolute liberty—is a standard leftist worldview. The poor and the weak are oppressed by a Corporate State—America is an imperialist oligarchy—Moscow wants peace and participates in an arms race only in order to keep up with our power-mad Pentagon planners—the Third World is being denied freedom and prosperity by America's ruling elite—all U.S. foreign policy, from Southeast Asia to Central America, is designed to achieve world domination—class struggle is the key to understanding the state of the world.

The role model for the Libertarian revolution is the New Left of the 1960s—"the first quasi-Libertarian mass movement in a hundred years," and one which "embodied the Libertarian values of respect for personal sovereignty, freedom, and peace," according to the Students for a Libertarian Society (SLS), the major Libertarian network on college campuses.[20]

Why did the New Left fail after its promising start? Because, a former director of SLS explains, it needed "a comprehensive philosophy of social change. Yet the only such philosophy immediately available was that of Marxism-Leninism. . . . The point is that those seeking a strategy for revolutionary change had nowhere else to go but toward Marxism."[21] Isn't the lesson, then, that radical change requires a *philosophical* alternative to Marxism? No, he says:

> Wherever and whenever there have been masses of people desirous of change—oppressed people, idealists, intellectuals— they have been drawn to Marxism as if by an invisible hand. I do not think that this can be explained fully by assuming that the people involved were statist, authoritarian, or collectivist. The drift to Marxism can be better explained by noting that, in the words of [the leader of the New Left's major campus organization], "there was—and is—no other coherent, integrative, and explicit philosophy of revolution.". . . We can inherit that kind of influence if we construct a new, distinctly Libertarian theory of revolution.[22]

In other words, the way that social change takes place is as follows. People somehow conclude that the existing political structure must be overthrown, they decide to make a revolution, they deliver rousing speeches and print up fiery pamphlets, they draw up plans to storm the gates of government—and then, like last-minute shoppers, they look around for the right brand of philosophy to grab off the counter in order to find out what the hell they are doing. And the brand they ultimately grab is not the one that presents the most persuasive explanation of the *ideas* they should be fighting for, but the one that happens to offer the best advice on how to get past the palace guards. If the New Left had had a Libertarian "model" for destroying the state in 1968, this analysis suggests, it would surely have abandoned Marxism. The future of Libertarianism, then, depends on its occupying more prominent shelf space than does Karl Marx in the supermarket of revolutionism.

The rabid desire, shared both by Libertarianism and the New Left, to bring down the U.S. government stems from a common root. As was true in the 1960s of the Molotov-cocktail thrower blowing up ROTC offices and chanting "Revolution, now!", the present-day Libertarian is a thorough emotionalist. He wants to act on whatever feelings he happens to feel, no matter how capricious and irrational. He wants no constraints on his behavior. As the Society for Libertarian Life puts it in a statement of principles, all people "have a natural right *to do their own thing,* providing that they do not physically harm or coercively restrict another individual's life, liberty or property." [Emphasis added.][23]

The Libertarian interprets liberty to mean the license to do whatever he feels like doing. Since he dismisses reason and philosophy, he has no way even to *define* force. To him, the pseudo-definition of "force" is that which interferes with somebody's desires; to him, any obstacle in the path of people's whims is undesirable. People ought to be "free" to act on any random impulses they feel. *That* is Libertarianism.

That is *not* liberty.

Libertarianism rejects all values and all morality because they are too "restrictive." Moral values establish standards for human conduct. This is too oppressive for the Libertarian, who cries that he wants to be "free" from all constraints.

If rights are a subjective matter, if the right to which men are inalienably entitled is subjectively to "do their own thing," then there is no basis for any objective concept of force. And regardless of how vociferously Libertarians proclaim their devotion to some fuzzy notion of noncoercion, they will inevitably *endorse* the use of force.

An individual who feels an urge to engage in child molestation, for example, is merely doing "his own thing" and should not be hindered by the state. Members of the North American Man/Boy Love Association—which advocates the legalization of sex between underage and adult males—"are among the most brutally state-oppressed individuals in this country," writes Marc Joffe in *Individual Liberty*, and support for them is the "acid test" of one's Libertarian credentials. "Any law which discriminates on the basis of age is unjust and un-Libertarian," he says.[24]

Since rights, in this view, are severed from the faculty of reason, children, like adults, are seen as having the right to do whatever they want. "We oppose all legally created or sanctioned discrimination against (or in favor of) children, just as we oppose government discrimination directed at any other artificially defined subcategory of human beings," says the Libertarian Party platform.[25] If a seven-year-old nods assent when asked whether he wants to engage in sex with an adult, that is his "right." If he wishes to drink liquor, one has a "right" to give it to him. If he wants to leave home and live with some strangers he has just met, he has a perfect "right" to do so. If he decides he wants to use heroin, buy a gun, drive a car, or fly a plane, neither he nor anyone willing to accommodate him should be stopped by law.

Should there be laws against libel and slander? No, say Libertarians; this is unduly restrictive of one's right to say whatever one feels like saying. "Libel laws were created by people with a vested interest in the status quo. Using libel laws stops the stirring up of controversy, and doesn't permit change," says a former vice president of the Cato Institute (a Libertarian policy-research organization). "Libel law is completely invalid," says the editor of *Inquiry* magazine. "The freedom to speak means the freedom to speak what others might consider untruth. [Apparently no statements are ever in fact untrue.] The central premise behind libel law is that a person has a right to his own reputation—but you can't own it or control it because it exists in the minds of others. Libel law is a monstrous threat to free speech."[26]

(So false advertising about one's product—or one's competitor's product—is acceptable because the item's reputation merely "exists in the minds of others.")

It should be plain why anarchism, far from being a viewpoint on the periphery of Libertarianism, is integral to it. Anarchism follows from amoralism. If people have a right never to be "constrained," then the state *must* be an illegitimate entity. If there are no objective standards of judging right and wrong, why shouldn't a person be entitled to act on his own feelings about what does and does not constitute force? If all views are subjective and no opinion is any less valid than another, by what right, and by what means, can a state establish any objective definition of crime?

If a man's fundamental goal is to define and validate individual rights objectively, and then to create a structure under which they are protected, he will discover laissez-faire capitalism and limited government. If, on the other hand, his basic concern is to allow people to do whatever they desire and to concoct a social arrangement by which that appears to be possible, then he will unearth Libertarianism and anarchism.

Of course, no social system can make the irrationalism of warring factions work. Dictatorship is the inevitable outcome of anarchism. Existentially, the chaos and destructiveness that anarchism encourages will make people turn to someone who promises order and security; intellectually, the people will have no grounds for resisting any despot who claims that his "private defense agency" is simply offering the marketplace the most "efficient" use of force—force that *he* feels is entirely "justified." In fact, there is no essential distinction between dictatorship and Libertarianism. The totalitarian maintains that the state may do whatever it wishes, without any restraints; the Libertarian insists that the individual may do whatever he wishes, without any restraints. Both agree that man is to be ruled by whim, and differ only on whether private whim or government whim takes precedence. They share the same anti-reason theory—and the same anti-freedom practice. (A term coined by author Ernest van den Haag to describe Libertarianism captures this aspect perfectly: anarcho-totalitarianism.)

The militant emotionalism of Libertarianism is succinctly conveyed by Walter Block. The virtue of Libertarianism, he writes,

> is that it allows for an amazing diversity. . . . We've seen priests, monogamists, family men as the fellow-Libertarians of the gays, the sado-masochists, the leather-freaks, and those into what they call "rational bestiality." . . . Only Libertarianism could gather together the homosexual motorcycle gang, the acid-dropper fascinated by the price of silver, and the Puerto Rican nationalist immersed in the Austrian school of economics.[27]

What unites all these creatures is a single premise: that human rationality is a dispensable element in politics and in life.

What Libertarianism entails is not just a trivialization of liberty, but an annihilation of the very concept. Block's crew is the dead end of the path that begins with the abdication of the mind.

But what is Libertarianism's goal? If it is anti-philosophy, anti-reason, anti-morality, anti-state, and anti-liberty—what is it *for*? A movement that is neutral about or indifferent to moral values does not launch a political crusade. Why would anyone who has renounced all values undertake a campaign to bring about radical social change?

The answer is that Libertarianism rests not on neutrality or apathy, but on hostility. The source of Libertarianism—the animating force behind its assaults on philosophy, on ethics, on ideas, on the institution of government, on the United States—is the desire not to neglect values, or even to evade their existence, but to *eradicate* them.

Walter Block, in *Defending the Undefendable*, argues that prostitution is no different from any business transaction and should not be viewed as demeaning. "We have to offer *something* to our prospective partners before they will consent to have sex with us," he says, such as the arrangement by which

> the male is expected to pay for the movies, dinners, flowers, etc., and the female is expected to reciprocate with sexual services. The marriages in which the husband provides the financial elements, and the wife the sexual and housekeeping functions, also conform clearly enough to the [prostitution] model.... *All* relationships where trade takes place, those which include sex as well as those which do not, are a form of prostitution. Instead of condemning all such relationships because of their similarity to prostitution, prostitution should be viewed as just one kind of interaction in which all human beings participate. Objections should not be raised to any of them—not to marriage, not to friendship, not to prostitution.[28]

Even pimps elicit moral praise from Block: "The pimp serves the function of bringing together two parties to a transaction at less cost than it would take to bring them together without his good offices." In doing so, the pimp "is, if anything, more honorable than many other brokers, such as [those in] banking, insurance and the stock market. They rely on restrictive state and federal laws to discourage their competition, whereas the pimp can never use the law to safeguard his position."[29]

This is not a demand for the repeal of laws against victimless crimes (laws that should be repealed). It is a blatant call for the repudiation of moral standards. Block is not defending an individual's right to engage in sordid behavior—he is denouncing the very idea of evaluating any behavior as sordid. He is insisting that pimps are actually honorable men, deserving of more respect than the typical businessman.

Who qualifies for Block's accolades? Only the dregs of society. They are applauded not in spite of their worthlessness, but because of it. It is because they are commonly regarded as scum that Block wants to elevate them to respectability—in order to debase the very idea of respectability. His "heroic" counterfeiter (whose activities "reduce and counteract the great evil of government counterfeiting")—the policeman who takes bribes for not enforcing certain laws ("the acceptance of money cannot be logically distinguished from the acceptance of a gift, and the mere acceptance of a gift is not illegitimate")—the habitual litterer ("who treats public property in much the same way that he would treat private property if he were but free to—namely, he leaves garbage around on it[!]" and thus exhibits "courage" and "can serve as a protest against an unjust system" of public streets)—the heroin pusher (who, "by acting so as to lower prices even at considerable personal risk," actually "saves lives and alleviates the tragedy somewhat")—all these are paragons of virtue to Block.[30] Why? Because they have rejected standards of behavior—not in favor of different or higher standards, but in the name of the *annihilation* of standards. As these reprobates choose to climb down into the slime, they do not uphold some new ethical criteria by which to claim that their lives are noble; they simply announce that they relish slime.

The "counterculture" of two decades ago was highly praised by Libertarians. In an article aptly titled "In Praise of Decadence," a former editor of *Libertarian Review* extols the hippies for demanding that "each person must be his own authority and must 'do his own thing.' "[31] The fact that they could articulate no alternatives, no philosophies, no arguments, no *values* to offer in place of the ones they were repudiating is immaterial to the Libertarian. What is significant to him is the repudiation per se.

The concept of "value" is irreconcilable with the Libertarian notion of "liberty." The existence of any value entails a certain "restraint" upon one's actions. It declares that X is good, that one ought to attain it, that one should pursue a particular end by using some defined means. It thereby limits man's behavior by pointing it in a specific direction. This is intolerable to those who want nothing to stand in the way of their whims.

In order for Libertarianism to bloom, therefore, values—not any particular code of values, but values as such—must be eliminated. This can be done either by debasing the good or by glorifying the depraved—by damning limited government or by upholding anarchism—by describing the Grenada invasion as "senseless militarism"[32] or by celebrating North Vietnam's victory over America as reflecting the people's determination "to dislodge dictatorial governments"[33]—by defaming Israel as "maniacally committed to the dread logic of empire, viz., . . . [of] slaughter and genocide"[34] or by praising the PLO as leading a "fight for justice and property rights"[35]—by vilifying the United States as the world's "main danger to peace and freedom"[36] or by hailing the Soviet Union for practicing a "proper and principled foreign policy."[37]

By either method, authentic values are sabotaged—and then anything goes.

Rothbard explains why the student rioters of the 1960s, who occupied university buildings and marched around campuses with loaded weapons, were quintessential Libertarians: "Perhaps the whole thing can be summed up by a sign carried by some of the kids at an antiwar march in New York City on April 5. The sign read simply: 'Death to the State. Power to the People.' How can you fault a movement having *that* as a slogan?"[38]

That sign does indeed reveal the essence of Libertarianism— the hostility, the anti-intellectualism, the utter philosophical void it represents. There is only one term that accurately describes this diseased viewpoint: nihilism. Libertarianism rests upon a pervasive desire to annihilate. There is to be no state, no ethics, no values, no standards, no ideas, no reason, no reality. No state—because it defines the use of force; no ethics—because it identifies proper behavior; no values—because they demand that actions have a purpose; no standards—because they establish right and wrong; no ideas—because they deny primacy to feelings; no reason—because it excludes the irrational; no reality— because it decrees that whims do not work.

Libertarianism starts with the brute observation that people have desires—where they come from and whether they are right or wrong are of no concern—and it offers, as the whole of its message, a single emotional ejaculation: act on those desires without restraint.

Liberty is the protector of man's values. It does not produce material goods, but it makes all production possible. It is comparable to the locks on doors: they do not create any wealth, but simply allow one to function in peace and to keep what one has already produced. Nobody could agitate for the universal installation of locks and burglar alarms in order to protect people's goods against theft, and at the same time declare that it does not matter to him whether the homes actually contain any goods or not; or whether material possessions should be valued or condemned; or even whether one's property really exists or is merely a figment of one's subjective consciousness.

Yet Libertarians do exactly this with respect to liberty. They want its protective shield, while nullifying everything that it safeguards. They want liberty—the *means*—while rejecting values—the *end*. Nothing matters to Libertarians—not even the value of life itself—but somehow the freedom to be a zero is of vital importance. They want to be free to act. To act how? Without purpose or reason. To achieve what? Nothing in particular. But the belligerent pursuit of nothing in particular is in fact the pursuit of . . . destruction. It is the quest not for political, but for metaphysical "freedom," which means: freedom from the demands of existence. Libertarians reject anything that tells them there is something they should not do, that there is something which will not yield to their emotions, that there is *something*. Reality itself is the limitation they ultimately resent. It is from the universe as such that Libertarians wish to be "liberated."

There are undoubtedly many Libertarians who would argue that the litany of irrationalities cited above does not represent their views. It is unjust, these "better" Libertarians would maintain, to denounce the entire movement on account of the absurd statements of those who do not typify or understand it.

It is these "better" Libertarians, however, who fail to understand the essence of Libertarianism.

The nature of an ideology is determined not by majority vote—but by logic, by analyzing its essence and its necessary implications. The logic of environmentalism, for example, leads to a society without technology; the logic of feminism leads to an egalitarian society in which men are not permitted to have anything which women do not; the logic of the New Right leads to theocracy—even if various environmentalists, feminists, and conservatives would deny this. And what the logic of Libertarianism inexorably leads to is nihilism, regardless of how many Libertarians protest that this is not their intention.

The full implications of an ideology's central principle are often evaded by its adherents. Many early supporters of Nazism in Germany, if asked, might very well have voted against the concentration camps. Does this mean that Hitler's atrocities reflect merely upon a number of sadistic Nazis but not upon Nazism per se? There are many Marxists who condemn the brutality of Soviet Russia, claiming that Moscow has abandoned the teachings of Karl Marx. Does this mean that Marxism itself is absolved of responsibility for such standard communist horrors as the machine-gunning of young children who try to escape across the Berlin wall? Obviously, all that this suggests is that many Nazis and Marxists are blind to the essential nature of their own philosophies.

Just as blind are those who claim that Libertarianism is compatible with laissez-faire capitalism, with morality, with reason, and with the requirements of human life.

The Libertarian movement was created in order to adopt a "united front" approach to liberty, that is, to spread out a broad umbrella under which a motley collection of people, irrespective of their philosophies, could gather in a joint effort to advance freedom. Libertarianism's one and only function is to bring together people who agree on nothing whatsoever except— ostensibly—the contextless claim that the use of force is evil. Its essence is precisely to bypass all the ideas underlying liberty and to jump directly to the assertion that the use of force is wrong.

But if there is no *why*, there can be no *what*. If Libertarianism announces that it need not offer any reason for its belief in liberty, then it cannot even state what it means by the term "liberty." Everyone from Karl Marx to Ralph Nader can then say that he is fundamentally in favor of liberty, and there is no objective means of disputing him. Why shouldn't anarchism be regarded as the implementation of genuine freedom? Why not describe libel and counterfeiting as actions fully consistent with individual rights? Why can't Moscow be said to be pursuing a foreign policy of worldwide liberation? Why not invite Timothy Leary to speak at Libertarian conventions—or label Jesus Christ "a Libertarian mystic"[39]—or glorify Yassir Arafat as a defender of "justice and property rights"[40]—or view God as "the Ultimate Noninterventionist"?[41] Once any *theory* is acceptable, any *practice* must be equally tolerable.

It is thus not just some Libertarians, but Libertarianism itself that is inherently subjectivist and therefore destructive. Imagine a group of physicians forming an umbrella organization in order to promote health in a society infected by disease. But, not wishing to be overly restrictive, they refuse to establish any basic principles. There are many avenues to health, they say; there is no need to take a position on *why* human health is desirable, or what values and premises the science of medicine presupposes—that could "prejudice" one's opinion against those who hold opposite premises. We just care about achieving health, they say; we don't care why people join us. Imagine further that as they go around lecturing on the importance of health, they are accompanied on the podium by Christian Scientists, faith healers, and witch doctors. They too support the value of "healing" —the physicians say—it does not matter why they do so or what they mean by it. After all, that is just a question about "grounding," not about the doctrine of health itself; so why care whether health is attained by exorcising demons inside one's body, or by following objective medical principles? It's all "health."

Those Libertarians who protest that *they* do not accept the premise of anarchism or of subjectivism or of nihilism simply refuse to see what is inherent in the fundamental nature and founding purpose of Libertarianism. Someone who agrees with the essence of capitalism—the principle of individual rights— and endorses tariffs or unemployment benefits does not understand capitalism's logical implications. By the same reasoning, someone who agrees with the essence of Libertarianism—"liberty" as a baseless assertion—and yet opposes unilateral U.S. disarmament or the terrorism of the PLO is likewise contradicting his basic premise.

Libertarianism's corrupt view of "liberty" also explains its attitude toward Objectivism.

Although Objectivism, unlike the rest of today's philosophies, advocates laissez-faire capitalism, it is those other philosophies that Libertarians tolerate and only Objectivism that elicits from them widespread hostility. Their policy of promiscuity in intellectual intercourse is suddenly replaced by one of extreme fastidiousness when they encounter Objectivism.

Libertarian writer Peter Breggin complains that the "books and philosophy of Ayn Rand have set back Libertarianism in their unabashed assault on anything that smacks of humanitarianism or humanism. Human beings are loved and hated strictly on the grounds of their ethical adherence to Objectivist principles and are granted no value whatsoever on the basis of their common humanity, their membership in the species."[42] Ayn Rand's "legacy has been a tragic one"—says another Libertarian writer—"a conservatarian millstone around the neck of the Libertarian movement. And that is why I say it's time to dissociate ourselves from Rand and everything she stood for."[43]

So while Libertarians believe that there are many avenues to their notion of liberty, they apparently draw the line at Objectivism—and they are entirely right to do so. Objectivism is incompatible with Libertarianism on every philosophical issue. Objectivism says: live by reason, follow a rational code of morality, practice self-interest as a virtue, establish the principles of limited government to define the appropriate use of retaliatory force. As its name implies, Ayn Rand's philosophy upholds an objective reality, objective cognition, objective values, and objective law.

Libertarianism's relationship to Objectivism is not merely that of an enemy, but of a parasite. Without Objectivism there would, ironically, be no Libertarian movement today. It is Objectivism that has offered a moral defense of liberty—which Libertarianism has stolen and mutilated. It is Objectivism that has imbued so many young people with a deep commitment to capitalism—which Libertarianism has seized on and corrupted.

Libertarianism seeks to appropriate some of the fruits of Objectivism while trying to uproot the tree. Its anti-conceptual nature makes it consistently desire effects without causes—politics without ethics, liberty without reason, social change without philosophy. It wants to use the words of Objectivism's noninitiation-of-force principle, but not the ideas that give them meaning. It wishes to feed off the by-products of Objectivism's defense of capitalism, while repudiating the nature and roots of that defense.

But the law of causality, like any metaphysical fact, cannot be circumvented. The attempt to do so can result only in that perversion of liberty which is the essence of Libertarianism.

NOTES

1. "Frank S. Meyer: The Fusionist as Libertarian Manqué," *Modern Age*, Fall 1981, p. 353.
2. From the 1978 Libertarian Party Platform, p. 2.
3. Michael Grossberg, "Let's Limit the Platform to Libertarianism," *Frontlines*, Sept. 1979, p. 4.
4. From the 1982 Libertarian Party Platform, p. 6.
5. Grossberg, *op. cit.*, p. 5.
6. "Letter to the *Free Libertarian*," *The Libertarian Forum*, April 1976, pp. 4, 5.

7. *Modern Age, op. cit.*, p. 355.
8. From "The Ten Points of the Libertarian Party Radical Caucus," issued July 1979.
9. "Draft Program of the Libertarian Party Radical Caucus," *Libertarian Vanguard*, Nov.–Dec. 1980, p. 8.
10. Justin Raimondo, "Why Evers and Rothbard Are Wrong," *Libertarian Vanguard*, Dec. 1982, p. 8.
11. Libertarian Party Radical Caucus, "Get in the Vanguard," *Libertarian Vanguard*, May 1979, p. 8.
12. Sheldon Richman, "Smash the Onion," *Individual Liberty*, Nov. 1981, p. 8.
13. From the 1984 Libertarian Party Platform, p. 3.
14. *Ibid.*, p. 8.
15. Kathleen Jacob Richman, "Nuclear Disarmament: A Survey," *Individual Liberty*, Oct. 1982, p. 5.
16. "Death of a State," *Reason*, July 1975, p. 31.
17. From "Draft Program," *op. cit.*, pp. 8, 9.
18. *For a New Liberty: The Libertarian Manifesto*, rev. ed. (Collier Books, 1978) pp. 270, 283.
19. Libertarian Party Radical Caucus, "Junta Launches Holocaust," *Libertarian Vanguard*, June 1981, p. 5.
20. From "Libertarianism: Challenging the Reign of Political Power" (brochure issued by Students for a Libertarian Society).
21. Milton Mueller, "Toward a Libertarian Theory of Revolution," *Libertarian Review*, Aug. 1978, pp. 14–16.
22. *Ibid.*, p. 17.
23. From "The Libertarian Statement," issued May 1973.
24. Letter to the editor, *Individual Liberty*, Sept. 1983; "News in Brief," Mar. 1983.
25. From the 1984 Libertarian Party Platform, p. 4.
26. David Theroux, Glenn Garvin, quoted in "Libertarians on Libel Law," *Libertarian Vanguard*, Oct. 1982, p. 7.
27. "Letter to the *Free Libertarian*," *op. cit.*, p. 3.
28. *Defending the Undefendable* (Fleet Press: 1976), p. 22.
29. *Ibid.*, p. 25.
30. *Ibid.*, pp. 105, 215, 216, 43.
31. Jeff Riggenbach, "In Praise of Decadence," *Libertarian Review*, Feb. 1979, p. 27.
32. "Why Are We in Grenada," *Update*, Nov. 1983, p. 5.
33. "Viewpoints," *Reason*, July 1975, p. 3.
34. "Israelis in Lebanon," *Frontlines*, July 1982, p. 3.
35. "Defend the Palestinians," *Libertarian Vanguard*, Aug. 1982, p. 5.
36. From "Draft Program," *op. cit.*, p. 9.
37. Rothbard, *For a New Liberty, op. cit.*, p. 283.
38. "The Student Revolution," *The Libertarian*, May 1, 1969, p. 3.
39. Letter to the editor, *Update*, Apr. 1983, p. 3.
40. "Defend the Palestinians," *op. cit.*, p. 6.
41. "Christian *and* Libertarian," *Frontlines*, Aug. 1980, p. 6.
42. "Why Libertarians Need Humanists," *Frontlines*, Nov. 1979, p. 6.
43. Bill Birmingham, "Rand: The Conscience of a Conservatarian," *Update*, May 1982, p. 6.

EPILOGUE

My Thirty Years With Ayn Rand: An Intellectual Memoir
by Leonard Peikoff

This lecture was delivered at the Ford Hall Forum on April 12, 1987, and published in The Objectivist Forum, *June 1987.*

Ayn Rand was unique—as a mind and as a person. If I could be granted a wish outside my power, it would be to meet and talk to someone like her again; unfortunately, I do not expect this wish to come true. The root of her uniqueness, which I had abundant opportunity to experience and enjoy in my thirty-year friendship with her, was the nature of her mental processes.

The purpose of this intellectual memoir is not to report on the content of the ideas I learned from Ayn Rand—whoever knows her books knows that already—but on her method of thinking as I observed it, her approach to the whole realm of ideas and therefore of living, her basic way of functioning cognitively in any situation. Method is fundamental; it is that which underlies and shapes content and thus all human achievement, in every field. Ayn Rand's method of thinking is an eloquent case in point: it is the root of her genius and of her distinctive art and philosophy. The mental processes she used in everyday life, from adolescence on, were the processes that led her, one step at a time, to all of her brilliant insights and to the principles of Objectivism.

Because of the role of method in human life, I have often thought that the greatest humanitarian service I could perform would be to leave the world a record and analysis of Ayn Rand's mind and how it worked. In the present discussion, I can offer you at least a glimpse of what I was privileged to see. Near the end, I will say something less epistemological—about Ayn Rand as a person.

When I met Ayn Rand, in the spring of 1951, I was an ignorant, intelligent seventeen-year-old, an admirer of *The Fountainhead*, but one who knew nothing about philosophy or how to think. Ayn Rand brought me up intellectually. In the nature of the case, therefore, some of my reminiscences are going to cast me in the role of naïve foil exhibiting her brilliance by contrast. This implication does not bother me, however, because alongside my confusions and errors, I claim one offsetting virtue: I did finally learn and come to practice what Ayn Rand taught me.

The strongest first impression I had of Ayn Rand on the fateful evening I met her—fateful to my life—was her passion for ideas. I have never seen its equal. I came to her California home that evening with a few broad questions suggested to me by *The Fountainhead*. One pertained to the issue of the moral and the practical, attributes which I had always been told were opposites. The character of Howard Roark, therefore, puzzled me, because he seemed to be both at once. So I asked Ayn Rand to tell me which one she intended him to represent. This was the sort of issue—relating to the nature of ideals and their role in life—which I had tried now and then, without much success, to discuss with family or teachers. Such issues were usually dismissed by the people I knew with a bromide or a shrug, amounting to the declaration: "Who knows and who cares?" Ayn Rand knew and Ayn Rand cared.

From the moment we started talking, she was vibrant, alert, alive. She listened intently to my words, she extracted every drop of meaning and of confusion, and then she answered. She spoke at length, first considering the question as I phrased it, then the deeper implications she saw in it. At each step, she explained what were the facts supporting her viewpoint, what kinds of objections might occur to me later if I pursued the topic, and what was the logical reply to them. She never suggested that I accept what she said on her say-so; on the contrary, she was working diligently to get me to see the truth with my own eyes and mind. The result was a brilliant extemporaneous dissertation on man's need of morality and therefore on the unity of the moral and the practical—in Roark and in any rational person—along with an eloquent demonstration of the disasters caused by the conventional viewpoint.

I was astonished not only by the originality of her ideas, but even more by her manner. She spoke as though it were urgent that I understand the issue and that she forestall every possible misinterpretation on my part. She was wringing out of herself every ounce of clarity she had. I have seen men lecturing to solemn halls of graduate students, and men running for national office, dealing in the most literal sense with issues of life and death; but I have never seen anyone work as hard as she did to be fully understood, down to the root. Yet she was doing it in a drawing room, in answer to a question from a boy she had just met. Clearly, it was not the boy who primarily inspired her; it was the subject (though she would not have answered as she did if she had doubted my sincerity).

Ayn Rand's performance that evening opened up the world to me. She made me think for the first time that thinking is important. I said to myself after I left her home: "All of life will be different now. If she exists, everything is possible."

As long as I knew Ayn Rand, her passion for ideas never abated. As a rule, she wrote in her office daily from noon until 6:30, and she often came out looking exhilarated but utterly spent. But then if I or someone else would drop over and make an intellectual observation or ask a question, she was suddenly, dramatically invigorated, and it might very well be midnight before she realized that she hadn't yet eaten dinner. A day or even an hour spent on legal contracts, or on business phone calls, or on shopping, or on having her hair done, tired her out thoroughly. But philosophy—ideas—was the stimulant that always brought her back.

She had such a passion for ideas because she thought that ideas are practical—that they are the most practical things in the world. In this regard, her approach was the opposite of that which philosophers call "rationalism." "Rationalism" amounts to the viewpoint that ideas are detached from reality, unrelated to daily events, and without significance for man's actual life—that they are nothing but floating abstractions to be manipulated by ivory-tower intellectuals for their own amusement, just as other men manipulate chess pieces. This viewpoint dominates twentieth-century thinkers. When I went to college, I routinely heard philosophical theories being discussed or debated by my professors as a purely academic matter. One professor was a follower of Immanuel Kant, say, another was an opponent of Kant, but they spoke and acted as though nothing separated them but dry, technical differences. After the debate, the two would go off arm in arm, buddies in spirit who had just finished a game or a show and were now returning to the real world. It reminds me of the logical positivist I heard about years ago who gave a lecture on why the word "God" is meaningless, then asked for directions to the nearest synagogue so he could say his prayers. The man was surprised that anyone was surprised by his request. "What has philosophy got to do with living?" he asked indignantly.

After a few weeks of classes with such professors, I would come running to Ayn Rand, chock-full of sophistry and fallacies, and she would spend twelve or even fifteen unbroken hours struggling to straighten out my thinking again. Why did it matter so much to her? Because her own mental practice was the antithesis of rationalism. To continue the same example, I remember asking her once long ago why she was so vehement in denouncing Kant's theories, particularly the abstract ideas at the base of his system, such as his view that the world we perceive by our senses and mind is not real, but is only a creation of man's subjective forms of awareness. I knew that Kant was wrong, but I did not understand at the age of twenty why the issue evoked in her so strong an emotion.

She replied, in essence: "When someone says that reality is unreal or that reason is subjective, he is, admittedly or not, attacking every conviction and every value I hold. Everything I love in life—my work, my husband, my kind of music, my freedom, the creativity of man's mind—all of it rests on my perception of reality; all of it becomes a delusion and an impossibility if reason is impotent. Once you concede Kant's kind of approach, you unleash the destroyers among men, the creatures who, freed of the need to be rational, will proceed—as in fact they have done since Kant—to expropriate the producers, sacrifice all values, and throw the rest of us into a fascist or communist dictatorship."

If you went up to an ordinary individual, itemized every object and person he cared for, then said to him seriously: "I intend to smash them all and leave you groveling in the muck," he would become indignant, even outraged. What set Ayn Rand apart from mankind is the fact that she heard the whole itemization and the intention to smash everything in the simple statement that "reality is unreal." Most people in our age of pragmatism and skepticism shrug off broad generalizations about reality as mere talk—i.e., as floating abstractions—and react only to relatively narrow utterances. Ayn Rand was the reverse. She reacted much more intensely to philosophical ideas than to narrow concretes. The more abstract an evil formulation, the more territory it covered, and the greater, therefore, the destructive potential she saw in it.

By the same token, if Ayn Rand heard a basic idea that she regarded as true—an idea upholding reality and reason, like many of the principles of Aristotle—she responded with profound respect, admiration, even gratitude. Ideas to her were not a parlor game. They were *man's form of grasping the world*, and they were thus an essential of human action and survival. So true ideas were an invaluable asset, and false ones a potential disaster.

Just as Ayn Rand did not detach abstractions from concretes, so she did not allow concretes to remain detached from abstractions. That is, she rejected today's widespread policy of staring at daily events in a vacuum, then wailing that life is unintelligible. What a man does, she held, is a product of what he thinks. To be understood, therefore, a man's actions have to be seen in relation to his ideas. Whether she encountered an inspiring novel by Victor Hugo, accordingly, or some horror spawned by Progressive education, or America's thrilling venture into space, or the latest catastrophe out of Washington, or the seemingly incomprehensible behavior of a friend she had trusted—whatever it was, she was always intent on explaining it by identifying the ideas at its root. Since abstractions, in her philosophy, are man's means of grasping and dealing with concretes, she actually used them for that purpose. She would not rest content either with floating theories or with unintelligible news items. She always required a crucial unity: theory *and* reality, or ideas and facts, or concepts and percepts.

Now I think you can see how Ayn Rand arrived at the most revolutionary element in Objectivism, her theory of concepts. I asked her about this once. She told me that she was talking one day to a Thomist and disagreed with the theory of concepts the man was advancing. "Well, then," Ayn Rand was asked, "where do *you* think concepts come from?" "Let me introspect a moment and see what my mind does in forming a concept," she replied, "because I haven't yet considered this question." Whereupon, after a few minutes of silence, she came up with her idea of measurement-omission as the essence of abstraction. I was always astounded by this feat of philosophic creativity; it seemed as though she had solved the problem of the ages by a casual glance inward. But now I think I understand it. What I see is that Ayn Rand's theory of concepts was implicit from the time of her adolescence in her basic mental approach—in her recognition of the fact that concepts are not supernatural or arbitrary, but rather are instruments enabling men to integrate perceptual data. The rest of her theory of concepts is really an elaboration of this fundamental, although of course it takes a genius to discover such an elaboration.

Ayn Rand regarded ideas as important to human life—as the shaper of man's character, his culture, his history, his future—because she knew what an idea is. She knew that an idea is not a social ritual, but a means of cognition.

If ideas are as crucial as this, then they must be dealt with properly—which brings me to the center of the present discussion: the specific steps of Ayn Rand's intellectual method. In her own thinking, she always distinguished the "what," as she called it, from the "how": what she knew, and how (by what means) she knew it. If you disagreed with her about a particular conclusion, you did not argue the point for long, because the discussion soon changed to method. To her, the "how" was *the* burning issue in life; it was the thing that gave rise to the "what." So let us look at some of the distinctive steps of Ayn Rand's method. The best way to approach this subject briefly is through the issue of *principles*.

Ayn Rand thought in terms of principles. In the sense I mean it, this is a rare phenomenon. I personally had never encountered or even imagined it before I met her, and most people have no idea of it at all. Let me start here by giving you an example; it is the one on which I first discovered the issue, about a year after I met Ayn Rand.

I had been taking an ethics course in college and was thoroughly confused about the virtue of honesty. I was not tempted to be dishonest myself, but I did not see how to prove the evil of lying. (I speak throughout of lying in order to gain some value from others, as against lying to defend oneself from criminals, which is perfectly moral.) On my own, I rejected the two dominant schools in regard to honesty: the religious school, which holds that lying is absolutely wrong because God forbids it; and the Utilitarian school, which holds that there are no absolutes and that one has to judge each case "on its own merits," according to the probable consequences of any given lie. I rejected the first of these as mystical, the second as brute expediency. But what could constitute a third interpretation? I had no idea, so I went to Ayn Rand.

She started her answer by asking me to invent the most plausible lie I could think of. I don't remember the details any longer, but I know that I did proceed to concoct a pretty good con-man scheme for bilking investors out of large sums of money. Ayn Rand then analyzed the example patiently, for thirty or forty minutes, showing me on my own material how one lie would lead necessarily to another, how I would be forced into contradictory lies, how I would gradually become trapped in my own escalating deceptions, and why, therefore, sooner or later, in one form or another, my con-man scheme would have to backfire and lead to the loss of the very things I was seeking to gain by it. If you are interested in the content of her analysis, I have re-created the substance of this lengthy discussion in my next book, *Objectivism: The Philosophy of Ayn Rand.*

The point now, however, lies in what happened next. My immediate reaction to her reply was to amend my initial scheme in order to remove the particular weaknesses she had found in it. So I made up a second con-man scheme, and again she analyzed it patiently, showing that it would lead to the same disastrous results even though most of the details were now different. Whereupon, in all innocence, I started to invent a third scheme (I was only 18). But Ayn Rand by this time was fed up. "Can't you think in principle?" she asked me.

Let me condense into a few paragraphs what she then explained to me at length. "The essence of a con-man's lie," she began, "of any such lie, no matter what the details, is the attempt to gain a value by faking certain facts of reality."

She went on: "Now can't you grasp the logical consequences of that kind of policy? Since all facts of reality are interrelated, faking one of them leads the person to fake others; ultimately, he is committed to an all-out war against reality as such. But this is the kind of war no one can win. If life in reality is a man's purpose, how can he expect to achieve it while struggling at the same time to escape and defeat reality?"

And she concluded: "The con-man's lies are wrong on *principle.* To state the principle positively: honesty is a long-range requirement of human self-preservation and is, therefore, a moral obligation."

This was not merely a new ethical argument to me. It was a whole new form of thought. She was saying, in effect: you do not have to consult some supernatural authority for intellectual guidance, nor try to judge particular cases in a vacuum and on to infinity. Rather, you first abstract the essence of a series of concretes. Then you identify, by an appropriate use of logic, the necessary implications or result of this essence. You thereby reach a fundamental generalization, a *principle*, which subsumes and enables you to deal with an unlimited number of instances—past, present, and future. The consequence, in this example, is an absolute prohibition against the con-man mentality—a prohibition based not on God, but on perception and thought.

Ayn Rand applied this method not only to lying or to moral issues, but to every fact and question she studied. She applied it in every branch of philosophy, from metaphysics to esthetics. If she saw that the sun rises every day, she did not, like David Hume, consider it a puzzling coincidence. She identified the essence of the event: an entity acting in accordance with its nature; and thereby was able to reach and validate the principle of causality. Or, if she admired the novels of Hugo and the plays of Friedrich Schiller, she did not say merely: "I like their grand-scale protagonists." She identified the essence of such art: the depiction of man as a being with volition; and thereby was able to reach and validate the principle of Romanticism in art. This kind of method is the root of a whole new approach to thought. It led her a step at a time to a philosophy that is neither mystical nor skeptical, but objective; one that neither bases knowledge on revelation nor succumbs to relativism, but that teaches men to conceptualize logically the data of observation. Such a philosophy enables us to discover absolutes which are not supernatural, but rational and this-worldly.

Ayn Rand started thinking in terms of principles, she told me once, at the age of twelve. To her, it was a normal part of the process of growing up, and she never dropped the method thereafter. Nor, I believe, did she ever entirely comprehend the fact that the approach which was second nature to her was not practiced by other people. Much of the time, she was baffled by or indignant at the people she was doomed to talk to, people like the man we heard about in the early 1950s, who was calling for the nationalization of the steel industry. The man was told by an Objectivist why government seizure of the steel industry was immoral and impractical, and he was impressed by the argument. His comeback was: "Okay, I see that. But what about the coal industry?"

The method of thinking in principle involves many complexities, about which I intend, someday, to write an entire volume. But let me mention here a few further aspects, to give you a fuller picture of Ayn Rand's approach. You recall that, to reach the principle that honesty is a virtue, we had first to grasp the essence of lying. Let us focus now on this issue, i.e., thinking in *essentials*, which was an essential part of Ayn Rand's method of thinking.

The concept of "essential" was originated by Aristotle in connection with his theory of definition. He used the term to name the quality that makes an entity the distinctive kind of thing it is, as against what he called the "accidental" qualities. For example, having a rational faculty is essential to being a man. But having blue eyes rather than green is not; it is a mere detail or accident of a particular case. Ayn Rand's commitment to essentials grew out of this Aristotelian theory, although she modified the concept significantly and expanded its role in human thought.

For Ayn Rand, thinking in essentials was not restricted to the issue of definitions. It was a method of understanding any complex situation by deliberately setting aside irrelevancies—such as insignificant details, superficial similarities, unimportant differences—and going instead to the heart of the matter, to the aspects which, as we may say, constitute the distinctive core or being of the situation. This is something Ayn Rand herself did brilliantly. I always thought of her, metaphorically, as possessing a special power of vision, which could penetrate beneath the surface data that most people see, just as an X-ray machine penetrates beneath the flesh that meets our eyes to reveal the crucial underlying structures.

This kind of penetration is precisely what was lacking in the man I just mentioned, who could see no connection between the steel and the coal industries. Ayn Rand, by contrast, knew at once that steel in this context is a mere detail. She went to the essence of nationalization: government force unleashed against the minds of productive, thinking men—a practice common to countless cases beyond steel, and one that will have a certain kind of effect no matter where it occurs. This is the kind of mental process that is required if one is to reach a generalization uniting many cases. It is the process that is required if one is to champion capitalism as a matter of principle, rather than, like today's conservatives, clamoring merely for the removal of some random controls.

In the deepest epistemological sense, Ayn Rand was the opposite of an egalitarian. She did not regard every aspect of a whole as equal in importance to every other. Some aspects, she held, are crucial to a proper understanding; others merely clutter up the cognitive landscape and distract lesser minds from the truth. So the task of the thinker is to distinguish the two, i.e., to analyze and process the data confronting him, not to amass mounds of information without any attempt at mental digestion. She herself always functioned like an intellectual detective, a philosophical Hercule Poirot, reading, watching, listening for the fact, the statement, the perspective that would illuminate a whole, tortuous complexity—the one that would reveal the essence and thereby suddenly make that complexity simple and intelligible. The result was often dramatic. When you were with her, you always felt poised on the brink of some startling new cognitive adventure and discovery.

Here is an example of what I mean. In the 1970s, Ayn Rand and I were watching the Academy Awards on television; it was the evening when a streaker flashed by during the ceremonies. Most people probably dismissed the incident with some remark like: "He's just a kid" or "It's a high-spirited prank" or "He wants to get on TV." But not Ayn Rand. Why, her mind wanted to know, does this "kid" act in this particular fashion? What is the difference between his "prank" and that of college students on a lark who swallow goldfish or stuff themselves into telephone booths? How does his desire to appear on TV differ from that of a typical game-show contestant? In other words, Ayn Rand swept aside from the outset the superficial aspects of the incident and the standard irrelevant comments in order to reach the essence, which had to pertain to this specific action in this distinctive setting.

"Here," she said to me in effect, "is a nationally acclaimed occasion replete with celebrities, jeweled ball gowns, coveted prizes, and breathless cameras, an occasion offered to the country as the height of excitement, elegance, glamor—and what this creature wants to do is drop his pants in the middle of it all and thrust his bare buttocks into everybody's face. What then is his motive? Not high spirits or TV coverage, but destruction—the satisfaction of sneering at and undercutting that which the rest of the country looks up to and admires." In essence, she concluded, the incident was an example of nihilism, which is the desire not to have or enjoy values, but to nullify and eradicate them.

Nor did she stop there. The purpose of using concepts—and the precondition of reaching principles—is the *integration* of observed facts; in other words, the bringing together in one's mind of many different examples or fields, such as the steel and the coal industries, for instance. Ayn Rand was expert at this process. For her, grasping the essence of an event was merely the beginning of processing it cognitively. The next step was to identify that essence in other, seemingly very different areas, and thereby discover a common denominator uniting them all.

Having grasped the streaker's nihilism, therefore, she was eager to point out some different examples of the same attitude. Modern literature, she observed, is distinguished by its creators' passion not to offer something new and positive, but to wipe out: to eliminate plots, heroes, motivation, even grammar and syntax; this represents the brazen desire to destroy an entire art form along with the great writers of the past by stripping away from literature every one of its cardinal attributes. Just as Progressive education is the desire for education stripped of lessons, reading, facts, teaching, and learning. Just as avant-garde physics is the gleeful cry that there is no order in nature, no law, no predictability, no causality. That streaker, in short, was the very opposite of an isolated phenomenon. He was a microcosm of the *principle* ruling modern culture, a fleeting representative of that corrupt motivation which Ayn Rand has described so eloquently as "hatred of the good for being the good." And what accounts for such widespread hatred? she asked at the end. Her answer brings us back to the philosophy we referred to earlier, the one that attacks reason and reality wholesale and thus makes all values impossible: the philosophy of Immanuel Kant.

Listening to Ayn Rand that evening, I felt that I was beginning to understand what it means really to understand an event. I went home and proceeded to write the chapter in *The Ominous Parallels* dealing with Weimar culture, which develops at length Ayn Rand's analysis of the modern intellectual trend. The point here, however, is not her analysis, but the method that underlies it: observation of facts; the identification of the essential; the integration of data from many disparate fields; then the culminating overview, the grasp of principle.

I use the term "overview" deliberately, because I always felt as though everyone else had their faces pressed up close to an event and were staring at it myopically, while she was standing on a mountaintop, sweeping the world with a single glance, and thus was able to identify the most startling connections, not only between streaking and literature, but also between sex and economics, art and business, William F. Buckley and Edward Kennedy. She was able to unite the kinds of things that other people automatically pigeonhole into separate compartments. Her universe, as a result, was a single whole, with all its parts interrelated and intelligible; it was not the scattered fragments and fiefdoms that are all most people know. To change the image: she was like a ballet dancer of the intellect, leaping from fact to fact and field to field, not by the strength of her legs, but by the power of logic, a power that most men do not seem fully to have discovered yet.

The unity of Ayn Rand's universe rested on more than I can indicate here. But I want to mention a last aspect of her method, one which is crucial in this regard: thinking in terms of *fundamentals*.

By "fundamental" I mean that on which everything else in a given context depends, that which is the base or groundwork on which a whole development is built. This concept is necessary because human knowledge, like a skyscraper, has a structure: certain ideas are the ground floor or foundation of cognition, while other ideas, like the upper stories of a building, are dependents, no better or stronger than the foundation on which they rely. Thinking in terms of fundamentals means never accepting a conclusion while ignoring its base; it means knowing and validating the deepest ideas on which one's conclusion rests.

For instance, in our discussion of honesty, we said that lying is wrong because it is incompatible with the requirements of self-preservation. What base were we counting on? Clearly, a certain ethical theory, the one that upholds self-preservation as man's proper goal—in contrast to the ethics that advocates self-sacrifice for the sake of others. If you accept this latter theory, our whole argument against lying collapses. Why should a man who is committed to selfless service necessarily tell the truth? What if, as often happens, others want him to lie and claim that it is essential to their happiness?

But this is just the beginning of our quest for fundamentals, because the field of ethics itself rests on the basic branches of philosophy, as you can see in this same example. How did we prove that lying is self-destructive? We said that a policy of lying leads to a war against reality, which no one can win. Well, why can't anyone? What ideas are we counting on here? Clearly, that there *is* a reality; that it is what it is independent of our desires; and that our minds are able to know these facts, i.e., to know reality. The issue of lying, in sum, whatever view of it one takes, is merely a consequence. It is a derivative, which rests on a complex philosophic foundation.

Thinking in terms of fundamentals is not an independent aspect of Ayn Rand's method; it is an inherent part of thinking in principle. If one ignored the issue of fundamentals, his so-called principles would be merely a heap of disconnected, random claims—like a catalog of divine commandments—and they would be of no help in understanding the world or guiding one's action. One would not be able to prove or even retain the items in such a heap; they would be nothing but floating abstractions. Only ideas organized into a logical structure can be tied to reality, and only such ideas, therefore, can be of use or value to man; and that means principles based on antecedent principles, going back ultimately to the fundamentals of philosophy.

Ayn Rand's real intellectual interest was emphatically *not* politics. Of course, she was a champion of capitalism and freedom. But unlike today's libertarians and conservatives, she was a thinker; she was not content to preach liberty or private property as though they were self-evident axioms. She wanted to know what they depend on and how they can be proved, all the way back to metaphysics and epistemology. This is why she admired Aristotle and Thomas Aquinas even more than she did Thomas Jefferson, and why, to the amazement of today's businessmen, she hated Kant and Hegel much more than income taxes. It is also why, starting with an interest in political questions, she was led eventually to formulate an overall system of thought, expressing a complete philosophy of life.

Ayn Rand's mind had an exalted quality, one shared by only a handful of kindred spirits across the ages. Hers was a mind with the profundity of a true philosopher; a mind that greeted the deepest issues of man's life with solemn reverence and ruthless logic; a mind that derived its greatest joy and its personal fulfillment from the rational study of fundamentals. In our age of mediocrity and anti-philosophy, this fact doomed her to a certain loneliness. It made her a unique personality, unable to find her equal, just as her product, the philosophy of reason that she called Objectivism, is unique and unequaled.

If you want to know what Ayn Rand was like as a person, I can now answer simply: you already know it, because she was just what she had to be given the nature of her intellectual processes. Ayn Rand the person was an expression and corollary of Ayn Rand the mind.

Ayn Rand herself repudiated any dichotomy between mind and person. Her mind, she held, was the essence of her person: it was her highest value, the source of her other values, and the root of her character traits. Thinking, to her, was not merely an interest or even a passion; it was a lifestyle. When she greeted you, for instance, she often asked not "How are you?" but "How's your universe?" Her meaning was: "How's your view of the universe? Have the problems of daily life swamped your philosophical knowledge? Or are you still holding on to the fact that reality is intelligible and that values are possible?" Similarly, when you left, she would say not "Goodbye," but "Good premises." In other words: "Don't count on luck or God for success, but on your own thinking." If self-esteem means confidence in the power of one's mind, then the explanation of Ayn Rand's profound self-esteem is obvious: she earned it—both in virtue of the value she ascribed to the mind, and of the meticulous method by which she used her own.

Another result of this method was that attribute men call "strength of character." Ayn Rand was immutable. I never saw her adapting her personality to please another individual. She was always the same and always herself, whether she was talking with me alone, or attending a cocktail party of celebrities, or being cheered or booed by a hall full of college students, or being interviewed on national television. She took on the whole world—liberals, conservatives, communists, religionists, Babbitts, and avant-garde alike—but opposition had no power to sway her. She knew too clearly how she had reached her ideas, why they were true, and what their opposites were doing to mankind. Nor, like Howard Roark, could she ever be tempted to betray her convictions. Since she had integrated her principles into a consistent system, she knew that to violate a single one would be to discard the totality. A Texas oil man once offered her up to a million dollars to use in spreading her philosophy, if she would only add a religious element to it to make it more popular. She threw his proposal into the wastebasket. "What would I do with his money," she asked me indignantly, "if I have to give up my mind in order to get it?"

Dedication to thought and thus to her work was the root of Ayn Rand's person; it was not, however, her only passion. As a result of this root, she held intense values in every department of life. She loved her husband of fifty years, Frank O'Connor, a sensitive, intense man, not nearly as intellectual as she but just as independent and deep in his own quiet way. He is the exception to my statement that she never found an equal. Frank did not have her mind; but his dedication to his work as a painter, his extravagant Romanticism, his innocent, sunlit sense of life, and, I may add, the visible joy he took in her work and in her person—all this made it plain that he did share her soul.

As to Ayn Rand's other values, I have hardly room here even to mention a sample. Some of them are obvious from her writings, such as America, skyscrapers, modern technology, man the hero, the great romantic artists of the nineteenth century, the silent German movies from her childhood that she always tried to find again, Agatha Christie, TV's Perry Mason—and there were so many more, from her cats to her lion pictures to her Adrian clothes to her vivid, outsize jewelry to her stamp collecting to her favorite candy (Godiva chocolates) and even her favorite color (blue-green). In every aspect of life, she once told me, a man should have favorites; he should define what he likes most and why, and then proceed to get it. She always did just that—from fleeing the Soviet dictatorship for America, to tripping her future husband on a movie set to get him to notice her, to ransacking ancient record shops to unearth some lost treasure, to decorating her apartment with an abundance of blue-green pillows, ashtrays, and even walls.

Ayn Rand was a woman dominated by values, values that were consistent expressions of a single view of life—which is what you might expect of a great thinker who was at once a moralist and an artist. The corollary is that she had strong dislikes in every department, too. You cannot love something without rejecting just as passionately that which you see as the antithesis of your love. Most people do not know their values clearly or hold them consistently; their desires are correspondingly vague, ambivalent, contradictory. To many such people, Ayn Rand's violent aliveness and assertiveness were shocking, even intimidating. To me, however, they were a tonic. I felt as though other people were drawn in wishy-washy shades of gray, whereas her soul was made of brilliant color.

Unfortunately—and here I turn for a moment to a somber topic—the wishy-washy people often wanted something from Ayn Rand and were drawn to her circle. A few of them wanted simply to advance their careers by cashing in on her fame and following. Others craved the security they found in her approval. Still others had an element of sincerity during their youth, but turned anti-intellectual as they grew older. These people did what they had to do in order to get from Ayn Rand what they wanted.

What they did usually was to give her the appearance of being the philosophical intelligence she desperately wanted to meet. They were glib, articulate, sometimes even brilliant people. They absorbed the surface features of Ayn Rand's intellectual style and viewpoint as though by osmosis and then mimicked them. Often, because she was so open, they knew what she wanted them to say, and they said it convincingly. Though uninterested in philosophy and even contemptuous of fundamentals, they could put on an expert act to the contrary, most often an act for themselves first of all. Ayn Rand was not the only person to be taken in by it. I knew most of these people well and, to be fair here, I must admit that I was even more deluded about them than she was.

All of these types ended up resenting Ayn Rand, and even hating her. They felt increasingly bored by the realm of ideas, and chafed under the necessity of suppressing their real self in order to keep up the pretense of intellectual passion. Above all, they found Ayn Rand's commitment to morality intolerable. In her mind, moral principles were requirements of man's survival proved by reference to the deepest premises of philosophy; they were thus the opposite of a luxury or a social convention; they were life-or-death absolutes. When she saw a moral breach, therefore—such as dishonesty or moral compromise or power lust or selling one's soul to the Establishment like Peter Keating— she knew what it meant and where it would lead, and she condemned the individual roundly.

To the types of people we are talking about, this was an unbearable reproach. They could accept Objectivism as pure theory for a while, but only as theory. When they were tested by life, they gave in guiltily, one at a time, to the sundry pressures they encountered, and they shrank thereafter from facing her. Usually they ended up artfully concealing their resentment, saying that they still admired, even adored, Ayn Rand and her philosophy, but not, as they put it, her "moralizing" or her "anger." Her "moralizing" means the fact that she pronounced moral judgments, i.e., applied her philosophy to real life. Her "anger" in this context means that she took her judgments seriously.

Several of these individuals are now publishing their memoirs in the hopes of getting even with Ayn Rand at last—and also of cashing in on her corpse. At this latter goal, regrettably, some of them seem to be succeeding.

Ayn Rand refused to make collective judgments. Each time she unmasked one of these individuals she struggled to learn from her mistake. But then she would be deceived again by some new variant.

Her basic error was that she took herself as the human standard or norm (as in a sense we all must do, since we have no direct contact with any human consciousness but our own). So if she saw all the outward signs of philosophical enthusiasm and activity, she took it to mean that the individual was, in effect, an intellectual equal of hers, who regarded ideas in the same way she did. After a long while, I came to understand this error. I realized how extraordinary her mind really was, and I tried to explain to her her many disappointments with people.

"You are suffering the fate of a genius trapped in a rotten culture," I would begin. "My distinctive attribute," she would retort, "is not genius, but intellectual honesty." "That is part of it," I would concede, "but after all I am intellectually honest, too, and it doesn't make me the kind of epochal mind who can write *Atlas Shrugged* or discover Objectivism." "One can't look at oneself that way," she would answer me. "No one can say: 'Ah me! the genius of the ages.' My perspective as a creator has to be not 'How great I am' but 'How true this idea is and how clear, if only men were honest enough to face the truth.' " So, for understandable reasons, we reached an impasse. She kept hoping to meet an equal; I knew that she never would. For once, I felt, I had the broad historical perspective, the perspective on her, that in the nature of the case she could not have.

In order to be fully clear at this point, I want to make one more comment about Ayn Rand's anger. Many times, as I have explained, it was thoroughly justified. But sometimes it was not justified. For instance, Ayn Rand not infrequently became angry at me over some philosophical statement I made that seemed for the moment to ally me with one of the intellectual movements she was fighting. On many such occasions, of course, she remained calm because she understood the cause of my statement: that I still had a great deal to learn. But other times she did not; she did not grasp fully the gulf that separates the historic master, to whom the truth is obvious, from the merely intelligent student. Since her mind immediately integrated a remark to the fundamentals it presupposes, she would project at once, almost automatically, the full, horrendous meaning of what I had uttered, and then she would be shocked at me. Once I explained that I had not understood the issue at all, her anger melted and she became intent on clarifying the truth for me. The anger she felt on such occasions was mistaken, but it was not irrational. Its root was her failure to appreciate her own intellectual uniqueness.

I should add here that I never saw her hold an unadmitted grudge. Her anger never festered unexpressed or turned into devious, brooding hatred. It was an immediate, open storm of indignant protest—then it was over. In this respect, she was the easiest person in the world to know and to deal with.

Did I ever get angry at Ayn Rand's anger at me? Certainly I did. But my anger did not matter to me and did not last. To me, her temper was an infinitesimal price to pay for the values I was gaining from her. The world, I knew, is full of kindly souls who specialize in loving everybody and forgiving everything; but these souls bored me. I wanted out of life that which Ayn Rand alone, in all her fiery genius, had to offer.

This brings me to my final topic. Whatever Ayn Rand's anger, her disappointments, her pain, they went down, as she said about Roark, only to a certain point. Beneath it was her self-esteem, her values, and her conviction that happiness, not pain, is what matters. People sometimes ask: "But did she achieve happiness in her own life?" My answer would consist of three images.

One is the memory of a spring day in 1957; we were walking up Madison Avenue toward the office of Random House, which was in the process of bringing out *Atlas Shrugged*. She was looking at the city she had always loved most, and now, after decades of rejection and bitter poverty, she had seen the top publishers in that city competing for what she knew, triumphantly, was her masterpiece. She turned to me suddenly and said: "Don't ever give up what you want in life. The struggle is worth it." I never forgot that. I can still see the look of quiet radiance on her face.

Then I see the image of her one night at a party, perhaps twenty years ago now; she was sitting on a couch with some other guests, looking shy, bored, and miserable. Then her husband, who had been working late, arrived, and she called out "Cubbyhole" (her pet name for him), insisting, as she always did, that he squeeze onto the couch beside her so that they could hold hands. And they smiled at each other, and she relaxed visibly, and he patted her hand and called her "Fluff" (his name for her).

Then I see her as she was turning seventy, on the morning when she, Frank, and I came home from the hospital after her lung surgery. It was still difficult for her to walk, but she wanted to play her "tiddlywink" music, as she always called it—gay, lighthearted, utterly cheerful popular tunes from the turn of the century, which have no counterpart today. And she got up and began to march around the living room to the music, tossing her head, grinning at us, marking the beat by waving her little baton, Frank all the while beaming at her from his easy chair. If ever I want to think of a *non*-tragic spectacle, I remember that.

Ayn Rand did experience unhappiness in her life. But if you ask me: was she a happy person? I have only one answer to give you. She was.

Ladies and gentlemen: in my judgment, Ayn Rand did live by her philosophy. Whatever her errors, she practiced what she preached, both epistemologically and morally. As a result, she did achieve in her life that which she set out to achieve; she achieved it intellectually, artistically, emotionally. But for you to judge these matters yourself and reach an objective view of Ayn Rand, you must be an unusually philosophical kind of person, because you are living in a Kantian, anti-value culture, and you are going to be offered some very opposite accounts of the facts of her life. So you have to know: what *is* objectivity? What sort of testimony qualifies as evidence in this context? What do *you* believe is possible to a man—or a woman? What kind of soul do *you* think it takes to write *Atlas Shrugged*? And what do you *want* to see in a historic figure?

I am not a Kantian. I do not believe that we can know Ayn

Rand only as she appeared to somebody or other. But if I were to grant that premise for a split second, if I were to agree that we all construe reality according to our own personal preferences, then I would still draw a fundamental moral distinction between two kinds of preferences: between those of the muckrakers and those of the hero-worshipers. It is the distinction between the people who, confronted by a genius, are seized with a passion to ferret out flaws, real or imaginary, i.e., to find feet of clay so as to justify their own blighted lives—as against the people who, desperate to feel admiration, want to dismiss any flaw as trivial because nothing matters to them in such a context but the sight of the human greatness that inspires and awes them. In this kind of clash, I am sure, you recognize where I stand.

I knew Ayn Rand longer than anyone now alive. I do not believe that my view of her is subjective. But if I am to go down in history as her apologist or glamorizer, then so be it. I am proud to be cursed as a "cultist," if the "cult" is unbreached dedication to the mind and to its most illustrious exponents.

According to the Objectivist esthetics, a crucial purpose of art is to depict man as he might be and ought to be, and thereby provide the reader or viewer with the pleasure of contemplating, in concrete, embodied form, his abstract moral ideal. Howard Roark and John Galt provide this kind of inspiration to me, and to many other people I know. What I want to add in closing is that Ayn Rand in person provided it, too. Because of the power of her mind and the purity of her soul, she gave me, when I was with her, what her novels give me: a sense of life as exaltation, the sense of living in a clean, uplifted, benevolent world, in which the good has every chance of winning, and the evil does not have to be taken seriously. I often felt, greeting her, as though I were entering the Atlantis of *Atlas Shrugged*, where the human ideal is not merely an elusive projection to be reached somehow, but is real, alive, here—seated across the room on the blue-green pillows, smiling delightedly, eager to talk philosophy with me, eyes huge, brilliant, penetrating.

That is the Ayn Rand I knew. And that is why I loved her.